ANNUAL EDIT

Human Resources   *08/09*

Seventeenth Edition

EDITOR

Fred H. Maidment

Western Connecticut State University

Dr. Fred Maidment is associate professor of management at Western Connecticut State University in Danbury, Connecticut. He received his bachelor's degree from New York University and his master's degree from the Bernard M. Baruch College of the City University of New York. In 1983 Dr. Maidment received his doctorate from the University of South Carolina. He resides in Connecticut with his wife.

 **Higher Education**

Boston   Burr Ridge, IL   Dubuque, IA   New York   San Francisco   St. Louis
Bangkok   Bogotá   Caracas   Kuala Lumpur   Lisbon   London   Madrid   Mexico City
Milan   Montreal   New Delhi   Santiago   Seoul   Singapore   Sydney   Taipei   Toronto

ANNUAL EDITIONS: HUMAN RESOURCES, SEVENTEENTH EDITION

Published by McGraw-Hill, a business unit of The McGraw-Hill Companies, Inc., 1221 Avenue of the Americas, New York, NY 10020. Copyright © 2008 by The McGraw-Hill Companies, Inc. All rights reserved. Previous edition(s) 1990–2007. No part of this publication may be reproduced or distributed in any form or by any means, or stored in a database or retrieval system, without the prior written consent of The McGraw-Hill Companies, Inc., including, but not limited to, in any network or other electronic storage or transmission, or broadcast for distance learning.

Some ancillaries, including electronic and print components, may not be available to customers outside the United States.

Annual Editions® is a registered trademark of The McGraw-Hill Companies, Inc.
Annual Editions is published by the **Contemporary Learning Series** group within the McGraw-Hill Higher Education division.

✪ This book is printed on recycled, acid-free paper containing 10% postconsumer waste.

1 2 3 4 5 6 7 8 9 0 QPD/QPD 0 9 8 7

ISBN 978–0–07–352847–2
MHID 0–07–352847–1
ISSN 1092–6577

Managing Editor: *Larry Loeppke*
Production Manager: *Beth Kundert*
Developmental Editor: *Dave Welsh*
Editorial Assistant: *Nancy Meissner*
Production Service Assistant: *Rita Hingtgen*
Permissions Coordinator: *Shirley Lanners*
Senior Marketing Manager: *Julie Keck*
Marketing Communications Specialist: *Mary Klein*
Marketing Coordinator: *Alice Link*
Project Manager: *Sandy Wille*
Design Specialist: *Tara McDermott*
Senior Administrative Assistant: *DeAnna Dausener*
Senior Operations Manager: *Pat Koch Krieger*
Cover Graphics: *Maggie Lytle*

Compositor: Laserwords Private Limited
Cover Image: Ryan McVay/Getty Images and Digital Vision

Library in Congress Cataloging-in-Publication Data
Main entry under title: Annual Editions: Human Resources. 2008/2009.
 1. Human Resources—Periodicals. I. Maidment, Fred H., *comp.* II. Title: Human Resources.
658'.05

www.mhhe.com

Editors/Advisory Board

Members of the Advisory Board are instrumental in the final selection of articles for each edition of ANNUAL EDITIONS. Their review of articles for content, level, currentness, and appropriateness provides critical direction to the editor and staff. We think that you will find their careful consideration well reflected in this volume.

Preface

In publishing ANNUAL EDITIONS we recognize the enormous role played by the magazines, newspapers, and journals of the public press in providing current, first-rate educational information in a broad spectrum of interest areas. Many of these articles are appropriate for students, researchers, and professionals seeking accurate, current material to help bridge the gap between principles and theories and the real world. These articles, however, become more useful for study when those of lasting value are carefully collected, organized, indexed, and reproduced in a low-cost format, which provides easy and permanent access when the material is needed. That is the role played by ANNUAL EDITIONS.

The environment for human resource management is constantly changing. The events of September 11, 2001, are only just a preview of the global environment that may be developing for human resource managers. This terrorist act changed the role of human resources and is certain to affect the human resources profession in the future. At the very least, what has transpired has and will continue to make the practice of human resources more difficult and more challenging. Meeting those challenges will be the continual task that will face human resource managers and will make it a key factor in the success of any organization.

Management must respond to these forces in many ways, not the least of which is the effort to keep current with the various developments in the field. The 46 articles that have been chosen for *Annual Editions: Human Resources 08/09* reflect an outstanding cross section of the current articles in the field. The volume addresses the various component parts of HRM (human resource management) from compensation, training, and discipline to international implications for the worker and the employer. Articles have been chosen from leading business magazines such as *Forbes* and journals such as *Workforce, HR Magazine* and *Monitor on Psychology* to provide a wide sampling of the latest thinking in the field of human resources.

Annual Editions: Human Resources 08/09 contains a number of features designed to be useful for people interested in human resource management. These features include a Table of Contents with abstracts that summarize each article with bold italicized key ideas and a Topic Guide to locate articles on specific subjects. The volume is organized into seven units, each dealing with specific interrelated topics in human resources. Every unit begins with an overview that provides background information for the articles in the section. This will enable the reader to place the selection in the context of the larger issues concerning human resources. Important topics are emphasized and key points to consider that address major themes are presented.

This is the seventeenth edition of *Annual Editions: Human Resources.* It is hoped that many more will follow addressing these important issues. We believe that the collection is the most complete and useful compilation of current material available to the human resource management student. We would like to have your response to this volume, for we are interested in your opinions and recommendations. Please take a few minutes to complete and return the postage-paid Article Rating Form at the back of the volume. Any book can be improved, and we need your help to continue to improve *Annual Editions: Human Resources.*

Fred Maidment
Editor

Contents

UNIT 1
Human Resource Management in Perspective

Part A. The Environment of Human Resource Management

Part B. Human Resources and Corporate Strategy

The concepts in bold italics are developed in the article. For further expansion, please refer to the Topic Guide.

UNIT 2
Meeting Human Resource Requirements

The concepts in bold italics are developed in the article. For further expansion, please refer to the Topic Guide.

UNIT 3
Creating a Productive Work Environment

The concepts in bold italics are developed in the article. For further expansion, please refer to the Topic Guide.

UNIT 4
Developing Effective Human Resources

UNIT 5
Implementing Compensation, Benefits, and Workplace Safety

The concepts in bold italics are developed in the article. For further expansion, please refer to the Topic Guide.

UNIT 6
Fostering Employee/Management Relationships

The concepts in bold italics are developed in the article. For further expansion, please refer to the Topic Guide.

UNIT 7
International Human Resource Management

The concepts in bold italics are developed in the article. For further expansion, please refer to the Topic Guide.

Topic Guide

This topic guide suggests how the selections in this book relate to the subjects covered in your course. You may want to use the topics listed on these pages to search the Web more easily.

On the following pages a number of Web sites have been gathered specifically for this book. They are arranged to reflect the units of this *Annual Edition*. You can link to these sites by going to the student online support site at *http://www.mhcls.com/online/*.

ALL THE ARTICLES THAT RELATE TO EACH TOPIC ARE LISTED BELOW THE BOLD-FACED TERM.

Americans with disabilities act

8. The Best 4 Ways to Recruit Employees with Disabilities
9. Making Reasonable Accommodations for Employees with Mental Illness under the ADA
11. The Disability Advantage
13. Some of 'Our Boys Overseas' Have Gray Hair
31. Doc in a Box
32. Building a Mentally Healthy Workforce
33. Employee Benefits of the Future

Benefits

8. The Best 4 Ways to Recruit Employees with Disabilities
9. Making Reasonable Accommodations for Employees with Mental Illness under the ADA
11. The Disability Advantage
13. Some of 'Our Boys Overseas' Have Gray Hair
25. Four Generations in the Workplace
26. The Face of Diversity Is More than Skin Deep
27. Philosophizing Compensation
28. Do Your Employees Qualify for Overtime?
30. Pay Setters
31. Doc in a Box
32. Building a Mentally Healthy Workforce
33. Employee Benefits of the Future
34. Benefits and the Bottom Line
40. Unregulated Work
42. Globalization and the American Labor Force
44. Learning from Our Overseas Counterparts
46. Don't Settle for Less: Global Compensation Programs Need Global Compensation Tools

Blue-collar jobs

2. Numbers Games
4. Alien Nation
8. The Best 4 Ways to Recruit Employees with Disabilities
9. Making Reasonable Accommodations for Employees with Mental Illness under the ADA
11. The Disability Advantage
13. Some of 'Our Boys Overseas' Have Gray Hair
17. Six Ways to Strengthen Staffing
25. Four Generations in the Workplace
26. The Face of Diversity Is More than Skin Deep
28. Do Your Employees Qualify for Overtime?
31. Doc in a Box
33. Employee Benefits of the Future
34. Benefits and the Bottom Line
40. Unregulated Work
42. Globalization and the American Labor Force
43. Immigration and the U.S. Economy: The Public's Perspective

Business ethics

2. Numbers Games
4. Alien Nation
8. The Best 4 Ways to Recruit Employees with Disabilities
9. Making Reasonable Accommodations for Employees with Mental Illness under the ADA
11. The Disability Advantage
12. Implementing Sexual Harassment Training in the Workplace
13. Some of 'Our Boys Overseas' Have Gray Hair
14. Fighting for Values
18. Balancing HR Systems with Employee Privacy

23. Banishing Bullying
26. The Face of Diversity Is More than Skin Deep
31. Doc in a Box
32. Building a Mentally Healthy Workforce
35. Setting up a Disciplinary Procedure
37. Hard-Core Offenders
39. Business Ethics: The Key Role of Corporate Governance
40. Unregulated Work
42. Globalization and the American Labor Force
43. Immigration and the U.S. Economy: The Public's Perspective

Communication

5. Strange Bedfellows
6. Understanding HRM-Firm Performance Linkages: The Role of the "Strength" of the HRM System
17. Six Ways to Strengthen Staffing
18. Balancing HR Systems with Employee Privacy
20. The Future of Work Motivation Theory
21. Managing in the New Millennium: Interpersonal Skills
22. Managing Employee Relations
23. Banishing Bullying
25. Four Generations in the Workplace
26. The Face of Diversity Is More than Skin Deep
29. Ten Steps to Designing an Effective Incentive Program
35. Setting up a Disciplinary Procedure
39. Business Ethics: The Key Role of Corporate Governance

Corporate strategy and human resources

4. Alien Nation
6. Understanding HRM-Firm Performance Linkages: The Role of the "Strength" of the HRM System
8. The Best 4 Ways to Recruit Employees with Disabilities
9. Making Reasonable Accommodations for Employees with Mental Illness under the ADA
11. The Disability Advantage
17. Six Ways to Strengthen Staffing
21. Managing in the New Millennium: Interpersonal Skills
25. Four Generations in the Workplace
26. The Face of Diversity Is More than Skin Deep
27. Philosophizing Compensation
28. Do Your Employees Qualify for Overtime?
29. Ten Steps to Designing an Effective Incentive Program
30. Pay Setters
33. Employee Benefits of the Future
34. Benefits and the Bottom Line
39. Business Ethics: The Key Role of Corporate Governance
40. Unregulated Work
42. Globalization and the American Labor Force
44. Learning from Our Overseas Counterparts
45. Human Resource Management in a Global Environment: Keys for Personal and Organizational Success

Disciplinary action

12. Implementing Sexual Harassment Training in the Workplace
20. The Future of Work Motivation Theory
23. Banishing Bullying
32. Building a Mentally Healthy Workforce
35. Setting Up a Disciplinary Procedure
37. Hard-Core Offenders
39. Business Ethics: The Key Role of Corporate Governance

Internet References

The following Internet sites have been carefully researched and selected to support the articles found in this reader. The easiest way to access these selected sites is to go to our student online support site at *http://www.mhcls.com/online/*.

AE: Human Resources 08/09

The following sites were available at the time of publication. Visit our Web site—we update our student online support site regularly to reflect any changes.

General Sources

Accountantsworld.com
http://www.accountantsworld.com

An online site dedicated to the field of accounting. Also included in the site are links to financial resources, including business, careers, e-commerce, insurance, and human resources.

American Psychological Association
http://www.apa.org

This site contains important information on workplace topics including revitalization of business and restructuring.

Bureau of Labor Statistics
http://stats.bls.gov:80

The home page of the Bureau of Labor Statistics (BLS), an agency of the U.S. Department of Labor, offers sections that include Economy at a Glance, Keyword Searches, Surveys and Programs, other statistical sites, and much more.

Economics Statistics Briefing Room
http://www.whitehouse.gov/fsbr/esbr.html

Easy access to current federal economic indicators is available at this site, which provides links to information produced by a number of federal agencies. Subjects are Output, Income, Employment, Production and Business Activity, Prices, Money, Transportation, and International Statistics.

Human Resource Professional's Gateway to the Internet
http://www.hrisolutions.com/index2.html

This Web site has links to other human relations locations, recruiting-related Web sites, HR–related companies, and search tools.

National Bureau of Economic Research Home Page
http://www.nber.org

The National Bureau of Economic Research does specialized research on every aspect of economics. These projects include, but are not limited to, pricing, labor studies, economics of aging, and productivity.

Society for Human Resource Management (SHRM)
http://www.shrm.org

SHRM is the world's largest association devoted to human resource management. Its mission is to serve the needs of HR professionals by providing essential and comprehensive resources. At this site, you'll find updates on methods, laws, and events as well as career information.

United States Department of Labor
http://www.dol.gov

This site provides a wealth of information on a number of labor-management issues. It has statutory as well as regulatory information and more.

United States Small Business Administration
http://www.sba.gov

The Small Business Administration encourages the establishment and development of small businesses through subsidized loans, business advice, and other forms of assistance.

UNIT 1: Human Resource Management in Perspective

Corporate Social Responsibility
http://www.aplink.net/~mikegree/career/social.htm

This article discusses balancing bottom line concerns with social responsibility.

Employment and Labor Law
http://www.lectlaw.com/temp.html

This site offers wide-ranging Web resources and articles covering electronic privacy rights, sexual harassment, discrimination, Americans with Disabilities (ADA) statutes, the Fair Labor Standards Act, and employment law.

Institute of Industrial Relations
http://www.iir.berkeley.edu

The Institute of Industrial Relations of the University of California, Berkeley, has links to research by the Center for Culture, Organization and Politics, the Center for Organization and Human Resource Effectiveness, and the Center for Work, Technology and Society.

Law at Work
http://www.lawatwork.com

From this site you can not only look at current labor laws, such as OSHA, but consider drug testing at work, unemployment questions, sexual harassment issues, affirmative action, and much more.

School of Labor and Industrial Relations Hot Links
http://www.lir.msu.edu/hotlinks

Links to newspapers, libraries, international intergovernmental organizations, as well as government statistics are provided here.

United States Equal Employment Opportunity Commission
http://www.eeoc.gov

Equal employment opportunity, employment discrimination, enforcement and litigation facts and figures are provided here.

UNIT 2: Meeting Human Resource Requirements

America's Job Bank
http://www.ajb.dni.us

You can find employers or job seekers and lots of job market information at this site. Employers can register their job openings, update them, and request employment service recruitment help.

International Association for Human Resource Information Management (IHRIM)
http://www.ihrim.org

IHRIM is a central network for its members to gain access and in-depth knowledge about HR information management and systems issues, trends, and technology.

Sympatico Careers
http://www.sympatico.workopolis.com

A Canadian site that provides a network with an outlet for finding solutions to everyday work problems.

Voice of the Shuttle: Postindustrial Business Theory Page
http://www.vos.scsb.edu/bfrowse.asp?=2727

Many subjects are included in this Web site, including: restructuring, downsizing, flattening, outsourcing, human resources, labor relations, learning organizations, and diversity.

UNIT 3: Creating a Productive Work Environment

American Society for Training and Development (ASTD)
http://www.astd.org

One of the largest organizations in the area of human resources. Publisher of *Training and Development* with local chapters all over the United States.

www.mhcls.com/online/

Commission on the Future of Worker-Management Relations
http://www.dol.gov/_sec/media/reports/dunlop/dunlop.htm

The report of the U.S. Federal Commission on the Future of Worker-Management Relations, which covers many issues, including enhancement of workplace productivity, changes in collective bargaining practices, and intervention in workplace problems by government agencies, may be found here.

The Downsizing of America
http://www.nytimes.com/specials/downsize/glance.html

The complete 7-week series on downsizing in America is printed on the Web by the *New York Times,* in which it appeared.

Employee Incentives and Career Development
http://www.snc.edu/socsci/chair/336/group1.htm

This site states that effective employee compensation and career development is an important tool in obtaining, maintaining, and retaining a productive workforce. There are links to Pay-for-Knowledge, Incentive Systems, Career Development, Wage and Salary Compensation, and more.

UNIT 4: Developing Effective Human Resources

Center for Organization and Human Resource Effectiveness
http://www.iir.berkeley.edu./cohre/cohre.html

The center for Organization and Human Resource Effectiveness Web page will allow you to navigate to policy papers, research in progress, as well as a virtual library. The center's mission is "Anticipating and creating new responses to a continuously changing business environment."

Discrimination and Diversity
http://www.domz.org/society/work/workplace.discriminatiorydiversity

A listing of sites to explore on workplace discrimination.

Employment Interviews
http://www.snc.edu/socsci/chair/336/group3.htm

The importance of proper interview techniques to the building of a workforce is discussed here. The page has links to related sites and refers to a book by Alder and Elmhorst, *Communicating at Work: Principles and Practices for Business and the Professionals.*

Feminist Majority Foundation
http://www.feminist.org

This site houses the Feminist Career Center, an Affirmative Action page, and information of interest to women.

UNIT 5: Implementing Compensation, Benefits, and Workplace Safety

BenefitsLink: The National Employee Benefits Web Site
http://www.benefitslink.com/index.php

This link offers facts and services for employers who are sponsoring employee benefit plans and for participating workers.

Equal Compensation, and Employee Ownership
http://www.fed.org

Sponsored by the Foundation for Enterprise Development, this site includes strategies for making critical decisions to help companies improve their profitability. There are interactive resources and cases.

Equal Pay Act and Pay Inequity
http://www.infoplease.com/spot/equalpayact1.html

Related links are included in this presentation of the Equal Pay Act and the history of pay inequity.

Executive Pay Watch
http://www.aflcio.org/corporateamerica/paywatch/

While keeping an eye on the issue of executive salaries, bonuses, and perks in CEO compensation packages, this labor union site offers suggestions to working families on what can be done to curb exorbitant pay schemes.

Job Stress
http://www.workhealth.org/news/nwprahn98.html

Research on job stress is available on this site.

Social Security Administration
http://www.ssa.gov

Here is the official Web site of the Social Security Administration.

WorkPlace Injury and Illness Statistics
http://www.osha.gov/oshstats/work.html

The Bureau of Labor Statistics Web site presents links to many issues of occupational injury and illness and offers a great deal of statistical information.

UNIT 6: Fostering Employee/Management Relationships

Management, Leadership and Supervision
http://humanresources.about.com/od/managementandleadership/

This site offers input as well as links on how to improve your management and leadership skills.

UNIT 7: International Human Resource Management

Cultural Globalization
http://www.inst.at/studies/collab/breidenb.htm

This paper by Joana Breidenbach and Ina Zukrigl discusses the dynamics and myths of cultural globalization.

Globalization and Human Resource Management
http://www.cic.sfu.ca/forum/adler.html

Dr. Nancy J. Adler, a faculty member at McGill University, discusses strategic international human resource development in this thorough summary for the Internet.

India Finance and Investment
http://www.finance.indiamart.com

A guide to investing in India. It addresses taxation, organization, capital market investment as well as other topics.

International Business Resources on the Web
http://www.globaledge.msu.edu/ibrd/ibrd.asp

The Center for International Business Education and Research at Michigan State University permits a key word search and has a great deal of trade information, government resources, and periodicals. It also has country and regional information.

International Labour Organization
http://www.ilo.org

The International Labour Organization's Web page leads to links that discuss the objectives of the organization and summarize international labor standards and human rights. The official United Nations Web site locator will point to many other resources.

Labor Relations and the National Labor Relations Board
http://www.snc.edu/socsci/chair/336/group2.htm

From this site you can explore labor relations in today's international marketplace.

We highly recommend that you review our Web site for expanded information and our other product lines. We are continually updating and adding links to our Web site in order to offer you the most usable and useful information that will support and expand the value of your Annual Editions. You can reach us at: *http://www.mhcls.com/annualeditions/.*

UNIT 1

Human Resource Management in Perspective

Unit Selections

1. **HR Is Dead, Long Live HR,** Shari Caudron
2. **Numbers Games,** Amy Burke Shriberg
3. **Why We Hate HR,** Keith H. Hammonds
4. **Alien Nation,** Michael Maiello and Nicole Ridgway
5. **Strange Bedfellows,** Jeff Smith and Kristiane Blomqvist
6. **Understanding HRM-Firm Performance Linkages: The Role of the "Strength" of the HRM System,** David Bowen and Cheri Ostroff
7. **Strategic Human Resources Management in Government,** Jonathan Tompkins
8. **The Best 4 Ways to Recruit Employees with Disabilities,** Yoji Cole
9. **Making Reasonable Accommodations for Employees with Mental Illness under the ADA,** Jonathan Hafen
10. **The Devil Is in the Details,** Thomas Clark
11. **The Disability Advantage,** Alison Stein Wellner
12. **Implementing Sexual Harassment Training in the Workplace,** Dave Gottwals
13. **Some of 'Our Boys Overseas' Have Gray Hair,** Allison Bell
14. **Fighting for Values,** Tony Blair

Key Points to Consider

- What are some of the possible changes you see occurring in the workforce in the next several generations? Do you think Human Resources can play a bigger and more important role in organizations?

- What are some of the ways that firms can better utilize the skills and talents of their employees?

- Do you think that the unemployment figures that are issued every month give an accurate picture of the state of unemployment and the U.S. economy?

- What were the most important changes for the American worker during the 20th century, and what changes do you see as likely in the next 20 years?

- In the past 30 years, the government has taken a more active role in the struggle of minorities and other groups in the workforce. How has the ADA changed the workplace?

- Sexual harassment is a very important area of concern for most organizations. What do you think organizations can and should do about it?

- How do you think September 11 will affect organizations and their relations with their employees? Do you think that things will change significantly?

Student Web Site
www.mhcls.com/online

Internet References
Further information regarding these Web sites may be found in this book's preface or online.

Corporate Social Responsibility
http://www.aplink.net/~mikegree/career/social.htm

Employment and Labor Law
http://www.lectlaw.com/temp.html

Institute of Industrial Relations
http://www.iir.berkeley.edu

Law at Work
http://www.lawatwork.com

School of Labor and Industrial Relations Hot Links
http://www.lir.msu.edu/hotlinks

United States Equal Employment Opportunity Commission
http://www.eeoc.gov

The only constant is change. Industrial society is dynamic, a great engine that has brought about many of the most significant changes in the history of the human race. Since the start of the Industrial Revolution in England, a little over 230 years ago, industrialized society has transformed Western civilization in a multitude of ways. Many great inventions of the last 200 years have significantly altered the way people live and the way they see the world.

At the time of the Declaration of Independence, the 13 colonies were an overwhelmingly agricultural society that clung to the Atlantic coast of North America. At the beginning of the 21st century, the United States is a continental nation with the world's largest industrial base and perhaps the smallest percentage of farmers of any major industrialized country. These changes did not happen overnight, but were both the result and the cause of the technological innovations of the Industrial Revolution. The technological marvels of today, such as television, radio, computers, airplanes, and automobiles, did not exist until after the Industrial Revolution, and a disproportionate number of them did not exist until after 1900.

Along with technological changes have come changes in the ways people earn their living. When Thomas Jefferson authored the Declaration of Independence in 1776, he envisioned a nation of small, independent farmers, but that is not what later developed. Factories, mass production, and economies of scale have been the watchwords of industrial development. Industrial development changed not only the economy, but also society. Most Americans are no longer independent farmers, but are, for the most part, wage earners, who make their living working for someone else.

Changes in the American labor force include the increase in women and minorities working next to white males. The nature of most jobs has changed from those directly associated with production to those providing services in the white-collar economy. Many other changes are developing in the economy and society that will be reflected in the workforce. For the first time since the early days of the republic, international trade represents a significant part of the American economy, having increased greatly in the past 30 years. The economic reality is that the GM autoworker competes not only with Ford and Chrysler, but also with Toyota and Volkswagen.

The society, the economy, and the workforce have changed. Americans today live in a much different world than they did 200 years ago. It is a highly diverse, heterogeneous world, full of paradoxes. When people think of American industry, they tend to think of giant-sized companies like IBM and General Electric, but, in fact, most people work for small firms. The relative importance of the Fortune 500 companies in terms of employment in the economy has been declining both in real and percentage terms. Today, economic growth is with small organizations.

Change has brought not only a different society, but a more complex one. Numerous rules and regulations must be followed

Digital Vision/PunchStock

that did not exist 200 years ago. The human element in any organization has been critical to its success, and knowing what the human resource needs of the organization are going to be 1, 5, or even 10 years into the future is a key element for continuing success.

Individual decisions have also changed. In the first part of the 20th century, it was common for a worker to spend his or her entire life with one organization, doing one particular job. Now the worker can expect to do many different jobs, probably with a number of different organizations in different industries. Mergers, technological change, and economic fluctuations all put a premium on individual adaptability in a changing work environment for individual economic survival.

The changes in industrial society often come at a faster rate than most people are willing to either accept or adapt to. Many old customs and prejudices have been retained from prior times, and while progress has been made with regard to certain groups— no American employer today would dare to end an employment notice with the letters "NINA" (No Irish Need Apply), as was common at one time—for other groups, the progress has been slow at best. Women represent about half of American workers but they are paid only about 70 percent of what men earn, and sexual harassment still represents a problem, as discussed in "Implementing Sexual Harassment Training in the Workplace."

African Americans, and other minorities, have been discriminated against for centuries in American society, to the point where the federal government has been forced to step in and legislate equal opportunity, both on and off the job. People with disabilities have also sought protection as seen in "The Best 4 Ways to Recruit Employees with Disabilities," "Making Reasonable Accommodations for Employees with Mental Illness under the ADA," and "The Disability Advantage."

The clash of differing cultures seems ever more pronounced in our society. America has traditionally viewed itself as a melting pot, but it is clear that certain groups have historically "melted" more easily than others, a situation that is reflected in the workplace.

Human resource management plays an important role in industrial America. Business leaders recognize the value of their employees to the future of their organizations. Increasingly, competition in world markets is becoming based on the skills and abilities of people, not machines. Indeed, among major competitors, virtually everyone has essentially the same equipment. The difference is often what the people in the organization do with the equipment.

Of special consideration are the recent events of 9/11. For the first time since the War of 1812, the United States was forcefully attacked on its' home soil with a greater loss of life than at Pearl Harbor. These events will mean changes in the way the economy operates and the way organizations will treat their employees. HR professionals must address these issues as seen in British Prime Minister Tony Blair's "Fighting for Values," and "Some of 'Our Boys Overseas' Have Gray Hair."

Society, the workplace, and the way they are viewed have all undergone major changes. Frederick W. Taylor and Elton Mayo, early writers in management, held certain views about industry at the beginning of the twentieth century, while Peter Drucker, W. Edwards Deming, and others have different ideas now, at the beginning of the twenty-first century. The American society and economy, as well as the very life of the average American worker, are different from what they were 200 or even 100 years ago, and both the workers and the organizations that employ them must respond to those changes.

HR Is Dead, Long Live HR

In this era of human capital, HR is experiencing seismic change. Outsourcing is swiftly taking over. If HR stands still, it's doomed. But if it changes, its business clout can be more potent than ever.

SHARI CAUDRON

The future of human resources has perhaps no greater champion than Kathleen S. Barclay, vice president of global human resources for General Motors. When asked if the function is becoming obsolete, Barclay is adamant. "I don't agree with that," she says. "I suppose it depends on the company that you're dealing with, but my view is that there has never been a more important time in any company to have a very strong, active HR organization. HR can have so much impact on the way the company works, how the culture feels, and the type of talent you have both now and in the future."

Is it an HR reality to become indispensable and more vital than ever? Or do the job losses signify a different trend? Could HR be on its way toward obsolescence?

In companies where HR has taken the reins and moved the function in a new direction, the financial results have been impressive. Research from Watson Wyatt's WorkUSA 2002 study indicates that companies with effective HR practices deliver shareholder returns that are three times higher than those of companies without such practices.

Despite the evidence and the firm belief in HR's potential among executives such as Barclay, the profession's rosy future is far from certain. In fact, the number of available HR jobs has dwindled significantly in recent years, and opportunities are not likely to increase anytime soon, says Frank Allen, president of Frank E. Allen and Associates in Florham Park, New Jersey. Allen, who has been in the HR recruitment field for more than 17 years, has placed thousands of HR professionals in jobs ranging from benefits manager to senior vice president. And right now, he's drowning in résumés. "I've got a database list-ing 18,000 HR professionals and out of that, somewhere around 7,000 active résumés," he says. "I'm also getting 200 to 300 résumés a week." The likelihood that Allen will be able to place all these people is pretty slim.

With the unemployment rate hovering around 6 percent, the same thing can be said of many jobs, including information technology, telecommunications, and marketing. But when the economy turns around, people in those positions are likely to find work again. That's not necessarily true for HR professionals, because the profession is enduring a wave of changes that by all accounts are likely to significantly reduce the number of people needed. David Ulrich, co-author of *The HR Scorecard: Linking People, Strategy, and Performance* (Harvard Business School Press, 2001), believes that the head count in HR will eventually plummet 25 percent—or more.

But wait. People like Barclay believe that HR is primed to lead knowledge-intensive companies into the future. Is she right? Is it an HR reality to become indispensable and more vital than ever? Or do the job losses signify a different trend? Could HR be on its way toward obsolescence?

First, the Bad News

If you are a pessimist who thinks that HR's cup is slowly draining, you'll find a lot of support for your position. The primary evidence comes in the form of outsourcing. Today, there are vendors available and champing at the bit to help with every single product and service offered by HR, including staffing, payroll, benefits administration, training, employee relations, and compensation. According to research by Gartner, Inc., 80 percent of companies now outsource at least one HR activity, and the number is swiftly growing.

Consequently, what started in the 1980s as simple payroll outsourcing has exploded into a $32 billion a year business involving all facets of HR. In the last two years alone, the value of the business-process outsourcing industry has grown 20

How Will the HR Profession Look Five Years from Now?

Steve VanNostrand, vice president, HR

The Raymond Corporation

(part of Toyota Industries Corporation) Greene, New York

"HR will take on more of a leadership role with the business units rather than a partnership role. I don't see radical change. I see continuous improvement. HR is now being held to the same standard as other functions such as marketing, manufacturing, and engineering. My expectation is that we will continue to deliver more value and our business expertise will continue to increase.

"I don't see HR becoming obsolete. I've got experience with both large and midsized organizations, and my network tells me our function continues to be valued more and more each year. In some cases, we'll see the line blur between historic HR and line management. But I see us becoming more relevant, not less."

How Do You Envision the Future of HR?

Lawrence B. Costello, senior vice president, HR

American Standard Companies, Inc.

Piscataway, New Jersey

"First off, [at American Standard] we're actively considering renaming the function. I think it's time. The typical image of HR is constraining and does not portray the visionary or leadership aspect we're trying to bring forward.

"That said, I think the future of HR is exciting because senior management is starting to look to HR for insight and perspective on how to guide the company. We're participating in the business process in a way we never have before.

"The new HR takes a different kind of person to succeed, and I'm having to do a lot more internal development work than I thought. The new HR takes people with business experience who are not afraid to state their point of view. Because of that, we in the HR community have to recognize that future HR leaders can't just come from HR. There is no reason we can't take people on a cross-functional basis and invite them into the profession."

percent, and analysts from Gartner estimate that it will become a $55 billion worldwide industry by 2005. In just four years, one outsource provider—Exult—has grown from a start-up with a handful of people to an established company with 1,500 employees and more than $400 million in annual revenues. Other big players include Accenture HR Services, ADP, Fidelity, Hewitt, and Convergys.

"Right now, it is primarily large companies that outsource their HR activities," says Rebecca Scholl, senior analyst with Gartner. "But we're definitely seeing an uptick in the number of medium-sized companies that are looking for providers to take on more HR processes."

Outsourcing has become popular because companies are finding that external vendors—through technology and economies of scale—can provide more efficient and cost-effective HR services than in-house departments. In 1999, BP (formerly British Petroleum) contracted with Exult to take over all of its transactional activities in the United States and United Kingdom, including all payroll, recruiting, expatriation, records management, vendor management, and relocation services for its 63,000 employees. The only function that remains in-house is BP's learning and development program in the United States.

Over the last two years, the company has reaped many benefits from the arrangement. Payroll processing is more timely and accurate. Employees get their benefits questions answered sooner. HR processes have been standardized across the company. And for the first time, BP has measurable data on which HR activities are effective.

Because BP is no longer handling routine transactional work in-house, a lot of its HR employees were deemed unnecessary.

As a result, its core HR staff has been slashed 65 percent—from 100 to 35 people.

This kind of staff reduction is fairly typical in outsource arrangements, says Jim Madden, chairman and president of Exult. "What usually happens when companies outsource with us is that one-half to two-thirds of the jobs in the HR department go away because the jobs are declared redundant."

External vendors have been so successful doing routine HR work that the list of companies handing over their HR activities continues to grow. In the last few months, Sony, Prudential, AT&T, and American Express have all inked deals with outsource providers. Chances are good that in the next few months, a lot of HR people in those companies will be looking for work.

But What about Strategy?

One of the primary arguments for downloading HR activities onto an external vendor is that getting rid of routine transactional tasks allows HR professionals to focus on the kind of transformational work that helps the bottom line. But despite all the talk about becoming strategic partners, research indicates that the majority of HR people still don't have what it takes to fulfill leadership roles.

Ed Lawler, director of the Center for Effective Organizations at the University of Southern California in Los Angeles, has been gathering data on the effectiveness of HR since 1995. In the last seven years, he's seen very little change in how HR professionals are spending their time. "It seems that instead of responding to this period of business turbulence by playing a central strategic business partner role," Lawler says, "HR has responded by maintaining the status quo."

His findings are supported by a recent survey of HR professionals conducted by the Society for Human Resource Management. When respondents were asked to identify two or three HR/workplace trends they believe will affect the HR profession, only 7 percent identified "HR as a strategic business partner" as a key trend. Much higher on the list were such things as managing diversity and administering health care. Clearly, HR professionals will never be able to transform the function—and hold on to their jobs—if they cannot embrace this new role.

Part of the problem is that many HR people simply don't understand what it means to be strategic. In a separate SHRM study entitled "The Future of the HR Profession," eight leading

What Are the Competencies Needed for Next-Generation HR Professionals?

Wayne Broadbank, clinical professor of business at the University of Michigan, Ann Arbor, has been studying HR competencies for the past 15 years. Over the course of his research, more than 27,000 HR professionals and their line management associates have participated.

Broadbank's most recent research, conducted last year (2002), revealed that HR professionals in high-performing firms demonstrate the following competencies:

1. **Strategic contribution:** HR professionals in high-performing companies manage culture, facilitate "fast change," are involved in strategic decision-making, and create market-driven connectivity.
2. **Personal credibility:** These HR professionals are credible to both their HR counterparts and the business line managers whom they serve. They also have effective writing and verbal skills.
3. **HR delivery:** Strategic HR people focus traditional HR activities in four key areas: staffing, development, performance management, and managing and measuring the impact of global HR practices.
4. **Business knowledge:** The most important areas of business knowledge for an HR professional include a keen understanding of how the firm creates wealth, how the firm is horizontally integrated (e.g., how sales and marketing relate to manufacturing), and what the industry challenges are.
5. **Knowledge of HR technology:** HR professionals must be able to leverage technology for HR practices and use e-HR/Web-based channels to deliver value to customers.

consulting firms shared their thoughts on the current and future state of HR. One of the themes that emerged is that few HR professionals possess both the business acumen and functional expertise necessary to move their companies and the HR profession forward.

Frank Allen, who's frequently given the task of finding high-level HR people for companies, estimates that of the 18,000 people in his database, "I'd say less than 1 percent of them are A players." And who are those A players? They are the people who not only have a solid understanding of HR, but also are conversant in finance, sales, marketing, and manufacturing, and know how HR can help companies meet their goals.

The dearth of business talent within HR is causing more and more companies to look outside the profession when seeking to fill top HR slots. Today, 75 percent of top HR executives have come up through the traditional ranks of HR. Four years ago, that number was 79 percent. What this means is that today, fully one quarter of the top HR jobs are going to people with backgrounds in marketing, manufacturing, finance, and other operational areas—and the number is growing. What hope does the profession have for its future if it is increasingly being managed by people from the outside?

To be fair, HR isn't solely to blame. Senior leaders have to recognize the role HR can play and give its HR team the time and resources necessary to make lasting changes. Unfortunately, not all CEOs understand that strategic workforce planning and management is an ongoing effort. Allen knows of some companies that have hired strategic high-level HR people only to let them go once they think they've achieved their objectives. "Either that, or a new chair will come in with a different idea of HR," he says. "Instead of viewing HR as an asset, they'll view it as an administrative function and fire the person who was trying to make strategic changes."

Fortunately, corporate leaders who do understand the role HR can play also realize that it takes time and a lot of serious effort to make changes.

The dearth of business talent within HR is causing more and more companies to look outside the profession when seeking to fill top HR slots.

Four years ago, when Barclay was promoted to vice president of global human resources at GM, it was the first time in the company's history that an HR person reported directly to the CEO. Barclay launched a company-wide HR transformation effort that involved standardizing processes, creating HR centers of excellence, and outsourcing routine activities. In a company with 362,000 global workers in 58 countries, a change of this magnitude obviously takes time. Barclay has already been at it for three years and says it will take three more years to fully complete the process—but that the CEO is committed to the change.

A key part of GM's global HR transformation involves developing HR people so that they understand and can take on the role of internal consultants. "We have a global HR curriculum that helps our people understand what we are attempting to accomplish in HR, what the transformation means to them, and where we're going as an HR community," Barclay says. "We have 15 to 20 courses out there now, and they are mandatory for all HR professionals." Among other things, these courses help HR professionals acquire business acumen, change-management skills, and the ability to forge relationships across the organization. As a result, in the not-too-distant future when a business unit is having trouble achieving its goals, GM's HR people will be able to work with that unit to diagnose its problem. It might be because the talent makeup is not adequate, the incentives are wrong, or goals have not been properly communicated. By training its HR people to understand—and address—such business issues, Barclay is slowly transforming the way the function operates.

In addition to training the HR people, her team has to train line managers to understand that HR is now there to help with strategy, not transactional work. "We have a global HR Web site that houses materials our HR people can use with their operating leaders to help those leaders understand how HR is changing, why it needs to, and why the value equation is better for the company," she says.

As in many other companies, a key part of the HR transformation at GM involves transferring responsibility for HR activities to line unit managers with the help of technology. For example, GM recently instituted a compensation plan for 40,000 employees that was implemented by managers entirely over the Web without any intervention from HR. "This experience helped managers understand how HR is working differently now," Barclay says.

However, this kind of change isn't always easy for organizations to accept, Lawler notes. "Line managers typically like the close, hand-holding type of relationship they've always gotten from their friendly HR person," he says. "The idea that transactional work might take place in an outsource company or disappear entirely because of employee self-service

technology is unattractive and anxiety-producing for many managers."

But blaming anxious line managers or noncommittal CEOs for presenting obstacles to HR's transformation does not a strategic, fully employed HR person make. The fact remains that the HR profession itself has a long way to go in developing the skills, competencies, and focus necessary to become internal business consultants. Until that happens, the slow decline of HR jobs and stature is likely to continue.

Finally, Some Good News

If you're an optimist who sees an unlimited future for HR, there's plenty of reason to celebrate.

Let's revisit the idea of outsourcing. Yes, it is reducing the number of HR jobs available in companies that choose to outsource. But those jobs tend to be lower-level administrative and technical positions. The good news is that outsourcing is finally giving higher-level HR professionals the time they need to tackle strategic workforce challenges. Even better, the demand for such strategists is higher than ever, for several reasons.

To begin with, demographic changes are making it harder and harder for companies to find and keep qualified employees. It will be up to HR to determine what kind of talent is needed to meet company goals and then devise recruitment and retention programs based on that need. Second, technology is making it possible for companies to become more and more decentralized, with employees distributed across wider geographic regions. HR people will be the ones who determine how to keep widely dispersed employees connected to corporate goals.

Third, although outsource vendors have proven their ability to handle routine transactional work, internal HR consultants will still be needed to determine what combination of pay, benefits, and learning opportunities is necessary to keep employees engaged. Finally, even if outsourcing does remove all the transactional work, someone with a solid understanding of HR and business will be needed to manage the multimillion-dollar vendor contracts. HR will always be responsible for ensuring the speed and accuracy of employee transactions, regardless of who is doing the work.

"Essentially, what's happened is that the field of HR has begun to split into two parts," Ulrich says. One half consists of administrative and transactional work, which is becoming more automated and routine and is increasingly being turned over to employee self-service or outsource providers. The second half consists of transformational work, in which HR develops organizational goals, determines what capabilities are needed to meet those goals, and then creates HR practices that make those capabilities come to life.

Put all of this together and you realize that the field is in the midst of an enormous transformation and its final form is not yet clear. However, the function is likely to be smaller and very different from what it is now. And there will be no shortage of challenging work. HR professionals can have an impact on their companies. And obviously, the need is there.

Is HR Becoming Obsolete?

Kathleen S. Barclay, vice president, global HR

General Motors

Detroit, Michigan

"I don't agree with that. I suppose it depends on the company that you're dealing with, but my view is that there has never been a more important time in any company to have a very strong, active HR organization. HR can have so much impact on the way the company works, how the culture feels, and the type of talent you have both now and in the future. HR has a huge role to play in helping senior leaders shape the culture and make sure that culture is driving business outcomes."

Is HR up to the task? In companies like General Motors, the answer is a definite yes. But as research shows, there's still a huge chasm between desire and reality when it comes to the future of HR.

Is HR becoming indispensable—or obsolete? Only the people currently working in the profession know the answer to that.

If they are able to forge a link between HR initiatives and corporate goals, their indispensability is all but assured. If not, a lot more HR résumés may be circulating in the near future.

Contributing editor **SHARI CAUDRON** lives in Denver. E-mail editors@ workforce.com to comment.

Numbers Games
Undercounting Unemployment and Its Consequences

AMY BURKE SHRIBERG

Although unemployment data from the U.S. Bureau of Labor Statistics (BLS) have been less discouraging of late, the news would be far worse if the media reported the total number of Americans currently out of work. And if the number of Americans who are under employed or who work full time but earn poverty wages were reported widely on a regular basis, the U.S. economic outlook would appear worse still. Instead, the official unemployment rate reflects a rather narrow definition of unemployment and obscures debates that we should be having about the overall health of the U.S. economy and its ability to provide decent, family-supporting jobs to all its citizens. Arguments about how to calculate the nation's unemployment rate aren't new, but the issue has fallen off the publics radar screen in recent years. Most Americans accept that the unemployment statistic is what it purports to be: an accurate assessment of those looking for work.

Mainstream media devote little attention to the limitations of the official unemployment rate, especially during periods of growth. During recessions, articles examining deeper economic issues may appear, but they almost never address just how many Americans are left out of the count—and how many others aren't doing well by other measures. Many middle- and lower income Americans have a visceral understanding that the economy is worse than our official economists admit, but their knowledge is not reflected in the nations unemployment statistics. Even during the boom years of the mid- and late 1990s, income inequality expanded for many Americans, and lower income Americans with less education enjoyed fewer opportunities for meaningful employment than the headlines about record low levels of unemployment suggested.

The government first began collecting simple information about the nations unemployed in 1880, but it wasn't until the Great Depression that efforts to collect unemployment statistics began in earnest. At the onset of that major calamity, estimates of the nations unemployed were unofficial and varied, often provided by private agencies. Inaccurate information about just how many Americans needed jobs made it more difficult for New Dealers to craft coherent employment policies. The depression firmly established the critical importance of more precise data, and the government instituted the monthly Current Population Survey in 1940. The CPS is a sample survey of (currently) sixty thousand households from which the official unemployment rate is derived. It was originally administered by the Works Progress Administration (WPA), a New Deal work relief program that ceased to exist in 1943, and it is now cosponsored by the U.S. Census Bureau and the BLS. The depression also gave birth in 1935 to our unemployment insurance system, which continues to provide benefits for unemployed Americans lucky enough to qualify. The system operates largely at the state level but with federal oversight, and its benefits only partially replace wages. Many of the unemployed are ineligible for benefits. According to the Economic Policy Institute (EPI), only 38 percent of currently unemployed workers qualify for unemployment benefits.

So how does the BLS define unemployment? For starters, those interviewed are never asked directly whether they are unemployed. To be classified as officially unemployed, individuals must meet the following Bureau criteria:

> They had no employment during the reference week; they were available for work at that time; and they made specific efforts to find employment sometime during the 4-week period ending with the reference week. Persons laid off from a job and expecting recall need not be looking for work to be counted as unemployed.

That leaves out many people without jobs who are available and want to work. These would-be workers, often the long-term unemployed, are left out of the official number if they have not sought work actively in the reference month—even though they may have spent months on a fruitless job search before giving up. Also left out are those working part time even though they would prefer full-time employment. The government does collect and publish this information, so it is there for people to find (if you know where to look for it), but it is almost never reported. Thus, when the official unemployment number is relatively low—as it was during the recent boom years—those interested in discussing poverty and the troubles confronting lower income Americans face an uphill battle. Policymakers and politicians consider low unemployment almost infallible evidence of economic health. Reliance on the official rate also stymies discussion of an expansive full-employment policy that would take into account the uncounted unemployed and the under employed as well.

An organization that works to highlight the discrepancy between the official unemployment rate and what is often called hidden unemployment is the National Jobs For All Coalition (NJFAC), which posts unemployment data each month after the BLS data are made public. In October (the latest figures available at this writing), the official U.S. unemployment rate was 6.0 percent or 8.8 million individuals. This marked a slight decrease from June's numbers, when the official unemployment statistic reached a more than nine-year high of 6.4 percent or 9.4 million individuals. Although the decrease may mark the beginning of an economic turnaround, growth remains sluggish in many sectors. To calculate hidden unemployment, the coalition includes BLS figures for those working part time because they can't find full-time employment. In October, 4.8 million Americans fell into that category. In addition, it also reports the number of people who want jobs but who are not included in the official statistic because they do not qualify as actively looking. That figure amounted to 4.9 million individuals in October. Combining the official unemployment rate with these additional figures provides a more realistic picture of the U.S. economy: it increases the number of unemployed from 6.0 percent to 12.2 percent or 18.5 million persons for October, according to the coalition (the BLS doesn't calculate that figure although it provides the components to do so).

We get an even better picture of the very large number of Americans facing economic hardship if we add in those working full time yet earning poverty level wages. Based on Census Bureau data for the year 2000, 16.8 percent of those working full-time, or 16.9 million individuals, earn less than the official poverty rate for a four-person family. In other words, about one in seven men and one in four women, employed full time all year, earned less than poverty level wages for a family of four.

In addition, the official unemployment figure excludes the incarcerated population from the labor force. During the 1980s and 1990s, the number of individuals held in federal and state prisons more than tripled, increasing from about 320,000 in 1980 to 1.3 million in 2000. And between 1980 and 2000 the total jail and prison population together increased from 503,586 to 1,937,482—a 284.7 percent increase, according to U.S. Bureau of Justice statistics.

The official unemployment rate has another flaw as well, namely that it is subject to the same under-coverage problems as all surveys are—and to any undercounting problems associated with the census from which CPS population controls are derived. Although efforts are made to correct for under-coverage, members of certain groups are more likely than others to be left out of census surveys. For instance, young black males are the most likely to be under-covered in the monthly CPS survey used to calculate the official unemployment rate. But they are not the only group inaccurately represented in the survey. Adjustments are made to correct for this under-coverage, yet the assumption is that members of the cohort left out of the survey resemble members of the cohort who responded to the survey. There is no way for statisticians at the Census and BLS to know for certain whether this is true, according to Ed Robison, a BLS statistician. Although he can't prove it one way or the other, Robisons assumption is that some of the under-covered groups experience at least slightly higher rates of unemployment than their covered counterparts.

Rather than developing a more broadly encompassing measure of unemployment, the BLS actually has narrowed the definition of those counted as officially unemployed over the years. It is interesting to note first how the BLS defines employment. Individuals are classified as employed if

> they did any work at all as paid employees during the reference week [working as little as an hour qualifies]; worked in their own business, profession, or on their own farm; or worked without pay at least 15 hours in a family business or farm. People are also counted as employed if they were temporarily absent from their jobs because of illness, bad weather, vacation, labor-management disputes, or personal reasons.

By including those who worked as little as an hour during the reference week, the number of employed individuals is already inflated. On top of that, the definition of "unemployed" has changed over the years to include fewer and fewer individuals. Several changes were made in 1967 and 1994 that winnowed the number of those officially out of work—most notably by excluding discouraged workers, who have stopped looking for work—from the labor force.

During recent boom years, unemployment hovered at such low levels that economists began redefining what they considered to be the natural rate of unemployment, or the non-accelerating inflation rate of unemployment (the NAIRU), which is the amount of unemployment considered necessary to keep inflation stable. The official unemployment rate fell from about 7.5 percent in 1992 to a thirty-year low of 4 percent in 2000. Such low unemployment precluded discussions of public jobs programs and ongoing job shortages, as employers often scrambled to fill positions, even though many Americans remained unemployed or underemployed at the same time.

Debates about joblessness in non-recessionary times usually revolve around how jobs are distributed among the population of job seekers. What is often overlooked is the perhaps more significant issue of whether there are enough total jobs, whether good or bad, to go around. "Even in periods of general prosperity, there are not enough jobs to satisfy the needs of everyone who wants to work, and the burdens of this joblessness tend to fall disproportionately on disadvantaged population groups," says Rutgers University law professor Philip Harvey in "Responding to Rising Unemployment: Can We Afford Jobs for All?"

Indeed, there is plenty of evidence that even in good times a low unemployment rate masks an underlying job shortage, especially if we are talking about jobs that offer individuals with a high-school diploma or less access to family-supporting wages and benefits. The U.S. manufacturing sector, which once provided the bulk of such jobs for Americans without college degrees, has continued to be pummeled by globalization and the movement of those jobs abroad. In 2002, the U.S. trade deficit soared to its highest level of $435 billion. Even during the most recent period of growth, the United States lost more than 2.4 million manufacturing jobs. White-collar jobs, such as computer programming positions, are increasingly being sent overseas as well, which raises further questions about the ability of the U.S. economy to provide enough jobs for its citizens.

Moreover, certain segments of the population have been disproportionately harmed by our current jobless recovery— although average job searches have lengthened across sub-groups and regardless of individuals educational background and previous work experience. A recent study by Northeastern University's Center for Labor Market Studies reveals that there are roughly 5.5 million young people who were out of school but jobless in 2002. The study, *Left Behind in the Labor Market,* documents a 12 percent, or six hundred thousand person increase, in the number of unemployed youths sixteen to twenty-four years old since 2000. Rather than boosting spending on youth programs, however, Congress cut more than three hundred million dollars last January for job training and youth employment programs.

One negative consequence of our system of officially under-estimating the number of unemployed is that many people perceive the unemployment rate as synonymous with the number of jobs needed to employ everybody who wants to work. "The more important failing in the U.S. statistics is our failure to measure job availability for purposes of comparison with unemployment statistics," as Harvey says. To correct this, the BLS should measure the number of jobs that employers are ready and willing to fill. The BLS has recently begun a new survey, the Job Openings and Labor Turnover Survey, which is designed to begin assessing the number of job openings in the country. While this is a start in the right direction, Harvey argues that more refined statistics are needed to evaluate how many full-time jobs are needed to employ all who want such jobs.

As long as there is a significant job shortage, it makes more sense to discuss how to increase the total number of jobs available rather than devoting scarce resources to trying to equalize the distribution of an insufficient number of jobs among different groups of Americans. This is unlikely while the official unemployment rate disguises the depth of unemployment and under employment plaguing the U.S. economy. It makes sense that the government would calculate the unemployment rate in such a way as to minimize the number of unemployed. But this poses severe problems for liberals and leftists because many contemporary policy debates, such as those about welfare reform, unemployment benefits, tax cuts, and more, revolve around an often false understanding of the economy and the opportunities it provides during periods of economic expansion and recession.

The welfare reform bill enacted by Congress in 1996, for instance, is predicated on the notion that those in need should have to work, but there was little significant debate about whether the economy could provide enough jobs, especially with decent wages, to those forced off the nations welfare rolls. The false idea that jobs await those who seek them undergirds the new welfare system, Temporary Assistance for Needy Families, which requires most recipients to work to remain eligible for benefits.

It is time to shift the terms of the debate, so that policymakers address the needs of all Americans in search of decent work. If more of our citizens understood how many more of us are unemployed, even during the best of times, support for a permanent public jobs program—modeled perhaps on Roosevelts WPA—might grow. Liberals might also be able to revive discussions of a full-employment agenda. Given the statistics as they are, and public knowledge about the economy as it is, we are left with a president and Congress whose only job creation proposals revolve around additional and continued tax cuts for the affluent and whose time in office has already coincided with the loss of at least 2.5 million jobs.

AMY BURKE SHRIBERG is a writer living in Ohio.

Why We Hate HR

In a knowledge economy, companies with the best talent win. And finding, nurturing, and developing that talent should be one of the most important tasks in a corporation. So why does human resources do such a bad job—and how can we fix it?

KEITH H. HAMMONDS

Well, here's a rockin' party: a gathering of several hundred midlevel human-resources executives in Las Vegas. (Yo, Wayne Newton! How's the 401(k)?) They are here, ensconced for two days at faux-glam Caesars Palace, to confer on "strategic HR leadership," a conceit that sounds, to the lay observer, at once frightening and self-contradictory. If not plain laughable.

Because let's face it: After close to 20 years of hopeful rhetoric about becoming "strategic partners" with a "seat at the table" where the business decisions that matter are made, most human-resources professionals aren't nearly there. They have no seat, and the table is locked inside a conference room to which they have no key. HR people are, for most practical purposes, neither strategic nor leaders.

I don't care for Las Vegas. And if it's not clear already, I don't like HR, either, which is why I'm here. The human-resources trade long ago proved itself, at best, a necessary evil—and at worst, a dark bureaucratic force that blindly enforces nonsensical rules, resists creativity, and impedes constructive change. HR is the corporate function with the greatest potential—the key driver, in theory, of business performance—and also the one that most consistently underdelivers. And I am here to find out why.

Why are annual performance appraisals so time-consuming—and so routinely useless? Why is HR so often a henchman for the chief financial officer, finding ever-more ingenious ways to cut benefits and hack at payroll? Why do its communications—when we can understand them at all—so often flout reality? Why are so many people processes duplicative and wasteful, creating a forest of paperwork for every minor transaction? And why does HR insist on sameness as a proxy for equity?

It's no wonder that we hate HR. In a 2005 survey by consultancy Hay Group, just 40% of employees commended their companies for retaining high-quality workers, just 41% agreed that performance evaluations were fair. Only 58% rated their job training as favorable. Most said they had few opportunities for advancement—and that they didn't know, in any case, what was required to move up. Most telling, only about half of workers below the manager level believed their companies took a genuine interest in their well-being.

None of this is explained immediately in Vegas. These HR folks, from employers across the nation, are neither evil courtiers nor thoughtless automatons. They are mostly smart, engaging people who seem genuinely interested in doing their jobs better. They speak convincingly about employee development and cultural transformation. And, over drinks, they spin some pretty funny yarns of employee weirdness. (Like the one about the guy who threatened to sue his wife's company for "enabling" her affair with a coworker. Then there was the mentally disabled worker and the hooker—well, no, never mind. . . .)

But then the facade cracks. It happens at an afternoon presentation called "From Technicians to Consultants: How to Transform Your HR Staff into Strategic Business Partners." The speaker, Julie Muckler, is senior vice president of human resources at Wells Fargo Home Mortgage. She is an enthusiastic woman with a broad smile and 20 years of experience at companies such as Johnson & Johnson and General Tire. She has degrees in consumer economics and human resources and organizational development.

And I have no idea what she's talking about. There is mention of "internal action learning" and "being more planful in my approach." PowerPoint slides outline Wells Fargo Home Mortgage's initiatives in performance management, organization design, and horizontal-solutions teams. Muckler describes leveraging internal resources and involving external resources—and she leaves her audience dazed. That evening, even the human-resources pros confide they didn't understand much of it, either.

This, friends, is the trouble with HR. In a knowledge economy, companies that have the best talent win. We all know that. Human resources execs should be making the most of our, well, human resources—finding the best hires, nurturing the stars, fostering a productive work environment—just as IT runs the computers and finance minds the capital. HR should be joined to business strategy at the hip.

Instead, most HR organizations have ghettoized themselves literally to the brink of obsolescence. They are competent at the administrivia of pay, benefits, and retirement, but companies increasingly are farming those functions out to contractors who can handle such routine tasks at lower expense. What's left is the more important strategic role of raising the reputational and intellectual capital of the company—but HR is, it turns out, uniquely unsuited for that.

Here's why.

1. HR people aren't the sharpest tacks in the box. We'll be blunt: If you are an ambitious young thing newly graduated from a top college or B-school with your eye on a rewarding career in business, your first instinct is not to join the human-resources dance. (At the University of Michigan's Ross School of Business, which arguably boasts the nation's top faculty for organizational issues, just 1.2% of 2004 grads did so.) Says a management professor at one leading school: "The best and the brightest don't go into HR."

Who does? Intelligent people, sometimes—but not business-people. "HR doesn't tend to hire a lot of independent thinkers or people who stand up as moral compasses," says Garold L. Markle, a longtime human-resources executive at Exxon and Shell Offshore who now runs his own consultancy. Some are exiles from the corporate mainstream: They've fared poorly in meatier roles—but not poorly enough to be fired. For them, and for their employers, HR represents a relatively low-risk parking spot.

Others enter the field by choice and with the best of intentions, but for the wrong reasons. They like working with people, and they want to be helpful—noble motives that thoroughly tick off some HR thinkers. "When people have come to me and said, 'I want to work with people,' I say, 'Good, go be a social worker,'" says Arnold Kanarick, who has headed human resources at the Limited and, until recently, at Bear Stearns. "HR isn't about being a do-gooder. It's about how do you get the best and brightest people and raise the value of the firm."

The really scary news is that the gulf between capabilities and job requirements appears to be widening. As business and legal demands on the function intensify, staffers' educational qualifications haven't kept pace. In fact, according to a survey by the Society for Human Resource Management (SHRM), a considerably smaller proportion of HR professionals today have some education beyond a bachelor's degree than in 1990.

And here's one more slice of telling SHRM data: When HR professionals were asked about the worth of various academic courses toward a "successful career in HR," 83% said that classes in interpersonal communications skills had "extremely high value." Employment law and business ethics followed, at 71% and 66%, respectively. Where was change management? At 35%. Strategic management? 32%. Finance? Um, that was just 2%.

The truth? Most human-resources managers aren't particularly interested in, or equipped for, doing business. And in a business, that's sort of a problem. As guardians of a company's talent, HR has to understand–how people serve corporate objectives. Instead, "business acumen is the single biggest factor that HR professionals in the U.S. lack today," says Anthony J. Rucci, executive vice president at Cardinal Health Inc., a big healthcare supply distributor.

Rucci is consistently mentioned by academics, consultants, and other HR leaders as an executive who actually does know business. At Baxter International, he ran both HR and corporate strategy. Before that, at Sears, he led a study of results at 800 stores over five years to assess the connection between employee commitment, customer loyalty, and profitability.

As far as Rucci is concerned, there are three questions that any decent HR person in the world should be able to answer. First, who is your company's core customer? "Have you talked to one lately? Do you know what challenges they face?" Second, who is the competition? "What do they do well and not well?" And most important, who are we? "What is a realistic assessment of what we do well and not so well vis à vis the customer and the competition?"

Does your HR pro know the answers?

2. HR pursues efficiency in lieu of value. Why? Because it's easier–and easier to measure. Dave Ulrich, a professor at the University of Michigan, recalls meeting with the chairman and top HR people from a big bank. "The training person said that 80% of employees have done at least 40 hours in classes. The chairman said, 'Congratulations.' I said, 'You're talking about the activities you're doing. The question is, What are you delivering?'"

That sort of stuff drives Ulrich nuts. Over 20 years, he has become the HR trade's best-known guru and a leading proponent of the push to take on more-strategic roles within corporations. But human-resources managers, he acknowledges, typically undermine that effort by investing more importance in activities than in outcomes. "You're only effective if you add value," Ulrich says. "That means you're not measured by what you do but by what you deliver." By that, he refers not just to the value delivered to employees and line managers, but the benefits that accrue to investors and customers, as well.

So here's a true story: A talented young marketing exec accepts a job offer with Time Warner out of business school. She interviews for openings in several departments—then is told by HR that only one is interested in her. In fact, she learns later, they all had been. She had been railroaded into the job, under the supervision of a widely reviled manager, because no one inside the company would take it.

You make the call: Did HR do its job? On the one hand, it filled the empty slot. "It did what was organizationally expedient," says the woman now. "Getting someone who wouldn't kick and scream about this role probably made sense to them. But I just felt angry." She left Time Warner after just a year. (A Time Warner spokesperson declined to comment on the incident.)

Part of the problem is that Time Warner's metrics likely will never catch the real cost of its HR department's action. Human resources can readily provide the number of people it hired, the percentage of performance evaluations completed, and the extent to which employees are satisfied or not with their

Stupid HR Tricks

Can Your Highly Trained Human-Resources Professional Do This? Or Has He Already?

In 2003, **FedEx** for the first time asked employees to make $10 copayments for doctors' visits. But Dave Haynes, a FedEx sales rep and author of *The Peon Book* (Berrett-Koehler, 2004), notes that "in order to ensure that all employees understood the policy and its impact, HR sent us three separate glossy four-color brochures and went to the expense of creating a Web site." Says a FedEx spokeswoman, "We do send four-color brochures to get the attention of employees and their families."

An editor at Disney Press, the **Walt Disney Co.**'s publisher of children's books, was worried about his relationship with his increasingly erratic supervisor. One morning, he arrived at work to find a voice mail from the boss that threatened physical violence. He played the voice mail to a human-resources manager, who told him, "Well, I think it's time for you to start looking for another job." "I said, 'You're kidding, right?'" the editor says now. "She said, 'That's my best solution.' I couldn't believe it." Disney declined to comment.

Regina Blus was managing a large software project across several departments at **Sun Microsystems**. In one department, a new manager, widely disliked, consistently berated and harassed the workers, Blus says, even while engaging one in an affair. Blus approached the local HR manager. "He said, 'Well, I certainly don't think it's appropriate to get involved in these witch hunts. And anyway, it's none of your business.'" The incident was never investigated. Sun says there is no record of Blus's complaint, that any such report would have sparked an investigation, and that it takes such issues seriously.

---

benefits. But only rarely does it link any of those metrics to business performance.

John W. Boudreau, a professor at the University of Southern California's Center for Effective Organizations, likens the failing to shortcomings of the finance function before DuPont figured out how to calculate return on investment in 1912. In HR, he says, "we don't have anywhere near that kind of logical sophistication in the way of people or talent. So the decisions that get made about that resource are far less sophisticated, reliable, and consistent."

Cardinal Health's Rucci is trying to fix that. Cardinal regularly asks its employees 12 questions designed to measure engagement. Among them: Do they understand the company's strategy? Do they see the connection between that and their jobs? Are they proud to tell people where they work? Rucci correlates the results to those of a survey of 2,000 customers, as well as monthly sales data and brand-awareness scores.

"So I don't know if our HR processes are having an impact" per se, Rucci says. "But I know absolutely that employee-engagement scores have an impact on our business," accounting for between 1% and 10% of earnings, depending on the business and the employee's role. "Cardinal may not anytime soon get invited by the Conference Board to explain our world-class best practices in any area of HR—and I couldn't care less. The real question is, Is the business effective and successful?"

3. HR isn't working for you. Want to know why you go through that asinine performance appraisal every year, really? Markle, who admits to having administered countless numbers of them over the years, is pleased to confirm your suspicions. Companies, he says "are doing it to protect themselves against their own employees," he says. "They put a piece of paper between you and employees, so if you ever have a confrontation, you can go to the file and say, 'Here, I've documented this problem.'"

There's a good reason for this defensive stance, of course. In the last two generations, government has created an immense thicket of labor regulations. Equal Employment Opportunity; Fair Labor Standards; Occupational Safety and Health; Family and Medical Leave; and the ever-popular ERISA. These are complex, serious issues requiring technical expertise, and HR has to apply reasonable caution.

But "it's easy to get sucked down into that," says Mark Royal, a senior consultant with Hay Group. "There's a tension created by HR's role as protector of corporate assets—making sure it doesn't run afoul of the rules. That puts you in the position of saying no a lot, of playing the bad cop. You have to step out of that, see the broad possibilities, and take a more open-minded approach. You need to understand where the exceptions to broad policies can be made."

Typically, HR people can't, or won't. Instead, they pursue standardization and uniformity in the face of a workforce that is heterogeneous and complex. A manager at a large capital leasing company complains that corporate HR is trying to eliminate most vice-president titles there—even though veeps are a dime a dozen in the finance industry. Why? Because in the company's commercial business, vice president is a rank reserved for the top officers. In its drive for bureaucratic "fairness," HR is actually threatening the reputation, and so the effectiveness, of the company's finance professionals.

The urge for one-size-fits-all, says one professor who studies the field, "is partly about compliance, but mostly because it's just easier." Bureaucrats everywhere abhor exceptions—not just because they open up the company to charges of bias but because they require more than rote solutions. They're time-consuming and expensive to manage. Make one exception, HR fears, and the floodgates will open.

There's a contradiction here, of course: Making exceptions should be exactly what human resources does, all the time—not because it's nice for employees, but because it drives the business. Employers keep their best people by acknowledging and rewarding their distinctive performance, not by treating them the same as everyone else. "If I'm running a business, I can tell you who's really helping to drive the business forward," says Dennis Ackley, an employee communication consultant. "HR should have the same view. We should send the message that we value our high-performing employees and we're focused on rewarding and retaining them."

Instead, human-resources departments benchmark salaries, function by function and job by job, against industry standards, keeping pay—even that of the stars—within a narrow band determined by competitors. They bounce performance appraisals back to managers who rate their employees too highly, unwilling to acknowledge accomplishments that would merit much more than the 4% companywide increase.

Human resources, in other words, forfeits long-term value for short-term cost efficiency. A simple test: Who does your company's vice president of human resources report to? If it's the CFO—and chances are good it is—then HR is headed in the wrong direction. "That's a model that cannot work," says one top HR exec who has been there. "A financial person is concerned with taking money out of the organization. HR should be concerned with putting investments in."

4. The corner office doesn't get HR (and vice versa). I'm at another rockin' party: a few dozen midlevel human-resources managers at a hotel restaurant in Mahwah, New Jersey. It is not glam in any way. (I've got to get a better travel agent.) But it is telling, in a hopeful way. Hunter Douglas, a $2.1 billion manufacturer of window coverings, has brought its HR staff here from across the United States to celebrate their accomplishments.

The company's top brass is on hand. Marvin B. Hopkins, president and CEO of North American operations, lays on the praise: "I feel fantastic about your achievements," he says. "Our business is about people. Hiring, training, and empathizing with employees is extremely important. When someone is fired or leaves, we've failed in some way. People have to feel they have a place at the company, a sense of ownership."

So, yeah, it's corporate-speak in a drab exurban office park. But you know what? The human-resources managers from Tupelo and Dallas are totally pumped up. They've been flown into headquarters, they've had their picture taken with the boss, and they're seeing *Mamma Mia* on Broadway that afternoon on the company's dime.

Can your HR department say it has the ear of top management? Probably not. "Sometimes," says Ulrich, "line managers just have this legacy of HR in their minds, and they can't get rid of it. I felt really badly for one HR guy. The chairman wanted someone to plan company picnics and manage the union, and every time this guy tried to be strategic, he got shot down."

Say what? Execs don't think HR matters? What about all that happy talk about employees being their most important asset? Well, that turns out to have been a small misunderstanding. In the 1990s, a group of British academics examined the relationship between what companies (among them, the UK units of

---

How to Do HR Right

Say the Right Thing

At the grand level, what HR tells employees has to match what the company actually believes; empty rhetoric only breeds discontent. And when it comes to the details of pay and benefits, explain clearly what's being done and why. For example, asks consultant Dennis Ackley, "When you have a big deductible, do employees understand you're focusing on big costs? Or do they just think HR is being annoying?"

Measure the Right Thing

Human resources isn't taken seriously by top management because it can't demonstrate its impact on the business. Statistics on hiring, turnover, and training measure activity but not value. So devise measurements that consider impact: When you trained people, did they learn anything that made them better workers? And connect that data to business-performance indicators—such as customer loyalty, quality, employee-replacement costs, and, ultimately, profitability.

Get Rid of the "Social Workers"

After Libby Sartain arrived as chief people officer at Yahoo, she moved several HR staffers out—some because they didn't have the right functional skills, but mostly because "they were stuck in the old-school way of doing things."

Human resources shouldn't be about cutting costs, but it is all about business. The people who work there need to be both technically competent and sophisticated about the company's strategy, competitors, and customers.

Serve the Business

Human-resources staffers walk a fine line: Employees see them as stooges for management, and management views them as annoying do-gooders representing employees. But "the best employee advocates are the ones who are concerned with advancing organizational and individual performance," says Anthony Rucci of Cardinal Health. Represent management with integrity and honesty—and back employees in the name of improving the company's capability.

Make Value, Not Activity

University of Michigan professor Dave Ulrich, coauthor of *The HR Value Proposition* (Harvard Business School Press, 2005), says HR folks must create value for four groups: They need to foster competence and commitment among employees, develop the capabilities that allow managers to execute on strategy, help build relationships with customers, and create confidence among investors in the future value of the firm.

Hewlett-Packard and Citibank) said about their human assets and how they actually behaved. The results were, perhaps, inevitable.

In their rhetoric, human-resources organizations embraced the language of a "soft" approach, speaking of training, development, and commitment. But "the underlying principle was invariably restricted to the improvements of bottom-line performance," the authors wrote in the resulting book, *Strategic Human Resource Management* (Oxford University Press, 1999). "Even if the rhetoric of HRM is soft, the reality is almost always 'hard,' with the interests of the organization prevailing over those of the individual."

In the best of worlds, says London Business School professor Lynda Gratton, one of the study's authors, "the reality should be some combination of hard and soft." That's what's going on at Hunter Douglas. Human resources can address the needs of employees because it has proven its business mettle—and vice versa. Betty Lou Smith, the company's vice president of corporate HR, began investigating the connection between employee turnover and product quality. Divisions with the highest turnover rates, she found, were also those with damaged-goods rates of 5% or higher. And extraordinarily, 70% of employees were leaving the company within six months of being hired.

Smith's staffers learned that new employees were leaving for a variety of reasons: They didn't feel respected, they didn't have input in decisions, but mostly, they felt a lack of connection when they were first hired. "We gave them a 10-minute orientation, then they were out on the floor," Smith says. She addressed the weakness by creating a mentoring program that matched new hires with experienced workers. The latter were suspicious at first, but eventually, the mentor positions (with spiffy shirts and caps) came to be seen as prestigious. The six-month turnover rate dropped dramatically, to 16%. Attendance and productivity—and the damaged-goods rate—improved.

"We don't wait to hear from top management," Smith says. "You can't just sit in the corner and look at benefits. We have to know what the issues in our business are. HR has to step up and assume responsibility, not wait for management to knock on our door."

But most HR people do.

Hunter Douglas gives us a glimmer of hope—of the possibility that HR can be done right. And surely, even within ineffective human-resources organizations, there are great individual HR managers—trustworthy, caring people with their ears to the ground, who are sensitive to cultural nuance yet also understand the business and how people fit in. Professionals who move voluntarily into HR from line positions can prove especially adroit, bringing a profit-and-loss sensibility and strong management skills.

At Yahoo, Libby Sartain, chief people officer, is building a group that may prove to be the truly effective human-resources department that employees and executives imagine. In this, Sartain enjoys two advantages. First, she arrived with a reputation as a creative maverick, won in her 13 years running HR at Southwest Airlines. And second, she had license from the top to do whatever it took to create a world-class organization.

Sartain doesn't just have a "seat at the table" at Yahoo; she actually helped build the table, instituting a weekly operations meeting that she coordinates with COO Dan Rosensweig. Talent is always at the top of the agenda—and at the end of each meeting, the executive team mulls individual development decisions on key staffers.

That meeting, Sartain says, "sends a strong message to everyone at Yahoo that we can't do anything without HR." It also signals to HR staffers that they're responsible for more than shuffling papers and getting in the way. "We view human resources as the caretaker of the largest investment of the company," Sartain says. "If you're not nurturing that investment and watching it grow, you're not doing your job."

Yahoo, say some experts and peers at other organizations, is among a few companies—among them Cardinal Health, Procter & Gamble, Pitney Bowes, Goldman Sachs, and General Electric—that truly are bringing human resources into the realm of business strategy. But they are indeed the few. USC professor Edward E. Lawler III says that last year HR professionals reported spending 23% of their time "being a strategic business partner"—no more than they reported in 1995. And line managers, he found, said HR is far less involved in strategy than HR thinks it is. "Despite great huffing and puffing about strategy," Lawler says, "there's still a long way to go." (Indeed. When I asked one midlevel HR person exactly how she was involved in business strategy for her division, she excitedly described organizing a monthly lunch for her vice president with employees.)

What's driving the strategy disconnect? London Business School's Gratton spends a lot of time training human-resources professionals to create more impact. She sees two problems: Many HR people, she says, bring strong technical expertise to the party but no "point of view about the future and how organizations are going to change." And second, "it's very difficult to align HR strategy to business strategy, because business strategy changes very fast, and it's hard to fiddle around with a compensation strategy or benefits to keep up." More than simply understanding strategy, Gratton says, truly effective executives "need to be operating out of a set of principles and personal values." And few actually do.

In the meantime, economic natural selection is, in a way, taking care of the problem for us. Some 94% of large employers surveyed this year by Hewitt Associates reported they were outsourcing at least one human-resources activity. By 2008, according to the survey, many plan to expand outsourcing to include activities such as learning and development, payroll, recruiting, health and welfare, and global mobility.

Which is to say, they will farm out pretty much everything HR does. The happy rhetoric from the HR world says this is all for the best: Outsourcing the administrative minutiae, after all, would allow human-resources professionals to focus on more important stuff that's central to the business. You know, being strategic partners.

The problem, if you're an HR person, is this: The tasks companies are outsourcing—the administrivia—tend to be what you're good at. And what's left isn't exactly your strong suit. Human resources is crippled by what Jay Jamrog, executive director of the Human Resource Institute, calls "educated incapacity: You're smart, and you know the way you're working today isn't going to hold 10 years from now. But you can't move to that level. You're stuck."

That's where human resources is today. Stuck. "This is a unique organization in the company," says USC's Boudreau. "It discovers things about the business through the lens of people and talent. That's an opportunity for competitive advantage." In most companies, that opportunity is utterly wasted.

And that's why I don't like HR.

KEITH H. HAMMONDS is *Fast Company*'s deputy editor.

Alien Nation

With 12 million illegals in America, immigration policy is a shambles. Businesses want to hire more foreigners and can't because of antiterrorist laws. What's to be done?

MICHAEL MAIELLO AND NICOLE RIDGWAY

Where do you get your workers? We ask a certain highly successful roofing contractor in Washington, D.C. Technically speaking, he allows, his employees are all legal. They have papers, and it's not his responsibility to determine if the papers are forged. But he lives on the edge. That's why he recently declined to bid on a lucrative deal offered by the National Security Agency. The spy agency didn't want foreigners working on its premises and could be expected to do a much better job than Immigration & Customs Enforcement does of enforcing the law against employing illegals.

This entrepreneur won't admit that he has hired illegals. But, he concedes, "[If] I need five or ten additional men, I let it be known amongst a certain circle of guys. And I have access to those people immediately."

It's not easy finding American citizens willing to push shingles around on a hot roof during 100-degree weather. It's not easy finding engineers, either. James Goodnight, chief executive of SAS, the world's largest privately held software company, recently went looking for Ph.D. engineers. He needed them for a project to help companies increase profits by getting a handle on their suppliers. Plenty of willing and able foreigners could have done the work but landing the H-1B visas, which allow foreigners with special skills to work in the U.S. for up to six years, would be next to impossible. As a result, Goodnight came close to opening an R&D center in Poland. "I wish I had done it," he laments.

America's immigration policy is a shambles. "The current situation can only be described as untenable," says Craig Barrett, chairman of Intel Corp., which has a voracious appetite for chip designers. The U.S. does a brilliant job educating foreigners in our engineering schools, and then, during the recruiting season, chases this human capital away. Australia and the U.K. have a much better system: They come pretty close to stapling a visa to an engineer's diploma. "If we had purposefully set out to design a system that would cripple our ability to be competitive, we could hardly do better than what we have today," says Barrett.

We've been here before. Twenty years ago Congress passed the Simpson-Rodino immigration reform, a bill four years in the making. The law was supposed to halt the flood of illegal immigrants swarming in to take low-paying jobs. It granted a one-year amnesty to aliens who had been living in the U.S. since before 1982 and let them apply for legal status; it also slapped businesses with criminal penalties for knowingly hiring illegals. But the government did not enforce the law. The public, it seems, does not have the appetite for chasing millions of workers back to Mexico. And so the government has settled on a half-hearted enforcement scheme that combines a game of tag played out in the Arizona desert with very few raids on employers. Every now and then some meatpacker or night cleaning firm is scolded and fined. The penalty for individuals caught employing an undocumented nanny is loss of a cabinet appointment.

Illegals keep cascading in, recently at the rate of 700,000 a year, and businesses and families keep hiring them. The Pew Hispanic Center estimates that in the last decade the number of undocumented aliens living in the U.S. has doubled to 12 million. This despite a growth in spending on domestic security averaging 13.4% a year. President Bush recently requested $42.7 billion for the Department of Homeland Security and $2.6 billion for guarding the border with Mexico, the source of no known terrorist.

Adding to this morass of ambivalence about foreigners doing our dirty work: the fear and xenophobia that grew out of Sept. 11. The resulting crackdown did nothing to stop the unskilled workers walking across the border, but it did choke off the engineers from India and China. Since 2001 Congress has whacked the number of H-1B visas from 195,000 to 65,000 a year. Separately, green cards—permanent resident visas that allow for work, among other things, and granted to noncitizens—are handed out at the rate of 140,000 a year. Rationing of these precious documents is done not by setting employment priorities but by trying applicants' patience and forcing them to spend money on lawyers. For employment visas the waiting period for an initial interview with the U.S. consulate in the home country can be up to 149 days. Homeland Security says it does 35 million security checks a year before issuing visas to workers, tourists, visiting lecturers and the like.

Chipmaker Texas Instruments was trying to secure 65 visas last summer when the federal limit ran out and was told it would have to wait for many of them until April, when applications for 2007 are accepted, to begin the process all over again. That means advertising the jobs for 30 days to find "minimally qualified" U.S. workers, sifting through résumés, submitting paperwork to the Labor Department and trying again to lure talented recruits from abroad, a process that can cost up to $30,000 for each employee—and increases the risk that a company will lose foreign candidates it has its eye on, as Texas Instruments did. "The more barriers we have in place and more process steps we have to take, the more we're going to see these things happen," says Steve W. Lyle, TI's director of worldwide staffing.

How to fix the mess? Herewith, a few proposals from the Beltway and the academic braintrust—and their chances of being adopted.

Compassionate Compromise

President Bush has a plan that he claims "serves the American economy and reflects the American dream." Those illegals already in the U.S. would receive temporary worker cards that allow them to stay for up to three years and renew once for an unspecified period—then, vamoose. The same offer would apply to new aliens once a U.S. employer identifies a job and certifies that no American is qualified for or wants to take it. This isn't an amnesty program, the administration has been at pains to point out to avoid torpedoes from the hard right. (A bill introduced by John McCain and Edward Kennedy last May would let illegals apply for citizenship, once they pay a fine, clear up tax problems and learn English.) "I oppose amnesty—placing undocumented workers on the automatic path to citizenship," the President has said. Nor would he give them a leg up on foreigners who come legally and apply for a green card, which offers permanent resident status. He also supports lifting the ceiling on H-1Bs, but his plan doesn't say by how much.

If we had set out to design a system to cripple our competitiveness, we could hardly do better.

On the tough side, Bush's proposal would turn the screws on businesses that wittingly break the law but doesn't spell out the penalties. Enforcement would fall under the Department of Homeland Security, working with the Labor Department and other federal agencies. "Our homeland will be more secure when we can better account for those who enter our country," said Bush. Hard to disagree with that nostrum.

What's the likelihood we'll see some version of the plan? Not high, considering that no one in Congress has run with it—and the President introduced the idea on Jan. 7, 2004.

Build up That Wall

Last December, by 260–159, the House passed an amendment that would mandate the construction of a 700-mile fence along the 1,952-mile border with Mexico. Calling for a series of steel barriers armed with motion detectors, floodlights and surveillance equipment, the plan has been the pet project of Representative Duncan Hunter (R-Calif.) for the past 20 years. He finally got it on the radar as part of a get-tough immigration bill that would beef up security and tighten enforcement. Construction costs: $2.2 billion by Hunter's estimate; proponents of the idea, like Colin Hanna, president of Weneedafence.com, think it could easily reach $8 billion.

Good fences don't always make good neighbors, as Israel's recent attempt to wall itself off from the Palestinians most vividly illustrates. The House amendment drew immediate fire from Mexican President Vicente Fox, who complained that Congress had given into "xenophobic groups that impose the law at will." It would be hard for Mexico to swallow any reform plan that threatens the flow of dollars from Mexican expats to their families back home. Chance of success: iffy; there isn't much support in the Administration.

Caps Off

Some people argue the best way to deal with illegals is to create so many opportunities for legal immigration that no rational migrant would risk a deadly trek through the desert. (Last year, 460 people died trying to get into the U.S., up from 61 in 1995.) Daniel Griswold, director of the Cato Institute's Center for Trade Policy Studies, suggests letting in at least 300,000 temporary workers on three-year, renewable visas each year. Undocumented workers here could receive the same visa. But unlike Bush's proposal, this one does not force illegal residents to go home; they could pursue citizenship, as long as they pay an unspecified fine ("not chump change," Griswold says) and have clean records. Douglas S. Massey, a Princeton University professor of sociology and public affairs and author of *Beyond Smoke and Mirrors: Mexican Immigration in an Era of Economic Integration* (Russell Sage, 2002), would also let in 300,000 temporary workers every year. Each of them would pay $400 or so, about one-third what a "coyote" charges to smuggle people across the border, giving immigrants a financial incentive to play by the rules. Griswold agrees, adding that such reform would "drain the swamp of human smuggling and document fraud that facilitates illegal immigration."

As for the illegals already in place, Massey would allow anyone who arrived as a minor to apply for permanent legal status right away. Their parents would have the option to apply for temporary status. But, in any event, Massey wants the U.S. to allow far more than the current 20,000 green cards for Mexicans each year. That would swell their contributions to the U.S. Treasury. Massey's surveys have shown that a surprising 62% of illegal workers have taxes withheld from their paychecks and 66% pay Social Security. In 2004, illegal workers contributed $7 billion to

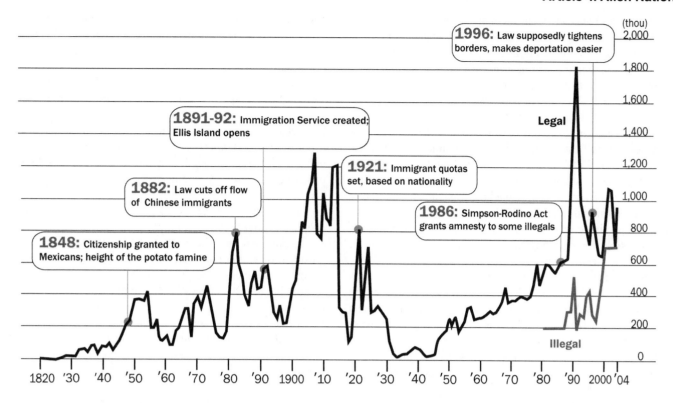

Figure 1 The Human Spigot. A nation of immigrants, the U.S. has long used legislation to control who—and how many people—can enter the country legally.

Sources: U.S. Census; estimates by Department of Homeland Security; Pew Hispanic Center.

Social Security and $1.5 billion to Medicare. Yet these workers seldom use social services because they fear getting busted. Massey found that only 10% of illegal Mexicans have sent a child to a U.S. public school, and just 5% have received food stamps or unemployment.

Chances for any legislative action? Maybe some tidbit from the guest-worker program. So far, it hasn't caught fire with feds or Joe Six-Pack. A recent Zogby International poll says 56% of likely voters oppose giving illegals any chance at citizenship.

Selling the American Dream— for a Price

Nobel laureate Gary Becker, who teaches economics at the University of Chicago, thinks the U.S. should welcome anyone who's not a criminal, a terrorist or a carrier of a communicable disease—for a fee of $50,000. That buys permanent status. Becker says the plan would lure skilled workers since they have more to gain. For those who can't afford a ticket, Becker would encourage commercial banks to make high-interest immigration loans.

$50,000 would buy permanent legal status for foreigners; it might help businesses lure more skilled workers.

Becker is tempted to push his own proposal a bit further. Why not auction off guest-worker visas—and the chance of citizenship—to the highest bidders? At a minimum, Becker thinks, such auctions could bring in $50 billion a year—enough to pay for the entire budget of the Department of Homeland Security.

Sound weird? There's a version already in place, known as the EB-5 visa, introduced in 1990. It's available to 10,000 foreigners a year who are willing to invest at least $500,000 (in some cases, $1 million) to create a new business or expand an existing one, creating ten or more jobs. But does the government really want to be in the business of marketing U.S. citizenship abroad?

Bring on Big Brother

What if we could open our borders and safeguard the country? Technology is a ministep in that direction. Last summer Homeland Security began a $100 million pilot program that embedded radio-frequency identification on the entry documents of those coming in from Canada and Mexico, tracking their arrival and departure, as Wal-Mart does pallets of toothpaste. The test didn't sit well with civil liberties groups or with Senator Patrick Leahy (D.–Vt.), who pointed out that the so-called pass card used an RFID chip that was incompatible with the one the State Department was using in passports. Could bad guys jam the systems or hack into them? That would make our borders less secure.

More plausible is an extension of a new practice that already exists. All foreign applicants for visas must schedule an interview with the U.S. consulate in their host country, where they submit to biometric fingerprint scans of their left and right index fingers and a digital photo. Such high-tech ID is also in 105 U.S. airports, as well as in all American seaports and border crossings. Draft legislation by Arlen Specter (R.–Pa.), the chairman of the Senate Judiciary Committee, would require the same kind of whiz-bang identification on the visas of all immigrants already in the States by 2007 and, by that time, would force compatibility between systems used by the FBI and Homeland Security. To curtail fraud, Specter would require companies to enter a social security number on an online government database for each prospective employee—and if it's bounced, the employer is responsible for reporting the culprit to the Immigration & Customs Enforcement agency.

The Specter bill is a melting pot of competing proposals that draw from the right and the left. Illegals already in the States could stay here indefinitely, as long as they have been employed since January 2004 and passed a background investigation by Homeland Security; whether they could become American citizens is still murky. Newly arrived aliens don't get quite as good a deal. Citizenship is off the table. But as guest workers, they would receive visas and have a chance to stay in the U.S., as long as they had jobs, for up to six years, when they would have to leave. However, they could apply for green cards from their home country. (A competing proposal by Senators John Cornyn [R.-Tex.] and Jon Kyl [R.-Ariz.] would allow temporary workers six years of employment in U.S., so long as they go home for a year every two years, with little chance to gain citizenship.) Specter would also almost triple H-1Bs to 180,000 the first year and thereafter adjust the number to market demand. Anyone with an advanced degree in science, technology, engineering or math is exempt from a visa cap.

Business has warmed to his proposals. "We have talented people we want to hire, whom we've offered a job to—and we can't bring them into the country," says Pamela Passman, vice president of global corporate affairs for Microsoft. "We think Specter's bill does address the [H-1B] crisis."

So what are its chances? It's a complex, omnibus package with many wiggling parts. Nothing will be enacted quickly. The 1986 reform took four years, and that was before Sept. 11. Xenophobia and protectionism combined to defeat an honest airing about whether an Arab ally should operate U.S. ports. Immigration probably won't fare any better.

Strange Bedfellows
Could HR be Marketing's New Best Friend?

JEFF SMITH AND KRISTIANE BLOMQVIST

In most companies, brands get limited traction outside of the marketing department. Historically, marketing has meant external communications and customer insights, so it generally has limited internal influence on employees' day-to-day activities. However, the world of brands and marketing is realizing that, to truly create a successful external brand, an organization's employees must be included. Marketing must shift its thinking about the brand and, perhaps most important, the internal partners with which it must collaborate.

The divide between marketing and the human resources (HR) department has developed under the banner of "we have different audiences and different objectives." The tension has grown by comparing ownership of initiatives like corporate vision and values vs. brand vision and brand values; internal communications vs. external communications; employee development vs. business development, and so on. Today, marketing and HR are realizing that, in creating sustainable change inside and outside the organization, the two functional areas need each other to survive. It is no longer one or the other; it is now "we are stronger together."

A truly collaborative partnership between the two departments can create a new kind of company with a culture and related behaviors that are on-brand, on-strategy, and ultimately more effective at delivering bottom-line results for the business. The notion of marketing and HR becoming bedfellows is not so strange when you consider the symbiotic requirements they both share and the tremendous benefits they deliver to an organization and its customers.

HR Supports Marketing

In fact, there are compelling reasons for marketing to team up with HR. These include HR's ability to "attach" the brand message to departmental areas where it may not previously have had a presence, and to provide marketing and brand access to employees in departments that may not have been recognized as needing that information in the past.

HR's primary constituents are the company's internal employees. With that audience, its work is truly cross-functional and company-wide. Therefore, in realizing that a brand's strength lies in its delivery and not just its communication, HR can be an effective conduit for influencing employees through recruiting, new employee orientation, training and development, performance evaluation, and compensation. By infusing the content of the brand into the programs, a brand-based culture starts to emerge.

One company we worked with makes a concerted effort to present a united front during new hire orientation, giving new employees a full day of introduction to the firm that includes basics about the facilities, the history of the company, the vision and key objectives for the future, and the strategies to achieve the stated vision. This is a most opportune time to involve the new employee in what the firm's customers want and what the firm is doing to satisfy them. Imagine a one hour discussion where a video is played of customers speaking about their key needs and wants. This video is then followed up by how the firm is planning to address these needs. External communications can then be shown, viewed in the context of solving these important issues. The combination creates a powerful story, enabling new employees to understand the customer and business better, understand they must behave in a certain way, and see the promises being made to customers by the firm. HR and marketing are completely intertwined in the story, and the result is a new group of brand ambassadors.

We also saw this collaboration in action at a global technology firm that used an interesting contest to create deeper appreciation and understanding for the new brand they were developing. HR and marketing teamed to develop a series of CD-ROM trading cards that had questions about how people would act if they were the brand. Once five questions were answered correctly, the card was traded for another. The first people to collect all six cards won a prize. This created an international network based on the ideals of the brand. Cards went back and forth to all corners of the globe. The more people got into it, the more distribution the cards received. The end result was an incredibly effective internal communications program.

As illustrated, HR can play a key role in helping marketing develop internal communications that demonstrate how employees "live" the brand. David Aaker, author of the new book, *Brand Portfolio Management* (The Free Press, 2004), asserts that the concept of internal role models is one of the most effective ways to enlist a broader population of employees. Traditionally, in change-management initiatives, these people a recalled "change agents." They are people that embody and live the ideals of the brand and are individuals respected by many people in the organization. By identifying these individuals and aligning their messages and behaviors, a very powerful force of internal role models is created for employees to emulate. No other function is more capable of identifying and encouraging these employees to participate than HR.

EXECUTIVE briefing
Companies are increasingly realizing that, for brand and business strategies to be aligned, the brand can no longer be driven solely by the activities of the marketing department. Delivering against the promises of a company's brand strategy requires every level of the organization to live the brand. Employees must not only accept these strategies, but actually change their behaviors and "walk the talk." However, integrating the brand into all facets of an organization does have its challenges.

Marketing Supports HR

The HR department also benefits from close collaboration with its marketing colleagues. By making its target audiences, positioning promises, and marketing strategies available to HR, marketing can bolster HR's ability to attract and retain employees that believe in and will support the company's brand and business strategies.

HR is increasingly discovering how marketing can help it attract and retain employees, which is critical in the ongoing competitive war for talent. Research has shown that a variety of factors play into what attracts the best candidates to a career opportunity, many of which rank equal to or higher than financial compensation. Sought-after candidates want to work for a company that reflects their own ideals and aspirations and maintains a strong customer focus.

A global services company recently conducted research on its recruiting efforts and found that there has been an evolution in how potential employees look at career opportunities. For example, it's no longer good enough to offer a long career; recruits today are seeking companies that clearly help them build their own market profiles. Candidates are seeking companies they can place on their resume that will build their overall market value, which suggests that marketing and the brand play an ever-increasing role in attracting the best talent. The brand is becoming a primary decision tool for recruits when considering a new career opportunity.

It's important not to forget that employees are often also your customers. They are learning about the organization from the

outside world as well through their exposure to the company's external communications. Many HR departments have realized the potential here: IBM (when it launched e-business), JPMorgan (with the "I am JPMorgan" campaign), and Southwest Airlines all spoke to their employees through their external advertising initiatives. These efforts built a great internal sense of pride in the companies and clearly communicated what the organization hoped its employees would deliver to customers. It also communicated a promise that included the employees.

This has elevated the importance of branding and increased HR's reliance on the marketing department to provide it with processes for developing internal and external communications that support the brand promises the company is making in the marketplace. The marketing group's in-depth understanding of the customer and its ability to develop communications targeted at this group can help HR determine what tools and messages will help current and potential employees deliver against the brand promises.

HR can accomplish this by leveraging the credibility marketing has acquired as a result of its focus on the customer. Generally, the marketing department "owns" market and customer research and thus has the greatest insight into the needs of the market. Whether employees believe in the concept of brand or not, they will always listen when being told what their customers want and how best to deliver against these needs. Providing them the sort of actionable data that's a specialty of marketing will help turn employee attention to other areas that support the needs and goals of the business, in turn making them ambassadors of the brand.

Brand Ambassadors

But creating such sweeping attitudinal change can be problematic. Changing behaviors is not a simple task, and many impediments block a successful implementation. These impediments include compensation systems that are not aligned with brand building, lack of senior management commitment, desire for immediate results, and management vs. leadership of an initiative.

Imagine if you worked in a call center for an insurance company. Typically, you would be compensated based on the number of calls you handle, not the depth and length of the calls. Now imagine the insurance company came out with a brand strategy where the company would understand customer needs better than anyone else. The compensation structure for the call center representative is actually prohibiting the desired experience from taking place. There is virtually no way customers are going to perceive that they are well-understood if they are handled according to the current measurement system. While this example is somewhat simplistic, it's illustrative of a problem faced by organizations of all sizes. How do you align the motivating factors of compensation with the promises the company must keep with customers?

Not only do HR and marketing need to know how the brand translates into specific employee competencies, but they also need to assess how these competencies deliver convincing customer experiences through distinct employee actions.

One company we worked with established a small task force with representatives from both HR and marketing to identify what competencies the target employee should have from the brand, business, and HR perspective. It was a rather lengthy but important process, as those competencies would become the foundation for the company's compensation and recruitment processes and therefore establish a behavioral role model. After primary and secondary research among employees and customers and multiple global workshops and teleconferences, a new target employee emerged. The target came complete with competencies, associated actions, and professional experience requirements by level.

How many "living the brand" initiatives have failed because they were nothing more than communications and a new mouse pad?

Having gone through the process together, marketing and HR had full clarity concerning what competencies this employee possessed and how these competencies were manifested in specific actions. HR could then easily proceed to align the compensation models so the right behaviors would be nurtured and rewarded. Marketing could start to think about the training programs, messages, and reward schemes that would further build the behaviors that supported the brand most strongly. This is the type of teamwork that creates strong customer experiences at Goldman Sachs Group Inc., Hertz Corp., and the Walt Disney Co.

Obviously the aligned compensation system isn't the answer to all problems, although its importance should not be underestimated. How many "living the brand" initiatives have failed because they were nothing more than communications and a new mouse pad? The surest way to end a great internal or external initiative is with a lack of senior management support. Senior managers of HR often hold on closely to their silo because that's how they believe they offer value to the organization. The marketing group often does the same. If an organization is unable to convince both groups to work together, the initiatives will forever be separate and will only confuse employees rather than motivate them. At many firms, the HR group owns the internal values of the organization, while the marketing group owns the values the company wants customers to experience. Each fights to keep its set of values and neither actually achieves its objectives. Each of these sets of values should be virtually the same. Since both departments are hoping to affect the behavior of employees, the message needs to be consistent.

Another impediment to making employees brand ambassadors is the rush to achieve immediate results—a great temptation when it comes to organizational change and brand development. With all of the work that goes into developing a strategy, many companies hope they will see immediate results. But it just doesn't happen when you're asking an organization to think and act differently. Short-term results are quicker to achieve but rarely sustainable and are usually a result of specific instructions from management. Sustainable change, like

enabling employees to see why they must think differently, comes from true leadership—managers demonstrating that changing the way employees think contributes to their personal commitment to the initiative ideals. Combining HR and marketing initiatives into a single program or initiative affords leaders greater clarity and focus and ultimately leads to more effective business results.

Sought-after candidates want to work for a company that reflects their own ideals and maintains a strong customer focus.

One such initiative was implemented at a global financial services company to determine the most effective way to attract the most valuable talent. A cross-functional, cross-geography, cross-business team that included marketing and HR was used to create a strategy. The outcome was a project that was single-minded, that enables the organization to hire the kinds of people who are able to deliver the brand promises, and is completely aligned with the external messages being communicated.

Collaboration Partnership

Truly reaping the benefits of collaboration between marketing and HR requires a solid partnership that strengthens the company's efforts to bring its brand to life internally. At Goldman Sachs, for example, the brand is at the very core of the company's culture. Each employee lives the Goldman Sachs brand—a result of a conscious effort to integrate the efforts of marketing and HR from strategy development to implementation. This sets the company apart and receives partial credit for the company's industry leadership. Internally, marketing employees talk about cultural practices, not branding programs. Recasting branding programs in this light is a far more effective way of engaging employees. Externally, marketing highlights the elements of the Goldman Sachs culture that are most important to its targeted customer segments. HR and marketing work together to ensure brand and business alignment during the intense new-hire training program. Among other things, the program explains how Goldman Sachs' culture and values relate to the client experience. Continuous employee research, including internal surveys, focus groups, and roundtables with senior management, are conducted to ensure that company initiatives always meet employee and customer expectations.

The biggest challenge that companies face in replicating the Goldman Sachs model is that integration isn't natural. Companies typically view vision, culture, and brand as distinct elements to be handled separately by different departments. Often, the company's vision resides with the management committee, its culture within HR, and its brand within marketing. This not only puts the company at risk of a strategic misalignment, but is also a source of tremendous internal and external confusion.

Bridge the Gap

So how can companies bridge the gap between marketing and HR, brand and culture, and inside and outside in order to better assimilate the brand internally?

Strategic alignment of company objectives, marketing and employee objectives, and ultimately communications to all constituents is the most critical pre requisite for success. It's not enough that marketing requests HR's assistance in implementing brand values across the firm or that HR requests marketing's help in adapting tools for HR purposes. If the goal is to deliver greater business value, the two departments need to work together seamlessly. The first step in forging this relationship is for each department to develop respect for the other's expertise. A mutual understanding can be achieved by slating a meeting of the minds where strategies can be exchanged, synergies can be discussed, and overlaps in responsibilities can be resolved. The alignment is best developed around the business objectives, not the departmental objectives. It's not about raising awareness with customers, nor is it about diversity. It's about delivering more profits to the bottom line.

Once marketing and HR are philosophically aligned, specific strategies for attracting and retaining employees and for the integration of the brand throughout the organization need to be discussed and agreed on. The two groups must proceed with a shared objective and a willingness to work together for a common purpose.

A shared objective, for example, might be to turn the company into a technology leader. On the HR side, supporting this objective would involve evaluating employee characteristics, rewards and compensation, management systems, and cultural values. Marketing's task is to specify the traits that are critical from a brand perspective (e.g., employees need to be creative and constantly pushing the envelope), then work with HR to define how these are translated into behaviors that are embedded into processes and systems. That's because the proof lies in the execution, not just in the promise. Another example of a shared objective might be generating employee excitement about recent company achievements or changes in strategic direction. Often, internal campaigns or employee contests are held where marketing leverages its work in external communications, or maybe sponsorship relationships, to bring additional flavor or interest to HR's employee activities.

After the two groups have developed their strategies, it comes down to implementation. The first step in this phase is to assess what needs to be done collectively and as individual functions. This is the time to see if things like rewards and compensation systems, training curriculums, and brand and recruitment communications are aligned with HR and marketing strategies. If not, this is the time to see that it's done. Once the tasks to align marketing and HR are outlined, a plan should be created that details how the brand is reflected across all key initiatives and the scheduled rollout for each initiative, complete with a summary of the roles and responsibilities of all those involved, sample brand actions, and/or language to be used.

Executing the plans becomes the responsibility of the functions themselves. However, there should be some joint management structure that enables frequent assessment of progress and required course corrections. This can be a steering committee made up of senior representatives from the two departments or it can be more of a joint working group that rolls up its sleeves and meets frequently to hammer out progress details and enable each others' programs.

Brand Alignment

The brand's alignment is critical for the implementation phase to be effective. A key step is for marketing to stop talking about the "brand." The reality is that "brand" is merely a buzzword to many in the organization, and discussions a round it often generate indifference. A better way to infuse brand into business practices is to relate it directly to employee benefits using language like: "If you act in this way, you will achieve these results." For example, telling a business machine salesperson that they have to treat their clients with kid gloves may not get the same response as if you said that their clients are looking to place business with someone that really takes care of their requirements.

It's also essential for marketing to be proactive in sharing the promises they intend to communicate internally with employees before the external market actually hears them. BMW Group, for example, has had great success cultivating enthusiasm and motivating employees by sharing its advertising campaigns with employees before they hit the general market. At Southwest Airlines, HR and marketing developed a list of eight employee "freedoms" to summarize the employment experience at Southwest, thereby creating an internal side to the external brand story. The brand identity of "freedom" internally has become: "At Southwest Airlines, freedom begins with me." As a result, employees know exactly what kind of experience they are to create. Successful brand alignment, as such examples illustrate, will help employees and the company as a whole to naturally act on-brand with an on-brand customer experience to follow.

The monitoring and management of the collaborative efforts is ongoing, and marketing and HR should provide updates on progress and relevant information regularly—at a minimum once per quarter. Measuring results can be done in a variety of ways, but conducting quantitative surveys and holding focus groups are two of the most effective. And while HR should continue to monitor the pulse of employees, marketing must stay focused on how best to deliver against the needs of the company's stakeholders. The combined results of internal understanding of the brand, quality of delivery at critical touch points, and customer awareness/loyalty to the brand should be reported back to the leadership team to ensure they have the necessary information to keep brand and business strategy in alignment.

Just how important a story HR and marketing can tell when the two work in tandem is illustrated by the results of HSBC's (Hong Kong Shanghai Banking Corporation) *Global International Brand Survey.* This survey is conducted periodically to test how well all 300,000 employees understand and live the brand as reflected by how they answer 10 statements. Results from the study are compared with a customer metrics system. In an interview with Peter Stringham, group general manager and head of marketing for HSBC, we learned that results correlate strongly. Branches that score high on "living the brand" have a tendency to score higher on both customer satisfaction and brand purchase consideration.

HR and marketing might not be natural bedfellows, but experience shows that, when they do cooperate and work together, an increase in successful recruiting, overall employee understanding, and support of the brand (and thus the work of the marketing group) follows. With a simple formula of communications and coordination, companies can create a strong foundation on which to build a compelling brand and strong culture and drive significant business impact.

About the Authors—Both of the authors work at Prophet, a management consultancy specializing in integrating business, brand, and marketing strategies. JEFF SMITH is an associate partner in the Zurich office and may be reached at jsmith@prophet.com. KRISTIANE BLOMQVIST is a senior associate in the London office and may be reached at kblomqvist@prophet.com.

Understanding HRM–Firm Performance Linkages: The Role of the "Strength" of the HRM System

Theory building has lagged on the intermediate linkages responsible for the relationship between HRM and firm performance. We introduce the construct "strength of the HRM system" and describe the metafeatures of an HRM system that result in a strong organizational climate, analogous to Mischel's "strong situation," in which individuals share a common interpretation of what behaviors are expected and rewarded. The strength of the HRM system can help explain how individual employee attributes accumulate to affect organizational effectiveness.

DAVID E. BOWEN AND CHERI OSTROFF

In recent years scholars have devoted a great deal of attention to examining the linkage between HR practices and firm performance. Based on research evidence to date, it is becoming increasingly clear that the HR system is one important component that can help an organization become more effective and achieve a competitive advantage (Becker & Huselid, 1998). However, a larger question remains unanswered: How does HRM contribute to firm performance?

> More specifically, if there is indeed an impact of HRM systems on firm performance, how do these effects occur? What are the mechanisms through which these effects manifest themselves?. . . These questions call for theory refinement and the development of more comprehensive models of the HRM-firm performance relationship that include intermediate linkages and boundary conditions. . . . this type of research should be given a high priority by HRM scholars (Ferris, Hochwarter, Buckley, Harrell-Cook, & Frink, 1999: 394).

In research on the HRM–firm performance relationship, scholars have often assumed two perspectives. One has been based on a systems approach. Research in this area has moved from a focus on *separate* HRM practices and *employee* performance to a more macro focus on the overall set of HRM practices and *firm* performance (e.g., Arthur, 1992; Huselid, 1995; Huselid & Becker, 1996; Huselid, Jackson, & Schuler, 1997). That is, the dominant trend in research on the HRM–firm per-

formance linkage has been to take a systems view of HRM by considering the overall configuration or aggregation of HRM practices (Ferris, Arthur, Berkson, Kaplan, Harrell-Cook, & Frink, 1998), rather than by examining the effects of individual HRM practices on firm performance (e.g., Delaney & Huselid, 1996; Delery & Doty, 1996) or on individual performance.

A second approach has been the strategic perspective on HRM, which has taken on different meanings in the literature (Ferris et al., 1999). In one strategic-based approach, researchers have examined the particular "fit" between various HRM practices and the organization's competitive strategy (e.g., Miles & Snow, 1994; Wright & Snell, 1991). Embedded in this view is the notion that organizations must also horizontally align their various HRM practices toward their strategic goal and that practices must complement one another to achieve the firm's business strategy (Schuler & Jackson, 1987a,b; Wright & Snell, 1991; Wright, McMahan, & McWilliams, 1994). The guiding logic is that a firm's HRM practices must develop employees' skills, knowledge, and motivation such that employees behave in ways that are instrumental to the implementation of a particular strategy. Similarly, researchers have taken a contingency perspective, with the assumption that the effectiveness of the HR system depends on contextual features such as industry, firm size, or manufacturing policies (e.g., MacDuffie, 1995; Youndt, Snell, Dean, & Lepak, 1996).

A related approach within the strategic perspective on HRM pertains to how the overall set of HRM practices is generally associated with firm performance and competitive advantage (Ferris et al., 1999). Central here is the resource-based perspective (Barney, 1991) such that, collectively, a firm's human resources are believed to have implications for firm performance and provide a unique source of competitive advantage that is difficult to replicate (Wright et al., 1994). The guiding proposition is that HRM practices are socially complex and intricately linked in ways that make them difficult for competitors to copy (Boxall, 1996). More fully, the complexities of the human resource value creation process make HRM a source of competitive advantage that is rare, inimitable, and nonsubstitutable (Barney, 1991; Ferris et al., 1999). The resource-based view has prompted recent work on how HRM practices contribute to firm performance by leveraging human capital, discretionary effort, and desired attitudes and behaviors (e.g., Becker & Gerhart, 1996; Lado & Wilson, 1994; Wright et al., 1994).

Taken together, these two perspectives on the HRM–firm performance relationship—the systems and strategic perspectives—help stage how HRM practices and their influence on employee attributes can lead to desired outcomes at the firm level, such as productivity, financial performance, and competitive advantage. Yet still left unanswered is the process through which this occurs. Although both perspectives take a macro approach, they assume implicit, multilevel relationships among HRM practices, individual employee attributes, and organizational performance (Huselid, 1995; Wright et al., 1994). The features of HRM that are necessary to facilitate these linkages have not been well addressed.

In what follows we develop a framework for understanding how HRM practices, as a system, can contribute to firm performance by motivating employees to adopt desired attitudes and behaviors that, in the collective, help achieve the organization's strategic goals. We first focus on climate as an important mediating variable in the HRM–firm performance relationship. The HRM system itself is discussed not so much in terms of content (e.g., the specific set of HRM practices necessary for achieving an organizational goal) but rather process (the features of an HRM system that send signals to employees that allow them to understand the desired and appropriate responses and form a collective sense of what is expected). We describe how a "strong climate" (Schneider, Salvaggio, & Subirats, 2002) can be viewed as a "strong situation" (Mischel, 1973, 1977), in which employees share a common interpretation of what is important and what behaviors are expected and rewarded. We then introduce the concept of "strength of the HRM system" and specify the metafeatures of the overall HRM system that would lead to strong climates, after which we examine the consequences of strong versus weak HRM systems, arguing that the emergence of the intended organizational climate from psychological climates is moderated by the strength of the HRM system. We close with directions for future research on this new strength of the HRM system construct and its antecedents and consequences. Our discussion is framed within the mesoparadigm that concerns the simultaneous study of organizational, group, and individual processes and specifies how levels are interrelated in the form of linking mechanisms (House, Rousseau, & Thomas-Hunt, 1995).

Climate as a Mediator of the HRM–Firm Performance Relationship

We begin our framework with the notion that different business strategies are linked to different sets of HRM practices, based on the contingency perspective of strategic human resource management (e.g., Schuler & Jackson, 1987b, 1995). For example, a strategy of innovation should foster adoption of HRM practices that share a focus on innovation; a strategy of customer service should be linked to a set of practices that center around service. We then build on the view that HRM systems influence employee attitudes and behavior, as well as organizational outcomes, through employee interpretations of the work climate (Ferris et al., 1998; Kopelman, Brief, & Guzzo, 1990).

Before developing climate as a mediator, it is important to note that other perspectives delineate different variables that can operate as a mediator in the HRM–firm performance relationship. For example, the technical subsystem perspective focuses on task requirements and task accomplishment (Katz & Kahn, 1978) and has historically dominated HRM research (Schuler & Jackson, 1995). The underlying assumption is that HRM practices lead to employee knowledge, skills, and abilities (KSAs) that, in turn, influence firm performance at the collective level (Schuler & Jackson, 1995).

Additionally, there are perspectives that focus on "higher-order" socially interactive constructs—what Ferris and his colleagues (1998) term *social context theory* views of the relationship between HRM and performance. By higher order, we mean social structures that cannot be reduced to an aggregation of the perceptions of the individuals currently composing the organization.

Although we focus on climate, two examples of higher-order social structures are organizational culture and the organization role structure. Culture, conceptualized as organizationally embedded assumptions and values, can function both as an antecedent to the HRM system and as a mediator of its linkage to firm performance (Denison, 1996). Organizational assumptions and values shape HRM practices, which, in turn, reinforce cultural norms and routines that can shape individual and firm performance. Role theorists conceptualize the organization as a system of formal roles, existing apart from any one current occupant, which serve to convey standardized information to employees about expected patterns of activity (Ashforth, 2001; Katz & Kahn, 1978). In this view the HRM system can be seen as part of the "maintenance subsystem" (Katz & Kahn, 1978) that defines roles, which, in turn, influence individual and firm performance.

Our focus on climate complements the technical and higher-order social structure perspectives on the HRM–firm performance relationship. We focus on climate because of our interest in multilevel relationships, since both psychological climates—as individual-level perceptions—and organizational climate—as a shared perception at the firm level—have been positioned as mediators of the relationship between HRM practices and performance (e.g., Kopelman et al., 1990; Ostroff & Bowen, 2000). Additionally, given our interest in strategic perspectives on HRM, climate is an appropriate construct for developing our framework, based on the recent emphasis on climates around strategic objectives that are purported to enhance effectiveness (e.g., Schneider, 2000).

Psychological climate is an experiential-based perception of what people "see" and report happening to them as they make sense of their environment (Schneider, 1990, 2000). This sense-making is relative to the goals the organization pursues; how employees are to perform their daily activities; the management practices under which employees work; and the perceptions of the kinds of behaviors that management expects, supports, and rewards (Schneider, Brief, & Guzzo, 1996). Organizational climate is a shared perception of what the organization is like in terms of practices, policies, procedures, routines, and rewards—what is important and what behaviors are expected and rewarded (e.g., James & Jones, 1974; Jones & James, 1979; Schneider, 2000)—and is based on shared perceptions among employees within formal organizational units.

Climate researchers have acquired a strategic focus over the years, with the move from viewing climate perceptions as shared perceptions about global, generic issues to linking climate perceptions to a shared, specific, strategic content criterion of interest, such as a climate for innovation (Delbecq & Mills, 1985; Klein & Sorra, 1996) or service (Schneider, 1990). Individual-level psychological climates may emerge as a shared organizational climate, which, in turn, ultimately relates to organizational performance.

Climate is a critical mediating construct in exploring multilevel relationships between HRM and organizational performance. Because climate is widely defined as the perception of these formal and informal organizational policies, practices, and procedures (Reichers & Schneider, 1990), it follows that the HRM practices and HRM system will play a critical role in determining climate perceptions. In turn, empirical demonstrations have indicated that organizational climate is related to higher-level behaviors and organizational performance indicators, including customer satisfaction, customer service quality, financial performance, organizational effectiveness, and total quality management outcomes (e.g., Borucki & Burke, 1999; Johnson, 1996; Ostroff & Schmitt, 1993; Schneider & Bowen, 1985).

Although the above variables are well established in the literature, the mechanisms by which they interrelate are poorly understood. For example, as Boxall (1996) has observed, knowledge of HRM practices is widespread, but knowledge of how to refine and implement them within a particular context (e.g., a particular strategic focus) may not be. With respect to climate, Schneider (2000) has observed that there is little research or understanding of how organizational climate actually develops. Intuitive acceptance of an HRM-climate linkage far exceeds theory development of the mechanisms responsible.

Integrating HRM Content and Process

Two interrelated features of an HRM system can be distinguished: content and process. By content, we mean the individual practices and policies intended to achieve a particular objective (e.g., practices to promote innovation or autonomy). The content of the HRM system refers to the set of practices adopted and, ideally, should be largely driven by the strategic goals and values of the organization. That is, given some strategic goal such as service, efficiency, or quality, a set of HRM practices should be devised to help direct human resources in meeting this goal. To be effective in terms of content, the foci of the HRM practices must be designed around a particular strategic focus, such as service or innovation.

While a number of different models detailing the appropriate HRM practices for different strategies have been offered (e.g., Dyer & Holder, 1988; Miles & Snow, 1994; Schuler & Jackson, 1987b), rhetoric about this contingency perspective outpaces data supporting it (cf. Huselid, 1995; MacDuffie, 1995; Schuler & Jackson, 1987a; Youndt et al., 1996). It is likely that there is not a single most appropriate set of practices for a particular strategic objective. Rather, different sets of practices may be equally effective (Delery & Doty, 1996), so long as they allow a particular type of climate around some strategic objective (e.g., climate for innovation or service) to develop (Klein & Sorra, 1996).

We propose that HRM content *and* process must be integrated effectively in order for prescriptive models of strategic HRM actually to link to firm performance. By process, we refer to how the HRM system can be designed and administered effectively by defining metafeatures of an overall HRM system that can create strong situations in the form of shared meaning about the content that might ultimately lead to organizational performance.

Given a desired content of the HRM system, the HRM system may still not elicit appropriate collective behaviors and attitudes needed for effectiveness, because individuals may interpret the HRM practices idiosyncratically, leading to variability in psychological climate perceptions. HRM practices can be viewed as a symbolic or signaling function by sending messages that employees use to make sense of and to define the psychological meaning of their work situation (e.g., Rousseau, 1995). All HRM practices communicate messages constantly and in unintended ways, and messages can be understood idiosyncratically, whereby two employees interpret the same practices differently (Guzzo & Noonan, 1994). Although much has been written about the substantive content of HRM—that is, the specific practices that can build task-relevant skills and motivations such as those for a climate for innovation (Delbecq & Mills, 1985), service (Schneider, 1990), change (Schneider et al., 1996), or safety (Zohar, 2000)—little attention has been given to the social constructions that employees make of their interactions with HRM across practices and time (Rousseau & Greller, 1984).

In what follows we focus on how HRM can send unambiguous messages to employees that result in a shared construction of the meaning of the situation. Thus, we concentrate on understanding what features of HRM process can lead employees to appropriately interpret and respond to the information conveyed in HRM practices. We develop the notion that characteristics of a strong HRM system must be present in order for a shared, strong organizational climate to emerge (at the aggregate level) from psychological climates (at the individual level) and propose that the strength of the HRM system is a linking mechanism that builds shared, collective perceptions, attitudes, and behaviors among employees.

Climate as the Situation: The Concept of Situational Strength

Kurt Lewin's early work on climate is the foundation of discussions of situationism in social psychology (Ross & Nisbett, 1991). Lewin and his associates (Lewin, Lippit, & White, 1939) demonstrated that different leadership styles created different climates, which, in turn, led to different behavioral reactions and attitudes of members in the groups studied. As Ross and Nisbett summarize, "The main point of Lewin's situationism was that social context creates potent forces producing or constraining behavior" (1991: 9).

Strength of Situation

The situation, as developed in situationism, entails the psychological meaning of situations for the individual *and* the behavior potential of situations for the individual (Endler & Magnusson, 1976). The interest is not in the physical or actual situation per se but, rather, the situation individuals "see" based on their perceptions, cognitive maps, schemata, enactments, and even behavior in the situation (Drazin, Glynn, & Kazanjian, 1999).

In an attempt to explain when the characteristics of a situation would most likely lead to consistency in behaviors, Mischel developed the concept of the relative power of situations to control individual behavior:

> Psychological "situations" and "treatments" are powerful to the degree that they lead all persons to construe the particular events the same way, induce uniform expectancies regarding the most appropriate response pattern, provide adequate incentives for the performance of that response pattern, and instill the skills necessary for its satisfactory construction and execution. Conversely, situations and treatments are weak to the degree that they are not uniformly encoded, do not generate uniform expectancies concerning the desired behavior, do not offer sufficient incentives for its performance, or fail to provide the learning conditions for successful construction of the behavior (Mischel, 1973: 276).

In sum, situational strength deals with the extent to which a situation induces conformity—a strong situation—or is interpreted as ambiguous—a weak situation (Mischel & Peake, 1982). The interest is in specifying situational contingencies that identify when individual differences will or will not control individual behavior Mischel (1997).

Strong Climates

Only when perceptions are shared across people does organizational climate become a meaningful construct (James, 1982). Recently, the notion of strong or weak climates has begun to emerge in the literature, with a focus on the extent to which employees interpret the situation similarly, thereby producing low variance in perceptions about the situation (Jackofsky & Slocum, 1988; Payne, 2000; Schneider et al., 2002). As such, an organizational climate can *act as* a strong situation when employees develop a shared interpretation of the organization's policies, practices, procedures, and goals and develop shared perceptions about what behaviors are expected and rewarded in the organization. Additionally, the work on strategic climate content—for example, for safety and innovation (e.g., Schneider, 1990)—assumes that the more HRM practices send strong signals about what strategic goals are most important and what employee behaviors are expected, supported, and rewarded relative to those goals, the more likely it is those goals will be achieved.

Strength of the HRM System

What are the features of an HRM system that allow for the creation of a strong situation? Although suggestions for appropriate process for separate practices have been offered (e.g., employee participation in the design and administration of performance appraisal), *metafeatures* of an HRM system overall have not been identified. Using social cognitive psychology and social influence theories, we propose a set of characteristics that allow HRM systems to create strong situations in which unambiguous messages are communicated to employees about what is appropriate behavior. These characteristics refer to the process by which a consistent message about HRM content can be sent to employees.

HRM practices can be viewed as communications from the employer to employee (Guzzo & Noonan, 1994; Rousseau, 1995; Tsui, Pearce, Porter, & Tripoli, 1997). The literature on message-based persuasion (Chaiken, Wood, & Eagley, 1996) has its roots in McGuire's (1972) two-step process of "reception"—encoding of the message (exposure to the message, attention to its content, comprehension of the content)—and "yielding"—acceptance of the message (agreeing with the message and storing it in memory). For a message to have its desired effect, both reception and yielding are necessary. Yet making sense of the environment often entails numerous cycles of attending to information, interpreting information, acting on it, and receiving feedback to clarify one's sense of the situation, particularly when events are highly ambiguous or subject to change (Weick, 1995; Wicker, 1992).

Attribution theory has been useful in helping explain message-based persuasion and in helping identify key features that will allow for messages to be received and interpreted uniformly among employees (Fiske & Taylor, 1991). In the HRM context, employees are required to infer cause-effect attributions from these communications to determine what behaviors are important, expected, and rewarded. Causal inference can be understood not solely as the inner workings of the mind but also as a process by which people gather and elicit causal explanations from others and communicate their explanations to others (Fiske & Taylor, 1991).

In order to function effectively in a social context and make accurate attributions about a situation, an employee must have adequate and unambiguous information. Although attributional frameworks have been used to explain whether an individual attributes the cause of another person's behavior to internal or external factors, Kelley's (1967) attribution theory details the process for making attributions not only to other people but to situational factors as well. According to Kelley's (1967) covariation model, an individual can make confident attributions about cause-effect relationships in situations depending on the degree of distinctiveness (the event-effect is highly observable), consistency (the event-effect presents itself the same across modalities and time), and consensus (there is agreement among individuals' views of the event-effect relationship). Indeed, Mischel's (1973, 1977) explication of a strong situation implies that it is one in which there is distinctiveness, consistency, and consensus.

We propose that when the HRM system is perceived as high in distinctiveness, consistency, and consensus, it will create a strong situation. Using literature on message-based persuasion and social influence, we elucidate nine metafeatures of HRM systems that build distinctiveness, consistency, and consensus, thereby creating a strong influence situation in which employees share constructions of the situation. As such, the features help foster the emergence of a strong organizational climate, as opposed to idiosyncratic psychological climate perceptions. The strength of the HRM system can be conceptualized in terms of its effectiveness in conveying the types of information needed to create a strong situation.

Distinctiveness

Distinctiveness of the situation generally refers to features that allow it to stand out in the environment, thereby capturing attention and arousing interest. We elucidate four characteristics of HRM that can foster distinctiveness: visibility, understandability, legitimacy of authority, and relevance.

Visibility. Visibility of the HRM practices refers to the degree to which these practices are salient and readily observable. This is a basic prerequisite for interpretation involving whether an HRM practice and its component parts are disclosed to employees, affording them the opportunity for sense-making. Visibility or salience has long been identified as an important characteristic in determining not only whether people attend to information but how they cognitively organize it (e.g., Tajfel, 1968) and make cause-effect attributions (Taylor & Fiske, 1978). For example, if performance criteria are not transparent or if pay administration outcomes are withheld, such as with pay secrecy, this certainly will not create Mischel's (1973) strong situation, in which everyone has shared constructions of the situation and uniform expectancies regarding the most appropriate response pattern and what incentives are available.

The creation of a strong organizational situation requires that situational characteristics be salient and visible throughout

much of employees' daily work routines and activities. When the HRM system includes a wide spectrum of HRM practices—for example, selection, training, diversity programs, employee assistance programs, and so forth—that affect a large number of employees, visibility is likely to be higher. Expanding the number and range of practices should enhance salience and visibility, because it increases complexity and allows for the set of practices to be more figural relative to other stimuli—both of which are principles of salience (Fiske & Taylor, 1991). Additionally, shared meanings cannot be developed unless most or all employees are subjected to and can perceive the same practices.

Understandability. Understandability of HRM content refers to a lack of ambiguity and ease of comprehension of HRM practice content. An organizational communication that cannot be understood can have no authority (Barnard, 1938). Features of the stimulus or situation evoke cognitive categories (e.g., schemas, scripts, cognitive maps), drawing attention to some features and away from others. Sometimes profound differences exist in category systems across people (Kelley, 1955). To the extent that the situational stimulus is ambiguous or unclear, multiple categorizations are likely (Feldman, 1981). That is, different people are likely to use different cognitive categories to attend to different aspects of the information, resulting in different attributions. For example, employees must be able to understand how the practice works. HRM practices such as benefit plans, gain-sharing plans, and succession plans are easily misunderstood or at least open to multiple interpretations.

Legitimacy of authority. Legitimate authority of the HRM system and its agents leads individuals to consider submitting to performance expectations as formally sanctioned behaviors. Influence by legitimate authority is essentially a perceptual process—that is, one sees the behavioral requirements of one's own role as subordinate to another that stands out as the legitimate authority (Kelman & Hamilton, 1989). It is the concept of authority whereby individuals are willing to submit to the necessities of cooperative systems (Barnard, 1938).

The HRM system is most likely to be perceived as an authority situation when the HRM function is perceived as a high-status, high-credibility function and activity. This is most likely when HRM has significant and visible top management support in the firm and can be achieved through investments in HR practices or the HRM function, or perhaps by placing the director of HRM in a high-level managerial position. This fits the observation about the requirements for the success of HRM systems generally; namely, success depends largely on top management support, including top managers' beliefs about the importance of people, investment in human resources, and involvement of HRM professionals in the strategic planning process (Ostroff, 1995). In such a way, the signal sent from top management is that HRM is "legitimate" or "credible."

This notion is related to message source in social cognition, since the characteristics of the message source are linked to attributions made and the outcomes of persuasion (Fiske & Taylor, 1991). Communicator credibility (Chaiken et al., 1996) is a critical component in attribution, persuasion, and influence attempts. However, the elaboration likelihood model of persuasion (Petty & Cacioppo, 1986) indicates that persuasion and influence are not simply functions of features of the communicator and credibility but, rather, joint functions of the communicator's credibility *and* the recipients' involvement in the outcomes (Hass, 1981). Relatedly, obedience to legitimate authority is a function of more than the individual's subordination to a position of "higher office"; it also involves an individual's interpretation of the *relevance* of influence attempts to them (Kelman & Hamilton, 1989).

Relevance. Relevance of the HRM system refers to whether the situation is defined in such a way that individuals sees the situation as relevant to an important goal (Kelman & Hamilton, 1989). Relevance, coupled with legitimate authority, means that influence is based on both a perception of superordinate authority and what Kelman and Hamilton (1989) term *motivational significance*. For the latter, individuals must perceive the situation as relevant to their important goals, that the desired behaviors are clear and optimally suited for goal attainment, and that influencing agents have the personal power to affect the achievement of these goals (Kelman & Hamilton, 1989).

Here, consideration of both individual goals and organizational goals—in our case, the strategic goal desired in the form of HRM content—is important in that individual goals should be fostered to align with those of the organization. Alignment or congruence between individuals' and managers' goals has been shown to have important consequences for both individual attitudes and behaviors, as well as for effective organizational functioning (Vancouver & Schmitt, 1991). Thus, the situation must be defined in such a way that individuals are willing to work toward goals that not only allow them to meet their own needs but, in doing so, also allow the organization to achieve its goals. For example, if the organization has a strategic goal of customer service and an employee values financial gain, then service-based bonuses will heighten relevance and allow both the individual and organization to achieve their goals. Relatedly, the relevant desired behaviors must be specified and obstacles to their performance removed.

Additionally, relevance is a function of the perceived power of the influencing agent(s) to help individuals achieve relevant goals (Kelman & Hamilton, 1989). Influence is based on the extent to which an agent (e.g., HRM staff member or line manager enacting HRM practices) is perceived as possessing *personal* capabilities and is willing to use them to aid goal achievement—separate from his or her influence based on position power and legitimate authority. Perceived power of the influencing agent(s) depends on two factors. One is whether the agent can affect some of the conditions necessary for the achievement of relevant goals through, for example, the application of unique expertise or the allocation of necessary resources. Characteristics of the agent that bear on this issue include his or her prestige, special knowledge or expertise, representativeness, control of resources, and ability to apply sanctions. A second is the perceived likelihood that the agent will actually use his or her relevant capabilities in ways that will affect the likelihood of goal achievement.

Taylor and Fiske (1991) explain the relationship between relevance and the credibility or legitimacy of the message source.

If outcomes (rewards, punishments, goal attainment) depend on someone else's actions as well as the individual's actions, then this creates a condition of outcome dependency, which, in turn, affects perceptions and attributions. When people are more outcome dependent, particularly when the outcomes are relevant, they direct more active attention to the person or source of communication. At the same time, when outcomes are particularly relevant, credibility of the message source has less of an influence. Thus, it appears relevance alone can enhance distinctiveness; when relevance is not strongly established, legitimacy plays a greater role.

Consistency

The above features of visibility, understandability, legitimacy of authority, and relevance help draw attention to the message and communicator, thereby increasing the probability that the HRM message will be encoded and interpreted uniformly among employees. However, distinctiveness alone is not likely sufficient enough for people to view the situation uniformly and to respond to the message sent by the set of HRM practices. For employees to make accurate attributions about what behaviors are expected and rewarded, attributional principles of causation must be present. Fundamental principles for causal attribution include priority, whereby causes precede effects, and contiguity with the effect, whereby causes occur close in time to an effect (Kassin & Pryor, 1985).

Similarly, as alluded to above, the literature on authority and influence indicates that individuals who are to be influenced must perceive instrumentalities in the situation whereby behaviors lead to rewards. That is, the distinctiveness characteristics ensure that the HRM system is viewed, overall, as significant in defining the social context for employee behavior; a consistent pattern of instrumentalities across HRM practices, time, and employees that link specific events and effects further enhances the likelihood that desired specific behaviors will be displayed.

These notions are related to Kelley's (1967) concept of consistency. Consistency generally refers to establishing an effect over time and modalities whereby the effect occurs each time the entity is present, regardless of the form of the interactions. Thus, we focus on features that establish consistent relationships over time, people, and contexts: instrumentality, validity, and consistent HRM messages.

Instrumentality. Instrumentality refers to establishing an *unambiguous* perceived cause effect relationship in reference to the HRM system's desired content-focused behaviors and associated employee consequences. It ensures that there are adequate incentives associated with performance of the desired behavioral pattern. Strong instrumentalities, combined with the earlier "relevance" of social influence, leverage influence within an expectancy theory of motivation perspective (e.g., Vroom, 1964).

Perception plays a central role in instrumentality because it emphasizes how employees anticipate likely consequences of behavior. Instrumentalities are shaped largely by reinforcement consistency and are established by consistency and repetition over time, particularly through application of reinforcement principles. Employees are more likely to perceive the instrumentality when behavior and outcomes are closely linked in time (evoking the contiguity causation attribution principle) and when they are administered consistently over some time schedule (evoking the priority causation attribution principle). To the extent that HRM staff and line managers have the resources and power to link outcomes to behavior or performance on a timely and consistent schedule, they will be able to influence cause-effect attributions.

Validity. Validity of HRM practices is important because message recipients attempt to determine the validity of a message in making attributions (Fiske & Taylor, 1991). Thus, HRM practices must display consistency between what they purport to do and what they actually do in order for them to help create a strong situation. Selection tests, for example, must validly screen on desired employee abilities, thereby making a substantive contribution to human capital development. Recall that one aspect of a strong situation is that employees have the skills necessary to execute the behaviors expected of them. Barnard (1938) long ago observed that employees would view a communication as authoritative only if they were able mentally and physically to comply with it.

Validity also makes a symbolic contribution by signaling to employees what KSAs are valued in a setting and by adding more employees with specified skills to the workforce. Further, when a practice is implemented and advertised to have certain effects, and then does not do what it was intended to do, the message sent to employees is contradictory, and employees are left to develop their own idiosyncratic interpretations.

Consistent HRM messages. These convey compatibility and stability in the signals sent by the HRM practices. Considerable evidence indicates that individuals desire consistency in organizational life (e.g., Kelley, 1973; Lidz, 1973; Siehl, 1985). The lack of consistency in "double-bind" communication can lead to particularly intense cognitive dissonance (Siehl, 1985). Double-bind communication occurs when a person is faced with significant communication involving two separate messages (Bateson, Jackson, Haley, & Weakland, 1956). The messages are related to each other and deal with the same content area, but they are incongruent or contradictory. Consequences of inconsistency can be severe (Lidz, 1973).

Three types of consistency are required, each of which entails the need to avoid sending double-bind communications to employees and to allow for HRM content to be perceived consistently. One is between what senior managers say are the organization's goals and values and what employees actually conclude those goals and values are based on their perceptions of HRM practices. Inconsistency here is a difference between what has been termed *espoused* values and *inferred* values (Martin & Siehl, 1983). For example, managers may espouse a value of risk taking, but employees may infer that performance appraisal and reward system practices reinforce playing it safe.

A second requirement for avoiding double-bind communication is internal consistency among the HRM practices themselves. In recent years, much has been written on the importance of designing an HRM system with practices that complement one another and fit together as a whole in achieving the organiza-

tion's goals (e.g., Becker & Gerhart, 1996; Delery & Doty, 1996; Schuler & Jackson, 1995; Wright & McMahan, 1992; Wright & Snell, 1991). Internal alignment among practices should result in performance advantages for firms, because the different sets of HRM practices will elicit, reward, and control the appropriate employee behaviors for achieving strategic objectives (Arthur, 1992; Ulrich & Lake, 1991; Wright et al., 1994). For example, if the ability to work in teams is a screening focus in selection, then internal consistency will be ensured if group, rather than individual, performance is the basis for rewards. Furthermore, if each employee encounter with an HRM practice (e.g., hiring decision, performance appraisal interview) is conceptualized as a separate situation, then, following Mischel (1968), the functional similarity of these situational stimuli will influence the generalizability of team-oriented behavior across on-the-job situations.

A third dimension of consistency is stability over time. HRM practices are situational stimuli, the meaning of which is acquired across time. Certainly, how one responds to a situation depends on one's prior history with the stimulus (e.g., Mischel, 1968). Behaviors and behavioral consequences remain stable when the evoking conditions remain stable. In organizations where practices have been in place a long time, there is stronger agreement among employees as to what is expected of them and what they expect of the organization in return (Rousseau & Wade-Benzoni, 1994).

Consensus

Consensus results when there is agreement among employees—the intended targets of influence by the HRM system—in their view of the event-effect relationship. More accurate attributions about what behaviors and responses lead to what consequences are more likely to be made when there is consensus (Kelley, 1972). Several factors can help foster consensus among employees and can influence whether individuals perceive the same effect with respect to the entity or situation in question. Among these are agreement among message senders, which can foster consensus (Fiske & Taylor, 1991), and the fairness of the HRM system, which can also influence consensus inasmuch as fairness involves whether employees understand the distribution rules by which they do, or do not, receive what they feel they deserve for their contributions.

It is also important to point out that consistency and consensus are distinct but interrelated concepts. For example, when individuals throughout the organization experience consistency in HRM practices, consensus is more likely to be fostered. At the same time, when message senders cannot agree among themselves on the intended message, consistency is likely to be hampered.

Agreement among principal HRM decision makers. Agreement among these message senders helps promote consensus among employees. Within a strategic HRM perspective, the principal decision makers in the organization (e.g., top managers, HR executives) set the strategic goals and design the set of HRM practices for achieving those goals. When individuals view message senders as strongly agreeing among themselves on the message, they are more likely to form a consensus

(Fiske & Taylor, 1991). This perception of agreement can be facilitated in several ways and is related to distinctiveness and consistency.

First, when multiple decision makers agree on the message, distinctiveness can be enhanced because a larger number of individuals can send similar communications (increasing visibility). As more employees "see" the practice and perceive that top decision makers agree on it, consensus can be facilitated. Further, integration and close interactions among HRM professionals, managers, and top managers foster the exchange of tacit knowledge for the formulation and implementation of an organizational strategy and HRM system that reflect the firm's strategic direction (Lado & Wilson, 1994). These integrations among decision makers can help promote relevance by clearly identifying important goals and means to goal attainment, as well as enhance legitimacy of authority of the HR managers and line managers enacting the HRM policies.

Second, to the extent that members of the top management team disagree among themselves about the goals of HRM and/or disagree with HRM professionals or managers, and to the extent that HRM managers and staff members disagree among themselves, it becomes difficult to send unambiguous and internally consistent messages to employees. Low consistency of HRM practices and lack of consensus are related in that disagreement among decision makers is likely to produce poor consistency in delivering practices; thus, different employees will experience different event-consequence relationships. Overall, then, agreement among top decision makers can help foster greater consensus among employees, since it allows for more visible, relevant, and consistent messages to be conveyed to employees.

Fairness. Fairness of the HRM system is a composite of employees' perceptions of whether HRM practices adhere to the principles of delivering three dimensions of justice: distributive, procedural, and interactional (e.g., Bowen, Gilliland, & Folger, 1999; Folger & Cropanzano, 1998). Research indicates that the perceived fairness of HRM affects how positively HRM activity is viewed and the capability of the HRM system to *influence* employee attitudes and behaviors. Researchers have argued that there is a positive relationship between perceptions of HRM fairness and what has been termed the *acceptability* criterion of HRM practices (Bretz, Milkovich, & Read, 1992; Waldman & Bowen, 1998), which refers to the extent to which employees contribute to and utilize HRM (e.g., complete 360 degree appraisals and use feedback from it to shape their behavior).

Agreement among employees' perceptions of event-effect relationships will be influenced by whether employees have similar perceptions of what distribution rules—principles of distributive justice—apply in what situations. Outcomes such as rewards can be distributed based on an "equality" rule, in which all receive the same outcome; an "equity" rule, in which subsets of employees receive different amounts based on relevant differences, such as in a merit pay system; or an "individual need" rule, such as flexible working hours for a single mother in unique circumstances (Bowen et al., 1999).

Management practices that lead to employee perceptions of procedural and interactional justice increase the transparency of these distribution rules (Bowen et al., 1999) and, by so doing, increase the likelihood that the HRM system will be characterized by consensus about event-effect relationships. Procedural justice can be enhanced by giving employees a voice in determining the methods by which outcome decisions are made—for example, involving employees in designing behavior or outcome-based performance appraisals. Interactional justice involves managers' openly and respectfully explaining to employees the reasons behind decisions and the distribution of outcomes. It can include clarifying what distribution formula was used in making individual pay increase decisions in situations where not all employees received the same pay increase.

Consequences of the Strength of the HRM System

HRM practices influence employee perceptions of climate at the individual level. Further, the characteristics of strong HRM systems are more likely to promote shared perceptions and give rise to the emergence of a strong organizational climate about the HRM content. That is, we propose that *the strength of the HRM system will foster the emergence of organizational climate (collective perceptions) from psychological climates (individual-level perceptions).*

In a strong situation, variability among employees' perceptions of the meaning of the situation will be small and will reflect a common desired content. In turn, organizational climate will display a significant association with employee attitudes and behaviors. This occurs because a strong HRM system can foster similar viewpoints such that the situation leads everyone to "see" the situation similarly, induces uniform expectancies about responses, provides clear expectations about rewards and incentives for the desired responses and behaviors, and induces compliance and conformity through social influence. Therefore, we propose that a *strong HRM system process can enhance organizational performance owing to shared meanings in promotion of collective responses that are consistent with organizational strategic goals (assuming the appropriateness of those goals).* More specifically, an *HRM system high in distinctiveness, consistency, and consensus should enhance clarity of interpretation in the setting, thereby allowing for similar "cognitive maps" or "causal maps" to develop among people, as well as to create an "influence situation" whereby individuals yield to the message and understand the appropriate ways of behaving.*

Further, while interactions and communication among employees are likely to result in collective sensemaking (Jackofsky & Slocum, 1988), regardless of the strength of the HRM system, we argue that in cases where the strength of the HRM system is strong, the sensemaking process will be most likely to result in the *intended* organizational climate. If the HRM system is weak, HRM practices will send messages that are ambiguous and subject to individual interpretation. Given ambiguity, one of two things may happen: variability or unintended sensemaking.

First, with a weak system, variability of individual responses may be large (Mischel, 1973). Considerable variance across individuals' perceptions of psychological climates will exist, and shared perceptions in the form of organizational climate will not emerge. Individuals can construct their own version of reality (House et al., 1995) or their own version of what messages are being communicated by HRM practices and use this to guide their own behavior. Thus, in *weak situations (low distinctiveness, consistency, and consensus), constructs at the individual but not the organizational level are likely to show strong relationships; psychological climate perceptions will have a significant association with individual attitudes and behaviors.*

While a weak situation is produced by low distinctiveness, consistency, and consensus, we also argue that *the most ambiguous or weakest situation is produced when distinctiveness is high, coupled with low consistency and consensus.* Distinctiveness drives up attention. That is, HRM practices are salient or visible, and employees are aware of them. However, if the messages that employees are now attending to are inconsistent or conflicting, as different individuals are subjected to different experiences with the HRM practices, confusion, disillusionment, or other negative reactions will likely result. In such a case, not only will shared perceptions about the practices and climate particularly be unlikely to emerge, but many employees may have negative attitudes.

Alternatively, the ambiguity inherent in weak situations may cause employees to engage in collective sensemaking (House et al., 1995). When faced with an equivocal situation or attributional uncertainty, individuals may attempt to reduce this uncertainty by engaging in a social process of interacting and consulting with one another to develop their own shared interpretations (Drazin et al., 1999; Fiske & Taylor, 1991; Weick, 1995). The danger here is that the collective interpretation that employees draw from the ambiguous situation is not the one intended by the organization. That is, the "strong" climate that emerges does not match the intended climate content; hence, it may conflict with organizational goals and strategies and may ultimately lead to conflicts, poor productivity, or low effectiveness. This is particularly likely to occur when "distinctiveness" is low (although low consensus and consistency will also play a role). When practices are not made salient, visible, and understandable, ambiguity is high, and employees are more likely to refer to one another in an attempt to define the situation in their own way. Thus, we propose that *low distinctiveness of the HRM system contributes to a collective sensemaking process that may result in unintended organizational climates. Further, a weak HRM system process is unlikely to promote organizational effectiveness because it creates a weak situation in which either individual processes dominate or collective sensemaking results in shared interpretations that may be inconsistent with organizational* strategic goals.

It is important to note that this process of emergence of similar perceptions of climate does not occur in a vacuum. While the HRM system and the strength of this system form the fundamental basis of whether similar perceptions will be derived, scholars have argued that interactions among employees are also relevant (Jackofsky & Slocum, 1988). Morgeson and Hofmann (1999) provide rationales for the importance of these interactions in forming collective constructs. Within any collective, individuals are likely to meet one another and interact. Each interaction results in a discrete event, and subsequent interactions are termed *event cycles*. The structure of any collective group can be viewed as a series of ongoing events, activities, and event cycles among the individuals. These interdependencies and interactions among individuals over time can result in jointly produced responses, and it is this structure that forms the basis for the eventual emergence of collective constructs—one that can transcend individuals, individual behaviors, and individual perceptions.

This process is similar to the emergence of overlapping "causal maps" through cognitive processing (e.g., Weick, 1995; Wicker, 1992). Individuals develop causal maps, which are cognitive representations of the entities in the situation, certain qualities of those entities, and perceived linkages among them. Overlapping causal maps can be facilitated through social exchange and transactions among employees. In such a way, *employees* can *collectively* agree on the appropriate aspects of the environment to attend to, as well as how to interpret these aspects and how to respond to them appropriately. Thus, we propose that *a strong HRM system facilitates interactions, interdependencies, and event cycles such that fewer event cycles are needed to develop shared interpretations.*

Context and HRM System Strength

In the preceding discussion we implicitly assumed an organizational climate. Yet researchers and theorists recognize the multidimensional nature of climate such that multiple types of organizational climates can exist within a firm and at different levels of analysis in the organization (Schneider, 1990). That is, different functional areas, departments, or groups may develop different subclimates (e.g., Payne, 2000). Likewise, cluster analysis has been used to demonstrate different collective climates within an organization—climates that represent clusters of employees who perceive the organization similarly and span formal organizational units (e.g., Jackofsky & Slocum, 1988; Joyce & Slocum, 1984).

We acknowledge that the content of the climate can vary across groups within the organization. Further, different HRM practices around a different content might be applied to different groups of employees. We propose that *if the process of the HRM system is strong, a shared perception of the climate will emerge in organizational subunits, albeit with some differences in content or strategic focus across groups.* Indeed, for many firms this may be strategically desirable—for example, in diversified firms, firms with multiple locations, international firms, or firms pursuing multiple strategic objectives in different parts of the organization. It is also likely that, for some groups in the organization, a shared climate will emerge, whereas for others it will not, owing to differences in the HRM process across different groups.

Another concern is the possibility that a strong climate might be inflexible and resistant to change, thereby compromising organizational effectiveness. The literature on strong cultures offers a resolution of this issue. A culture whose content comprises values and beliefs that support flexibility can be strong, without limiting the organization's ability to adapt to its environment (e.g., Sathe & Davidson, 2000). Similarly, we propose that a strong climate that has elements of what has been termed a *climate for innovation* (e.g., Klein & Sorra, 1996), for example, can be simultaneously strong and adaptable. In other words, *the process of the HRM system can create a strong climate adaptable to change, if the content of the climate includes elements that focus on flexibility and innovation.* Although individual employees' behaviors may differ so as to be innovative or flexible, all employees should still share the idea that this type of adaptability is what is expected of them. Thus, perceptions of the climate will be the same with a strong system that encourages innovation or flexibility, but there may be variance and changes in actual behavior over time.

Future Research and Theory Development

Research is needed on the properties of the HRM *process,* as distinct from research on the properties of practices (e.g., reliability) and the content of HRM practices and systems (e.g., the specific practices that make up different systems). That is, research is needed to delineate how these processes influence the attributes of the work situation as perceived by employees.

Little is known about the important parameters underlying organizational situations (e.g., Bem & Funder, 1978; Chatman, 1989; Fredrickson, 1972). We have proposed a set of features, based on social influence and social cognition theories, that should help create a strong situation and shared meaning. It is critical that the viability of these metafeatures of the organization be tested as important elements that create strong situations. Frederiksen (1972) proposes a number of different means for attempting to classify and develop taxonomies of situations. In this case, it may be useful to attempt to group or cluster situations on the basis of their tendency to elicit similar behaviors. This would require a three-dimensional data matrix, with the dimensions representing person, behavior, and situational attributes (Frederiksen, 1972). With such a procedure, one could derive clusters of responses or behaviors that differentially correspond with the nine HRM process features.

In addition, research is needed to determine the most appropriate means for "combining" the metafeatures of the HRM system. As suggested earlier, it is likely that some features are more critical than others in creating a strong situation. For example, without consistent HRM messages, distinctiveness and consensus may lose impact. Alternatively, although we believe this is less likely, a compensatory model may be appropriate in that a high level of one feature will make up for a low level of another feature. Thus, one could compare and test the viability of an additive model (i.e., the sum across all features), a configural model (i.e., different profiles of features), and a multiplicative or contingency model (i.e., interactions among the features).

Further, it is important to determine the relative impact of and interrelationships between HRM system strength and other determinants of strong situations or climates. Factors such as leadership, social relationships, and structural design features can also affect the strength of the situation and can foster the development of a shared climate (Ashforth, 1985; Ostroff, Kinicki, & Tamkins, 2003). HRM features are likely to interact with these other factors to further foster a shared sense of the situation. For example, supervisors can serve as interpretive filters of HRM practices, and when they are visible in implementing practices or promote high-quality exchanges with employees, they can introduce a common interpretation among unit members (Kozlowski & Doherty, 1989; Naumann & Bennett, 2000).

Thus, a strong HRM system coupled with a visible supervisor may foster stronger relationships among HRM, climate, and performance than each would individually. Similarly, while our primary intent was to elucidate the characteristics of an HRM process that would allow for shared perceptions of climate to emerge, additional research is needed to determine the extent to which these HRM system characteristics can also impact other social structures such as culture, roles, communication patterns and networks, and social capital, all of which may enhance the relationship between HRM and performance.

Relationships between Content and Process

Research is needed to test interrelationships between HRM process strength and content. The configural approach examines how a pattern of numerous HRM practices is related to firm performance so that the total effect of HRM is greater than the sum of the individual practices themselves (Becker & Gerhart, 1996; Delery & Doty, 1996; Ichniowski, Shaw, & Prennushi, 1997). The focus of this approach is on the sets of mutually reinforcing practices that may be related to firm performance. The strength of the HRM system may be a factor influencing whether the configural approach to HRM–firm performance relationships is supported in empirical studies. The likelihood that individual HRM practices would function as a set, in a mutually reinforcing manner, may be a function of the internal consistency of those practices and the effectiveness with which they are implemented together.

A similar case can be developed for assessing interactions between strength and content across climates *for* different strategic foci. For example, on the one hand, it may not be difficult to incorporate features of a strong HRM system for a climate focused on cost leadership or safety, given that the desired outcomes and behaviors associated with those criteria can be specified clearly. On the other hand, it may be more difficult to create a strong HRM system for a climate for service, given that the intangibility of service makes it difficult to specify service quality goals and the employee behaviors that will lead to them (Bowen & Schneider, 1988). This may either complicate the ability to create a strong HRM system or moderate the relationship between that strength and the uniformity of employees' perceptions in the form of organizational climates.

Methodological and Measurement Issues

Two interrelated methodological issues are raised by our proposals. The first of these concerns appropriate measurement for the strength of the HRM system. The second concerns levels of analysis and aggregation issues in moving from individual-level perceptions of climate to collective constructs. A full discussion of these issues is beyond the scope of this article.

New measures will need to be developed to assess the strength of the HRM system. It is important to note that this construct is a situational context variable, and, as we have defined it, it represents a higher-level construct. In past research on HRM practices and systems, scholars have typically relied on reports from a higher-level manager or HR executive. In our case, HR directors and top managers could be asked to evaluate the dimensions of strength of the system. This procedure has the obvious advantage of obtaining a single, global measure for each dimension of strength of the system. However, this measurement technique focuses only on measures of the attributes from a single source that is at a higher level in the organization, while our primary theoretical focus lies in the impact these practices have on perceptions of employees. Because the concept of strength requires judgments and perceptions of employees, we suggest that a better alternative is to assess these characteristics of the HRM system from employees themselves. That is, the appropriate unit of measurement of assessing strength is the individual, since employee attributions and perceptions reside in the individual.

Future work should be directed at developing a valid measure of HRM strength. For example, to assess visibility, employees could be given a list of a variety of HRM practices and asked to indicate the extent to which each is utilized in the firm. A comparison between those practices that agents of the HRM function assert are in place and those that employees indicate are used would provide some assessment of how visible the practices are to employees.

Similarly, to assess consistency, employees could be asked to what extent they have actually participated in or experienced each of these practices (e.g., received a semiannual performance review). The percent of people indicating they experienced the practice would provide some indication of how consistently the practice is administered across employees in the organization. As an alternative, employees could be asked to indicate the extent to which they believe the practice applies to all employees.

Agreement might be assessed by asking top decision makers to delineate the strategic goals related to HRM and the intended message of the HRM practices (e.g., promote innovation and risk taking, promote loyalty and longevity, promote safety). High agreement among decision makers should be related to higher consensus among employees as to what practices are salient, visible, administered consistently, and so forth.

Such measures would be useful from multiple perspectives. First, the mean score on the dimension would provide an indication as to the level at which these characteristics are present. That is, a higher mean score on measures tapping distinctiveness, consistency, and consensus would be one indicator of strong HRM process. Second, researchers could assess the extent to which employees perceive characteristics in the same way—that is, they could assess the extent of agreement or variability in responses among employees. Higher agreement would support consensus and a strong system, whereas high variance in responses would indicate a weak system.

As to assessments of climate, agreement among employees about their perceptions must be demonstrated before aggregated measures of psychological climate perceptions can be used to represent a unit-level or organizational level climate construct (James, 1982). Further, it is important to examine both the level (e.g., the level of rating on a dimension of climate) and the variability in responses. Level is an indicator of "content," whereas variability is an indicator of situational "strength." At the individual level of analysis, if one is interested in examining the relationship between perceptions of the climate and individual responses, the level of the individual's responses on the variables is most useful. However, when moving to higher levels of analysis, additional measurement issues emerge. Strong and well-designed HRM systems produce greater homogeneity of perceptions and responses within the organization, resulting in organizational climate. The strength of the climate is indicated by the degree of variability in responses, regardless of the level of the aggregate rating on the content of climate. An indication of whether the HRM system creates a strong situation is the extent of agreement on climate ratings (Payne, 2000).

Final Thoughts

In listing challenges that the HRM community faces in the future, Ulrich cites the need for HR practice to be guided by HR theory. He reminds HRM professionals that theory helps explain the manner in which outcomes emerge:

> To make HR practices more than isolated acts, managers and HR professionals must master the theory behind HR work; they need to be able to explain conceptually how and why HR practices lead to their outcomes . . . Regardless of the preferred theory, managers and HR professionals should abstract from it a higher level of reasoning for their day-to-day work and thus better explain why their work accomplishes its goals (1997: 238; emphasis added).

Recently, in the literature scholars have developed "why" HR practices lead to sustainable competitive advantage. Hopefully, this present effort at theory building on the strength of the HRM system can begin to help explain "how" HRM practices lead to outcomes the organization desires.

References

Arthur, J. B. 1992. The link between business strategy and industrial relations systems in American steel mini-mills. *Industrial and Labor Relations Review,* 45: 488–506.

Ashforth, B. E. 1985. Climate formation: Issues and extensions. *Academy of Management Review,* 10: 837–847.

Ashforth, B. E. 2001. *Role transitions in organizational life.* Mahwah, NJ: Lawrence Erlbaum Associates.

Barnard, C. I. 1938. *The functions of the executive.* Cambridge, MA: Harvard University Press.

Barney, J. 1991. Firm resources and competitive advantage. *Journal of Management,* 17: 99–120.

Bateson, G., Jackson, D. D., Haley, J., & Weakland, J. H. 1956. Toward a theory of schizophrenia. *Behavioral Science,* 1: 251–264.

Becker, B., & Gerhart, B. 1996. The impact of human resource management on organizational performance: Progress and prospects. *Academy of Management Journal,* 39: 779–801.

Becker, B. E., & Huselid, M. A. 1998. High performance work systems and firm performance: A synthesis of research and managerial implications. *Research in Personnel and Human Resources Management,* 16: 53–101.

Bem, D. J., & Funder, D. C. 1978. Predicting more of the people more of the time—assessing personality of situations. *Psychological Review,* 85: 485–501.

Borucki, C. C., & Burke, M. J. 1999. An examination of service-related antecedents to retail store performance. *Journal of Organizational Behavior,* 20: 943–962.

Bowen, D. E., Gilliland, S. W., & Folger, R. 1999. HRM and service fairness: How being fair with employees spills over to customers. *Organizational Dynamics,* 27(3): 7–23.

Bowen, D. E., & Schneider, B. 1988. Services marketing and management: Implications for organizational behavior. *Research in Organizational Behavior,* 10: 43–80.

Boxall, P. 1996. The strategic HRM debate and the resource based view of the firm. *Human Resource Management Journal,* 6: 59–75.

Bretz, R. D. Jr., Milkovich, G. T., & Read, W. 1992. The current state of performance appraisal research and practice: Concerns, directions, and implications. *Journal of Management,* 18: 321–352.

Chaiken, S., Wood, W., & Eagly, A. H. 1996. Principles of persuasion. In E. T. Higgins & A. W. Kruglanski (Eds.), *Social psychology: Handbook of basic principles:* 702–744. New York: Guilford Press.

Chatman, J. A. 1989. Improving interactional organizational research: A model of person-organization fit. *Academy of Management Review,* 14: 333–349.

Delaney, J. T., & Huselid, M. A. 1996. The impact of human resource management practices on perceptions of organizational performance. *Academy of Management Journal,* 39: 949–969.

Delbecq, A., & Mills, P. K. 1985. Managerial practices that enhance innovation. *Organizational Dynamics,* 14(1): 24–34.

Delery, J. E., & Doty, D. H. 1996. Modes of theorizing in strategic human resource management: Tests of universalistic, contingency, and configural performance predictions. *Academy of Management Journal,* 39: 802–835.

Denison, D. R. 1996. What is the difference between culture and organizational climate? A native's point of view on a decade of paradigm wars. *Academy of Management Review,* 21: 619–654.

Drazin, R., Glynn, M. A., & Kazanjian, R. K. 1999. Multilevel theorizing about creativity in organizations: A sensemaking perspective. *Academy of Management Review,* 24: 286–307.

Dyer, L., & Holder, G. W. 1988. A strategic perspective of human resource management. In L. Dyer (Ed.), *Human resource management: Evolving roles and responsibilities:* 1–45. Washington, DC: Bureau of National Affairs.

Endler, N. S., & Magnusson, D. 1976. Personality and person by situation interactions. In N. S. Endler & D. Magnusson (Eds.), *Interactional psychology and personality:* 1–25. New York: Hemisphere.

Feldman, J. M. 1981. Perception, cognition, and the organization. *Journal of Applied Psychology,* 66: 128–138.

Ferris, G. R., Arthur, M. M., Berkson, H. M., Kaplan, D. M., Harrell-Cook, G., & Frink, D. D. 1998. Toward a social context theory of the human resource management organization effectiveness relationship. *Human Resource Management Review,* 8: 235–264.

Ferris, G. R., Hochwarter, W. A., Buckley, M. R., Harrell-Cook, G., & Frink, D. D. 1999. Human resource management: Some new directions. *Journal of Management,* 25: 385–415.

Fiske, S. T., & Taylor, S. E. 1991. *Social cognition.* New York: McGraw-Hill.

Folger, R., & Cropanzano, R. 1998. *Organizational justice and human resource management.* Newbury Park, CA: Sage.

Frederiksen, N. 1972. Toward a taxonomy of situations. *American Psychologist,* 26: 114–123.

Guzzo, R. A., & Noonan, K. A. 1994. Human resource practices as communications and the psychological contract. *Human Resource Management,* 33: 447–462.

Hass, R. G. 1981. Effects of source characteristics on cognitive responses and persuasion. In R. E. Petty, T. M. Ostrom, & T. C. Brock (Eds.), *Cognitive responses in persuasion:* 141–172. Hillsdale, NJ: Lawrence Erlbaum Associates.

House, R., Rousseau, D. M., & Thomas-Hunt, M. 1995. The meso-paradigm: A framework for the integration of micro and macro organizational behavior. *Research in Organizational Behavior,* 17: 41–114.

Huselid, M. A. 1995. The impact of human resource management practices on turnover, productivity, and corporate financial performance. *Academy of Management Journal,* 38: 635–672.

Huselid, M. A., & Becker, B. E. 1996. Methodological issues in cross-sectional and panel estimates of the human resource management-firm performance link. *Industrial Relations,* 35: 400–422.

Huselid, M. A., Jackson, S. E., & Schuler, R. S. 1997. Technical and strategic human resource management effectiveness as determinants of firm performance. *Academy of Management Journal,* 40: 171–188.

Ichniowski, C., Shaw, K., & Prennushi, G. 1997. The effect of human resource management practices on productivity: A study of steel finishing lines. *American Economic Review,* 87: 291–313.

Jackofsky, E. F., & Slocum, J. W., Jr. 1988. A longitudinal study of climates. *Journal of Organizational Behavior,* 9: 319–334.

James, L. R. 1982. Aggregation bias in estimates of perceptual agreement. *Journal of Applied Psychology,* 67: 219–229.

James, L. R., & Jones, A. P. 1974. Organizational climate: A review of theory and research. *Psychological Bulletin,* 81: 1096–1112.

Johnson, J. W. 1996. Linking employee perceptions of service climate to customer satisfaction. *Personnel Psychology,* 49: 831–852.

Jones, A. P., & James, L. R. 1979. Psychological climate: Dimensions and relationships of individual and aggregated work environment perceptions. *Organizational Behavior and Human Decision Processes,* 23: 201–250.

Joyce, W., & Slocum, J. 1984. Collective climate: Agreement as a basis for defining aggregate climates in organizations. *Academy of Management Journal,* 27: 721–742.

Kassin, S. M., & Pryor, J. B. 1985. The development of attribution processes. In J. Pryor & J. Day (Eds.), *The development of social cognition:* 3–34. New York: Springer-Verlag.

Katz, D., & Kahn, R. L. 1978. *The social psychology of organizing.* New York: Wiley.

Kelley, G. A. 1955. *A theory of personality: The psychology of personal constructs.* New York: Norton.

Kelley, H. H. 1967. Attribution theory in social psychology. In D. Levine (Ed.), *Nebraska symposium on motivation:* 192–240. Lincoln: University of Nebraska Press.

Kelley, H. H. 1972. Causal schemata and the attribution process. In E. E. Jones, D. E. Kanouse, H. H. Kelley, R. E. Nisbett, S. Valins, & B. Weiner (Eds.), *Attribution: Perceiving the causes of behavior:* 151–174. Morristown, NJ: General Learning Press.

Kelley, H. H. 1973. The processes of causal attribution. American Psychologist, 28: 107–128.

Kelman, H. C., & Hamilton, V. C. 1989. *Crimes of obedience: Toward a social psychology of authority and responsibility.* New Haven, CT: Yale University Press.

Klein, K. J., & Sorra, J. S. 1996. The challenge of innovation implementation. *Academy of Management Review,* 21: 1055–1080.

Kopelman, R. E., Brief, A. P., & Guzzo, R. A. 1990. In B. Schneider (Ed.), *Organizational climate and culture:* 282–318. San Francisco: Jossey-Bass.

Kozlowski, S. W. J., & Doherty, J. L. 1989. Integration of climate and leadership: Examination of a neglected issue. *Journal of Applied Psychology,* 74: 721–742.

Lado, A. A., & Wilson, M. C. 1994. Human resource systems and sustained competitive advantage: A competency based perspective. *Academy of Management Review,* 19: 699–727.

Lewin, K., Lippit, R., & White, R. 1939. Patterns of aggressive behavior in experimentally created social climates. *Journal of Social Psychology,* 10: 271–299.

Lidz, T. 1973. *Origin and treatment of schizophrenic disorders.* New York: Basic Books.

MacDuffie, J. P. 1995. Human resource bundles and manufacturing performance: Organizational logic and flexible production systems in the world auto industry. *Industrial and Labor Relations Review,* 48: 199–221.

Martin, J., & Siehl, C. J. 1983. Organizational customer and counterculture: An uneasy symbiosis. *Organizational Dynamics,* 12(2): 52–64.

McGuire, W. J. 1972. Attitude change: The information processing paradigm. In C. G. McClintock (Ed.), *Experimental social psychology:* 108–141. New York: Holt, Rinehart & Winston.

Miles, R. E., & Snow, C. C. 1994. *Fit, failure and the hall of fame.* New York: Free Press.

Mischel, W. 1968. *Personality and assessment.* New York: Wiley.

Mischel, W. 1973. Toward a cognitive social learning conceptualization of personality. *Psychological Review,* 80: 252–283.

Mischel, W. 1977. The interaction of person and situation. In D. Magnusson & N. S. Endler (Eds.), *Personality at the crossroads: Current issues in interactional psychology:* 333–352. Hillsdale, NJ: Lawrence Erlbaum Associates.

Mischel, W. 1997. Personality dispositions revisited and revised: A view after three decades. In R. Hogan, J. Johnson, & S. Briggs (Eds.), *Handbook of personality psychology:* 113–132. New York: Academic Press.

Mischel, W., & Peake, P. K. 1982. Beyond déjà vu in the search for cross-situational consistency. *Psychological Review,* 89: 730–755.

Morgeson, F. P., & Hofmann, D. A. 1999. The structure and function of collective constructs: Implications for multilevel research and theory development. *Academy of Management Review,* 24: 249–265.

Naumann, S. E., & Bennett, N. 2000. A case for procedural justice climate: Development and test of a multilevel model. *Academy of Management Journal,* 43: 881–889.

Ostroff, C. 1995. SHRM/CCH survey. *Human Resources Management: Ideas and Trends in Personnel* (356): 1–12.

Ostroff, C., & Bowen, D. E. 2000. Moving HR to a higher level: Human resource practices and organizational effectiveness. In K. J. Klein & S. W. J. Kozlowski (Eds.), *Multilevel theory, research, and methods in organizations:* 211–266. San Francisco: Jossey-Bass.

Ostroff, C., Kinicki, A. J., & Tamkins, M. M. 2003. Organizational culture and climate. In W. C. Borman, D. R. Ilgen, & R. J. Klimoski (Eds.), *Comprehensive handbook of psychology, volume 12: Industrial and organizational psychology:* 565–594. New York: Wiley.

Ostroff, C., & Schmitt, N. 1993. Configurations of organizational effectiveness and efficiency. *Academy of Management Journal,* 36: 1345–1361.

Payne, R. L. 2000. Culture and climate: How close can they get? In N. M. Ashkanasy, C. P. M. Wilderom, & M. F. Peterson (Eds.), *Handbook of organizational culture and climate:* 163–176. Thousand Oaks, CA: Sage.

Petty, R. E., & Cacioppo, J. T. 1986. The elaboration likelihood model of persuasion. In L. Berkowitz (Ed.), *Advances in experimental social psychology,* vol. 19: 123–205. San Diego: Academic Press.

Reichers, A. E., & Schneider, B. 1990. Climate and culture: An evolution of constructs. In B. Schneider (Ed.), *Organizational climate and culture:* 5–39. San Francisco: Jossey-Bass.

Ross, L., & Nisbett, R. E. 1991. *The person and the situation: Perspectives of social psychology.* Philadelphia: Temple University Press.

Rousseau, D. M. 1995. *Psychological contracts in organizations.* Thousand Oaks, CA: Sage.

Rousseau, D. M., & Greller, M. M. 1994. Human resource practices: Administrative contract-makers. *Human Resource Management,* 33: 385–402.

Rousseau, D. M., & Wade-Benzoni, K. A. 1994. Linking strategy and human resource practices: How employee and customer contracts are created. *Human Resource Management,* 33: 463–490.

Sathe, V., & Davidson, E. J. 2000. Toward a new conceptualization of culture change. In N. M. Ashkanasy, C. P. M. Wilderom, & M. F. Peterson (Eds.), *Handbook of organizational culture and climate:* 279–296. Thousand Oaks, CA: Sage.

Schneider, B. 1990. The climate for service: An application of the climate construct. In B. Schneider (Ed.), *Organizational climate and culture:* 383–412. San Francisco: Jossey-Bass.

Schneider, B. 2000. The psychological life of organizations. In N. M. Ashkanasy, C. P. M. Wilderom, & M. F. Peterson (Eds.), *Handbook of organizational culture and climate:* xvii–xxii. Thousand Oaks, CA: Sage.

Schneider, B., & Bowen, D. E. 1985. Employee and customer perceptions of service in banks: Replication and extension. *Journal of Applied Psychology,* 70: 423–433.

Schneider, B., Brief, A. P., & Guzzo, R. A. 1996. Creating a climate and culture for sustainable organizational change. *Organizational Dynamics,* 24(4): 7–19.

Schneider, B., Salvaggio, A. N., & Subirats, M. 2002. Climate strength: A new direction for climate research. *Journal of Applied Psychology,* 87: 220–229.

Schuler, R. S., & Jackson, S. E. 1987a. Organizational strategy and organization level as determinants of human resource management practices. *Human Resource Planning,* 10: 125–141.

Schuler, R. S., & Jackson, S. E. 1987b. Linking competitive strategies and human resource management practices. *Academy of Management Executive,* 1(3): 207–219.

Schuler, R. S., & Jackson, S. E. 1995. Understanding human resource management in the context of organizations and their environment. *Annual Review of Psychology,* 46: 237–264.

Siehl, C. J. 1985. After the founder: An opportunity to manage culture. In P. Frost, L. Moore, M. Louis, C. Lundberg, & J. Martin (Eds.), *Organizational culture:* 125–140. Beverly Hills, CA: Sage.

Tajfel, H. 1968. Social and cultural factors in perception. In G. Lindzey & E. Aronson (Eds.), *Handbook of social psychology:* 315–394. Reading, MA: Addison-Wesley.

Taylor, S. E., & Fiske, S. T. 1978. Salience, attention, and attributions: Top of the head phenomena. In L. Berkowitz (Ed.), *Advances in experimental social psychology:* 249–287. New York: Academic Press.

Tsui, A. S., Pearce, J. L., Porter, L. W., & Tripoli, A. M. 1997. Alternative approaches to employee-organization relationship: Does investment in employees pay off? *Academy of Management Journal,* 40: 1089–1121.

Ulrich, D. 1997. *Human resource champions: The next agenda for adding value and delivering results.* Boston: Harvard Business School Press.

Ulrich, D., & Lake, D. 1991. Organizational capability: Creating competitive advantage. *Academy of Management Executive,* 5(1): 77–91.

Vancouver, J. B., & Schmitt, N. W. 1991. An exploratory examination of person-organization fit: Organizational goal congruence. *Personnel Psychology,* 44: 333–352.

Vroom, V. 1964. *Work and motivation.* New York: Wiley.

Waldman, D. A., & Bowen, D. E. 1998. The acceptability of 360-degree appraisals: A customer-supplier relationship perspective. *Human Resource Management,* 37: 117–130.

Weick, K. E. 1995. *Sensemaking in organizations.* Thousand Oaks, CA: Sage.

Wicker, A. W. 1992. Making sense of environments. In W. B. Walsh, K. H. Craik, & R. H. Price (Eds.), *Person-environment psychology:* 157–192. Hillsdale, NJ: Lawrence Erlbaum Associates.

Wright, P. M., & McMahan, G. C. 1992. Theoretical perspectives for strategic human resource management. *Journal of Management,* 18: 295–320.

Wright, P. M., McMahan, G. C., & McWilliams, A. 1994. Human resources and sustained competitive advantage: A resource-based perspective. *International Journal of Human Resource Management,* 5: 301–326.

Wright, P. M., & Snell, S. A. 1991. Toward an integrative view of strategic human resource management. *Human Resource Management Review,* 1: 203–225.

Youndt, M. A., Snell, S. A., Dean, J. W., Jr., & Lepak, D. P. 1996. Human resource management, manufacturing strategy, and firm performance. *Academy of Management Journal,* 39: 836–866.

Zohar, D. 2000. A group-level model of safety climate: Testing the effect of group climate on microaccidents in manufacturing jobs. *Journal of Applied Psychology,* 85: 587–596.

DAVID E. BOWEN is dean of faculty and programs and professor of management at Thunderbird, The American Graduate School of International Management. His research interests are organizational behavior issues in service quality and the linkage between human resource management effectiveness and competitive advantage. **CHERI OSTROFF** is a professor of psychology and education at Teachers College, Columbia University. She received her PhD in industrial-organizational psychology from Michigan State University. Her current research interests include levels of analysis issues, human resource management systems, and person-environment congruence.

We thank Blake Ashforth, College of Business, Arizona State University, and Art Brief, then associate editor for *AMR,* for their comments and time.

Strategic Human Resources Management in Government
Unresolved Issues

The concept of strategic human resources management (SHRM) holds considerable promise for improving government performance. However, to realize this promise, it is necessary to invest the concept with clear meaning. This article explores unresolved issues regarding the meaning of SHRM and its relevance to public organizations. Arguing that the value of the concept is undermined by tying it too closely to strategic planning, the article offers an expanded, two-pronged understanding of SHRM. The personnel office, in addition to helping the agency implement strategic initiatives, also carries out an integrated personnel program guided by a coherent theory about what it should be doing and why.

JONATHAN TOMPKINS

The concept of strategic human resources management (SHRM) is well established in business literature.[1] It refers to ongoing efforts to align an organization's personnel policies and practices with its business strategy. The recent interest in SHRM reflects a growing awareness that human resources are the key to success in both public and private organizations. Yet, despite this growing awareness, the relevance of SHRM to public organizations is far from clear. Government agencies rarely operate in competitive markets and thus do not develop business strategies in the same sense that private organizations do. And because they function within larger systems of authority, they do not enjoy the same degree of autonomy that private organizations do to alter their personnel policies or provide performance-based incentives to employees. Given these inherent differences, SHRM cannot be transferred successfully from the private to the public sector without tailoring its design and implementation to the unique characteristics of public organizations.

At present there remain many unresolved issues about what modifications are required and the probabilities of their success. If SHRM is to succeed in fundamentally altering the role of the personnel department and the practice of public personnel management, greater clarity is required regarding the concept of SHRM and how it is to be implemented in public organizations. Accordingly, this article examines unresolved issues regarding the relevance of SHRM for government agencies and closes with an argument for an expanded understanding of what it means to manage human resources strategically.

Procedural and Structural Prerequisites: Unresolved Issues

Figure 1 presents a conceptual framework representative of the kind found in the business literature. It depicts SHRM as a process that merges strategic planning and human resource management. Specifically, it views SHRM as a continuous process of determining mission-related objectives and aligning personnel policies and practices with those objectives. The personnel department plays a strategic role to the extent that its policies and practices support accomplishment of the organization's objectives. Key components include analyzing the agency's internal and external environments, identifying the agency's strategic objectives, developing HR objectives and strategies consistent with the agency's goals (vertical integration), and aligning HR policies and practices with each other (horizontal integration). For this conceptual understanding of SHRM to be implemented successfully, certain structural and procedural requirements must be satisfied. These core requirements include the following:

1. An established strategic planning process.
2. Involvement of the HR director in the strategic planning process and full consideration of the personnel-related implications of the strategic objectives or initiatives under discussion.
3. A clear statement, written or unwritten, of each agency's mission and the strategic objectives to be achieved in pursuit of mission.

Analysis of Internal Environment		Analysis of External Environment	
	Statement of Agency's Mission and Strategic Objectives		
VERTICAL INTEGRATION			
	HR Objectives and Strategies		
	Function-Specific HR Policies and Practices		
Classification & Pay	Recruitment & Selection	Training & Development	Employee Benefits	Performance Management	Employee & Labor Relations
	HORIZONTAL INTEGRATION		

Figure 1 SHRM: A Conceptual Framework.

4. The vertical alignment of personnel policies and practices with an agency's mission and strategic objectives, and the horizontal integration of personnel policies and practices with each other.

5. A personnel office whose organizational role and structure are consistent with and contribute to the attainment of the agency's mission and strategic objectives.

These prerequisites capture what is required to integrate strategic planning with human resources management in a way that enhances organizational performance. Such an integration is difficult to achieve, for example, if there is no strategic planning process in place, no participation by the personnel director, and no subsequent development of personnel initiatives designed to support identified objectives. These prerequisites are explored below, along with unresolved issues about how to fulfill them in governmental settings.

An Established Strategic Planning Process

The role of strategic planning is to provide agencies with a clear sense of direction by clarifying mission, setting priorities, and identifying goals and objectives. NAPA's *Guide for Effective Strategic Management of Human Resources* recommends a short and simple planning process, five to seven days in length, which establishes five or six key objectives to be accomplished during the next few years.[2] A short and simple process has the advantage of providing a clear sense of direction to line and staff officials without becoming an overly elaborate and ultimately hollow planning exercise.

Most federal agencies engage in strategic planning because they are required to do so by the Government Performance and Results Act of 1993. The extent of its use among state and local governments, although somewhat less clear, is indicated by the results of two studies. Of those responding to a national survey of state agencies conducted by Berry and Wechsler, 60 percent said they had strategic planning processes in place.[3] Similarly, in a study of municipalities with

populations between 25,000 and 1,000,000, Poister and Streib found that 60 percent had adopted strategic planning in at least one department or program area.[4] These findings indicate that a large and growing number of state and local agencies are using strategic planning as a basic way of doing business.

One unresolved issue is whether the goals of SHRM are best achieved through a single, top-down, jurisdiction-wide strategic planning process or by separate agency-level planning processes. The business literature promotes strategic planning as a company-wide process in which top executives identify strategic objectives for the entire organization and managers develop their operational plans accordingly. But however appropriate this may be in the private sector, it is less so in the public sector. The essential task of government agencies is to execute public law. Because each agency has a unique mission and set of mandates to carry out, a single, top-down strategic planning process is less appropriate for purposes of SHRM. As Poister and Streib observed in their study of municipal governments, strategic planning may be "more useful for major organizational units with a unified sense of mission rather than a highly diversified and fragmented municipal jurisdiction as a whole."[5] While it is true that states such as Oregon[6] and communities such as Rock Hill, South Carolina[7] have engaged in strategic planning, such efforts are typically short-term exercises designed to resolve jurisdiction-wide problems or policy issues rather than institutionalized processes designed to enhance agency performance. Enhanced performance is the purpose that SHRM is intended to serve. Because each agency has a unique mission and set of mandates, SHRM logically requires agency-level strategic planning processes guided by legislative intent as well as the chief executive's policy or political agenda. The subsequent integration of agency plans into a jurisdiction-wide strategic plan is not required for purposes of SHRM.

A second unresolved issue is whether SHRM requires a particular kind of strategic planning to deliver on its promise of enhanced organizational performance. Strategic planning may be practiced in a variety of ways.[8] It may be externally-oriented, bringing together a diverse range of stakeholders to resolve issues of mutual concern, or internally-oriented, bringing together a cross-functional team of agency officials to set internal priorities and objectives. It may be mandated from above for purposes of accountability, or adopted voluntarily by an agency to establish a clear sense of direction. It may comprise a temporary, problem-specific process that ends when the immediate problem has been resolved, or an ongoing, institutionalized process for goal setting and issues management. Lastly, it may follow the Harvard policy model and call for extensive analysis of the agency's internal and external environments, or it may avoid lengthy analyses, opting instead for simple goal-setting exercises.[9] Process characteristics are important because they affect how seriously strategic planning is taken by agency staff, its perceived value as a management tool, and how much it ultimately contributes to organizational performance.

Advocates of SHRM tend to assume an institutionalized, internally-oriented strategic planning process adopted by agencies to clarify their missions, set priorities, and decide upon strategic objectives. There are, however, two contrasting approaches in current use. Little attention has been given to which of these is best suited to SHRM. The **performance management approach,** which is typically mandated by law or executive order, aims to ensure accountability. Under this approach, strategic objectives are stated in terms of desired results, such as a ten percent increase in the number of criminal cases closed successfully, and appropriate performance measures are identified to track success in achieving identified objectives. Although touted as an important governmental reform by members of the managing-for-results movement,[10] this approach relies upon several problematic assumptions. Among these are that agencies do not and will not pursue meaningful results on their own initiative, that rational planning models are appropriate for use in the public sector, that agencies can in fact translate their missions into measurable outcomes, and that agencies should be rewarded and sanctioned according to their degree of success in achieving their stated objectives. Despite the difficulties inherent in this approach, it has been mandated for use in the federal government as well as in many states. By contrast, the **issues management approach** is undertaken voluntarily to address emerging issues, internal or external to the agency, that are likely to affect its ability to carry out its mission.[11] Its primary purpose is adaptability rather than accountability. Under this approach, strategic objectives are stated in terms of the actions required to achieve a desired future state. Although the planning process is sometimes institutionalized and ongoing, in many cases it is undertaken on a limited basis to address emerging areas of concern. Examples of the latter include a federal agency seeking to maintain program quality in the face of budget cuts, a suburban school district wishing to explore educational reform initiatives, and a public library struggling to maintain employee morale as demand for its services continue to rise.[12] The issues management approach tends to emphasize political rationality (doing what is politically acceptable to powerful stakeholders) over formal rationality (utilizing objective criteria and cost-benefit calculations to determine

how best to attain agency goals). Key stakeholders are often brought together to negotiate an agreement about what to do and how. This approach also tends to be more pragmatic than ideological, reflecting the assumption that strategic planning is a valuable management tool for adjusting an organization to its external environment and keeping it focused on desired future states. Although tracking success with quantitative measures is not excluded under this approach, emphasis is placed on addressing issues affecting the agency's ability to carry out its mission rather than managing performance through the use of outcome measures.

Although this issue remains unresolved, it is possible to cite three reasons why the performance management approach is less suited to the purposes of SHRM. First, its underlying assumptions are difficult to satisfy in practice, potentially leaving participants frustrated and undermining their commitment to the process. As Bryson and Roering have cautioned, "a strategic planning system characterized by substantial comprehensiveness, formal rationality in decision making, and tight control will work only in an organization that has a clear mission; clear goals and objectives; centralized authority; clear performance indicators; and information about actual performance available at reasonable cost. Few public-sector organizations—or functions or communities—operate under such conditions."[13] Second, performance management systems are usually mandated from above and monitored by budget and planning offices. The problems associated with mandating strategic planning for purposes of control are well established.[14] Such systems tend to create an underlying air of distrust, which undermines commitment to the process. They tend to skew goal statements, choice of performance measures, and actual behaviors towards those results that are easiest to achieve, whether or not they truly enhance organizational performance. Third, the model of SHRM presented in Figure 1 calls for the alignment of personnel policies and practices with strategic initiatives designed to help the agency adapt to or cope with internal and external pressures. It does not call for their alignment with performance measures as such. Managing issues and measuring program results may be complementary processes, but planning for action and planning for control are two very different things. In the final analysis more research is required to determine whether the issues management approach is best suited to the purposes of SHRM or, alternatively, whether it is possible to integrate the two approaches successfully.

Involvement of the Personnel Director in Strategic Planning

SHRM as conceptualized in Figure 1 requires more than an established strategic planning process. It also requires the full involvement of the personnel director in that process. This is necessary to ensure that the strategic initiatives under discussion are evaluated in terms of their implications for human resources. When a new program initiative is under consideration, for example, the personnel director can offer an analysis of the gap between current human resources capabilities and projected needs. Similarly, if an agency wishes to adopt a customer-service orientation, the personnel director can explain the difficulties inherent in changing an organization's culture and the kinds of training and incentives required to accomplish it successfully. Involvement by the personnel director is also necessary so that the personnel staff can obtain a better and more complete understanding of the agency's mission and the issues confronting line managers.

Although examples of strategic partnerships are increasingly heralded in professional journals and at management conferences, many jurisdictions still do not include human resource professionals in strategic deliberations. An unresolved issue here is how to forge such a partnership. Traditionally, agency executives have tended to view the personnel office as a staff agency performing relatively routine functions and occupying a relatively low status in the organizational scheme of things. Consequently, they have not been inclined to involve personnel directors in strategic deliberations. At the same time many personnel directors have been slow to insist upon a strategic role because their professional training has not prepared them to perform such a role. Training in personnel management tends to emphasize the administration of personnel systems rather than general management or organizational development.

A Clear Statement of Strategic Objectives

Strategic goals and objectives, key products of the planning process, are often stated in a written plan. This plan provides a useful guide to the personnel office as it seeks to align existing policies and practices with strategic objectives. A written plan is not, however, an essential requirement of SHRM. As noted in NAPA's *Guide for Effective Strategic Management of Human Resources,* "the absence of a written plan developed at the agency level does not mean that SHRM cannot exist. The HR office can develop its own plan for linking its goals to the agency's goals, or the staff can be reminded of the need to factor the agency's strategic goals into its daily operations."[15] For purposes of SHRM, all that is required is that members of the personnel staff know and understand the agency's strategic objectives so that they can contribute to their attainment.

Although this requirement appears straightforward enough, most discussions of strategic planning fail to define what the term strategy or strategic objective means in a public context. In private sector firms practicing SHRM, a business strategy is designed to give them a competitive edge over other firms in their industry. They have three basic strategies from which to choose.[16] The **innovation strategy** involves developing a unique product or service, or concentrating on a specific market niche; the **quality enhancement strategy** involves offering products or services that are superior in quality; and the

cost reduction strategy involves reducing costs so that the firm can offer goods and services at the lowest possible price. Firms may also explore different growth strategies, such as those involving mergers and diversification. Once business strategies are selected, specific objectives are identified and the task of aligning personnel policies and practices begins.

Because public agencies are embedded in authority networks rather than economic markets, what it means to select a "business strategy" is much less clear. As Wechsler and Backoff have noted, the "strategies of public organizations, unlike business strategies, are produced in response to a variety of competing signals that emanate not from markets but from complex political, economic, legal, and organizational structures, processes, and relationships."[17] Whereas business executives are relatively unconstrained in making strategic decisions, the constraints encountered by public administrators often cause them to make strategic choices other than those they believe are best suited to mission attainment. Factors influencing choice of strategy include the political goals of elected officials, demands of powerful stakeholders, judicial mandates, budgetary constraints, the organization's capacities and resources, and its relationships with other organizations. Agencies are more likely to engage in strategic planning and more likely to succeed in implementing their intended objectives when they possess internal capacity for performance (adequate funding, personnel, and management systems), a supportive political environment, and a weak or divided external influence field. Conversely, strategies tend to be shaped by external demands rather than internal intentions when an agency experiences a hostile environment and low internal capacity.

An agency's strategy may be understood as the basic pattern reflected in its policy decisions and actions. Wechsler and Backoff's analysis of state agencies in Ohio revealed three basic patterns. **Developmental** strategies involve actions taken to enhance the agency's resources, status, influence, and capacity for future action, presumably as it relates to mission attainment. Developmental strategies are often products of a formal planning process in which strategists and planners deliberately seek to develop capacity so as to maintain internal control and enhance organizational performance. **Political** strategies involve actions taken either to balance competing stakeholder demands or to reward supporters of the administration by moving the agency in specific policy or programmatic directions. For example, control over internal operations may be tightened in order to further a specific political agenda. Such strategies are adopted where political and partisan pressures are high. **Protective** strategies involve actions designed to accommodate external pressures or appease external stakeholders while maintaining the organizational status quo. It is a reactive strategy more or less forced on an agency by an overtly hostile environment and weak internal capacity for strategic action. It is a pattern that is highly frustrating for agency staff.

Steeped in the rationalistic assumptions of planning theory, discussions of SHRM tend to envision agencies pursuing developmental, capacity-building strategies rather than political or protective strategies. In practice, however, a developmental strategy requires widely shared objectives, the capacity to plan and carry out strategic initiatives, extensive discretion, adequate resources, and relatively weak or divided external forces—conditions which often cannot be satisfied. Although Backoff and Wechsler do not address issues relating to SHRM, their analysis strongly suggests that SHRM may look very different in agencies engaged in political or protective strategies. Rather than helping an agency develop its capacity for mission attainment, the personnel office may be asked, for example, to help the agency secure the political loyalty of career civil servants, recruit and reward based on partisan or political criteria, or tighten control over employee performance. In short, although the concept of SHRM, with its emphasis on linking means and ends, strongly implies an institutionalized process utilized by agencies pursuing a developmental strategy, it must be kept in mind that agency performance can be defined in terms of political and protective objectives as well, and that SHRM, as it is generally understood, may be undermined or derailed as a result.

Alignment of HR Policies and Practices with Strategic Objectives

Although their mandates are set by external actors, agencies still must interpret their mandates, clarify their missions, and seek agreement among key stakeholders regarding how their missions will be carried out. Statements of strategic objectives, written or unwritten, emerge from these decision processes. The core requirement of SHRM is the alignment of personnel policies and practices with the agency's strategic objectives. Although many examples of alignment have been reported in the literature, no classification system has yet been proposed to capture how alignment is accomplished. In general, the reported examples tend to fall into one or more of the following categories:

1. **Adapting to environmental change.** This category includes actions taken by the personnel office in response to external events or trends, such as budget cuts, tight labor markets, changing demographic characteristics of workers, and new technologies. During a period of retrenchment, for example, the personnel office can help managers communicate to staff members the reasons behind staff cutbacks and how they will be accomplished, develop and introduce an early retirement incentive program, counsel those who must be laid off about alternative job opportunities, provide stress management programs for those anxious about their jobs or struggling to cope with increased workloads, and explore the use of temporary or contract employees to ease workload burdens. Adaptive responses of this kind may or may not be guided by a formal statement of agency objectives.

2. **Building human capacity to support strategic initiatives.** Human resources planning is a traditional personnel function. It involves forecasting future staffing needs and taking steps to recruit new employees or train existing employees to meet the forecasted demands. What is unique in the context of SHRM is analysis of the gap between current and required capacity for each new strategic initiative. If an agency has decided to serve a new clientele group, expand services into new areas, or take on an entirely new program, the personnel office can play a strategic role by recruiting new employees with the requisite skills or enhancing the skills of existing personnel through training and development.

3. **Changing organizational culture.** Many public organizations have followed their private sector counterparts by reinventing and reengineering themselves. Major reform initiatives often require new organizational cultures, cultures driven by different values and requiring different behaviors. Adopting a "customer-service" orientation, for example, has become a common strategic objective in both the private and public sectors. The personnel office can help develop a shared commitment to service quality and customer satisfaction through its employee orientation sessions and training programs. It can also redesign performance appraisal and incentive systems so that employees are rewarded for emphasizing quality and customer service. The personnel office can undertake similar efforts in agencies seeking to move from a process-oriented to a results-oriented culture.[18]

4. **Preparing employees for change.** Staff members often resist the implementation of major reforms because of implicit or explicit threats to personal security. Thus, in addition to taking steps to develop a new organizational culture, the personnel office can also take steps to prepare employees for impending changes. It can, for example, encourage managers to involve employees in the design and implementation of the new program or reform initiative, help communicate the purposes behind the changes and the benefits to be derived from them, and provide additional training opportunities so that staff members are prepared to function successfully under the new order.

5. **Supporting a specific "business strategy."** This category, which overlaps with the preceding ones, is distinguished by the selection of a specific business strategy for success. Many of the examples of alignment in the business literature envision this kind of situation. When Marriott, for example, decided to gain a competitive advantage by being "the employer of choice," the personnel office altered its policies and practices so as to attract and retain the very best workers available.[19] Another business strategy is to become "a high commitment" organization. In this instance the personnel office is charged with altering its policies and practices to encourage employee development and empowerment. Indeed, some advocates tend to equate SHRM with the adoption of "progressive" policies designed to boost employee commitment and performance.[20] The common denominator in these business strategies is the belief that human resources are the key to organizational success.

These five kinds of actions are undertaken to achieve vertical integration. Vertical integration is a measure of how well personnel policies and practices, individually and collectively, contribute to organizational objectives. As indicated in Figure 1, horizontal integration is important as well. This is a measure of how well personnel policies mesh with each other in contributing to organizational objectives. The goal is to develop an integrated personnel program in which policies and practices in one functional area do not work at cross purposes with those in other areas.

Changing the Role and Structure of the Personnel Office

The first four requirements of SHRM cannot be satisfied unless the personnel office fundamentally alters the way it does business. An unresolved issue is how to do so. Advocates of SHRM have offered several recommendations in this regard. First, the personnel office must develop the capacity it needs to support strategic initiatives. This means it must develop staff expertise in job design, organizational development, change management, employee motivation, and human resource theory. The personnel staff must also develop knowledge of general management, agency mission, and the specific personnel problems facing managers. Whether this strategic role should be assigned to a special unit within the personnel office or should be expected of all personnel staff remains an unanswered question. Because the strategic and operational roles of the personnel office are contradictory in many respects, performing both roles in an integrated fashion will remain an ongoing challenge.

Second, the traditional control orientation must be superseded by a service orientation. The required line-staff partnership cannot be forged as long as the personnel office is perceived by agency managers as an enforcer of rules and a source of suffocating red tape. According to SHRM advocates, a service orientation can be established by assigning primary responsibility for human resource management to managers and creating service teams comprised of personnel generalists to assist managers in achieving mission-related objectives.[21] Under this proposal, personnel generalists are to perform a service-oriented role both when administering personnel systems such as classification and pay and when consulting with managers about specific personnel problems or objectives. Adopting a service orientation does not require that the personnel office abdicate its responsibility for safeguarding merit, employee rights, and equal employment opportunity. Rather, it means carrying out this responsibility as legal counselors rather than police officers. If the personnel office is to contribute more directly to an agency's mission, shifts in role orientation are important. For SHRM to be implemented successfully, according to NAPA, "the HR staff must believe that their mission is helping the agency accomplish its mission by assisting supervisors in managing their human resources."[22]

Lastly, many advocates of SHRM believe that highly centralized personnel systems must be decentralized and deregulated. Perry and Mesch argue, for example, that the implementation of SHRM is incompatible with highly centralized personnel systems.[23] Possessing unique missions and mandates, and facing unique situations, agencies must be able to tailor their personnel policies and practices to their strategic needs. Centralized personnel systems deny them the flexibility they need. Structural reforms may include reducing the number of centralized personnel regulations to the bare minimum needed to enforce statutory requirements, devolving responsibility for classification and applicant screening to the agency and bureau level, and delegating policy making authority downwards so that agencies can establish personnel policies suited to their individual needs. Advocates of structural reform believe that certain positive effects will follow, including greater flexibility and timeliness in personnel decision making and improved line-staff relations.

In fact, however, decentralization and deregulation may not be a prerequisite for the successful implementation of SHRM. Structural reform efforts tend to encounter serious obstacles and create new problems. For example, devolution of authority means that agency personnel must be trained to handle personnel transactions formerly handled by a central personnel office and new ways must be found to coordinate the efforts of all line and staff officials engaged in performing the personnel management function. Some of these obstacles may prove insurmountable, creating additional redundancies and waste and further undermining agency performance. From the perspective of SHRM, structural reform may not be necessary as long as each agency has sufficient authority and flexibility to align its personnel policies and practices with its strategic objectives. This, too, remains an unresolved issue.

An Expanded Understanding of SHRM

What it means to manage human resources strategically can be understood in more than one way. The difficulty with the understanding discussed above is that it lacks an integrated and sustained focus on the organization's human resources. Because it is closely tied to the practice of strategic planning, it envisions the personnel office taking only those actions necessary to support a specific strategic objective. In this instance the role of the personnel office may be strategic but it is also somewhat ad hoc and reactive. In actuality there is much the personnel office can do to advance an agency's strategic interests other than, or in addition to, supporting the initiatives that emerge from a strategic planning process.

An alternative understanding of what it means to manage human resources strategically has been suggested by Eugene McGregor.[24] The role of the personnel office, according to this understanding, is to help "manage strategic resources strategically." It begins from the premise that many, if not most, government jobs are knowledge-intensive, involving the creation of knowledge or the creation of "smart products" through the application of "trained intelligence." Where this is the case, the intellectual capital stored within the workers becomes the critical resource for the organization and must therefore be viewed as a strategic resource. Managing this strategic

HR Strategies	Underlying Values	Desired Outcomes
Cost Containment Strategy. Containing labor costs by setting salaries at or below market levels, adopting wellness programs and managed care to reduce benefit costs, and using part-time, temporary, and contract employees whenever possible.	economy	cost-effective staffing
Performance Management Strategy. Setting measurable objectives for employees and making rewards contingent upon performance.	productivity	mission-related results
Involvement Strategy. Providing employees, individually or in teams, with considerable work autonomy, decision-making authority, and responsibility for a "complete" task.	empowerment	sense of ownership; enhanced motivation and contribution; employee commitment and retention
Retention Strategy. Providing the conditions necessary to retain valuable human resources, including generous benefit packages, pay that is at or above market, positive work environment, and family-friendly policies such as flextime and day care assistance.	need satisfaction	job satisfaction; employee commitment and retention
Investment Strategy. Increasing individual competence and organizational capacity by investing heavily in training and development.	human development	personal competence; agency adaptability; employee commitment and retention
Cohesion Strategy. Establishing a sense of community and strong social bonds through agency newsletters, picnics, and recreational activities, and by fostering open and trusting relationships between employees and managers and retention	comradeship; openness; trust	job satisfaction; cooperative relations; employee commitment

Figure 2   Human Resource Strategies

resource strategically involves determining essential knowledge, skills, and abilities; improving recruitment and selection methods; developing the capacities of all employees so that the agency can respond to any opportunity or threat appearing on the horizon; and fostering employee commitment so that human capital is not lost to other employers. In short, this alternative understanding envisions a personnel office pursuing an ongoing, integrated program for enhancing organizational performance by acquiring, developing, and managing human resources strategically.

With these observations in mind, it is possible to suggest an expanded, two-pronged approach to SHRM in which the personnel office, in addition to helping the agency implement strategic initiatives, also carries out an integrated personnel program guided by a coherent theory or philosophy about what it means to manage human resources strategically. A theory or philosophy of this kind specifies how human resources must be treated, how much money must be invested in developing human capital, the kind of culture and work climate that must be established, and the specific attitudes and behaviors that must be elicited if the agency is to achieve its vision of success. That personnel offices are rarely guided by such a theory has been cited as the primary reason for their low institutional

standing.[25] If the personnel office succeeds in developing such a theory in consultation with agency officials and legislative bodies, the next step is to identify and implement appropriate human resource strategies. Six human resource strategies are identified in Figure 2. Although these strategies are neither exhaustive nor mutually exclusive, they nonetheless serve to illustrate the connections between values and vision, desired outcomes, and the programmatic means by which to realize them.

The cost-containment strategy tends, in practice, to serve as a default strategy. Although it is antithetical to McGregor's understanding of what it means to manage strategic resources strategically, it is often the strategy of choice among elected officials concerned with holding the line on labor costs and budget increases. Where there is no agreed upon vision of success, nor any theory regarding the strategic importance of human resources to agency performance, other strategies tend to receive little attention. However, the convergence of several factors in recent years, including tighter labor markets, a growing proportion of high-skill and knowledge-intensive jobs, a better educated workforce with heightened growth needs, and political pressures to improve government performance, has turned attention to alternative strategies. The performance management strategy, for example, has been adopted in jurisdictions where the values and assumptions of the managing-for-results movement have gained sway.[26] Similarly, because most government employees are knowledge workers who can sell their intellectual capital on the open market, many agencies are turning to a combination of the investment, involvement, and retention strategies to attract, develop, and retain the human resources they need to provide knowledge intensive services in an ever changing environment. The investment strategy in particular reflects a growing awareness that human competence is the engine behind the creation of value.[27]

The strategies or combination of strategies chosen, if any, depends on situational factors such as the nature of the work performed by agency staff, the agency's capacity for pursuing excellence, and the priorities of its leaders. Political and practical factors often divert attention from developing a human resource philosophy or expending funds to put it into practice. Indeed, as McGregor has noted, "in the minds of many a case-hardened practitioner, the idea of strategic public-sector human resource management may well be an oxymoron."[28] But if the prospects for implementing SHRM in the public sector are uncertain, the concept itself represents a valuable goal toward which to strive.

Conclusion

The concept of SHRM as outlined above calls upon the personnel office to adopt a strategic role in addition to its operational roles as rule enforcer and guardian of the integrity of personnel systems. For the personnel staff, adopting a strategic role means being more responsive to agency goals by acting as consultants and service providers to line managers; supporting the attainment of the agency's strategic objectives; and carrying out an integrated, philosophy-driven personnel program. Although the concept of SHRM is steeped in problematic, rationalistic assumptions, it nonetheless holds considerable promise for enhancing government performance. Its success depends on whether the personnel office can integrate its strategic and operational roles successfully and whether it can satisfy the norms of political and formal rationality simultaneously. Too much is at stake for this potentially valuable concept to become a label for yet another failed management initiative.

Notes

1. Tichy, Noel M., Charles J. Fombrun, and Mary Anne Devanna, "Strategic Human Resource Management," *Sloan Management Review* 23 (Winter 1982): 47–61; Cynthia A. Lengnick-Hall and Mark L. Lengnick-Hall, "Strategic Human Resources Management: A Review of the Literature and a Proposed Typology," *Academy of Management Review* 13 (July 1988): 454–470; Randall Schuler, "Strategic Human Resource Management and Industrial Relations," *Human Relations* 42 (No. 2 1989):157–184.

2. National Academy of Public Administration (NAPA), *A Guide for Effective Strategic Management of Human Resources* (Washington D.C.: NAPA, 1996).

3. Berry, Frances Stokes and Barton Wechsler, "State Agencies' Experience with Strategic Planning: Findings from a National Survey," *Public Administration Review* 55 (March/April 1995): 159–168.

4. Poister, Theodore H. and Gregory Streib, "Management Tools in Municipal Government: Trends over the Past Decade," *Public Administration Review* 49 (May/June 1989): 240–248.

5. Poister and Streib, "Management Tools," 244.

6. Kissler, Gerald R., Karmen N. Fore, Willow S. Jacobson, William P. Kittredge, and Scott L. Stewart, "State Strategic Planning: Suggestions from the Oregon Experience," *Public Administration Review* 58 (July/August 1998): 353–359.

7. Wheeland, Craig M., "Citywide Strategic Planning: An Evaluation of Rock Hill's Empowering Vision," *Public Administration Review* 53 (January/February 1993): 65–72.

8. Bryson, John M., *Strategic Planning for Public and Nonprofit Organizations: A Guide to Strengthening and Sustaining Organizational Achievement* (San Francisco: Jossey-Bass, 1995).

9. Bryson, John M. and William D. Roering, "Applying Private-Sector Strategic Planning in the Public Sector," *Journal of the American Planning Association* 53 (Winter 1987): 9–22.

10. Osborne, David and Ted Gaebler, *Reinventing Government* (Reading, MA: Addison-Wesley, 1992).

11. Bryson, *Strategic Planning;* Paul C. Nutt and Robert W. Backoff, *Strategic Management of Public and Third Sector Organizations* (San Francisco: Jossey-Bass, 1992).

12. Bryson, *Strategic Planning.*

13. Bryson and Roering, "Applying Private-Sector Strategic Planning," 15.

14. Mintzberg, Henry, *The Rise and Fall of Strategic Planning* (New York: Free Press, 1994).

15. NAPA, *A Guide for Effective Strategic Management of Human Resources,* 17.

16. Porter, Michael E., *Competitive Strategy: Techniques for Analyzing Industries and Competitors* (New York: Free Press, 1980); Schuler, "Strategic Human Resource Management and Industrial Relations."

17. Wechsler, Barton and Robert W. Backoff, "The Dynamics of Strategy in Public Organizations," *Journal of the American Planning Association* 53 (Winter 1987): 34–43.

18. Popovich, Mark G. (ed.), *Creating High-Performance Government Organizations* (San Francisco: Jossey-Bass, 1998).

19. Ulrich, Dave, "Strategic and Human Resource Planning: Linking Customers and Employees," *Human Resource Planning* 15 (June 1992): 47+.

20. NAPA, *A Guide for Effective Strategic Management of Human Resources.*

21. Perry, James L. and Debra J. Mesch, "Strategic Human Resource Management," in *Public Personnel Management: Current Concerns, Future Challenges* edited by Carolyn Ban and Norma M. Riccucci (New York: Longman, 1997), 21–34.

22. NAPA, *A Guide for Effective Strategic Management of Human Resources,* 53.

23. Perry and Mesch, "Strategic Human Resource Management."

24. McGregor, Eugene B., *Strategic Management of Human Knowledge, Skills, and Abilities* (San Francisco: Jossey-Bass, 1991).

25. Christensen, Ralph, "Where is HR?" *Human Resource Management* 36 (Spring 1997): 81–84.

26. Lawler, Edward E., *Strategic Pay: Aligning Organizational Strategies and Pay Systems* (San Francisco: Jossey-Bass, 1990); Popovich, *Creating High-Performance Government Organizations.*

27. Christensen, "Where is HR?"; Lee Dyer and Gerald W. Holder, "A Strategic Perspective of Human Resource Management," in *Human Resource Management: Evolving Roles and Responsibilities* edited by Lee Dyer (Washington D.C.: Bureau of National Affairs, 1988): 1–46.

28. McGregor, *Strategic Management,* 33.

JONATHAN TOMPKINS is professor of political science at The University of Montana. His primary teaching responsibilities include courses in human resources management, strategic planning, and organization theory. He has published several articles relating to human resource management and a text entitled *Human Resource Management in Government.*

Reprinted with permission from *Public Personnel Management,* Spring 2002, published by International Personnel Management Association for Human Resources (IPMA-HR), 1617 Duke Street, Alexandria, VA 22314, (703) 549–7100. www.ipma-hr.org

The Best 4 Ways to Recruit Employees with Disabilities

YOJI COLE

Kathy Martinez, who is blind, was shocked to be asked questions such as "How will you find the restroom?" and "What should we do about employees who wonder if they'll have to pick up your slack?" at the end of a job interview. She felt she had proved she was well suited for the job, but those questions told her that the interviewer only saw her disability. Fortunately, she had the opportunity to choose another company.

"Now I'm managing a $2.1-million company," says Martinez, executive director of the Oakland, Calif.–based World Institute on Disability (WID).

Her experience is not unique. People with disabilities face stigmas and stereotypes daily, especially when they enter the corporate world, which is why those who are able to hide their disabilities often choose to do so. And that, Martinez believes, is a tragedy for companies, employers and potential employees.

Fear of the unknown is the main reason so many in corporate America struggle to recruit and retain its employees with disabilities. "As a person with a disability, you have a different perspective because thinking outside the box happens for someone with a disability every day," says Alan Muir, executive director of the group Career Opportunities for Students with Disabilities (COSD). "People with learning disabilities figure out how to do things differently every day, and companies want people who think outside the box and who think creatively."

However, even among the most active companies that recruit for people with disabilities, networks are relatively new. General knowledge about where to find recruits with disabilities is just beginning.

To learn how to best recruit people with disabilities, DiversityInc interviewed companies from the DiversityInc Top 10 Companies for People With Disabilities list. The companies included Merrill Lynch (No. 1), SSM

Healthcare (No. 3), Eastman Kodak (No. 5) and Citigroup (No. 7).

1. Partnerships

Merrill Lynch partners with the Eden Institute, which provides services for people with autism. The firm also partners with the Special Olympics and with groups for students with disabilities for recruiting purposes on college campuses.

SSM Healthcare has found success partnering with ParaQuad, an organization designed to highlight the capabilities of people who are paraplegic or quadriplegic.

Citigroup partners with the National Business & Disability Council and the American Association of People with Disabilities. The company works as a corporate sponsor for both organizations and participates at their events.

"We've partnered with the National Business & Disability Council to bring in students and professionals from the metro area [of New York]; we tap into them to recruit and to find mentors for people with disabilities and to educate our human-resources community," says Ana Duarte-McCarthy, chief diversity officer for Citigroup.

Meanwhile, Eastman Kodak has partnered as a sponsor and employer of choice for the past three years with the National Technical Institute for the Deaf, which is associated with the Rochester Institute of Technology.

"These efforts put you in touch with folks you wouldn't otherwise meet," says Duarte-McCarthy.

Relationships with organizations are built through networking, calling disability organizations to tell them the company is interested in recruiting people with disabilities.

"We're trying to normalize disabilities," says Chris Fossel, national leader for Merrill Lynch's Disability

Awareness Professional Network, adding, "Through working with the Special Olympics and having volunteers go there, it's helped employees understand disability."

"This is a community where you could be born with disabilities, you could become disabled, your spouse, partner or child could become disabled and everyone knows someone with a disability."

Ana Duarte-McCarthy, Citigroup

Finding qualified recruits with disabilities is so important to Merrill Lynch that the firm is creating a list of core suppliers who help candidates find jobs. "Centralizing this list and leveraging it to increase our ability to source talent will be a key focus for the remainder of 2006 and 2007," says Fossel.

2. Human-Resources Training

Sensitizing employees to the capabilities of people with disabilities and the issues they face is critical.

SSM Healthcare's Mission Awareness Team educated employees who do not have disabilities to the lives of employees with disabilities by putting them in situations that made them feel disabled for a period of time. The Mission Awareness Team put SSM Healthcare employees in wheelchairs, plugged their ears with wax and covered their eyes for up to two hours. Following the exercise, employees talked about their frustration and ways they had to think outside the box to accomplish tasks.

Training at Citigroup occurs on a local basis: "In the businesses, we do offer training, some in class, some online, and some training that occurs at the point of hire," says Duarte-McCarthy. "Citigroup is focusing on integrating disability awareness in its leadership training.

"We've always talked about the idea that anyone can be a member of this community at any time," says Duarte-McCarthy. "This is a community where you could be born with disabilities, you could become disabled, your spouse, partner or child could become disabled, and everyone knows someone with a disability."

Cingular features a disability task-force team that focuses on policies, practices, training and accommodating the needs of employees with disabilities, says Bob Reed, vice president of diversity for Cingular.

"All of our diversity training incorporates creating an inclusive work environment, which includes people with disabilities," says Reed. "We train all hiring managers in Targeted Selection, which covers EEO/AAP—appropriate questions in this area, and others."

3. Use Employee-Resource Groups

"If people [with disabilities] get a sense they're welcomed in a company, they will apply," says Martinez.

An employee group for employees with disabilities can help a company provide amenities to make recruits with disabilities feel welcome. Kodak's chief technology officer, Bill Lloyd, is the champion of its employee group for employees with disabilities. The group—along with Lloyd—meets with CEO and Chairman Antonio Perez at least once a year to update him on the various issues they face in the workplace.

At Cingular, the employee-resource group, ENABLE, helps the company keep its pulse on the community, says Reed.

"ENABLE helped us ensure the on-boarding experience and work environment are welcoming," says Reed. ENABLE made Cingular aware that providing accessibility for employees with disabilities, such as computers screens for people who have vision impairments, attracts recruits.

At Merrill Lynch, during a discussion with his network's sponsor, Fossel recently asked what he would do in the following scenario: If two applicants, both suitable for the position, came across his desk and one of the applicants happened to be a college student with a disability while the other was not, who would he choose for the position?

"He said the one with the disability because that showed they could go through issues and deal with their disability—that shows creativity, persistence," says Fossel, whose Disability Awareness Professional Network at Merrill Lynch works with the Princeton University Development Institute for People with Autism, talking to students with disabilities about the career opportunities offered at Merrill Lynch.

4. Use Government Organizations/Job Boards

The Department of Labor's Vocational Rehabilitation and Employment Service group is geared toward helping veterans with disabilities. It is used by SSM Healthcare and Cingular.

"We publish our job openings at local military-transition offices," says Yvonne Tisdel, corporate vice president of human resources and system diversity at SSM Healthcare. Tisdel suffered a back injury while in the military.

"It is likely that people coming out of the military have a technical background," she adds.

Reed serves on the Department of Labor's Corporate Executive Advisory Council's Circle of Champions and also serves on the board of the Georgia Council for Employing People with Disabilities. Cingular, on a state-by-state basis,

Helping Companies Find Students with Disabilities

There are more than 2.6 million reasons why organizations such as Career Opportunities for Students with Disabilities (COSD) and Entry Point! are necessary.

Recent census data shows that there are 2.6 million people with disabilities between the ages of 5 and 15. Organizations such as COSD and Entry Point! are working to make sure that by the time these children enter college and then the work force, corporations will be ready for them and—more importantly—know how to find them.

While 78 percent of The 2006 DiversityInc Top 50 Companies for Diversity® have active programs to recruit people with disabilities, most Fortune 500 companies don't—and even those that do report difficulty finding "qualified" candidates. This is because they don't know where to look and they don't actively start a pipeline for future employees.

"We know students with disabilities are an untapped talent pool ... Businesses have to understand that being disabled does not mean your intelligence is disabled," says Virginia Stern, the director of the American Association for the Advancement of Science's (AAAS) Entry Point! internship program.

Students with disabilities often learn about organizations and programs such as Entry Point! and COSD through career-services offices or disability student centers, according to Laureen Summers, an Entry Point! program associate.

Entry Point!, which started in 1996, matches students with disabilities who have demonstrated high motivation and achievement in STEM (science, technology, engineering and mathematics) fields in internships in research and development throughout the United States. Students are paired up with mentors who provide guidance for future undergraduate coursework, plans for graduate study, and often potential employment opportunities.

"The reason employers may say they do not know where to find them is because of the law (the ADA). Students with disabilities are attending just about every higher-education institution in United States," says Stern. "Employers can't go to one place as they could by going to an HBCU or a predominantly Latino campus and just find 1,000 students with disabilities who meet their skills or needs. Our focus is on the skill needs of the employers. We don't generalize about hiring people with disabilities just because they are disabled. This is not a social program. This is a program to find talent among graduate and undergraduate students who have skills."

Entry Point! places students in internships with organizations such as Merck & Co. (No. 34 on The 2006 DiversityInc Top 50 Companies for Diversity® list, and No. 4 in the Top 10 Companies for People With Disabilities), IBM, Google, the National Aeronautic and Space Administration and the National Oceanic and Atmospheric Administration. To be eligible for the 10-week program, students first have to apply and submit their transcripts and two letters of recommendation from professors. Students considered also must have a 3.0 average or better.

"Our goal is to bring the best and brightest and we recognize that there are multiple sources to find them. Entry Point! is definitely one of those resources," says Regina Flynn, the director of university relations at Merck, which has had partnerships with Entry Point! and COSD for several years.

"It took a bit, but I would do this again in a heartbeat," says Chad Cheetham, a recent graduate of the University of California at Riverside who wrapped up his first internship through Entry Point! at Merck's Rahway, N.J., research laboratory in the department of metabolic disorders of obesity. Cheetham, who is partially blind, will be attending the University of Alabama at Birmingham for his graduate studies.

"The way [Entry Point! selects] students, you know they are already the best. You know you are not getting a student because of a disability, you know you are getting talent that could have been overlooked elsewhere," says Cheetham. "I highly recommend any student out there to do what I did. It has been the best experience."

"Every year we get approximately 600 inquiries and end up with about 120 to 150 students in the pool of possible applicants," says Summers, who adds that approximately 25 percent of students selected return the following year. "We have made [approximately] 500 placements [to the work force] over our 11-year existence, and we know that 74 are currently pursuing graduate degrees, 18 of which are pursuing or have achieved Ph.D.'s. Students begin with internships, but there is a lot more to it."

COSD was started in 2000 by Alan Muir, executive director, and Robert Greenberg, the former director of career services (he has since retired), because the two realized that students with disabilities were simply not receiving necessary career-planning services and job-placement assistance. There was a gap in communication between the disability-services and career-services offices, limiting exposure for people with disabilities to recruiters visiting their campuses. COSD educates career counselors in colleges and universities around the United States on the various internships, fellowships and career-training programs available for students with disabilities. It also makes companies and their recruiters aware of this talent pool. "Before COSD, career services and recruiters did not focus on this student population," Muir says.

"Our students are really outstanding, and that's what the companies want. It's about the skills, and if you have the skills, the disability is minor," says Stern.

—Brenda Velez

also taps into the databases of Employment Security Career Centers and State Workforce Commissions and the Department of Blind Services.

Companies utilize diversity-related Internet job boards, such as DiversityInc.com, where they know their job posting will be seen not only by people of color, women and GLBTs but also by people with disabilities. Besides DiversityInc.com, DiversityWorkings.com and Project EARN's online job board are used by companies on the Top 10.

"Folks with disabilities like to integrate into the work force," says Muir. "To call themselves out as different and say they need this and this, unless they have a strong advocacy sense, that could be difficult . . . It all comes down to the supervising managers and how enlightened they may be."

Making Reasonable Accommodations for Employees with Mental Illness under the ADA

Jonathan Hafen

Title I of the Americans with Disabilities Act (ADA) is an elaborate set of regulations designed to provide protection for "qualified" employees in the workplace. Although the ADA restricts qualifying a disability to "a physical or mental impairment that substantially limits one or more of the major life activities of such individual," its reference to "neurological systems, mental or psychological disorders," has paved the way for employees to bring lawsuits against employers in an attempt to prove various mental conditions should be eligible for accommodations under the Act.

Moreover, as the stigma of mental illness diminishes in this society, employees may find less reason to conceal such illnesses on the job. In fact, some may try to exploit coverage under the ADA as a way to change their jobs or work environments into something more preferable for themselves.

Fortunately for employers, various jurisdictions as well as the Supreme Court have acted to narrow the scope of impairment and limit the protection Title I provides employees with disabilities. Even with this guidance, understanding ADA coverage for mental illness as well as compliance obligations for accommodations can pose challenges for employers.

Does the Employee's Mental Disorder Warrant ADA Protection?

Broadly speaking, the ADA only protects employees who have severe mental disabilities meeting ADA standards yet who are nevertheless able to perform the essential functions of the jobs they hold or for which they could be considered. The first issue, therefore, is to determine whether the employee actually has a qualifying mental illness. While this may seem an obvious place to start, most ADA litigation focuses on whether an impairment "substantially limits . . . a major life activity," not whether an individual actually has an impairment.

In case after case, plaintiff employees have tried to benefit from the ADA by claiming behavioral difficulties such as not getting along with co-workers or supervisors, poor concentration, being depressed, and poor judgment are conditions that deserve ADA protection. The good news for vigilant employers is that the courts have been fairly clear on distinguishing between qualifying mental illness and non-

qualifying employee personality or behavior problems. For example, in one case, an employee claimed to have a qualifying mental illness which made it hard to get along with co-workers. The court rejected the claim, ruling that "paranoid, disgruntled, oppositional, difficult to interact with, unusual, suspicious, threatening, and distrustful" were behavioral characteristics, not qualifying mental impairments. Many other court rulings also have supported the premise the ADA was never intended to categorize people with common personality traits as disabled.

Assuming a mental illness exists, employees have two more hurdles to overcome before establishing a right to a "reasonable accommodation." Employees must demonstrate that the mental illness causes a substantial limitation to a major life activity and, despite this disability, can perform functions essential to their job.

As discussed below, employers should require proof of a qualifying mental illness and an ability to perform essential job functions before making a commitment to provide workplace accommodations.

Does the employee actually have a qualifying mental illness? Employers often do not spend enough time determining whether an employee requesting accommodation has a qualifying disability. In general, short-term conditions are not covered by the ADA, while permanent or long-term impairments may be eligible. Confusion still exists within the courts regarding the cross-over point from short to long-term and, unfortunately, there is no definite answer.

Some courts have concluded that disorders such as ADHD and depression are not qualifying disabilities, if the conditions can be effectively treated with medication. On the other hand, depression with an indefinite duration could be considered a disability. Episodic disorders also may be covered by the ADA, provided employees can prove the underlying reasons for the episodes are long-term conditions and are not rare occurrences.

When possible, it is advisable to have the employee obtain and provide a medical diagnosis from a qualified professional, though this is not always supported by the courts. In some cases, the courts have stated that a medical diagnosis is not always needed to support an individual's claim of impairment.

Is there a "substantial limitation" to a "major life activity?" A majority of litigation centers on whether an alleged disability substantially limits an employee's ability to perform a job and whether the limitation impacts a major life activity. This area continues to be controversial as there is a fair amount of disagreement over what constitutes a major life activity and, furthermore, whether there need be a strong connection between the limitation, life activity and the workplace. There have been cases where courts have maintained an employee is eligible for ADA protection even though the major life activity did not impact the employee's ability to perform in the workplace. For the most part, though, courts have employed common sense when it comes to ADA eligibility and the impact a disability has in the workplace.

The US Supreme Court defined "substantially limits" as "considerable" or "to a large extent" and a major life activity as something of central importance to daily life. Under this definition an employee seeking ADA protection must have a disability preventing or severely restricting the individual from doing activities of central importance to most people's lives. The EEOC's description of this analysis suggest that an individual must be unable to perform a major life activity the average person in the general population can perform and is significantly restricted compared with the manner or duration the average person could perform the activity. In one Third Circuit court case, the court found that an employee's ADHD did not substantially limit her ability to think, learn, remember, or concentrate and that "many people who are not suffering from ADHD/ADD must regularly cope with" such limitations.

As for major life activities, the EEOC lists caring for oneself, performing manual tasks, walking, seeing, hearing, speaking, breathing, learning, and working. Due to the broad nature of the activities described by the EEOC, many cases have tried to create more precise direction on what constitutes a disability. For instance, bipolar disorder is a disability, but the resulting inability to sit and think is not a major life activity. Often the criteria which employees use to establish that an impairment impacts a major life activity miss the mark and are dismissed by the courts.

On the topic of whether the major life activity must have a connection to the workplace, most courts have agreed it does not, sometimes making the direct impact of the disability on the job an irrelevant issue.

Is the employee "qualified?" The ADA defines the term "qualified" as having the requisite education, skills, experience, licenses, or certifications for the job and the ability to perform the essential functions of the job, with or without reasonable accommodation. Therefore, employees claiming mental disorders must nevertheless be able to perform the essential functions of the job with or without an accommodation.

Courts have made it clear the burden of proof as to whether an employee is qualified for a job rests with the individual. According to a case in the Sixth Circuit court, the employee must also prove how they remain qualified with a reasonable accommodation. The employer's burden is to prove which aspects of an employee's job are essential functions.

It stands to reason that an employee without the appropriate background may not qualify for a particular job. If an employee is not qualified for the job due solely to a disability, however, the employer may find itself in a position to defend the requirements, standards or prerequisites of a job. Licenses or certifications necessary to perform a job allow straightforward explanations. Other job requirements may not be as easy to support, but the consistency and uniformity with which an employer enforces the essential job requirements among like kinds of employees strengthens the legitimate need for the functions.

What are the essential functions of the job? Not only must an employer be prepared to address what the essential functions of a job are, they must also address why the functions are essential. When essential function is the issue, courts often have relied on an employer's judgment of what is necessary to perform a particular job and written job descriptions prepared in advance of advertising for or interviewing candidates. While an employer's judgment is never conclusive, it does carry a lot of weight with the court provided there is consistent application of the requirement among similar employees. Carefully crafted job descriptions detailing essential job functions can provide compelling evidence against ADA claims where specific aspects of the job are in dispute. As a word of caution, incomplete or inaccurate job descriptions can work against employers just as effectively.

It is advisable to include all functions deemed essential to the effective execution of a job in a written description prior to the interview process. It is also critical to understand the difference between whether a specific task is an essential function or whether it is a way of performing the function. The EEOC states a task becomes essential when the position exists to perform the function. Additionally, justification for a function can include the degree of specialization required, the amount of time devoted to the task, terms of a collective bargaining agreement, the consequences of not performing the function, as well as the experience of those who have performed or are currently performing the same job. All of these factors should be considered when drafting job descriptions.

A Cautionary Note: The "Regarded as Disabled" Employee. Any employee who has been "regarded as" having a mental (or physical) disability, whether it impacts a major life activity or not, is covered under the ADA. In situations where employers base their actions on perceptions of an employee's condition rather than fact, the employer may open itself to a discrimination case under the ADA. Regarding an employee as disabled can come in many forms such as a notation in an employee file, passing the employee up for a job because of the perceived limitation, moving an employee to a new position based on the disability perception, or restricting job responsibilities. On the flip side, the courts have generally agreed with the EEOC in stating that employers that make requested changes to a job to help an employee with a medical condition have not necessarily regarded the employee as disabled. In an ADHD case, the court concluded an employer did not regard the employee as disabled simply because modifications such as installing a partition and allowing a radio to block noises were made.

The ADA does not try to discourage employers from assisting employees, but doing so may set precedents and inadvertently open the door to litigation should "regarded as" employees decide they have a case for a "better" accommodation under the regulations. Fortunately, courts seem to fairly consider these types of cases and are often reluctant to punish the employer for showing goodwill towards employees.

Process for Investigating "Reasonable" Accommodation

Once it is determined an employee is qualified for the job and has a qualifying disability that substantially limits a major life activity, employers are obligated to make reasonable accommodations so the employee can continue to experience the same workplace opportunities that those without disabilities would automatically enjoy.

The basic steps recommended for investigating accommodations include:

1. *Requiring written requests for accommodations.* Employers are under no obligation to provide accommodations for employees if they are unaware a disability exists. In cases involving mental disorders, courts have ruled

that an employee cannot remain silent about limitations caused by a disability and expect the employer to bear the burden of identifying the need and finding appropriate accommodations. Employers may have a policy requiring employees to submit written requests which include a description of the disability, the major life activity being substantially limited, and suggestions for accommodations. The courts have been favorable to employers when requests were ambiguous and did not adequately describe the accommodation being sought.

Employers cannot, however, require employees to use specific or magic language when requesting an accommodation. The requests should be reviewed with a fair and open mind, provided the fundamental criteria for accommodation are met. Further, if an employer is aware of both the qualifying disability and need for accommodation, it may be obligated to begin an investigation into finding a suitable solution even if an employee request was not made.

2. *Engaging in an interactive process.* When a request has been made or a need discovered, the employer should engage in a productive interaction with the employee regarding accommodation possibilities. On appeal, some courts have suggested that an interactive process may be mandatory. During this part of the process, the employer should analyze which job functions are essential. The interaction should always be conducted in good faith and involve direct contact with the employee to identify the nature of the limitations, the barriers to successfully performing the essential job tasks and discussion about potential accommodations.

Courts have held that employees must participate in the interactive process or risk having their claims denied. They must be willing to discuss and try accommodations suggested by the employer as well as provide requested documentation on the disability and the nature and extent of the limitation. Courts generally agree with the EEOC's position allowing employers to ask for documentation, particularly for non-obvious disabilities. Additionally, the employer may require cooperation from the employee in future investigations regarding the ongoing need for the accommodation.

3. *Offering an accommodation.* An employer's obligation is to find an effective accommodation for the employee-one that allows the employee to successfully complete essential job functions without causing an undue hardship to the employer. Selecting an appropriate accommodation is the employer's choice and no pressure need be felt in accepting the employee's preference for modification.

Should an employee refuse the offered, effective accommodation, the employer has no further obligation under the ADA. It has met its obligation to offer reasonable accommodation. The employee is free to dispute the nature of the accommodation, particularly if the accommodation could be considered ineffective. If there is a dispute over the offered accommodation, the employer must be able to explain and support its effectiveness.

4. *Telling other employees.* Employers hands are often tied in discussing why one employee receives seemingly preferential treatment. Revealing why an employee has been given an accommodation can violate federal laws restricting the disclosure of medical information. Nonetheless, the employer is sometimes put in a position of needing to provide an explanation. To avoid violating ADA and HIPAA laws, it is advisable to work with legal counsel to draft a statement indicating the accommodation was made to comply with federal law, but other federal laws prohibit additional disclosure. For supervisors, especially if the employee is being reassigned, disclosure should inform the supervisor that the employee has a disability and the ADA requires the reassignment, assuming the employee is qualified.

Considerations for Reasonable Accommodation

An accommodation is reasonable if the costs and benefits of providing it are properly weighted. Employers are not required to make accommodations which create an undue hardship, but proving a hardship in court can be difficult. Accommodations can include physical barriers, procedures, or rules. Employers cannot, however, demand employees take medication as an accommodation. Medication and other treatments are deemed personal choices. Should an employee wish to take medication or get treatment, a reasonable accommodation could be made allowing the individual time to do so.

Other reasonable accommodations can include, but are not limited to:

- A leave of absence;
- A job reassignment;
- A shift change;
- Job restructuring;
- A modified work schedule;
- Working at home;
- Modifying equipment or the work environment; and
- Changing or modifying policies, procedures or standards.

If an employee cannot fulfill the essential tasks of a job even with an accommodation, they are not qualified for the job. The employer can seek other alternatives, but is not obligated to create a new position, reallocate essential functions, promote the employee, put the employee in a job for which they are not qualified or reassign another employee to create a vacancy.

A frequently asked question is whether the employer must continue to pay the original salary and benefits if the job changes or the employee is reassigned. There is broad agreement that the employer need only pay salary and benefits commensurate with the new duties.

The complexity of the ADA and nuances from state to state make it advisable to seek legal counsel when developing and implementing policies for handling ADA claims as well as when investigating requests for accommodations by employees.

JONATHAN HAFEN, a shareholder with Parr Waddoups Brown Gee & Loveless in Salt Lake City, has extensive experience in federal and state courts with employment law issues and has published and lectured widely on a variety of topics including legal ethics, litigation strategy, and employment. He can be reached at joh@pwlaw.com.

From *Employee Benefit Plan Review*, by Jonathan Hafen, September 2006, pp. 10–13. Copyright © 2006 by Aspen Publishers. Reprinted by permission of Wolters Kluwer Law & Business.

The Devil Is in the Details

More than a decade later, the ADA is still a tricky law to follow.

THOMAS CLARK

After 13 years, the Americans with Disabilities Act still cause facility owners to stumble.

It's been more than a dozen years since the Americans with Disabilities Act became law, guaranteeing those with a variety of handicaps the right to work and access to public buildings. While the landmark civil rights legislation has had a profound impact in many ways, its myriad rules and standards still pose a problem for all institutions, including long term care facilities.

Cynthia Leibrock—a Livermore, Colo., interior designer who now specializes in universal design and aging, and the author of *Design Details for Health* (John Wiley & Sons)—says she's still never found a nursing home that is ADA compliant.

But that doesn't mean that Leibrock finds problems in the form of steep staircases and inaccessible bathrooms. The problems for most facilities are usually in the smaller issues that muddy the ideal of being fully compliant with the ADA.

"People don't get the nuances of the ADA," says Leibrock. "They get the basics right, but they miss the details."

It's those details that Leibrock closely examines when she surveys a nursing home. When she does, she can be sure that she'll literally find "hundreds of violations"—even in facilities built since the ADA became law.

"Not many [of the violations] are life-threatening," she says. "They are smaller matters."

A typical example, Leibrock said, is a Dutch door. Many facilities use these divided doorways to give residents a view of a room or hall without fully opening the door. But ADA restrictions say that any object that is lower than 80 inches above the floor and higher than 27 inches can't protrude more than three inches. The top half of the Dutch door is therefore non-compliant.

But "even the smaller details can disable someone," says Leibrock. The height requirements are to protect blind people who use a cane to sweep the landscape in front of them: They would have no way of knowing that the top half of the Dutch door would open in their path.

States of Inconsistency

Perhaps the biggest obstacle to a facility being 100 percent compliant with the ADA is the lack at consistency in regulations and restrictions from state to state. Federal ADA standards and state building codes differ, and state building codes aren't uniform from place to place.

Jim Terry, a Birmingham, Ala, architect and chief executive officer of Evan Terry Associates, P.C., routinely hears the complaint from

---

The Act Itself

The AMERICANS WITH DISABILITIES ACT of 1990

S. 933

One Hundred First Congress of the United States of America at the second session

Begun and held at the City of Washington on Tuesday, the twenty-third day of January, one thousand nine hundred and ninety

An Act

To establish a clear and comprehensive prohibition of discrimination on the basis of disability.

Sec. 2

(b) Purpose.—It is the purpose of the Act—

1. to provide a clear and comprehensive national mandate for the elimination of discrimination against individuals with disabilities;
2. to provide clear, strong, consistent, enforceable standards addressing discrimination against individuals with disabilities;
3. to ensure that the Federal Government plays a central role in enforcing the standards established in this Act on behalf of individuals with disabilities; and
4. to invoke the sweep of congressional authority, including the power to enforce the fourteenth amendment and to regulate commerce, in order to address the major areas of discrimination faced day-to-day by people with disabilities.

Sweating the Small (and Not So Small) Stuff

Long term care facilities typically provide good patient care, but they fall down in providing good visitor care, according to Jim Terry, an Alabama architect specializing in accessibility and ADA issues.

The places that are good at it are making accommodations for visitors as well as patients, according to Terry. They know that the people who are deciding where to place a spouse or family member may need some type of accommodations themselves. "Their first impression is going to be, 'Hey, I got a parking spot,'" Terry says. "You can let them decide whether to go or not, rather them shooing them out of your building."

Terry tells building managers to "look out your window and see if your handicapped places are full most of the time. If they are, you need more spots." Other building details Terry suggest looking at:

- **Water fountains.** Some low for people in wheelchairs, others high for people who have trouble bending.
- **Furniture.** Firm, raised (18–20 inches) seats, with armrests that extend to the chair's edge.
- **Signage.** Visual impairments make low-contrast, high-glare and warm colors hard to read.

- **Bathrooms.** "The ADA doesn't require grab bars in every room, but the more you have, the better," says Terry.
- **Easy-to-operate hardware.** Try to operate any hardware with your fingers taped together or your hand balled into a fist. That's why levers are better than knobs.
- **Door forces.** Non-fire rated doors shouldn't require more than five pounds of force.
- **Floor surfaces.** Walk the route from the parking lot to the rooms. Pay close attention to thresholds and to transitions between different flooring types.
- **Curb ramps.** Keep the slope gentle and never paint them (the paint is slippery). If they aren't right, says Terry, "rip 'em out. It's cheaper to rip out 100 ramps than defend one lawsuit."

"None of these are really expensive," says Terry, "and they serve a huge portion of the population. They also say a lot about your care of people who need these accommodations. They pay off in goodwill, new business and references."

—T.C.

---

clients who operate facilities throughout the United States. "They tell us it would be great if there were one national standard so they could have a national model to duplicate." But, says Terry, "that's not possible. Something that one state requires, another won't allow."

One state, for instance, requires a bathroom grab bar to be 33 inches off the floor. Another mandates a height of between 34 inches and 36 inches. Even toilet paper holders defy uniformity: In California and many other states. The holder must be 7 inches to 9 inches in front of the water closet. The ADA regulations say the holder may not be more than 36 inches from the rear wall. "So, in a 30-inch water closet," says Terry, "the holder would be too close for the state standard."

States are making an effort to align their accessibility standards to at least be compatible with, the ADA standards, says Terry. And, a revised set of combined ADA/ABA (Architectural Buildings Act) regulations now open to comment may help down the road. But it's unlikely that all the involved parties will ever get together on a single code.

"There's so much politics involved," says Terry. "These issues are emotional and critically important to people. Advocates have worked hard to win battles, and they don't want to give them up to harmonize with standards won by other people with different agendas."

"Everyone's pulling for their own needs on different sides of each issue," Terry continues, "and there may be three or four sides to the issue. Politics don't even land in the same place twice. We don't wind up with the same sorts of compromises."

Courts of Enforcement

The result is that litigation has become the chief enforcer of the ADA. "There are lots of advocacy groups out there," says Terry, "and they're saying people aren't doing anything until we sue them. So we're going to file as many suits as possible."

"These groups' members are saying the law's been in place a long time now. It's time for these places to be compliant."

Terry believes most lawsuits could be stopped through preventive work. "Ninety-nine percent of the companies that call us have a lawsuit because they had a problem with patient care. After that, the plaintiffs began looking for everything they could find."

Leibrock and Terry advocate hiring ADA specialists to survey a facility and identify non-compliance issues. Services vary: Terry's architectural firm performs five types, ranging from a "high-speed walkthrough" to a "standard barrier survey." Costs increase with thoroughness, says Terry. The simple walkthrough costs as little as $2,000, but may identify only 25 percent of the issues noted in the most detailed survey. The barrier survey—which also prioritizes problems and suggests solutions—can run between 25 and 40 cents per square foot.

For all its complexities, the ADA "has done a lot of good," says Leibrock. "The United States is the most accessible nation in the world." Still, she believes the law could be improved. "There are many problems that actually work against older people."

Leibrock cites Japanese research that led to the development of angled bathtub grab bars. These bars don't demand the same upper-body strength as the horizontal bars mandated by the ADA, making them more appropriate for older, weaker residents. But in some places, the angled bars aren't compatible with what's required by the ADA and state codes.

"You can claim [the modified bars] are a conditional equivalent to what's required," says Leibrock. "The law allows that. But no one will sign off on it—no state inspector and no one in the federal government."

"In the future," says Leibrock, "the regulations should be based on performance specifications. We need to stop giving lip service to the idea of meeting people's needs and really design an environment that allows people to do things for themselves."

The Disability Advantage

Even as the number of workers with disabilities grows because of factors like the Iraq war, fewer of them are finding jobs. Here's one employer that bucks the trend.

ALISON STEIN WELLNER

On a recent morning, Connie Presnell pulled into the parking lot of Habitat International, a carpet, turf, and contract manufacturing company in Chattanooga. She drove past towering lawn ornaments (one's a metal giraffe), and then parked near the building, where she manages the factory floor. As the company's 30 employees punched in, Presnell received word that Habitat had to ship 13,000 boxes to a Tropicana cannery overnight. She assigned a dozen of her fastest workers to the task and, as the sound system cranked up rock music, they got down to work. As usual, the order was delivered on time.

What makes this story remarkable is that Presnell's A-team was made up entirely of people with cerebral palsy, Down syndrome, schizophrenia, and other disabilities. At Habitat, in fact, nearly every employee (including some managers) has a physical or mental disability or both. And yet, Habitat excels by many measures. Its quality-control statistics are especially enviable. During peak season, from January to June, the factory turns out up to 15,000 rugs a day, five or six days a week. Yet the plant's defect rate is less than one-half of 1%. Only about 10 rugs have been cut incorrectly in the company's history. "We've never had a back order" boasts David Morris, Habitat's owner and CEO. "If we fall behind one day, we'll all work hard to catch up."

Morris credits his workers—who are paid regionally competitive wages for factory work—with the company's impressive financial performance. Profits have risen every year for the past decade, against a steady $14 million in sales. And to think, Morris says, shaking his head, that at first, giving these workers a chance "had to be forced down my throat."

More Disabled, but Fewer Are Employed

It's been 15 years since the first President Bush signed into law the Americans With Disabilities Act, which prohibits discrimination against people with disabilities in all parts of society, including the workplace. Nearly 50 million Americans—a segment of the population larger than the number of either Hispanics or African Americans—are covered by the ADA.

But while the ADA improved the treatment of people with disabilities in many tangible ways—think curb cuts and wheelchair ramps—its legacy with respect to employment has been mixed. In fact, since the ADA went into effect, employment among people with disabilities has declined. Between 1990 and 2004, employment rates dropped by 30% for people with disabilities, according to research conducted by Andrew J. Houtenville, a researcher at Cornell University (see chart). "And this in a time frame when employment rates for other people increased" notes Pamela Loprest, of the Urban Institute.

Economists and policy experts argue over why this is so. Some think specific language in the ADA scares employers, others contend that Social Security's disability insurance program compels people not to work. Whatever the cause, one thing is clear: People with disabilities constitute a growing share of the available work force—their ranks swelling because of medical advancements, the aging population, and importantly, the war in

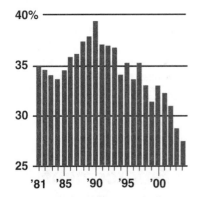

DECLINING JOB PROSPECTS.
Employment among people with disabilities peaked in 1990.

Source: Andrew J. Houtenville/Cornell

Hiring Employees with Disabilities

Three in four firms have no ADA workers. Rookie employers should:

1. Temper their enthusiasm

Go slow at first. "Don't hire 20 people with disabilities if you've never been around someone with a disability," says Nancy Henderson Wurst, author of *Able!,* a new book about Habitat International.

2. Find expertise

Make sure at least one manager really understands how to work with people with disabilities. A person who has had a family member with a disability is probably a good candidate, says Wurst.

3. Do adequate screening

Interview prospective workers' caregivers because their commitment is crucial. "The biggest failures are with the family or the caregivers, not the employees," says David Morris, Habitat's CEO.

4. Team up with a school

Habitat has an internship program with the special ed department of a nearby school. The school is only too happy to share information and help with training.

Iraq. More than 15,000 troops are likely to be wounded this year, and the rate of amputation, in part because of the prevalence of roadside bombings, is twice that of any previous war. Meanwhile, Social Security and Medicaid are in the midst of reforms aimed at encouraging employment among people with disabilities, says Houtenville. One proposal would move people into training programs more quickly following an injury. Another would allow people to keep federally funded benefits while they get back on the job, he says. But who will hire these workers?

Managers' Concerns, Real and Imagined

Managers who employ people with disabilities often say that many of the perceived concerns are exaggerated. Hidden costs are rare, for example. Researchers at Rutgers University found that 73% of companies employing people with disabilities spent nothing on accommodations, while those that did spent $500 on average. What's more, federal and state tax credits are available to defray the costs. Fears that disabled workers are injury-prone also seem to be overblown.

Still, managing workers with disabilities does require sensitivity and stamina. At Habitat, workers have had seizures on the factory floor. Every couple of weeks, an employee loses bowel or bladder control. To cope, Morris installed showers in the factory. Employees clock out, clean up, and change into a fresh set of clothes that they keep on hand. Then there are workers who have chronic behavioral issues. "I have one employee who has temper tantrums a couple of times a week" says Presnell. "He hits himself, and jumps up and down and screams."

The outbursts can happen without warning, although they are sometimes triggered when Presnell assigns a new task to the worker, who has autism and doesn't always adapt well to change. At first, Presnell was frightened by these episodes. Now she calmly tells the employee to punch out, then sends him to the break room for 15 minutes. "This is a very bad punishment for him" she says, "because he knows he's not making money."

Forfeiting a Million-Dollar Account

Some employers rely on a middleman—either a sponsoring public agency or a nonprofit group—to take responsibility for their workers. Though many companies stand by this model, Habitat's Morris thinks it's bad to have a buffer. Early on, he worked with a nonprofit whose mission was to offer "clients" as many work experiences as possible. As a result, the nonprofit rotated workers from company to company, which meant a good staffer might disappear the day before a shipment deadline. When Habitat couldn't persuade the agency to change this policy, Morris ended the relationship.

Today Habitat eschews sponsors and applies for no government funds because these programs sometimes cap workers' salaries, which drives Morris crazy. "I hate red tape," he says.

He also hates an inescapable fact of human nature, which is that some people treat people with disabilities poorly. Nine years ago, Morris worked with a group of independent sales representatives to gain distribution to a large West Coast chain. On a visit to Chattanooga, two of the reps made derogatory comments about Habitat's workers.

Though none of his employees heard the comments, Morris was furious. But he couldn't ignore the $1 million the account was worth. The head of the rep firm called to apologize, and that settled matters, but only for a while. Subsequently, some of the reps said still more hurtful things, and so Morris dropped the firm. It took Habitat two years to get revenue back to where it had been before, but it's a tradeoff he's happy that he made.

Just as some people display prejudice, he says, others give Habitat their business specifically because of the company's work force. And while he faces challenges that other business owners do not, Morris prefers them to the challenges he'd face if he ran a typical factory. He doesn't have to worry about turnover or absenteeism. During the winter, his employees often try to sleep at the plant so they can be sure to get in the next day if it snows. "A lot of companies have token ADA employees," Morris says; the difference at Habitat, he explains, is that "we're run by them."

ALISON STEIN WELLNER can be reached at Alison@wellner.biz.

Implementing Sexual Harassment Training in the Workplace

DAVE GOTTWALS

As sexual harassment becomes more prevalent in the workplace, states are incorporating requirements in addition to the federal harassment laws that protect businesses and employees. These laws are established to prevent potential lawsuits and to teach companies to be proactive by training their employees about how to avoid sexual harassment. The laws may seem burdensome, but businesses will benefit in the long run from the requirements.

Sexual harassment training is more than a good idea in California, it is now the law. Along with only four other states (Connecticut, New Jersey, Massachusetts, and Maine) that have their own sexual harassment laws, California joined the list with its recently passed AB 1825.

California was not the first state to add a requirement to the federal law. In fact, California's law is modeled after Connecticut's existing statute. The new requirement calls for companies to implement sexual harassment training for all supervisory employees.

Converting to any new corporate process can be a consuming and costly matter. The burden of initiating a new training program along with the proper documentation practices can place a strain particularly on a company's human resource department.

National Harassment Requirements

Title VII of the Civil Rights Act of 1964, which outlaws discrimination in the workplace based on protected classes, is overseen by the Equal Employment Opportunity Commission. Harassment training is highly recommended, but there are no specific requirements for it. Companies are not obligated by federal law to provide sexual harassment training. However, it is strongly recommended and considered to be an excellent idea. Besides encouraging employees to treat each other with respect and professionalism in hopes of creating a positive and productive work environment, harassment training can reduce your company's liability, should a suit be brought at the state and federal levels.

California's AB 1825 Requirements

The requirements and definitions of AB 1825 are more comprehensive than most people realize. Effective January 1, 2006, all supervisory employees will be required to receive at least two hours of harassment training every two years. In addition, all supervisory employees who have been employed as of July 1, 2005, must have completed their two hours of training by the end of December 2005.

Supervisory employees that are hired or promoted after July 1, 2005, must complete their initial two hours of sexual harassment training within the first six months of their hire or promotion date. This basic requirement triggers several follow up questions with respect to who needs to comply, how do you count employees, how is a supervisor defined, and what is included in the training?

Companies Required to Comply

AB 1825 directly affects all businesses that have 50 or more employees regardless of where the 50 employees are located. All 50 do not have to be located in California. For example, a company with 100 employees, with 80 employees outside of California and 20 employees in California, must comply. Furthermore, whether the supervisory employee for the 20 California employees is located in California or not, that supervisory employee must be trained in compliance with AB 1825.

Counting 50 Employees

AB 1825 requires anyone that is "regularly employed" or "regularly providing services" to count toward the 50 employees. Therefore, employers must count temp-agency staff, independent contractors, and consultants, along with their regular employees. It does not matter if workers are part time or full time, they all count.

Defining Supervisory Employees

This is another part of AB 1825 that can be overlooked accidentally. Though AB 1825 does not have a specific definition of supervisory employee, the Fair Employee and Housing Act (FEHA) does. And since AB 1825 is a new section of FEHA, it is considered prudent to review supervisory employee in other parts of FEHA.

Besides the usual and obvious language of "any individual having the authority to . . . hire, transfer, lay off, promote, . . .", it also includes "the ability to direct other employees," as a criteria for a supervisor as defined by the law.

Therefore, any employee having the ability to direct other employees may be considered a supervisory employee and must be trained in compliance with AB 1825. The employee does not need "supervisor" or "manager" in their title.

For example, in many instances in the high tech industry, engineering leads frequently are responsible for directing engineers on specific assignments within projects. Therefore, it would meet FEHA's definition of supervisory employee.

Although, it is mandatory for only supervisory employees to undergo harassment training, it is good practice to inform and train all employees on this issue. Harassment training is a form of risk management and it allows a company to manage and limit future liability.

Requirements of the Training Content

The training time of two hours is a minimum and it should not discourage a company from additional training time as needed. Although the words "Sexual Harassment" are frequently used for AB 1825, the law requires additional topics be covered in the training session for it to be considered compliant. The training must cover:

- State and federal level laws prohibiting all forms of harassment (not just sexual harassment);
- Discrimination and the protected classes;
- Prevention techniques;
- Correction of harassment;
- Remedies available to harassment victims; and
- Practical examples to help supervisory employees prevent harassment, discrimination, and retaliation.

Additionally, the employer is required to provide at least two hours of "classroom or other effective interactive training." This can be tricky. Usually "effective interactive training" means participants should be able to ask questions and get answers from trainer to trainee and from trainee to trainer.

If your company cannot feasibly provide classroom training to all its employees, compliance can be met with effective online training. Just understand the interactive requirement before setting up a training program.

Penalties and Liability

Although the penalty for noncompliance of AB 1825 itself is minimal (FEHA issues an order to provide the training), the liability for noncompliance in a harassment lawsuit can bring a company to its knees. This includes noncompliant training programs as well as those companies that have neglected to complete the harassment training within the training timelines.

Companies that are confronted by the court of law face heavy disciplinary action if they have not taken all "reasonable measures" to prevent harassment and have not kept good records (documentation). In these instances, the judge will view the company as having bad practices or being negligent about the issue. This obviously can contribute to a verdict against the company and awarding the plaintiff with punitive damages. Historically, courts tend not to be lenient since most of the jury's are comprised of employees, not employers.

HR and Harassment Training

Many companies throughout the United States are unaware or have little understanding of the sexual harassment laws in California. Of the employers who are aware of the requirements, many do not have the time and resources to examine AB 1825 in great detail.

We have found that many human resource departments are aware that the training is a good defense mechanism, yet they do not have a compliant sexual harassment training program in place. This is often because there is no person in the company who is equipped with the expertise needed to lead the training.

It is often helpful to bring in a third-party consultant, who is an expert in AB 1825, to deliver effective sexual harassment training. Also, bringing in a third-party consultant may be beneficial as they can discuss scenarios with your employees and deliver what can be an awkward message about what behaviors are acceptable for your company.

Companies that do not have an internal employee or lawyer that concentrates in employee benefits and human resource practices can refer to outside sources that specialize in consulting for human resource departments in its legal practices and risk management.

Additional Information Liberty Benefit Insurance Services Provides during a Training Session

Listed below are a sampling of items reviewed by your consultant that provides sexual harassment training that will enhance the required contents of harassment training.

A clear explanation of what the government mandates: supervisory employees are required to participate in harassment training and that is a necessary starting point for the training.

Sexual harassment training participants are handed a pretest upon the entry of the training session. The pretest encompasses basic harassment concerns in the workplace and assesses what employees know about sexual harassment prior to the training. Most employees are aware of the concerns; however, the pretest helps to show them some things they are not aware of. The test is reviewed at the end of the training session and corrected.

In the training, employees learn about two forms of sexual harassment—*quid pro quo,* when something is given or received for something else, and *hostile work environment,* unwelcome conduct of a sexual nature that inhibits the employee's ability to work.

Trainers inform the employees of harassment statistics, share multiple examples and discuss cases that have gone to court and their outcomes. One such case that proves that even large established companies can make mistakes is that of, Agilent Technologies, formerly of Hewlett Packard. It lost a court case in March of 2005, which cost the company $438,000 in punitive damages.

Participants will also learn which forms of sexual harassment are on the rise and which are most common in the workplace.

Trainers will then explain discrimination and the protected classes.

Participants will learn that harassment is not about the intent—it's about the perception by the individual who feels that they were harassed. Participants will be made aware of the "reasonable woman" test that the state of California applies to each case to determine if it was harassment or not.

Participants will learn about the need for a formal investigation process. Sexual harassment complaints must be taken seriously and handled with a rapid response. Action should be taken within 24 to 48 hours upon receiving the complaint. This action should include the company delegating trained personnel to initiate an investigation. An alternate person should be on standby to handle the investigation if the delegated employee is not available. Any delay in action may lead to a penalty.

Trainers also review techniques for conducting interviews while doing the investigations, as well as who should be interviewed. And after the investigation has been conducted, the company then needs to determine what its response will be.

Participants will learn that if by chance they have a claim that goes to court, the court will review the entire process a company implements. This includes the training process, as in which employees were trained and when, the harassment policy, the required posters, communications, the response time to a complaint, the investigation process, the interviews, the remedy, the follow-up after the remedy, and of course, all the supporting documentation.

Participants will learn that prevention techniques work to help a company avoid liability. Supervisory employees become knowledgeable about company policy in a training session, and discuss how to make sure their staff knows the company policy.

In the training they should learn how to maintain a neutral attitude and create a climate of respect among their employees. The supervisory employees need to be trained to be cognitive of the office environment and of how not to allow offensive behavior to persist. They should reflect neutral behavior towards gender, race, and all the protected classes. Supervisory employees should learn how to be "model citizens," setting an example for their employees to follow.

Participants will learn that even though the harasser is the one to blame, the company can be held liable for his or her actions. The employer can be determined responsible if it has not provided adequate training, made efforts to prevent harassment, or does not have its efforts documented. And, more alarming, the individuals who are a supervisory employee may be held liable in certain circumstances.

Trainers will also discuss the fact that associates other than employees of your company can be the harasser. Your company may be liable for their actions as it would an employee. For example, vendors, suppliers, and customers of a company can initiate harassment and a company may be held liable if it is aware and did not take appropriate actions.

Trainers may also present a video with several vignettes that display situations of harassment in the workplace. Each vignette shows how a common situation can easily lead to comments or jokes that can be considered as harassment.

Third-Party Consultants and Risk Management

A good third-party human resource consultant can not only provide a sexual harassment trainer but it can help manage the company's risk, compliance issues, benefit costs, turnover, morale, and overall have a positive impact on the company's bottom line and growth. They focus on finances, legal compliance, and performance issues—not just insurance renewals.

Compliance Check is a strategic risk management tool from Liberty that has 18 modules, including sexual harassment. This risk management tool allows it to review and audit the company from a human resource perspective, identifying the noncompliant components and suggesting fixes to be compliant and reduce risk. Both companies work together strategically to create remedies for these issues. Some examples of the 18 modules include the review of the Employee Handbook, COBRA practices, FMLA practices, FLSA practices, HIPAA practices, and ADA practices. By keeping these practices up to code, companies are able to manage their liability.

What Should Human Resource Departments Do Next?

The best next step for human resource departments is to hire an experienced consultant to handle their sexual harassment training. Select a consultant who will become a strategic partner with its clients to help the human resource department contribute to the reduction of the company's bottom line. Instead of hiring a company for a fee of $2,000 to $3,000, or more, it should partner with a firm that offers sexual harassment training as part of its services. It has four qualified members with extensive industry service to provide the harassment training.

DAVE GOTTWALS is a Benefit Consultant for Liberty Benefit Insurance Services, Inc., a nationwide, full service benefit and human resource consulting firm based in San Jose, CA. He is certified as a Compliance Check auditor helping companies manage their risk.

Some of 'Our Boys Overseas' Have Gray Hair

Advisors should be aware of laws affecting boomer citizen soldiers on active duty.

ALLISON BELL

Financial advisors who work with baby boomers and their employers might want to learn something about the laws that protect the rights of members of Guard and Reserve units who go away on active duty.

Years ago, the military was dominated by young recruits and career military personnel who had only limited economic ties to the civilian world. Today, the Army, the Navy, the Marine Corps, the Air Force and the Coast Guard have 173,335 citizen soldiers on active duty, according to the latest U.S. Department of Defense mobilization report.

The Pentagon does not have an official count of baby boomer service members. But, in 2002, when boomers were between the ages of 38 and 56, 72% of the military Guard and Reserve officers and 36% of the enlisted personnel were over age 35, according to estimates based on age distribution figures published in the military's 2002 Demographics Report.

Advisors who work with boomer doctors and nurses with no military ties also may want to know something about government rules that affect the finances of citizen soldiers: *The Seattle Post Intelligencer* reported in May that the Pentagon has sketched out an emergency medical draft system that, in some cases, could call civilian doctors and nurses as old as 44 to active military service.

Although many members of the Guard and Reserves have low incomes in civilian life, about 12% suffer a drop in income of $5,000 or more when they are activated, and 2.4% suffer a drop of more than $25,000, according to a report released by the U.S. Government Accountability Office in March 2003.

Many of the citizen soldiers who see the steepest drops in income are boomers who work in the civilian world as doctors, lawyers or pilots, says Dr. Linda Eagle, president of Edcomm Group Ltd., New York, a company that has developed a free SCRA tutorial to serve as a sample of its course-development services.

Major federal laws that protect citizen soldiers include the Uniformed Services Employment and Re-employment Rights Act of 1994 and the Servicemembers Civil Relief Act of 1993.

USERRA requires employers of all sizes to hold citizen soldiers' jobs open for them while they are away on active duty for at least 5 years.

The law also requires employers to offer activated employees and dependents a chance to buy continuation health benefits for at least 18 months. At press time, Congress was working to extend the minimum coverage continuation period to 24 months.

Employers can exclude health coverage for service-related medical problems when the employees return. But employers, their health carriers and their benefits administrators cannot apply any other exclusions, waiting periods or other limitations to health coverage for returning service members, according to the law.

Once employees return, they have a chance to catch up on any employee contributions that they missed while they were away. Proposed guidance released in September by the U.S. Labor Department suggests that, under normal conditions, employers may have to make up for any retirement plan contributions missed while an employee was on military leave within 30 days after reemploying the employee. If it were "impossible or unreasonable" for the employer to make the payments within 30 days, the employer would have to make the contributions "as soon as practicable," according to the guidance.

The other law, SCRA, does everything from limiting interest rates on activated service members' debts to 6% to preventing landlords from evicting the families of activated service members who pay less than $1,200 per month in rent.

One major insurance section of SCRA requires life insurers to keep service members' life insurance policies in effect for at least 2 years after the service members return to civilian life, even if the service members fail to pay the policy premiums.

Another section of SCRA requires companies that have sold individual health insurance to activated service members to reinstate the coverage without any exclusions or waiting periods once the service members return to civilian life.

A Touch of Gray Age of Members of Guard and Reserve Units in 2002

Age	Officers	Enlisted
▶ 25 or younger	2,186	254,797
▶ 26–30	9,634	109,286
▶ 31–35	25,146	114,607
▶ 36–40	33,764	111,479
▶ 41 and older	60,604	160,639
▶ Total	131,334	750,808

Source: U.S. Department of Defense, 2002 Demographics Report.

Sellers of individual health insurers can withhold coverage or impose extra restrictions only if the returning service members have employer-sponsored coverage or suffer from disabilities incurred or aggravated in the line of duty, according to the text of the law.

USERRA and SCRA protect workers who are drafted or volunteer for regular military service as well members of the Guard and Reserve.

The GAO now is conducting a study that looks at compliance with USERRA and SCRA insurance provisions, and an arm of the Labor Department is starting to survey service members to assess their views on USERRA compliance.

Robert Kaplan, education director at McKay Hochman Company Inc., Butler, N.J., a benefits consulting firm, has written about USERRA and talks about USERRA legal developments in discussions with employers. So far, though, he has not run into many questions about real-life incidents involving returning service members.

Because many citizen soldiers are still on active duty, handling the workers' return "is an issue that probably hasn't kicked in yet," Kaplan says.

Many activated service members need help with SCRA concerns long before they need help with returning to their civilian jobs.

Edcomm, the company that developed the SCRA tutorial, is starting to get questions from employers and returning boomers who need immediate help with SCRA and some who need help with USERRA, Eagle says.

Eagle has heard from some returning boomers who were shut out of their old jobs and some whose employers have tried to impose waiting periods or pre-existing condition limits on health coverage.

In most cases, "that's illegal," Eagle says.

Kaplan is not sure how much advisors who work with individual consumers have to do to explain USERRA and SCRA to members of the Guard and Reserve.

"The military does a pretty good job of explaining the law," Kaplan says.

But Kaplan points to the recommendation in the proposed USERRA guidance about making up missed retirement plan contributions as an example of why employers who employ boomers should hear something from their benefits advisors about USERRA.

"The employer could be on the hook for making up the contributions within 30 days," Kaplan says.

Eagle argues that individuals, employers, advisors and financial services companies all need to hear more about SCRA and USERRA.

Employers and financial services companies usually want to do the right thing, but they often are unfamiliar with the laws because, up till now, the laws have been used so little, Eagle says.

Fighting for Values

The struggle against Islamic extremism is not a clash between civilizations, the British prime minister argues. It is a clash *about* civilization.

TONY BLAIR

Over the past nine years, Britain has pursued a markedly different foreign policy, justifying our actions at least as much by reference to values as to interests. The defining characteristic of today's world is its interdependence. Whereas the economics of globalization are well matured, the politics of globalization are not. Unless we articulate a common global policy based on common values, we risk chaos threatening our stability, economic and political, through letting extremism, conflict or injustice go unchecked.

The consequence of this thesis is a policy of engagement, not isolation; and one that is active, not reactive.

Confusingly, its proponents and opponents come from all sides of the political spectrum. So it is apparently a "neoconservative" or right wing view to be ardently in favor of spreading democracy around the world. Others on the right take the view that this is dangerous and deluded—the only thing that matters is an immediate view of national interest. Some progressives see intervention as humanitarian and necessary; others take the view that, provided dictators don't threaten our citizens directly, what they do with their own is up to them.

The debate on world trade has thrown all sides into an orgy of political cross-dressing. Protectionist sentiment is rife on the left. On the right, there are calls for "economic patriotism." Meanwhile some voices, left and right, are making the case for free trade not just on grounds of commerce but of justice.

The true division in foreign policy today is between those who want the shop "open" and those who want it "closed;" between those who believe that the long-term interests of a country lie in it being engaged—and those who think the short-term pain of such a policy and its decisions is too great. This division has strong echoes in debates not just over foreign policy and trade but also over immigration.

Progressives are stronger on the challenges of poverty, climate change, and trade justice. It is impossible to gain support for our values unless the demand for justice is as strong as the demand for freedom; and the willingness to work in partnership with others is an avowed preference to going it alone, even if that may sometimes be necessary.

We will not ever get real support for the tough action that may well be essential to safeguard our way of life unless we also attack global poverty and environmental degradation or injustice with equal vigor.

Neither in defending this interventionist policy do I pretend that mistakes have not been made or that major problems do not confront us.

I also acknowledge that the standoff between Israel and Palestine remains a genuine source of anger in the Arab and Muslim world that goes far beyond usual anti-Western feeling. Yet it is in confronting global terrorism today that the sharpest debate and disagreement is found. Nowhere is the supposed "folly" of the interventionist case so loudly trumpeted as in this case. Here, so it is said, as the third anniversary of the Iraq conflict took place, is the wreckage of such a world view. Under Saddam Iraq was "stable." Now its stability is in the balance. Ergo, it should never have been done.

This is the conventional view of foreign policy since the fall of the Berlin Wall. Countries should manage their affairs and relationships according to their narrow national interests. The basic posture represented by this view is not to provoke, to keep all as settled as it can be, and to cause no tectonic plates to move. It has its soft face in dealing with issues like global warming or Africa and reserves its hard face only if directly attacked by another state, which is unlikely. It is a view which sees the world as not without challenge but basically calm, with a few nasty things lurking in deep waters, which it is best to avoid. It believes the storms have been largely self-created.

This is the majority view of a large part of Western opinion, certainly in Europe. According to this opinion, the policy of America since 9/11 has been a gross overreaction; George Bush is as much if not more of a threat to world peace as Osama bin Laden; and what is happening in Iraq, Afghanistan, or anywhere else in the Middle East is an entirely understandable consequence of U.S./U.K. imperialism or worse, of just plain stupidity. Leave it all alone or at least treat it with sensitivity and it would all resolve itself in time; "it" never quite being defined, but just generally felt as anything that causes disruption.

This world view—which I would characterize as a doctrine of benign inactivity—sits in the commentator's seat, almost as a matter of principle. It has imposed a paradigm on world events that is extraordinary in its attraction and its scope. The effect of this paradigm is to see each setback in Iraq or Afghanistan, each revolting terrorist barbarity, each reverse for the forces of democracy or advance for the forces of tyranny as merely an illustration of the foolishness of our ever being there; as a reason why Saddam should have been left in place or the Taliban free to continue their alliance with al Qaeda. Those who still justify the interventions are treated with scorn.

Then, when terrorists strike in the nations like Britain or Spain, who supported such action, there is a groundswell of opinion formers keen to say, in effect, that it's hardly surprising—after all, if we do this to "their" countries, is it any wonder they do it to "ours"?

So the statement that Iraq or Afghanistan or Palestine or indeed Chechnya, Kashmir, or half a dozen other troublespots is seen by extremists as fertile ground for their recruiting—a statement of the obvious—is elided with the notion that we have "caused" such recruitment or made terrorism worse, a notion that, on any sane analysis, has the most profound implications for democracy.

The easiest line for any politician seeking office in the West today is to attack American policy. Earlier this year, as I was addressing young Slovak students, one got up, denouncing U.S./U.K. policy in Iraq, fully bought in to the demonization of the United States, utterly oblivious to the fact that without the U.S. and the liberation of his country, he would have been unable to ask such a question, let alone get an answer to it.

I recall the video footage of Mohammed Sadiq Khan, the man who was the ringleader of the 7/7 bombers in London. There he was, complaining about the suppression of Muslims, the wickedness of America and Britain, calling on all fellow Muslims to fight us. And I thought: here is someone, brought up in this country, free to practice his religion, free to speak out, free to vote, with a good standard of living and every chance to raise a family in a decent way of life, talking about "us," the British, when his whole experience of "us" has been the very opposite of the message he is preaching.

There was something tragic but also ridiculous about such a diatribe. He may have been born here. But his ideology wasn't. And that is why it has to be taken on, everywhere.

This terrorism will not be defeated until its ideas, the poison that warps the minds of its adherents, are confronted, head-on, in their essence, at their core. By this I don't mean telling them terrorism is wrong. I mean telling them their attitude to America is absurd; their concept of governance pre-feudal; their positions on women and other faiths, reactionary and regressive; and then since only by Muslims can this be done: standing up for and supporting those within Islam who will tell them all of this but more, namely that the extremist view of Islam is not just theologically backward but completely contrary to the spirit and teaching of the Koran.

But in order to do this, we must reject the thought that somehow we are the authors of our own distress; that if only we altered this decision or that, the extremism would fade away.

The only way to win is to recognize this phenomenon is a global ideology; to see all areas in which it operates as linked; and to defeat it by values and ideas set in opposition to those of the terrorists.

A reforming book. The roots of global terrorism and extremism are indeed deep. They reach right down through decades of alienation, victimhood, and political oppression in the Arab and Muslim world. Yet this is not and never has been inevitable. The most remarkable thing about reading the Koran is to understand how progressive it is. I speak with great diffidence and humility as a member of another faith. I am not qualified to make any judgments. But as an outsider, the Koran strikes me as a reforming book, trying to return Judaism and Christianity to their origins, rather as reformers attempted with the Christian Church centuries later. It is inclusive. It extols science and knowledge and abhors superstition. It is practical and way ahead of its time in attitudes to marriage, women, and governance.

Under its guidance, the spread of Islam and its dominance over previously Christian or pagan lands was breathtaking. Over centuries it founded an empire, leading the world in discovery, art, and culture. The standard bearers of tolerance in the early Middle Ages were far more likely to be found in Muslim lands than in Christian.

But by the early 20th century, after renaissance, reformation, and enlightenment had swept over the Western world, the Muslim and Arab world was uncertain, insecure, and on the defensive. Muslims began to see the sorry state of Muslim countries as symptomatic of the sorry state of Islam. Political radicals became religious radicals and vice versa. Those in power tried to accommodate the resurgent Islamic radicalism by incorporating some of its leaders and some of its ideology. The result was nearly always disastrous. The religious radicalism was made respectable, the political radicalism suppressed, and so in the minds of many, the cause of the two came together to symbolize the need for change. So many came to believe that the way of restoring the confidence and stability of Islam was the combination of religious extremism and populist politics.

The extremism may have started through religious doctrine and thought. But soon, in offshoots of the Muslim brotherhood, supported by Wahabi extremists and taught in some of the madrassas of the Middle East and Asia, an ideology was born and exported around the world.

The different aspects of this terrorism are linked. The struggle against terrorism in Madrid or London or Paris is the same as the struggle against the terrorist acts of Hezbollah in Lebanon or the PIJ in Palestine, or rejectionist groups in Iraq. The murder of the innocent in Beslan is part of the same ideology that takes innocent lives in Saudi Arabia, Yemen, or Libya. And when Iran gives support to such terrorism, it becomes part of the same battle with the same ideology at its heart.

Clash about civilization. Which brings me to the fundamental point. "We" is not the West. "We" are as much Muslim as Christian or Jew or Hindu. "We" are those who believe in religious tolerance, openness to others, to democracy, liberty, and human rights administered by secular courts.

This is not a clash between civilizations. It is a clash about civilization. It is the age-old battle between progress and reaction, between those who embrace and see opportunity in the modern world and those who reject its existence; between optimism and hope on the one hand, and pessimism and fear on the other. And in the era of globalization where nations depend on each other and where our security is held in common or not at all, the outcome of this clash between extremism and progress is utterly determinative of our future. We can no more opt out of this struggle than we can opt out of the climate changing around us. Inaction, pushing the responsibility on to America, deluding ourselves that this terrorism is an isolated series of individual incidents rather than a global movement and would go away if only we were more sensitive to its pretensions; this too is a policy. It is just that; it is a policy that is profoundly, fundamentally wrong.

And this is why the position of so much opinion on how to defeat this terrorism and on the continuing struggle in Iraq and Afghanistan and the Middle East is, in my judgment, so mistaken.

It ignores the true significance of the elections in Iraq and Afghanistan. The fact is: Given the chance, the people wanted democracy. OK, so they voted on religious or regional lines. That's not surprising, given the history. But there's not much doubt what all the main parties in both countries would prefer, and it is neither theocratic nor secular dictatorship. The people—despite violence, intimidation, inexperience, and often logistical nightmares—voted. Not a few. But in numbers large enough to shame many Western democracies. They want government decided by the people.

"This terrorism will not be defeated until its ideas, the poison that warps the minds of its adherents, are confronted, head-on, in their essence, at their core."

And who is trying to stop them? In Iraq, a mixture of foreign jihadists, former Saddamists, and rejectionist insurgents. In Afghanistan, a combination of drug barons, Taliban, and al Qaeda.

In each case, the United States, the U.K., and the forces of many other nations are there to help the indigenous security forces grow, to support the democratic process, and to provide some clear bulwark against the terrorism that threatens it.

Of course, and wholly wrongly, there are abuses of human rights, mistakes made, things done that should not be done. There always were. But at least this time, someone demands redress; people are free to complain.

So here, in its most pure form, is a struggle between democracy and violence. People look back on the three years since the Iraq conflict; they point to the precarious nature of Iraq today and to those who have died—mainly in terrorist acts—and they say: How can it have been worth it?

But there is a different question to ask: Why is it so important to the forces of reaction and violence to halt Iraq in its democratic tracks and tip it into sectarian war?

The answer is that the reactionary elements know the importance of victory or defeat in Iraq. Right from the beginning, to them it was obvious. For sure, errors were made on our side. It is arguable that de-Baathification went too quickly and was spread too indiscriminately, especially amongst the armed forces. Though in parenthesis, the real worry back in 2003 was a humanitarian crisis, which we avoided; and the pressure was all to de-Baathify faster.

But the basic problem from the murder of the United Nations staff in August 2003 onwards was simple: security. The reactionary elements were trying to derail both reconstruction and democracy by violence. Power and electricity became problems not through the indolence of either Iraqis or the multinational forces but through sabotage.

These were not random acts. They were and are a strategy. When that strategy failed to push the multinational forces out of Iraq prematurely and failed to stop the voting, they turned to sectarian killing and outrage.

They know that if they can succeed either in Iraq or Afghanistan or anywhere else wanting to go the democratic route, then the choice of a modern democratic future for the Arab or Muslim world is dealt a potentially mortal blow. They play our own media with a shrewdness that would be the envy of many a political party. Every act of carnage somehow serves to indicate our responsibility for disorder, rather than the act of wickedness that causes it.

What happens in Iraq or Afghanistan today is not just crucial for the people in those countries. In their salvation lies our own security.

This is a battle of values and progress; and therefore it is one we must win.

TONY BLAIR is prime minister of Britain. This article is adapted from a speech he gave on March 21.

UNIT 2

Meeting Human Resource Requirements

Unit Selections

Key Points to Consider

- Job requirements and working conditions have changed over the past several years. What new changes do you foresee in the workplace in the next 10 years? How do you see the impact of the 24/7 work schedule on employers and employees? What impact do you think telecommuting will have on the workplace? Do you think you will be working in the same kind of position as your parents? Do you think you will be working 9 to 5?

- The first step in the process of working is getting hired. The last step is termination, whether for cause, leaving for a new job, retirement, or a "reduction in force." What trends do you see in the workforce concerning individuals and their careers? What do you think the impact of race or diversity in the workforce is? What about globalization? Do you see any changes coming?

- How do you see computerization being applied to human resources, and how will this change human resources? What do you see as some of the issues concerning computerization of employee records?

- What are some of the trends in the workforce? How do you see organizations responding to those trends? What are some of the strategies that organizations are now using and/or could use in the future to hire and develop their workforces?

Student Web Site

www.mhcls.com/online

Internet References

Further information regarding these Web sites may be found in this book's preface or online.

America's Job Bank
   http://www.ajb.dni.us
International Association for Human Resource Information Management (IHRIM)
   http://www.ihrim.org
Sympatico Careers
   http://www.sympatico.workopolis.com
Voice of the Shuttle: Postindustrial Business Theory Page
   http://www.vos.scsb.edu/bfrowse.asp?=2727

Organizations, whether profit or nonprofit, are more than collections of buildings, desks, and telephones. Organizations are made of people—people with their particular traits, habits, and idiosyncrasies that make them unique. Each individual has different needs and wants, and the employer and the worker must seek a reasonable compromise so that at least an adequate match may be found for both.

The importance of human resource planning is greater than ever and will probably be even more important in the future. As Thomas Peters and Robert Waterman have pointed out in their book *In Search of Excellence*:

> Quality and service, then, were invariable hallmarks of excellent firms. To get them, of course, everyone's cooperation is required, not just the mighty labors of the top 200. The excellent companies require and demand extraordinary performance from the average man. Dana's former chairman, Rene McPherson, says that neither the few destructive laggards nor the handful of brilliant performers are the key. Instead, he urges attention to the care, feeding and unshackling of the average man. We labeled it "productivity through people." All companies pay it lip service. Few deliver.
>
> —Thomas Peters and Robert Waterman,
> *In Search of Excellence,* New York, Warner Books, 1987

Keith Brofsky/Getty Images

In the future, organizations are going to have to pay more than just lip service to "productivity through people" if they want to survive and prosper. They will have to practice it by demonstrating an understanding of not only their clients' and customers' needs, but also those of their employees. The only way they will be able to deliver the goods and services and achieve success is through those same employees. Companies are faced with the difficult task of finding the right people for the right jobs—a task that must be accomplished if the organization is going to have a future.

Organizations are trying to meet the needs of their employees by developing new and different approaches to workers' jobs. This means taking into account how society, the labor force, the family, and the nature of the jobs themselves have changed. Training and development will be key in meeting future human resource requirements. Employers will have to change the way they design their positions if they are to attract and keep good employees. They must consider how society has changed and will change in the future. They will learn from experience that there are fewer young people and more middle-aged employees, as well as dual-career couples in the workforce who struggle with raising children and deal with aging parents. They will have to consider how the very nature of jobs has changed in society, especially from predominantly blue-collar to white-collar jobs, from "9 to 5" to "24/7." Meeting these problems will entail new and different approaches to how jobs are structured.

Human resource planning, selection, and recruitment are going to be more critical in the future. Companies will have to go to extraordinary lengths to attract and keep new employees. There is no mystery about the reasons for this situation. America is aging, and there are fewer people in their late teens and early twenties to take the entry-level jobs that will be available in the future. Women, who for the past 20 years have been the major source of new employees, now represent almost half the workforce. As a result, new groups must be found, whether they are retirees, high school students, workers moonlighting on a second job, minority group members, people with disabilities, or immigrants. One

thing is certain: the workforce is changing and organizations will need to unlock the potential of all their employees. Other means of recruitment will need to be employed in the future, and old ideas and prejudices will have to go by the boards in all industrialized societies. Organizations will be faced with the problem of staffing, which is discussed in "Six Ways to Strengthen Staffing." But, this will be no easy task.

Another aspect of human resource planning involves both the selection process and the termination process. The days of working for only one company and then retiring with a gold watch and a pension are over. People are going to change jobs, if not companies, more frequently in the future, and many of the tasks they will be doing in the next 10, 15, or 20 years do not even exist today because of technological change. Mid-life and mid-career changes are going to be far more common than they have been in the past, requiring people to change and adapt.

Human resource information systems offer important tools in managing human resources. The ability of computers to handle large amounts of data is now being applied to human resource management with very interesting results. These practices, applied to hiring and internal information management, promise much greater automation of human resources in the future as well as reduced costs. There are, however, concerns. Privacy, security, and confidentiality are all key issues for employees who have their employment records encoded in a computer system. These concerns are highlighted in "Balancing HR Systems with Employee Privacy."

Meeting the human resource needs of any organization in the future will prove a difficult task. Assuming that the economy continues to grow at an acceptable rate, the need for workers will continue to increase, but many of the traditional sources of supply for new workers will be either exhausted or in decline. Management must plan for this shortage and consider alternative sources of potential employees. In turn, the individual employee must be ready to adapt quickly and efficiently to a changing environment. Job security is a thing of the past, and workers must remain flexible in order to cope with increased uncertainty.

Too Old to Work?

If you're over 40 and work for a big company, your future may well be tied to the fate of 6,400 Allstate agents who refused to be 'streamlined.'

ADAM COHEN

Allstate recruited new insurance agents in the 1980's with a brochure aimed at the dreams of time-clock punchers everywhere. The cover, which featured tidy-looking offices sporting the company's iconic blue-and-white logo, promised that signing on was "better than being in business for yourself." Inside, it offered prospective agents nothing less than a piece of the American dream. "Have you ever wanted a proprietary interest in a business?" the brochure beckoned. How about "unlimited income potential"? And "job security"?

Ron Harper, the son of a tractor salesman from Gainesville, Ga., wanted all of those things. A 38-year-old father of two, he had worked his way up in the supermarket business, starting as a bagger at 16 and rising to district sales manager in charge of 17 stores. But the supermarket industry was hurting, and after trying out a couple of other managerial jobs, he was looking for something more stable.

That was when he heard that Allstate was hiring. Its Neighborhood Office Agent program offered just the mix of opportunity and security he wanted. Allstate would give him policies to sell, money to run his own agency and a brand whose slogan— "You're in Good Hands"—was a marketing legend. He understood that the money would not be great at first. He would have to hustle to build a "book of business," and Allstate's commissions were less than he could earn as an independent broker. As an Allstate employee, though, he would receive generous benefits, including a pension. If he honed his skills and worked hard, he figured, there was no limit to what he could earn. And once he got past the preliminaries, he was told, he could be terminated only for dishonesty.

In August 1989, Harper was assigned to the small town of Thomson, Ga., and he uprooted his family and began hunting for customers in difficult terrain. Most of Thomson's older residents already had car and home insurance, and the younger ones were clearing out for better jobs in Augusta and Atlanta. But Harper "bled blue," as the company's saying goes. He lived off savings at first, pouring his commissions back into the agency, and used his own money for rent, an assistant's salary and ads in the Yellow Pages. After a few years, he had his book of business and was making a modest living. Then, in 1998, Allstate reduced the commissions it paid its neighborhood agents. To make up the lost revenue, Harper's wife quit her job and worked for him at below-market wages.

In November 1999, just past Harper's 10-year anniversary with Allstate, his supervisor called him in to his office in Augusta. Harper and about 17 of his fellow agents were handed a box of documents—the "job in a box," they would come to call it—radically redefining their relationship with Allstate. Harper and the others would now be independent contractors. Their benefits, pensions included, would end.

The box also contained what Harper now calls the "damnable release," which guaranteed that the agents would not sue. They didn't have to sign, but if they refused, their days selling for Allstate were over. "I read that thing, and honest to God, I felt nauseous," Harper says. The agents were filled with questions. Prime among them, What happened to the job security they were promised? But the managers were "on transmit, no receive," Harper recalls. "All they wanted to do was read to us from the script."

The same meeting was being played out in Allstate offices nationwide. The company, which had more than 15,000 agents of various kinds, was offering all of its 6,400 employee agents— the longest-serving agents, and those with the best benefits—the same unrelenting terms. They could keep their jobs by forfeiting benefits that were, in some cases, worth hundreds of thousands of dollars. Or they could give up their benefits and their jobs.

Allstate's reneging on its promise was, Harper insists, "totally wrong." But he also knew that he couldn't afford to walk away. In the end, he did what all but a handful of the employee agents did—he signed the release. Then he sued for age discrimination.

According to the federal government, age-discrimination complaints filed with the Equal Employment Opportunity Commission are up more than 24 percent over the past two years. Pick up the paper, and the cases are everywhere. Ford Motor Company is paying more than $10.5 million to settle suits by older managers who claim that its evaluation system discriminates against them. A Pennsylvania judge has cleared the way for 5,665 employees over 40 in the state Department of Transportation to bring a discrimination class action. McDonnell-Douglas is paying $36 million in partial settlement of a suit by about 1,100 older workers who say that the company laid them off to save on pension costs and medical benefits.

It's an odd time for age bias to be on the upswing. With the vast improvements in medicine, nutrition and lifestyle in recent years, old simply isn't what it used to be. The problem is that workplace culture has, for the most part, stuck to old ways of thinking about older workers. In many elite job markets—investment banking, computer programming, publishing—youth is celebrated, and regardless of how young older workers may feel, they only have to look around to realize that they represent the old school, not the new wave.

Hollywood has been rocked by a recent round of lawsuits charging television networks, production companies, studios and agencies with "gray listing"—refusing to hire older talent. (In the case of some television writing jobs, "old" actually refers to the early 30's.) Last September, Doris Roberts, the septuagenarian actress who plays Ray Romano's mother on "Everybody Loves Raymond," told the Senate Special Committee on Aging that society views people her age as discardable. "My contemporaries and I are denigrated as old," she said. "Old coots, old fogies, old codgers, geezers . . . hags and old-timers."

Roberts was testifying about the entertainment industry, but she could have been describing almost any workplace in America. Look through the reams of age-discrimination documents, and you'll see that the biggest cases come not from Hollywood and Madison Avenue but from Old Economy sectors like auto manufacturing and retailing. (And some of the cruelest comments about old workers appear in litigation involving plumbing supplies and fiberglass sales.)

The disconnect between workers who look at themselves in the mirror and feel young and companies that look at them and think "old-timer" has fueled much of the explosion in age-discrimination claims. But there are also some more basic social factors at work. With the graying of America, there are simply many more people eligible to be discriminated against—and to sue. The more than 70 million baby boomers now make up about half of the work force, and by next year even the youngest boomers will be 40—and therefore covered by federal age-discrimination laws. The oldest workers, who are most likely to face bias, are among the fastest-growing part of the work force. Workers over 65 increased by 20 percent in the 1990's; workers over 75 were up more than 80 percent from 1980 to 2000.

Couple these demographics with a faltering economy, and the conditions are perfect for a surge in discrimination suits. It's a typical pattern: when hard times hit, the ax falls disproportionately on older workers, who may be the most highly paid and who are often stereotyped as being less efficient. In a bad economy, with few other jobs available and retirement holdings taking a hit, fired workers are also more willing to sue.

The old face of age discrimination was the solitary worker quietly tapped on the shoulder and put out to pasture (Willy Loman, fired when the boss's son took over, left to complain, "You can't eat the orange and throw the peel away—a man is

not a piece of fruit!"). These days, however, age discrimination is more often the product of broad-based company policies, like decisions to phase out entire job categories disproportionately held by older workers.

That is precisely what Harper and his fellow agents have charged Allstate with doing. At the heart of their lawsuit is the claim that Allstate executives singled out one category of workers—employee agents—because more than 90 percent of them were over 40. If Harper and his 28 fellow plaintiffs win an early procedural battle and are allowed to represent a class of 6,400 onetime employee agents, this could be the biggest case ever charging a company with age discrimination.

The suit is still in its early stages, but the agents have retained two top Washington firms, and AARP has assigned two lawyers to the case. In late 2001, the Equal Employment Opportunity Commission jumped in on the agents' side, filing its own suit charging that Allstate violated federal pension and age-discrimination laws when it forced the agents to sign away their benefits and promise not to sue in order to keep working.

The stakes are high. If the plaintiffs win, Allstate could be forced to pay hundreds of millions of dollars. But more important is what the suit could mean for older workers nationwide. Thousands—maybe millions—of older workers are discriminated against on the job every year, but many have no idea what their rights are. Age discrimination is ready for a high-profile case that serves—like Brown v. Board of Education did for race discrimination, or the Clarence Thomas-Anita Hill Senate hearings did for sexual harassment—as a lightning rod.

"I've been looking for a case like this for years," says Raymond Gregory, an employment lawyer and the author of a book on age-discrimination law. A victory in the case, he says, could generate the kind of enormous damage awards and nationwide publicity that would force corporate America to rethink its approach to age in the workplace.

A llstate (the nation's second-largest auto and home insurer and No. 57 on the Fortune 500 list) got its start in 1931 as a mail-order insurance division of Sears, Roebuck & Co. After the 1933 Chicago World's Fair, where an Allstate agent sitting at a card table in the Sears exhibit was mobbed by customers, Sears began putting agents in booths in its stores—usually under the escalator, the least valuable space on the sales floor.

In 1984, Allstate initiated the Neighborhood Office Agent program to get agents out of stores and onto Main Street. The N.O.A. program recruited agents as exclusive salesmen for Allstate's insurance products. Allstate offered lower commissions, in many cases, than the competition, and the office-expense allotments it paid—as Ron Harper learned—often did not cover an agency's costs. But what Allstate was really offering was a relationship that turned the job of insurance agent—often a lonely seat-of-the-pants existence—into the equivalent of an executive post with a major corporation. In addition to a great benefits package, Allstate's neighborhood agents would receive the best training in the industry and would be eligible for an array of old-style sales incentives—Honor Rings, Chairman

Conference Awards and trips to sunny islands and European capitals.

The Neighborhood Office Agent program was initially a great success, but things began changing at Allstate in the 1990's. In an I.P.O. in '93, Sears spun off 20 percent of its Allstate stake, and two years later it sold off the rest. As Allstate began to fend for itself, its managers began rethinking the role of agents. It stopped hiring employee agents and, the plaintiffs say, began a campaign to switch the existing ones over to independent-contractor status.

Allstate dangled carrots, like bonuses for managers whose agents switched. And it wielded sticks, including tougher rules for neighborhood offices. But even as Allstate was apparently trying to prod its employee agents, it reassured them that the choice was theirs to make. "Rest easy, there is *no* plan to convert N.O.A. employee agents to . . . independent contractors effective 4/1/98!!!!" a December 1997 sales update promised.

The late 90's was a time of intense competition in the insurance business, and agent-oriented companies were worried. Insurgents like Geico were eliminating agents and selling directly to customers. And with the dot-com frenzy at a fever pitch, the conventional wisdom was that commerce of all kinds was moving online. The Internet's rise looked like bad news for Allstate, whose costly infrastructure of agents and offices would be a drag on earnings. Wall Street, certainly, was worried. In a booming stock market, Allstate shares plunged more than 50 percent, even as the company was furiously rebuying stock to prop it up.

In January 1999, Allstate's C.E.O., Jerry Choate, stepped down. Choate, the creator of the N.O.A. program, had worked his way up on the sales side and was well regarded by the agents. His replacement, Ed Liddy, a onetime Sears executive, lacked Choate's ties to the agents and came with a take-no-prisoners reputation. At Sears, he had helped to shutter the company's famed catalog, marveling to C.F.O. Magazine, "It's amazing how quickly you can dismantle a business that took a hundred years to build."

It was 10 months after Liddy took charge that Harper and the other employee agents were given Allstate's take-it-or-leave-it offer. Inside the "job in a box" packages handed out that day was a booklet titled "Preparing for the Future," which redefined the employment rules for employee agents. The tough new rules coincided with, and seemed designed to bolster, Allstate's widely heralded new plans to "aggressively expand the company's sales . . . and streamline the way the company operates."

The future that employee agents were supposed to prepare for was a grim one. As the plaintiffs see it, Allstate's motives were clear. The company was trying to cut costs by taking away their health insurance and freezing their pensions. At the same time, they say, Allstate was focused on "re-energizing" to compete against the Geicos and the dot-coms, and younger workers were the key. "We used to hear it in meetings all the time: 'We have these young people and they really go out and work,' " says Sylvia Crews-Kelly, a Tampa agent who was cut off after working 19 years, 8 months and 27 days—three months before she would have been eligible to start drawing her pension.

"They said older workers just want to sit on their policies and collect commissions."

Allstate sees things differently. "There was no discrimination," insists Sue Rosborough, a lawyer for the company. "We reorganized our agency force for a lot of very good business reasons." Allstate says that its new business model cut costs by $600 million but that almost all the savings came through closing regional offices and eliminating 4,000 nonagent positions.

The "Preparing for the Future" program was never intended to cut back on the cost of agent benefits, says Barry Hutton, the executive who oversaw it. Employee agents were asked to become independent contractors, he says, to "streamline" operations. Allstate's 6,400 employee agents were part of a force of more than 15,000 agents hired under different rules at different times. There were 11 categories of agents, Hutton says, each with its own commission rates. Simplifying the categories made Allstate more efficient. "We just flat-out had to make a business decision so we could be nimble, as nimble as a large company can be," Hutton says.

What about Allstate's supposed promises that employee agents would not be terminated except for dishonesty? If these promises were made, Rosborough says, they are not legally binding on the company.

It is unlikely that any prominent social theorist has ever put forth a vision of reform with insurance agents in the vanguard. The Allstate plaintiffs—who were highly compensated and are overwhelmingly white and male—do not look like typical victims of an unjust order. And the facts and legal issues in their suit are muddy. The animosity against older workers, if it was there, may be hard to find under all the layers of corporate cost-cutting and business strategizing.

Still, because of the number of workers affected, the prominence of the defendant, the size of the potential awards and the brazenness of Allstate's actions, this could represent the next wave in protecting the rights of older workers.

American workers are invariably surprised when they first learn, often when they have just been fired, about the concept of "employment at will." The general rule in American law is that employees hold their jobs at the whim of their bosses. Employers are free to fire workers, as the Tennessee Supreme Court explained in 1884, for "good cause, for no cause or even for cause morally wrong, without being thereby guilty of legal wrong."

Modern employment law has largely been a prolonged battle to whittle away at this doctrine. There are now a number of exceptions: workers generally can't be fired for union activity, say, or for whistle-blowing. But the largest carve-out is discrimination law. Employers may, as the Tennessee court said, fire workers for good cause or for no cause, but they cannot fire them on the basis of race, religion, sex or other prohibited factors.

Just where age fits in this list has long been unclear. It has been a kind of forgotten stepchild of the civil rights revolution. When the granddaddy of all employment-discrimination laws, Title VII of the Civil Rights Act of 1964, was adopted, there was general agreement on most of the categories. But Congress was uncertain what to do about age. The secretary of labor was asked to study age discrimination in employment and advise whether it should be covered. The secretary found that age discrimination was a real problem. At the time, about 50 percent of job listings were not open to applicants over 55, and 25 percent were closed off to those over 45. Relying on the report, Congress passed the Age Discrimination in Employment Act (A.D.E.A.).

Based on its language, which almost exactly tracks Title VII, older workers *should* be well protected. But it hasn't worked out that way. "The passage of the A.D.E.A. was the biggest victory," says Michael Lieder, a lawyer for the Allstate plaintiffs. "It's been downhill ever since."

It is almost always harder for older workers to win a bias claim than it is for the groups covered by Title VII. One of the biggest differences is the availability of an evidentiary theory known as "disparate impact." The Supreme Court has held since 1971 that plaintiffs suing under Title VII do not need to show that they were intentionally discriminated against (what the law calls "disparate treatment"); it is enough to show that a supposedly neutral policy disproportionately hurt a protected group. Once that is shown, the employer has the burden of showing that the challenged policy (a new kind of aptitude test, say, or a height requirement) is necessary for the job. Disparate impact is a powerful tool, since it is often hard for workers to prove intentional discrimination. Many of the biggest race- and sex-discrimination lawsuits could not have been won without it.

There is no reason that disparate impact shouldn't be available under the A.D.E.A., but many federal courts won't allow it. Even with intentional discrimination claims, older workers are worse off. Many judges just don't like age-discrimination lawsuits. One federal judge complained in a decision that older workers feel they can file age suits with no more evidence "than a birth certificate and a pink slip."

As a result, courts go to great lengths not to see age bias when it is obviously there. In case after case, judges excuse blatantly discriminatory comments as mere "stray remarks" and strain to find alternative reasons that older workers were fired. In one egregious case, a 56-year-old worker at a North Carolina company was fired. Two weeks before the firing, a supervisor said to him, "O'Connor, you are too damn old for this kind of work." This, a federal appeals court held, did not constitute sufficient evidence for discrimination.

Even when older workers make their case, courts are more willing to accept employers' defenses. Early in the civil rights era, it was established that a company cannot defend a race-discrimination claim by saying it acted for economic reasons. In the classic case, a restaurant that pleads "customer preference"—that it would happily hire black waitresses, but its racist customers would stop coming—still loses.

But in age cases, courts are all too willing to accept economic defenses. A company that says it laid off older workers because they were highly paid will often prevail. This can be a potent weapon for a company like Allstate, which can argue that when it pushed out all of those agents who were 40 or older, it was looking to get rid of expensive employees, not old ones.

There are many reasons that courts have been grudging about age claims. In part, judges do not see old people as a "discrete and insular minority," the classic legal formulation for a protected class. Blacks are separate and apart from the majority culture, the theory goes, but every family has old people in it, and anyone not currently in the class eventually will be. That logic ignores the fact that Congress established to its satisfaction 36 years ago that bias against older workers is real and pervasive—and passed the A.D.E.A. to do something about it.

Judges are also inclined to see pushing older workers out as part of the natural order, because they are less able, or to make room for the next generation. But stereotypes like these, about who is capable, or deserving, of employment are just what Congress was taking aim at with the A.D.E.A. There is no small contradiction in the fact that some of the worst age-discrimination law has come from Supreme Court justices, who serve for life. Lawyers for older workers have been reluctant to use the word "hypocrisy," but they have noted in their arguments that Justice Oliver Wendell Holmes stayed on the court into his 90's.

Advocates for older workers say, perhaps too hopefully, that the Supreme Court may be softening on age discrimination. They point, in particular, to a case from 2000 reinstating a jury verdict in favor of a Mississippi plumbing-products factory employee who was fired after his supervisor told him that he "must have come over on the Mayflower" and that he was "too damn old" for the job. Reversing a lower court, the Supreme Court unanimously held that the fired worker had put forth enough evidence to prove that his firing violated the A.D.E.A.

But also important, the E.E.O.C. recently signaled a willingness to challenge the court's stingy view of age discrimination. After the Supreme Court ruled in 2000 that individuals cannot sue state entities for damages under federal age-bias laws, the E.E.O.C. stepped in to represent 1,700 retired police officers, firefighters and other safety officers who charged the California Public Employees Retirement System with discriminating in benefits. In January, the retirement system agreed to pay $250 million—the largest settlement, for any kind of discrimination, in E.E.O.C. history.

Ron Harper and his fellow plaintiffs know they have their work cut out for them. If disparate impact were available to them, they would be off to a fast start. The ratio of terminated agents who were in the protected class—more than 90 percent—is enormous by the standards of discrimination law. Under disparate impact, the burden would shift to Allstate to explain what it was up to.

As things now stand, the plaintiffs will need to come up with more proof of intentional discrimination to show that Allstate was biased against its older workers. If they can make the legal claims work, the plaintiffs say, they believe they have the sort of human stories that will put Allstate on the defensive. There are certainly plenty of plaintiffs like Harper who have stayed with the company and are struggling to stay afloat. More than 2,500 have left, and many of them describe it as if they have been fired. Gene Romero, 54, a 13-year Allstate agent in Overland Park, Kan., sold his book of business and has been unemployed ever since. He has looked for work, but the job market is weak, he says, and he hasn't found anyone who "wants to hire an old man." Michael Wilson, a lawyer for the Allstate plaintiffs, says that his clients are suffering the usual fallout of involuntary job loss—depression, divorce, alcoholism and worse. "I've had people call me and say, 'I was sitting out in my backyard with a gun in my mouth,' " he says.

Even if they don't prevail on the age-discrimination claims, they may win—as often happens in these cases—on a related claim. With sentiment running strongly against large companies that leave their retired workers in the lurch, they may do well with their challenge to the take-it-or-leave-it release.

However things work out for the Allstate plaintiffs, the case could reshape the legal landscape for older workers. Given the nation's demographic trends—and the persistence in stereo-typed thinking about older people—there is every reason to believe that the age-bias complaints from television writers and teachers, bus mechanics and bankers will continue their explosive growth.

Now the law may have a chance to catch up. If the Allstate plaintiffs prevail, the case could give older workers their first true landmark case, with damage awards large enough to make corporate America recalculate the costs of discriminating.

Win or lose, advocates for older workers say, this case could be indispensable to the process of improving age-discrimination law—making it the equal of race, sex and religion. They have not given up, they say, on getting the courts to rethink the economic-defense excuse and their antipathy toward disparate impact. "We are not going to cower in front of these precedents," vows Laurie

McCann, a senior AARP lawyer. "We're going to chip away to show that they're wrong."

The Allstate plaintiffs—who were highly compensated and are overwhelmingly white and male—do not look like typical victims of an unjust order.

They also want Congress to get involved. It could amend the A.D.E.A. to bring age-discrimination rules in line with the more generous ones available under Title VII. This may seem like a uniquely inauspicious time to ask Congress to expand a civil rights law, particularly with the Republicans in control of both houses. But advocates for older workers point out that their constituents are one of the most potent voting blocs around. Politicians ignore older workers at their peril.

Harper is hoping that his dispute with Allstate rewrites the legal rules. Except for marrying his wife and rearing "two fine boys," he says, taking on Allstate is the most important thing he has ever done. "I'd be lying if I said we're not fighting for our-selves and our families," he says. "But every one of us knows that we're also carrying the ball for other people—people who will be hit by something like this in the future."

ADAM COHEN is a lawyer and a member of the editorial board of *The Times.*

Can You Interview for Integrity?

Yes, and you don't need a lie detector to do it.

WILLIAM C. BYHAM

After a thorough search for a new employee, one candidate has risen to the top, and he has the look of a winner. Impeccable résumé. Extensive relevant experience. Great interpersonal skills. Plenty of energy and enthusiasm. Great new ideas he's eager to set in motion.

So you hire him. And it turns out to be one of the biggest mistakes you've ever made.

That glowing individual, so impressive sitting across the conference-room table, lies to clients and misrepresents your products. He can't satisfactorily explain the irregularities in his expense reports. He backstabs co-workers and takes credit for work he didn't do. You have to let him go. But in his wake the questions remain: How were we so misled and so wrong? Why couldn't we have seen what kind of person we were *really* hiring?

Scenarios like this one are all too familiar, perhaps painfully so. But in light of the numerous examples of illegal and unethical behavior that have garnered headlines in recent months and years, managers are more interested than ever in making sure that they hire people, for positions at all organizational levels, who are trustworthy and share the organization's ethical values.

But despite their interest in doing a better job of hiring for honesty and integrity, too many managers continue to believe that their hands are tied. This is a mistake: They *can* screen for integrity and ethical behavior when selecting new employees. It might be as simple as doing background checks and checking references—steps that many organizations had tended to skip in recent years but are resurrecting. Then there is the often-overlooked yet substantial information on ethical behavior that managers can obtain during the interviewing process—by having properly trained interviewers seek examples of how candidates have handled ethical situations in the past, and by having everyone who interviews a candidate share, cross-check, and evaluate the information.

"Doesn't Everyone Do It?"

Some people are understandably skeptical that dishonest and unethical individuals can be ferreted out simply by asking them questions about their past behavior. After all, won't a dishonest or

unethical person just lie, anyway? Psychology suggests that the answer is no, they won't. People with low integrity tend to think that everybody else has the same degree or an even lower degree of integrity than they do; they readily admit to integrity lapses because they think that their behavior is normal and assume that the interviewer feels the same way.

I have seen this theory borne out many times in my own interviewing experiences and in those of others. On one occasion, I interviewed a prominent politician's administrative assistant who bragged about how she helped her boss pad his expense account. Another time, a candidate I interviewed for a sales position told me how he had obtained "gold status" on a major airline by taking needless flights—paid for out of his employer's travel budget.

Organizations must have leaders and associates who will share and live their ethical values.

The real key to effectively interviewing for integrity is seeking multiple examples of behaviors and asking probing follow-up questions that reveal the thinking behind the behaviors described. While integrity-focused questions need be only a small part of the total interview, any ethical issues that arise must be explored fully so that the examples can be accurately evaluated and the best hiring decision reached.

Timing Is Everything

It is important to incorporate integrity questions into an interview—and equally important to know when to ask those questions. Interviewers are wise to save sensitive ethical questions for late in the interview, after rapport has been developed. And, of course, as with all interview questions, once you have asked an ethical question, remember to listen and respond with empathy.

Empathy does not mean acceptance or agreement—it means understanding. You can be empathetic with a person who is telling you about an unethical behavior, without having to bend or sacrifice your own ethical standards, by reflecting the interviewee's feelings ("So you felt really good after the presentation," or "So you had second thoughts after the sales call"). And by showing empathy, you can keep the individual talking, providing other examples of behavior that will foster your understanding.

The recent bad behavior of high-profile executives has been nothing short of alarming. But it's an alarm that conscientious managers needed to hear—and to heed. Organizations must have leaders and associates who will share and live their ethical values, and extra care must be taken to ensure that these individuals are the ones who are brought into the organization—and promoted.

The Top 11

The first step in an interviewing process to screen for honesty and integrity is for interviewers to ask the right questions. These questions need to be geared toward gathering information on past behaviors that illustrate whether a candidate's own ethical values are compatible with those of the organization.

Following is a list of questions, any of which could be incorporated into an interview to elicit examples of a candidate's past ethical behavior and to reveal insights about the candidate's honesty and integrity. While I've included 11 questions, most interview situations will dictate using only two or three such questions to obtain examples of past ethical behavior.

I've also given examples of good and questionable answers that candidates might give to these questions. The "rightness" or the "wrongness" of the answers is up to the interviewer's judgment. As such, it's important to train interviewers to follow up answers with more questions to pin down behavior and the thinking behind the behavior, to ask for additional examples, and to have a systematic integration of data so that multiple interpretations of the answers can be obtained and discussed.

1. "We are often confronted with the dilemma of having to choose between what is right and what is best for the company. Give at least two examples of situations in which you faced this dilemma and how you handled them."

Good answer: Once, we discovered a technical defect in a product after it had been shipped and used by a client. The client did not notice the defect. We debated whether to tell the client and admit we had made a stupid error, or just let things go because the client seemed to be using the product with no problem. We decided to tell the client and replace the product at no cost.

Questionable answer: We discovered that our sales clerks were making errors in charging for certain combinations of products and that the errors were almost always in favor of the company. In no way were the clerks encouraged or trained to make these errors. We also learned that, with training, the errors could be eliminated, but the training would be fairly expensive. I decided not to institute the training.

2. "How would you describe the ethics of your company? In which areas do you feel comfortable and uncomfortable with them? Why?"

Good answer: My company is extremely ethical, and I've never, ever run into a situation in which I disagreed with a deci-

sion made because of ethics. In fact, we bend over backward in the treatment of our customers—such as taking back out-of-date products and providing free service past warranty, whenever there is any question about our products and services.

Questionable answer: I'm not sure what the ethics of our company are. People seem to do what's necessary to get the job done.

3. "Give me an example of an ethical decision you have had to make on the job. What factors did you consider in reaching this decision?"

Good answer: We had a customer return a large shipment. While technically it was in the second quarter, it would have been very easy to move the revenue hit to the third quarter. Including it in the second quarter meant that we would not meet sales expectations. To me, it was a matter of borrowing from Peter to pay Paul, and we probably wouldn't meet our expectations the next quarter. Anyway, I felt that it was better to take the bad results when you were supposed to, rather than cook the books.

Questionable answer: I've never really had to make a tough decision regarding ethics.

4. "Have you ever observed someone stretching the rules at work? What did you do about it?"

Good answer: One of my fellow executives took a company car to use for a weekend vacation. I spoke to him, and he agreed that it was not right and that he would not do it again.

Questionable answer: Everybody stretches the rules sometimes.

5. "Have you ever had to bend the rules or exaggerate a little bit when trying to make a sale?"

Good answer: My experience is that when salespeople misrepresent products and services, customers buy less from them. Having credibility with customers brings in better long-term sales. For example, when I was selling servers, we had a proprietary server and operating system. The client asked me why my machine was really worth the higher cost. I listed the advantages and disadvantages, which indicated for him that the cheaper solution would work. I lost that sale but came back to win a much larger sale six months later.

Questionable answer: Sometimes when selling to a doctor, the doctor will state that he's heard that one of my products is effective against a certain disease. I listen and nod my head and say, "Interesting." I don't correct him even though I know that the drug is not recommended for that purpose. I'm not saying that it *does* work the way he thinks it does; I'm just not disagreeing with the doctor. You can't give advice to physicians.

6. "Have you ever been in a situation in which you had to make something seem better than it really was?"

Good answer: That's a big temptation in the high-tech field, particularly with new products. Often you know that there are errors in the program and that there are going to be some problems—what do you do? I try to be as honest as I can and give people realistic expectations.

Questionable answer: Our product has a very long sales cycle, and very often when we come out with a new release, it's not really done. It's "vaporware." We talk about it and sell it as if it were really done, with the expectation that by the time we make the sale and the client gets ready to have it installed, it *will* be ready. Most of the time we meet the client's deadlines,

Why You Need to Read Between the Lines

While interviews can uncover examples of a candidate's past unethical behavior or his lack of integrity, employers also are wise to closely scrutinize résumés. Studies find that 40 to 60 percent of résumés contain meaningful errors, such as dramatically inflated education, experience, or employment history.

These statistics and examples are hard to ignore, and demand that employers examine résumés with greater care.

Short of doing a background check before you interview an individual, there is little you can do about errors on résumés until you get into the interview. Then there are two things you *can* do.

First, look for holes, obvious or not, in the candidate's employment record and ask about those omissions.

Second, assign at least one interviewer to do a thorough review of the person's work or education record, asking questions like, "How did you get the job?" "What did you do?" "Why did you leave?" and, "How did you leave?" All dates should be verified. Often at this point an interviewee admits that perhaps the way that he presented information in the résumé is misleading: He didn't really graduate—he just attended courses; his title was sales manager but he didn't manage anybody. Often such education/job reviews are "assigned" to someone from HR and are done over the phone as part of a screening process. The interviewer covers the areas in a friendly way—"I just want to be sure that we're clear on everything so we can set you up for success if you come in for one-to-one interviews."

Sometimes dates don't line up for good reasons. For example, a candidate could show the date he received his master's degree well into the time that his résumé would indicate that he was living in another town and had a full-time job. The reason may well be that the university awards degrees only at certain times but the candidate finished his coursework for his master's degree months or even a year earlier. You should go over the dates with him and offer the chance to explain these discrepancies. Don't take action on a discrepancy without giving the candidate an opportunity to explain it.

Ultimately, recruiters and hiring managers must judge for themselves how important a particular résumé error is. But certainly the intentional deletion of critical information or inclusion of misinformation is a telling sign about what kind of person the candidate really is.

—W.C.B.

---

but we've had some really embarrassing situations when we didn't.

7. "Tell me about an instance when you've had to go against company guidelines or procedures in order to get something done."

Good answer: Like any manager, I move budget money around in order to get projects done with the resources that I have been allocated—for example, by reassigning people. That's what managers are expected to do. You can't precisely follow detailed budget allocations that are made six or nine months in advance.

Questionable answer: My wife works for one of our suppliers, and I actually buy things from her. This is technically in violation of company rules, but it doesn't hurt anything, and, frankly, it's the best product.

8. "We've all done things that we regretted. Can you give me an example that falls into this category for you? How would you handle it differently today?"

Good answer: When I first took over my job, I let seven people go without a whole lot of knowledge about their skills and contributions. Later I found that three of them were actually outstanding employees who should not have been let go. My jumping to conclusions hurt them and the company's operations. It took us several years to replace their knowledge of our equipment.

Questionable answer: I've never regretted anything about business. It's a game. I play the game to win.

9. "Have you ever had anyone who worked for you do or say something that was misleading to the company or to a client? How did you handle it?"

Good answer: I had a salesperson misrepresent a feature of one of our products in a presentation made to a client. I knew that the feature was important to the client. I asked the salesperson to meet again with the client to correct the misrepresentation, and I made a follow-up phone call to ensure that the discussion occurred.

Questionable answer: I was part of a sales presentation by one of my best salespeople to a very, very big client. In the presentation, the salesperson absolutely misrepresented one of our product's features. It was an important misrepresentation because a competitor for that business had that feature. I sat through the rest of the meeting thinking about what to do but decided that I just couldn't let the misunderstanding stand. So after we left the presentation, I asked him to call the client and clarify the situation. I think he did, but I'm not sure.

10. "There are two philosophies about regulations and policies. One is that they are to be followed to the letter; the other is that they are just guidelines. What is your opinion?"

Good answer: Regulations and policies are made for important reasons. A regulation seems to me to be stronger, and I feel that I follow all regulations, such as getting reports in at a certain time and accounting for expenses in a certain way. Policies are a little bit more indefinite. They express more of a guideline and a philosophy. There are circumstances when you fall into the "gray area" when applying a policy. When I have had questions, I've checked with my boss.

Questionable answer: In order to get things done, you can't be held back by old-fashioned policies of your organization. You have to know what's right and do the right thing. You have

The Art of the Ego Boost

People don't want to look bad in an interview and will very naturally put their best foot forward. An effective interviewer makes the interviewee feel at ease in giving what potentially could be negative information about himself. The interviewer does this in three ways:

- Provide a rationale for talking about poor or unethical behavior prior to asking a question. For example, "Everyone in an organization breaks the rules sometime. Can you tell me about some times when you've broken the rules?" With the opening phrase, the interviewer is giving an excuse to the interviewee up-front to offer an example of negative behavior.
- Help the interviewee maintain self-esteem when the interviewee has offered a behavior about which she is embarrassed or uncertain (e.g., the interviewee admits she got in trouble for overstating a product's functionality). The interviewer should help the individual rationalize the behavior disclosed by saying something like, "We all make mistakes sometimes, and at least they provide an opportunity for learning" or, "That's a common mistake made by new people in sales." Such post-confession affirmation maintains self-esteem and keeps the individual talking and providing information that will help the evaluation of ethical behavior.
- Do not take notes on negative behaviors at the time the interviewee shares the information. If the interviewer begins to write on his notepad, it is doubtful that the candidate will continue to open up or give additional, meaningful examples. Rather, the interviewer should just remember the negative behavior and later on in the interview, when the subject is more positive, write down a few notes.

—W.C.B.

to have good ethics and make decisions based on those ethics. You may have to bend the rules sometimes.

11. "Have you ever felt guilty about receiving credit for work that was mostly completed by others? If so, how did you handle it?"

Good answer: I frequently encounter this situation. By nature of being the boss, I get the credit for many of the things that my people do. I try my best to redirect that credit to them. For example, I insist that everyone who works on a proposal has her name on that proposal. We have celebrations when we win a contract at which we particularly point out the contributions of various people.

Questionable answer: No, I've never felt guilty. The person at the top gets credit when things go well, and he gets the blame when things go poorly. It's the nature of the job.

Interviewers should gather multiple examples from each question by employing a simple follow-up query: "Can you give me another example?" This will tell the interviewer whether the dishonest or unethical behavior was a one-time event or if there is a pattern. Also, interviewees tend to be more truthful in later examples than they are in their first example, which may be more of a PR effort.

Finally, it is vitally important for the interviewer to pin down the circumstances of the behavior so that a fair evaluation can be made. Interviewers do this by seeking the situation or task in which the behavior occurred, the actions of the individual, and the results from that action. If an interviewer doesn't have all three of these elements, it's very easy to misinterpret the response.

A candidate might relate a story in which he had to "bend the rules" on what could be put on his expense account. At first blush, this might seem like a negative behavior, but when you fully understand the circumstances—for example, "There was an opportunity to obtain some critical competitive information" and the result "that a project launch was more successful"—a different interpretation might be appropriate.

For example, when I was working as an industrial/organizational psychologist at J.C. Penney, a professional acquaintance at Sears offered to share some information on his company's selection system for management trainees. He loved to eat and drink, so I took him out for a nice lunch with wine when I flew to Chicago to meet him. He gave me two suitcases of research reports that catapulted my work ahead. I didn't have to make the same mistakes that Sears had made. The meeting and lunch were certainly worth hundreds of thousands of dollars to J.C. Penney. However, my company had a very low expense cap for taking people to lunch and refused to reimburse any alcoholic beverages. With my boss's knowledge and approval, I covered the difference elsewhere on the expense form.

Once you have uncovered examples of questionable behavior, be sure to accurately report the candidate's response to the others who have interviewed the same candidate when you meet to compare notes and arrive at a hiring decision. By obtaining multiple perspectives, you can better understand the examples' importance and check your standards before arriving at a final decision. This sharing and open discussion is a crucial step, as ethical behavior is best evaluated by a consensus decision among several knowledgeable managers.

Yes, you can interview for honesty and integrity. What's more, it's critically important that you do.

WILLIAM C. BYHAM is president and CEO of Development Dimensions International Inc., an HR organization based in Pittsburgh. His last article was *"Bench Strength"* in February 2000.

From *Across the Board*, March/April 2004, pp. 35–38. Copyright © 2004 by William C. Byham. Reprinted by permission of the author.

Six Ways to Strengthen Staffing

A company's performance hinges on the quality of its people. And that means your staffing activities need to be in tip-top shape.

ADRIENNE HEDGER

You know the drill. There's an open job and you need to find an ideal candidate—someone with the perfect mix of talent, knowledge and personality. Someone who will exceed the company's expectations. Oh—and you need to find that person right away.

Make a mistake, and it could cost dearly. Indeed, experts place the cost of losing an employee at somewhere between 30 and 150 percent of the person's yearly salary.

Staffing has never been an easy endeavor—but over the next five years the playing field will become even more interesting and challenging. With a labor shortage, changing work preferences and the rapid evolution of online recruiting, the industry is entering an era unlike any other.

"The next few years will be dynamic," says Mike Lafayette, Director of Product Development for the Staffing business segment at Monster.com.

"There is no status quo," agrees Diane Shelgren, Executive Vice President of Strategy and Client Development at Veritude, which provides a range of strategic human resources services. "Companies that understand the changes will be able to attract the best talent."

What should you consider as you fine-tune your staffing strategies? Here are six areas of focus that leading companies will be addressing over the next year.

1: Get Better at Finding the Needle in the Haystack

Currently there are more than 52 million resumes sitting in the Monster.com database. And roughly 40,000 resumes are added every week. That's more than 280 added every hour, around the clock.

Meanwhile, profiles are constantly being created and updated on networking sites like LinkedIn, Plaxo, Jobster and Spoke.

All this is creating pathways to millions of potential employees—and while this certainly improves the odds of finding the right person, it can also lead to resume overload.

In response, companies are becoming more sophisticated about searching for qualified candidates. The Web site Zoominfo, for instance, extracts information from online sources including Web sites, press releases and electronic news services and bundles it in one report. Services such as W3 Data and Accurint also allow for targeted searches.

Advances in search technology are underway at sites like Monster.com as well. There, the company's SmartFind Resume Search helps employers and staffing companies quickly identify the most qualified applicants, reducing the number of resumes that need to be reviewed.

Meanwhile, companies are also working niche job sites into their recruiting strategies. In fact, media research firm Borrell and Associates predicts a "proliferation of specialized job sites" in 2007.

No matter which strategy-or combination of strategies-a company takes, the ability to conduct a fast, targeted search will be crucial in the years ahead.

2: Knock on New Doors to Find Talent

With a labor shortage inching closer and closer, more companies are investigating alternative talent sources, such as retirees or stay-at-home moms who want part-time work.

In fact, according to one survey by CareerBuilder.com, 20 percent of employers plan to rehire retirees from other companies or provide incentives so their own employees delay retirement.

At The RightThing, Inc., an end-to-end provider of recruitment process outsourcing, the staff knows firsthand that tapping into these talent sources can be good for business.

"We've built a culture that values flexible work schedules," says Jamie Minier, Vice President of The RightThing. "Our company routinely employs retirees and work-at-home moms as part-time staff, and we help our clients recruit from these unique groups as well."

In part because of this strategy The RightThing was named one of the "25 Best Small Companies to Work for in America" by the Great Place to Work Institute.

Similarly, Veritude has tapped into an alternative talent source—this one in India. The team in India searches online for qualified job candidates, then sends the names to the company's recruiters in the United States.

"When our recruiters arrive at work in the morning, they already have a list of people to contact," says Shelgren. "This speeds the entire process."

Alternative talent sources will only become more essential as the pool of available workers begins to drain. "At this point," adds Minier, "if you're not tapping into alternative talent sources or looking globally, you're not ahead of the game."

3: Embrace Flexibility

Tapping into alternative talent sources dovetails with another emerging trend: more flexibility.

Indeed, 19 percent of employers say they are "very" or "extremely" willing to provide more flexible work arrangements for employees, according to a survey by CareerBuilder.com.

Meanwhile, the American Staffing Association reports that people are looking for flexibility in their employment arrangements—and an increasing number of people are deciding to become temporary or contract workers instead of entering traditional employment contracts.

In fact, according to the association's 2006 staffing employee survey, two-thirds of respondents said flexible work time was an important factor in their decision to become a temporary or contract employee. And a recent report by Veritude predicts that independent and contract workers will make up 25 percent of the workforce in the next five years.

This rise in flexible arrangements is inspiring companies to design creative staffing solutions. Shelgren points to one example: "We're seeing an increase in an arrangement known as 'homeshoring,'" she says. "Basically, organizations are establishing technology that allows employees to conduct call center activities from home offices."

4: Get to (Really!) Know Your Candidates

Shelly Wheeler, Human Resources Director at Roche Diagnostics, remembers a recent close call in staffing.

"We had a candidate we thought was perfect for the job," she recalls. "But after he completed our assessment tool, we realized there were some gaps that we couldn't fill. Without the assessment data, we likely would have hired him."

Assessment tools have been around for a long time, but lately there has been an increase in the number of companies using them—and this upward trend is expected to continue.

In fact, according to a 2006 survey by Rocket-Hire, the number of companies using assessment tools to gauge personality measures hit 65 percent in 2006, up from 34 percent in 2005.

And 53 percent were using the tools to measure a candidate's "fit," up from 35 percent in 2005.

"One of the key benefits is that these tools allow you to look ahead," says Gary Schmidt, Ph.D. and President of Saville Consulting. The company provides an online assessment tool called The Wave that is used by Roche Diagnostics and others. "For example, instead of just talking to the candidate about their previous jobs, you can assess whether they have the talent, skills and motivation to do something they've never done before."

The key to finding a good assessment tool: "Look for one that is scientifically validated, customizable, Internet-based and easy to use," says Schmidt. "You also don't want it to be too long—30 to 40 minutes maximum is a good target."

Some assessment tools can even deliver benefits after the candidate is hired. "We continue to rely on The Wave assessment tool to develop and coach our employees," says Jim Messina, Vice President of Sales for Maritz Learning, a division of Maritz Inc. "It's been a great tool for us."

"It doesn't cost much to have that other check in the system," adds Wheeler. "And it can save you from hiring the wrong person."

Another similar trend underway: giving prospective employees a "test drive." From simulated job environments to company tours, companies like Veritude, The RightThing and others are incorporating creative strategies to make sure the employee/employer fit is just right.

"These strategies work," says Shelgren. "We recently used a simulated environment to help reduce turnover at a call center by 50 percent."

5: Think "Temp to Hire"

Assessment tools and trial runs are powerful, but some companies are going a step further and using "temp to hire" scenarios, where an employee starts on a temporary basis through a staffing company, then later gets hired.

One telling statistic: When the American Staffing Association surveyed current and former temporary and contract employees, it found that more than 53 percent of the survey participants who remained in the workforce had moved on to permanent jobs.

"These arrangements seem to be growing in popularity," says Steven Berchem, Vice President of the American Staffing Association. "It's a win for the candidate as well as the customer because it's a great way to determine if there actually is a good fit."

Some professionals see temporary work as a good way to get a foot in the door at highly sought-after companies. Indeed, companies like Veritude and The RightThing routinely place highly skilled workers in industries such as pharmaceuticals, advanced technology, product development and animation.

Still others prefer the flexibility and lifestyle that temporary and contract work provides.

Either way, this growing body of highly skilled and highly educated professionals is rapidly debunking the myth that only low-skilled workers or recent college graduates align themselves with staffing companies.

For their part, businesses are waking up to this fact and increasingly looking to staffing firms as a good source for talent—and potentially permanent employees.

"More businesses are using staffing strategically," confirms Berchem. "They are using temporary and contract workers to fill specific, targeted needs—projects that demand highly skilled workers."

"One way to look at it," says John Hennessy, Senior Vice President of the Staffing business segment at Monster.com, "is that there are roughly 145 million employed people in the U.S.—and 35 million are currently employed or have had a relationship with a staffing company during their career. That's a significant number."

Taking all this into account it makes sense that, according to the Bureau of Labor Statistics, the U.S. staffing industry will grow faster and add more jobs over the next decade than just about any other industry.

6: Consider the Outsourcing Option

As the staffing industry continues to change and evolve, employers will need to rely on new technologies, new strategies and new online tools to stay ahead. Some companies will manage this internally—but for others the answer will be outsourcing.

"We've definitely seen an increase in business over the past 12 months," says Minier at The RightThing. "And we expect this boom to continue over the next 18 to 24 months."

The advantages of outsourcing can be compelling. Many RPO vendors are equipped with the latest technology and have the broad, deep networks required to fill a large number of jobs—even highly specialized jobs—very quickly. Companies also find that an RPO strategy allows them to tap into a more diverse workforce, as well as outsource the labor-intensive work of tracking compliance.

"If a company does decide to outsource recruitment activities, it is essential to find a vendor that understands your culture," says Shelgren. "Ideally, the vendor will assign someone on site, so that person experiences the company the same way any employee would."

"Client expectations are very high in the RPO arena," adds Minier. "Companies want service providers who consistently deliver quality, use robust and unique strategies to find talent, and are highly reliable."

In response, RPO providers are stepping up their offerings to go beyond recruiting and deliver end-to-end talent management. "Our consulting practice at Veritude is growing rapidly," Shelgren notes.

Putting It All Together

A number of trends are reshaping the staffing world, but the industry's ultimate goal remains the same: find great employees as cost effectively and quickly as possible.

The challenge in the year ahead will be to stay on top of emerging trends and adapt staffing strategies in response. The staffing teams who get it right will secure the top talent, and will fuel their company's success.

"Selecting and hiring people is one of the most important skills a manager can have," says Jim Messina of Maritz. "If you pick the right person, that's 99 percent of the battle."

Shelgren agrees, adding, "The thing that ends up differentiating a company is the people. Every day they are a living embodiment of your brand, your values, and your culture. If you get the right ones, it's so powerful."

Balancing HR Systems with Employee Privacy

Breaches of employee data continue to make headlines and extra work for HR professionals at the organizations that have had problems. The growing reliance on systems for corporate functions including HR is one cause of the heightened risk, despite the many rewards that technology can provide.

How can your organization balance its needs for efficiency and productivity that HR systems can provide with its efforts to protect the privacy and security of employee information? A presentation at the IHRIM conference in Washington, D.C., helped shed light on the effectiveness of a joint approach by HR and HRIT working together. Carolyn Anker of the HR Data Privacy Office and Brenda Striggo, employee privacy architect in the Global Business Integration Project (GBIP; global SAP implementation and integration) at Eli Lilly and Company (Indianapolis), discussed this issue from both the HR and IT points of view.

They acknowledged that there is no perfect solution. "HRIT [HR information technology] versus privacy is a conundrum," Anker said. "HRIT is about accessibility, but privacy should be limited access on a need-to-know basis. How can the HR organization handle this?"

What's Causing the Conflict?

Anker explained some trends that are affecting the security of data, including:

- Multiple states/countries. In the U.S., there is no national law; information privacy is a state issue.
- More telecommuters and distance workers.
- More use of vendors and outsourcing.
- Enterprise resource planning.
- Demand for ease of use via email, downloads, and so forth.

There are privacy realities for all organizations, she said, including a more complex business and regulatory environment. Privacy law is growing and changing throughout the world, while state laws keep changing in the United States.

Eli Lilly has devoted resources to addressing the privacy versus technology challenge, in part because of a consent decree from the Federal Trade Commission in response to an e-mail accidentally sent to a list of Prozac users instead of a "bcc" message, Striggo acknowledged.

The company has been additionally challenged through the need to adapt its centralized SAP installation, which inadvertently set up violations of multinational privacy laws. The system is being adjusted so that it can adhere to local privacy requirements.

Another challenge has been adapting technology so that the company could obtain safe-harbor certification, which enables the use of data from European nations in the U.S.

From the technology side, there have been privacy challenges from the use of test data (personal information in an environment where development work is being conducted) in a production environment, Striggo noted. *A related issue:* A systems life cycle approach that includes the use of production data in test environments violates European laws. These challenges have meant that the Lilly HRIT team has had to address issues such as the effects of scrambling data within SAP.

All of these situations call for a coexistence of HRIT and HR privacy issues, noted Anker. "Practicality must be the reality" in finding a middle ground. Hard copies are risky, but e-records are even riskier if systems pre-date privacy issues (and so aren't designed to protect privacy). As a result, errors are often only "one click away." The solution to this latter problem was developed jointly by the HRIT and HR business team. A tool was used with rules to convert and scramble data, making the people anonymous in the development environment.

This is just one example of how joint efforts by both HR and HRIT personnel help address the conflict between privacy and technology. Eli Lilly has made this an official arrangement through its privacy audits initiative.

Privacy Audits

The company has a dedicated privacy audit team, with a regular schedule approved by its board. The audit looks at system privacy, including HR business process audits, site audits, and vendor audits. This process helps to identify new challenges and enables you to start work toward solving existing challenges. IT people are often "loaned" to the audit teams, since it is crucial to understand IT to perform the privacy audits. Other privacy issues that have to be considered are consumer and medical privacy, such as clinical trials.

HR privacy proves to be especially challenging, Anker noted. "HR privacy is the sleeping giant of HR issues," she said. "Everyone has employees, and employee data is everywhere.

People feel a lot freer and looser with HR data since it is inside the company."

Using the U.S. recruiting and staffing as an example, Anker and Striggo explained how the HR business process audit tracks where employee information goes within the system. Most personal information (more than 90%) enters the system through recruiting. The data then may move through manual processes and IT systems to vendors. Each destination for the information must be examined to make sure it is being protected and properly conveyed to the next place in the system.

Any findings that violate Eli Lilly's global privacy policy must be resolved via action plans, to which HR must commit with HRIT agreement on feasibility, budget, and timeline. HRIT can't commit to any actions unless the privacy office signs off.

The issue of privacy protection when information goes out to vendors can be another problem. "Vendors processing data on your behalf is a big risk," Striggo pointed out. "Relationships and communication are very important here." Requiring vendor protections through a certification process developed by the IT department is helping Eli Lilly with this issue.

"It's all about containing risk," Anker concluded. "The more people you can restrain from making a mistake, [the more you can] reduce risk."

Tomorrow's World

A new generation of HR software should provide the tools to pursue the holy grails of productivity, performance and governance. Is your system up to date?

CAROL GLOVER

With increasing focus on the measurement and evaluation of HR activities, technology is becoming the catalyst for changing how HR works.

Michael Howard, managing director of Frontier, says: "Self-service kiosks where staff can change their own data will grow across all sectors." In fact, Tony Price, senior sales executive at Snowdrop, says: "Over 60 percent of our new clients are implementing web-enabled solutions currently." There are clear advantages. Marketing manager at KCS, Nicola Smith, says: "Self-service removes the danger of Chinese whispers and data distortion by layers of bureaucracy as it streamlines processes."

Organisations are even investigating biometrics to measure attendance, although sceptics still see it as a "black art." For example, staff may be resistant to identification through iris reading, fearing it damages eyes, and no HR department is going to push a measure if there are safety concerns—however unfounded. But full facial recognition—similar to a photograph—may be on its way.

Management of system "evolution"—for example, keeping up with EU employment legislation—is important to clients in any sector. Frank Beechner, CEO of Vizual, says that new technology will enable multinational, multi-lingual firms to have consistent practices across continents.

James Bennett, head of Workforce Solutions Oracle UK, who has been in the HR software business since 1986, says that performance, productivity and governance have long been HR's "holy grails" but they've never before had the tools to make it happen. "Conversations with HR departments revolve around how software can help HR improve workforce performance, productivity, and governance leading to greater shareholder value," he says. "Technology gives HR the tools to measure workforce performance and ensure that it's consistent with law and best practice."

Christopher Berry, managing director of Computers in Personnel, says: "More demands are being put on HR by the business. This automatically extends to the question of systems security, as with increased use of Internet, intranets and wireless networks HR must be more IT and security savvy." HR will have to understand the technical capabilities to be able to justify "spend" to the board.

Wayne Carstensen, CEO of Arinso, believes that "people services manager" will replace the title HR manager. Arinso has confirmed a partnership contract with Shell for its SAPHR deployment. By the end of the year over two-thirds of Shell's 115,000 employees will be using the Shell People Services system that uses a single global HR IT solution across 45 countries. This is increasingly common for multinationals. Since 2001 Arinso has supported Shell in rolling out a global HR management system and 80 Arinso consultants are working with Shell HR teams in North America, Europe and Asia Pacific.

Tony Flannigan, marketing manager at ASR, says that the feel of self-service centres is important for buy-in. "For line managers and employees we've given our system an 'online banking' feel as it's not such an alien concept to people." Employee buy-in is crucial, agrees Snowdrop's Tony Price: "HR managers need to put the users first."

Eric Smart, CEO of Smart Human Logistics, says: "The Web has allowed attendance to be deployed in multi-site companies more effectively. This is a great leap forward for centralised control. This goes for manufacturing or retailers with many sites. As long as they have a PC and a phone point it's as if everyone is in the same building."

For example, police forces had to change how they measure ethnicity, but Cedar HR Software, which is a provider to a number of forces, could make one change to the system centrally and distribute it to all its customers, rather than having to repeat it 16 times. This dilutes the cost of system evolution or updating.

Insiders believe that the HR software market is ripe for consolidation. "We've seen several acquisitions to create economies of scale and this trend will probably continue over the next year," Flannigan says. HR outsourcing and software supplier Northgate Information Solutions plc is buying payroll software supplier Rebus HR Group in a reverse takeover bid, doubling its own size in the process.

Whatever the future of the market, this new generation of HR managers with HR software purchasing experience is clued up and ready to champion projects.

Learning Curve

The learning management systems (LMS) market is entering a new phase. While value for money used to be a concern, a new generation of market-savvy buyers has led to the growth in more cost-effective products.

Buyers of the first wave of LMS often challenged the value they gained from them, says Tim Drewitt, consultant at Balance Learning. "Organisations may have features that they never use and systems that are more costly to maintain than they envisaged. Now, when contracts are up for renewal, system providers are having to work harder to convince clients of the return on investment."

However, there is a shift in this trend and observers see the LMS market entering a new phase of maturity and adoption. Donald Clark, CEO of Epic, says: "We've always believed that LMSs shouldn't be regarded as essential to e-learning, although they can be useful for large corporates." The industry predicts than only a few LMS providers will survive. "LMSs became too big, expensive and hard to integrate and buyers were using only a fraction of their capabilities. Sociology always wins over technology—you can't make people use resources," Clark says.

Even so, the market is adapting. Matthew Borg, consultant and partner at Information Transfer, says: "We're seeing a trend towards providing extra learning resources through portals and the creation of knowledge or reference centres for ongoing learner support." Borg says clients want to integrate LMSs with existing HR systems such as self-service centres. This is important since line managers are now more involved in staff development and individuals are taking responsibility for self-learning. Web-based systems mean that people can access learning from home PCs.

One-stop-shops are the norm as customers demand service integration because implementation has been hard. Because of these problems some larger organisations have spent a large amount on getting made-to-measure LMSs, especially since past pricing policy has often been "per employee", regardless of whether they all used the system. We have witnessed an explosion in low-to-medium cost solutions.

Jamie Johnson, business manager at DeltaNet, says: "Customers prefer a bespoke approach to managing their learning." Partial LMSs are available if organisations only want certain features.

There has also been a growth in corporate use of virtual learning environments (VLEs), originally designed for the academic community, mainly as they are cheaper. VLEs mean you can get on the learning management ladder sooner. Organisations often do their own authoring and so want tools that are compatible with their LMS, making understanding the IT architecture and engaging the IT team essential.

From *People Management*, April 2004, pp. 65–70. Copyright © 2004 by Chartered Institute of Personnel and Development. Reproduced with permission of Chartered Institute of Personnel and Development.

UNIT 3

Creating a Productive Work Environment

Unit Selections

Key Points to Consider

- What are some things you might do to motivate employees, especially in a downsizing environment? What are some of the things that motivate you?

- In today's environment, do you think people should be viewed more as partners or as workers?

- What strategies could you employ to communicate more effectively with your peers or your instructor? What things can destroy effective communication? What role does correct communication play in projecting a desired image?

- Do you think feedback is important? In conversation? In your career?

- How would you deal with a bully in the workplace?

Student Web Site
www.mhcls.com/online

Internet References
Further information regarding these Web sites may be found in this book's preface or online.

American Society for Training and Development (ASTD)
http://www.astd.org
Commission on the Future of Worker-Management Relations
http://www.dol.gov/_sec/media/reports/dunlop/dunlop.htm
The Downsizing of America
http://www.nytimes.com/specials/downsize/glance.html
Employee Incentives and Career Development
http://www.snc.edu/socsci/chair/336/group1.htm

Whenever anything is being accomplished, it is being done, I have learned, by a monomaniac with a mission.

—Peter Drucker

For years, management theorists have indicated that the basic functions of management are to plan, direct, organize, control, and staff organizations. Unfortunately, those five words only tell what the manager is to do. They do not tell the manager how to do it. Being a truly effective manager involves more than just those five tasks. It involves knowing what goals to set for the organization, pursuing those goals with more desire and determination than anyone else in the organization, communicating the goals once they have been established, and having other members of the organization adopt those goals as their own.

Motivation is one of the easiest concepts to understand, yet one of the most difficult to implement. Often the difference between successful and mediocre organizations is that the usual 20 percent in successful organizations are motivated, and the other 80 percent are also motivated. They are excited about the company, about what they do for the company, and about the company's products or services. Effective organizations build upon past successes. All of the employees are performing at very high levels. If people feel good about themselves and good about their organization, then they are probably going to do a good job. Whether it is called morale, motivation, or enthusiasm, it still amounts to the same fragile concept—simple to understand, difficult to create and build, and very easy to destroy.

In order to maintain a motivated workforce for any task, it is necessary to establish an effective reward system. A truly motivated worker will respond much more effectively to a carrot than to a stick. Turned-on workers are having their needs met and are responding to the goals and objectives of the organization. They do an outstanding job because they want to, which results in an outstanding company.

Scholars have studied motivation for many years, attempting to determine what, exactly, motivates people and are continuing to do so as can be seen in "The Future of Work Motivation Theory."

Perhaps the single most important skill for any manager, or, for that matter, any human being, is the ability to communicate. People work on this skill throughout their education in courses such as English and speech. They attempt to improve communication through an array of methods and media, which range from the printed word, e-mail, and television, to rumors and

Manchan/Getty Images

simple conversation. Yet managers often do not do a very good job of communicating with their employees or their customers. This is very unfortunate, because ineffective communication can often negate all of the other successes that a firm has enjoyed. "Managing in the New Millennium: Interpersonal Skills," and "Managing Employee Relations," address this issue. This is something that a manager must strive for if you want to have people working together for a common goal. Managers, and the firms they represent, must honestly communicate their goals, as well as their instructions, to their employees. If the manager does not do so, the employees will be confused and even distrustful, because they will not understand the rationale behind their instructions. If the manager is successful in honestly communicating the company's goals, ideals and culture to the employees, and is able to build the motivation and enthusiasm that are necessary to successfully accomplish those goals, then he or she has become not just a manager, but a leader, and that is, indeed, rare.

Positive work environments are also work environments that are free of fear and intimidation. Bullying in the workplace is being recognized as a problem in the workplace, just as it is in the society. While some people may scoff at bullying as being a problem, they should be reminded that twenty years ago sexual harassment was also scoffed at as a problem too. Many lawsuits and millions if not billions of dollars later, nobody underestimates the importance or potential danger of sexual harassment in the workplace, and "Banishing Bullying," should be a top priority for any organization.

Creating a positive work environment is not easy. Communicating with and motivating people, whether employees, volunteers, citizens, or Boy Scouts, is difficult to do. Managers, however, are faced with the task of doing exactly that.

The Future of Work Motivation Theory
Introduction to Special Topic Forum

RICHARD M. STEERS, RICHARD T. MOWDAY, AND DEBRA L. SHAPIRO

The topic of employee motivation plays a central role in the field of management—both practically and theoretically. Managers see motivation as an integral part of the performance equation at all levels, while organizational researchers see it as a fundamental building block in the development of useful theories of effective management practice. Indeed, the topic of motivation permeates many of the subfields that compose the study of management, including leadership, teams, performance management, managerial ethics, decision making, and organizational change. It is not surprising, therefore, that this topic has received so much attention over the past several decades in both research journals and management periodicals.

Whereas several recent articles have examined how far we have come in researching work motivation, this special forum focuses on where we are going.[1] That is, we ask the questions: What is the future of work motivation theories? What are the critical questions that must be addressed if progress in the field is to be made? What is the future research agenda? How can we extend or modify current models of work motivation so they continue to be relevant in the future? And where are entirely new models of motivation needed to further our understanding of employee behavior and job performance in contemporary organizations?

To understand where the field is going, however, we must first understand where it has been. This introduction represents an overview of the field of work motivation from a theoretical standpoint and lays the foundation for the articles that follow.[2]

The term *motivation* derives from the Latin word for movement (*movere.*) Building on this concept, Atkinson defines motivation as "the contemporary (immediate) influence on direction, vigor, and persistence of action" (1964: 2), while Vroom defines it as "a process governing choice made by persons . . . among alternative forms of voluntary activity" (1964: 6). Campbell and Pritchard suggest that

> motivation has to do with a set of independent/dependent variable relationships that explain the direction, amplitude, and persistence of an individual's behavior, holding

constant the effects of aptitude, skill, and understanding of the task, and the constraints operating in the environment (1976: 63–130).

These and other definitions have three common denominators. They are all principally concerned with factors or events that energize, channel, and sustain human behavior over time. In various ways, contemporary theories of work motivation derive from efforts to explicate with increasing precision how these three factors interrelate to determine behavior in organizations.

Early Developments in Motivation Theory

The earliest approaches to understanding human motivation date from the time of the Greek philosophers and focus on the concept of hedonism as a principle driving force in behavior. Individuals were seen as focusing their efforts on seeking pleasure and avoiding pain. This principle was later refined and further developed in the works of philosophers like Locke, Bentham, Mill, and Helvetius, in the seventeenth and eighteenth centuries.

Toward the end of the nineteenth century, the issue of motivation began to migrate from the realm of philosophy to the newly emerging science of psychology. Challenges immediately arose over the use of hedonism as the basis for the study of motivation. As Vroom explains, hedonism had

> no clear-cut specification of the type of events that were pleasurable or painful, or even how these events could be determined for a particular individual; nor did it make clear how persons acquired their conceptions of ways of attaining pleasure or pain, or how the source of pleasure or pain might be modified by experience. In short, the hedonistic assumption has no empirical content and was untestable (1964: 10).

As a result, behavioral scientists began searching for more empirically based models to explain motivation.

Among these early models were instinct theories, such as those proposed by James, Freud, and McDougall. Instead of viewing behavior as highly rational, these theorists argued that much behavior resulted from instinct, defined by McDougall as

an inherited or innate psychological predisposition which determined its possessor to perceive, or pay attention to, objects of a certain class, to experience an emotional excitement of a particular quality upon perceiving such an object, and to act in regard to it in a particular manner (1908: 4).

James identified a list of such instincts that included locomotion, curiosity, sociability, fear, jealousy, and sympathy.

Beginning around the 1920s, however, as increased limitations of the theory began to emerge, instinct theories began to be replaced by models based on drive or reinforcement. Led by such psychologists as Thorndike, Woodworth, and Hull, drive theorists introduced the concept of learning in motivated behavior and posited that decisions concerning present or future behaviors are largely influenced by the consequences of rewards associated with past behavior. Allport (1954) referred to this as *hedonism of the past.* Past actions that led to positive outcomes would tend to be repeated, whereas past actions that led to negative outcomes would tend to diminish. Thorndike (1911) referred to this as the *law of effect,* while Hull (1943) suggested that effort or motivation was largely determined by *drive × habit.*

Skinner (1953) and others later built on these principles with the introduction of operant conditioning (referred to by some as *reinforcement theories*), arguing that, over time, individuals learn contingent relationships between actions and their consequences and that these contingencies guide future behavior. Reinforcement models continue to thrive today as explanatory vehicles for understanding work motivation and job performance, as well as in the workplace in various performance management programs (e.g., Komaki, 2003).

While psychologists were focusing on instincts and drives, managers were focusing on more pragmatic issues. A key development here was the work of Frederick Taylor and his colleagues in the scientific management movement. Coming from an industrial engineering background, Taylor (1911), along with many of his associates, focused his attention on the inefficiencies of factory production in an increasingly industrialized age. These colleagues proposed a new and paternalistic approach to managing workers that relied on a combination of job training, pay-for-performance incentive systems, improved employee selection techniques, and job redesign, including the introduction of ergonomics. Far from being exploitative in intent, Taylor and his associates saw scientific management as an economic boon to both workers and management through the use of improved manufacturing techniques, increased operating efficiency, and shared rewards. However, the subsequent rise of an increasingly sophisticated workforce, coupled with company efforts to maximize productivity without simultaneously increasing employee rewards, eventually served to discredit this system, leading to the widespread rise of unionization efforts in the 1930s.

Meanwhile, social scientists and managers began to consider the role of social influences on behavior in the 1930s. The role of group dynamics and the need to view employees as complex beings with multiple motivational influences were recognized as powerful influences on performance. Best noted among these research endeavors are Mayo's (1933) and Roethlisberger and Dickson's (1939) works. Bendix summarized the principle contribution of this human relations movement by observing that the "failure to treat workers as human beings came to be regarded as the cause of low morale, poor craftsmanship, unresponsiveness, and confusion" (1956: 294). McGregor (1960) later built on this in his classic early work, *The Human Side of Enterprise.*

By the 1950s, several new models of work motivation emerged, which collectively have been referred to as *content theories,* since their principal aim was to identify factors associated with motivation. Included here is Maslow's (1954) need hierarchy theory, which suggests that, as individuals develop, they work their way up a hierarchy based on the fulfillment of a series of prioritized needs, including physiological, safety and security, belongingness, esteem, and self-actualization. Maslow argued that the first three needs on the list represent deficiency needs that people must master before they can develop into a healthy personality, while the last two represent growth needs that relate to individual achievement and the development of human potential. Alderfer (1972) later adapted this model to encompass just three needs: existence, relatedness, and growth.

A second need theory of the same era, first introduced by Murray (1938) but more fully developed by McClelland (1961, 1971), ignored the concept of a hierarchy and focused instead on the motivational potency of an array of distinct and clearly defined needs, including achievement, affiliation, power, and autonomy. McClelland argued that, at any given time, individuals possess several often competing needs that serve to motivate behavior when activated. This contrasts with Maslow's notion of a steady progression over time up a hypothetical hierarchy as individuals grow and mature. By far, most of the attention in McClelland's model focused on the needs for achievement (defined as behavior directed toward competition with a standard of excellence) and power (defined as a need to have control over one's environment). McClelland's conceptualization offered researchers a set of clearly defined needs as they related to workplace behavior, in contrast to Maslow's more abstract conceptualizations (e.g., need for achievement versus need for self-actualization) and, thus, has found considerable popularity in research on individual factors relating to work motivation.

While Maslow and McClelland and their colleagues focused on the role of individual differences in motivation, Herzberg (1966; Herzberg, Mausner, & Snyderman, 1959) sought to understand how work activities and the nature of one's job influence motivation and performance. In his motivation-hygiene theory, Herzberg argued that work motivation is largely influenced by the extent to which a job is intrinsically challenging and provides opportunities for recognition and reinforcement. Herzberg saw the context surrounding a job (which he referred to as *hygiene* factors) as being far more temporal in terms of leading to satisfaction and future motivation. Herzberg deserves credit for introducing the field to the role of job design—specifically, job enrichment—as a key factor in work motivation and job attitudes. In subsequent work, Hackman and Oldham (1976) and others have extended this line of research as it relates to work design, motivation, and job performance, while others, including Deci (1975; Ryan & Deci, 2000), have articulated theories focusing specifically on task-based intrinsic versus extrinsic factors in motivation (e.g., self-determination theory).

The "Golden Age" of Work Motivation Theories

Beginning in the mid 1960s, a new approach to the study of work motivation emerged, which focused on delineating the processes underlying work motivation. Process theories contrast sharply with the earlier content theories, which focused on identifying factors associated with motivation in a relatively static environment. Process theorists view work motivation from a dynamic perspective and look for causal relationships across time and events as they relate to human behavior in the workplace.

Central to the process theory genre is a series of cognitive theories of motivation that collectively attempt to understand the thought processes that people go through in determining how to behave in the workplace. In our view, the theories generated during the late 1960s and early 1970s make this period something of a "golden age" of work motivation theories. Never before and, some would argue, never since has so much progress been made in explicating the etiology of work motivation.

Perhaps best known of the cognitive theories is expectancy (or expectancy-valence) theory. Expectancy theory derives from the early work of Lewin (1938) and Tolman (1959), who saw behavior as purposeful, goal directed, and largely based on conscious intentions. Vroom (1964) presented the first systematic formulation of expectancy theory as it related to the workplace. He argued that employees tend to rationally evaluate various on-the-job work behaviors (e.g., working harder) and then choose those behaviors they believe will lead to their most valued work-related rewards and outcomes (e.g., a promotion). Thus, the attractiveness of a particular task and the energy invested in it will depend a great deal on the extent to which the employee believes its accomplishment will lead to valued outcomes.

Porter and Lawler (1968) expanded Vroom's initial work to recognize the role of individual differences (e.g., employee abilities and skills) and role clarity in linking job effort to actual job performance. Porter and Lawler also clarified the relationship between performance and subsequent satisfaction, arguing that this relationship is mediated by the extent and quality of the rewards employees receive in exchange for good job performance. Finally, Porter and Lawler incorporated a feedback loop to recognize learning by employees about past relationships. That is, if superior performance in the past failed to lead to superior rewards, future employee effort may suffer as incentives and the reward system lose credibility in the employee's eyes.

Since its initial publication, a number of scholars have worked to extend or further refine the basic cognitive expectancy framework to reflect emerging research findings and new theoretical developments (e.g., Kanfer, 1990; Mitchell, 1997). For example, expectancy theory has been used to study forms of work behavior other than job performance, including employee absenteeism, turnover, and organizational citizenship behavior (Mobley, 1977; Mowday, Porter, & Steers, 1982; Organ, 1988; Porter & Steers, 1973; Steers & Rhodes, 1978). Researchers have also linked group expectations and social influences to individual work motivation decisions (Porter, Lawler, & Hackman, 1975). Finally, basic expectancy principles have been incorporated into several emerging models of cross-cultural influences on work motivation and job performance (Bhagat & McQuaid, 1982; Earley, 1997; Steers & Sanchez-Runde, 2001; Triandis, 1995).

In addition to expectancy theory, a number of other important cognitive theories of work motivation have been developed since the 1960s, each with its own focus. Adams (1963), for example, introduced equity theory to explain how employees respond both cognitively and behaviorally to perceived unfairness in the workplace (see also Mowday & Colwell, 2003, and Weick, Bougon, & Maruyama, 1976). Adams argued that both conditions of underpayment and overpayment can influence subsequent behavior. Recent work on procedural and distributive justice further develops this area using the fundamental concept of equity and its consequences (Cropanzano & Rupp, 2003; Folger, 1986; Greenberg, 1993; Sweeney & McFarlin, 1993).

Goal-setting theory also emerged in the late 1960s, as researchers began to discover that the simple act of specifying targets for behavior enhanced task performance (Locke, 1968, 1996; Steers & Porter, 1974). Research in this arena showed that goal specificity, goal difficulty, and goal commitment each served to enhance task performance. Based on numerous empirical studies, Locke and Latham (1990) subsequently proposed a formal theory of goal setting. Earley and Erez (1991) later added a time dimension to this topic by examining the role of cognitive processing on motivation, while Crown and Rosse (1995) examined the role of group goals, in addition to individual goals, on performance. Applications of goal-setting theory in the form of individual and team management-by-objectives programs are now used widely throughout industry (Ambrose & Kulik, 1999).

Finally, this period saw significant developments focusing on the role of social cognition and self-efficacy on behavior and performance by such leading researchers as Bandura (1977a,b, 1997). Bandura proposed a social cognitive theory, suggesting that self-confidence lies at the heart of an individual's incentive to act or to be proactive. Indeed, after a major review of the research literature on social cognition and self-efficacy,

Stajkovic and Luthans (1998, 2003) found considerable support for the role of self-efficacy in determining workrelated performance, particularly as moderated by task complexity and locus of control. Based on this research, Luthans (2001) has proposed extending this concept into the workplace through a model labeled *positive organizational behavior.*

Recent Developments in Work Motivation

Many of the ideas emerging from the 1960s and 1970s have subsequently been extended and further developed to reflect an expanded pool of research findings and more sophisticated research methods. Indeed, the 1980s witnessed a series of refinements and extensions of existing theories. For example, researchers made great strides in conceptual developments and empirical work focusing on social learning theory, as they did in new work focusing on goal-setting theory, job design, reward systems, punishment, procedural justice, innovation and creativity, and cross-cultural influences on work behavior.

However, by the 1990s, intellectual interest in work motivation *theory*—at least as measured by journal publications—seemed to decline precipitously. As evidence of this, consider the number of theoretical (as opposed to empirical) articles published in leading behavioral science journals over the past decade (e.g., see Ambrose & Kulik, 1999, or Mitchell & Daniels, 2002). You will find few articles that focus on genuine theoretical developments in this area. Instead, you will see minor extensions, empirical tests, or applications of existing theories. While clearly helpful, this hardly leads to breakthrough developments in our understanding of the principles underlying work motivation. At the same time, a review of the most recent editions of textbooks in the field of management and organizational behavior reveals that most of the theories discussed date from the 1960s and 1970s, with only fleeting references to more recent work. (It is also curious that some early motivation theories that have subsequently been widely discredited continue to permeate such texts.) In short, while other fields of management research (e.g., leadership, decision making, negotiations, groups and teams, and organization design) continue to develop conceptually, substantive theoretical developments focusing on work motivation have not kept pace.

An outside observer might conclude from this situation that either we have lost interest in the subject of work motivation (perhaps because it is no longer a pressing issue in organizations) or that we solved the work motivation problem long ago, thereby eliminating the need for additional work. Neither of these conclusions seems very plausible. On the contrary, in the new economy, replete with its dot.coms, e-commerce, and increased globalization (as well as the more traditional manufacturing and service firms), a motivated workforce is frequently cited as a hallmark of competitive advantage. Indeed, MIT economist Lester Thurow (1992) observed over a decade ago that successful companies (and countries) will compete in the future based principally on the quality of both their technology and their human resources. A motivated workforce becomes a critical strategic asset in such competition.[3] Why, then, has there been so little intellectual activity focusing on this important topic? Perhaps we have yet to develop the breakthrough ideas that can push us to the next level of understanding.

While theoretical developments on work motivation may have declined in recent years, the world of work has changed dramatically. Indeed, one can argue that the past decade has witnessed greater workplace changes than any other decade in memory. Companies are both downsizing and expanding (often at the same time, in different divisions or levels of the hierarchy). The workforce is characterized by increased diversity with highly divergent needs and demands. Information technology has frequently changed both the manner and location of work activities. New organizational forms (such as those found in e-commerce) are now commonplace. Teams are redefining the notion of hierarchy, as well as traditional power distributions. The use of contingent workers is on the rise. Managing knowledge workers continues to perplex experienced managers across divergent industries. And globalization and the challenges of managing across borders are now the norm instead of the exception.

These changes can have a profound influence on how companies attempt to attract, retain, and motivate their employees. Yet we lack new models capable of guiding managerial behavior in this new era of work. As Cappelli notes, "Most observers of the corporate world believe that the traditional relationship between employer and employee is gone, but there is little understanding of why it ended and even less about what is replacing that relationship" (1999: 1). We believe that the time has come to redirect our intellectual energies into discovering new models—and research toward new models—of work motivation and job performance commensurate with this new era.

References

Adams, S. J. 1963. Towards an understanding of inequity. *Journal of Abnormal and Social Psychology,* 67: 422–436.

Alderfer, C. P. 1972. *Existence, relatedness, and growth.* New York: Free Press.

Allport, G. W. 1954. The historical background of modern psychology. In G. Lindzey (Ed.), *Handbook of social psychology.* Cambridge, MA: Addison-Wesley.

Ambrose, M. L., & Kulik, C. T. 1999. Old friends, new faces: Motivation research in the 1990s. *Journal of Management,* 25: 231–292.

Atkinson, J. W. 1964. *Introduction to motivation.* Princeton, NJ: Van Nostrand.

Bandura, A. 1977a. Self-efficacy: Toward a unifying theory of behavioral change. *Psychological Review,* 84: 191–215.

Bandura, A. 1977b. *Social learning theory.* Englewood Cliffs, NJ: Prentice-Hall.

Bandura, A. 1997. *Self-efficacy: The exercise of control.* New York: Freeman.

Bendix, R. 1956. *Work and authority in industry.* New York: Wiley.

Bhagat, R. S., & McQuaid, S. J. 1982. Role of subjective culture in organizations: A review and directions for future research. *Journal of Applied Psychology,* 67: 653–685.

Campbell, J. P., & Pritchard, R. D. 1976. Motivation theory in industrial and organizational psychology. In M. D. Dunnette

(Ed.), *Handbook of industrial and organizational psychology:* 63–130. Chicago: Rand McNally.

Cappelli, P. 1999. *The new deal at work.* Boston: Harvard Business School Press.

Cropanzano, R., & Rupp, D. E. 2003. An overview of organizational justice: Implications for work motivation. In L. W. Porter, G. A. Bigley, & R. M. Steers (Eds.), *Motivation and work behavior* (7th ed.): 82–95. Burr Ridge, IL: Irwin/ McGraw-Hill.

Crown, D. F., & Rosse, J. G. 1995. Yours, mine and ours: Facilitating group productivity through the integration of individual and group goals. *Organizational Behavior and Human Decision Processes,* 64: 138–150.

Deci, E. L. 1975. *Intrinsic motivation.* New York: Plenum.

Earley, P. C. 1997. *Face, harmony, and social structure: An analysis of organizational behavior across cultures.* New York: Oxford University Press.

Earley, P. C., & Erez, M. 1991. Time dependency effects of goals and norms: The role of cognitive processing on motivational models. *Journal of Applied Psychology,* 76: 717–727.

Folger, R. 1986. Rethinking equity theory: A referent cognitions model. In H. W. Beirhoff, R. L. Cohen, & J. Greenberg (Eds.), *Justice in social relations:* 145–162. New York: Plenum.

Greenberg, J. 1993. The social side of fairness: Interpersonal and informational classes or organizational justice. In R. Cropanzano (Ed.), *Justice in the workplace: Approaching fairness in human resources management:* 79–103. Hillsdale, NJ: Lawrence Erlbaum Associates.

Hackman, J. R., & Oldham, G. R. 1976. Motivation through the design of work: Test of a theory. *Organizational Behavior and Human Performance,* 16: 250–279.

Herzberg, F. 1966. *Work and the nature of man.* Cleveland: World Publishing.

Herzberg, F., Mausner, B., & Snyderman, B. 1959. *The motivation to work.* New York: Wiley.

Hull, C. L. 1943. *Principles of behavior.* New York: Appleton-Century-Crofts.

Kanfer, R. 1990. Motivation theory and industrial and organizational psychology. In M. D. Dunnette & L. D. Hough (Eds.), *Handbook of industrial and organizational psychology:* 75–170. Palo Alto, CA: Consulting Psychologists Press.

Komaki, J. 2003. Reinforcement theory at work: Enhancing and explaining what employees do. In L. W. Porter, G. A. Bigley, & R. M. Steers (Eds.), *Motivation and work behavior* (7th ed.): 95–113. Burr Ridge, IL: Irwin/McGraw-Hill.

Lewin, K. 1938. *The conceptual representation and the measurement of psychological forces.* Durham, NC: Duke University Press.

Locke, E. A. 1968. Towards a theory of task motivation and incentives. *Organizational Behavior and Human Performance,* 3: 157–189.

Locke, E. A. 1996. Motivation through conscious goal setting. *Applied and Preventive Psychology,* 5: 117–124.

Locke, E. A., & Latham, G. P. 1990. *A theory of goal setting and task performance.* Englewood Cliffs, NJ: Prentice-Hall.

Luthans, F. 2001. The case for positive organizational behavior. *Current Issues in Management:* 1(1): 10–21.

Maslow, A. H. 1954. *Motivation and personality.* New York: Harper & Row.

Mayo, E. 1933. *The human problems of an industrial civilization.* New York: Macmillan.

McClelland, D. C. 1961. *The achieving society.* Princeton, NJ: Van Nostrand.

McClelland, D. C. 1971. *Assessing human motivation.* New York: General Learning Press.

McDougall, W. 1908. *An introduction to social psychology.* London: Methuen.

McGregor, D. 1960. *The human side of enterprise.* New York: McGraw-Hill.

Mitchell, T. R. 1997. Matching motivational strategies with organizational contexts. *Research in Organizational Behavior,* 19: 57–94.

Mitchell, T. R., & Daniels, D. 2002. Motivation. In W. Borman, D. Ilgen, & R. Klimoski (Eds.), *Comprehensive handbook of psychology. Volume 12: Industrial and organizational psychology:* 225–254. New York: Wiley.

Mobley, W. H. 1977. Intermediate linkages in the relationship between job satisfaction and employee turnover. *Journal of Applied Psychology,* 62: 237–240.

Mowday, R. T., & Colwell, K. A. 2003. Employee reactions to unfair outcomes in the workplace: The contributions of Adams' equity theory to understanding work motivation. In L. W. Porter, G. A. Bigley, & R. M. Steers (Eds.), *Motivation and work behavior* (7th ed.): 65–82. Burr Ridge, IL: Irwin/McGraw-Hill.

Mowday, R. T., Porter, L. W., & Steers, R. M. 1982. *Employee organization linkages: The psychology of commitment, absenteeism, and turnover.* New York: Academic Press.

Murray, H. A. 1938. *Exploration in personality.* New York: Oxford University Press.

Organ, D. W. 1988. *Organizational citizenship behavior: The good soldier syndrome.* Lexington, MA: Lexington Books.

Pinder, C. 1998. *Work motivation in organizational behavior.* Upper Saddle River, NJ: Prentice-Hall.

Porter, L. W., Bigley, G. A., & Steers, R. M. 2003. *Motivation and work behavior* (7th ed.): Burr Ridge, IL: Irwin/McGraw-Hill.

Porter, L. W., & Lawler, E. E. 1968. *Managerial attitudes and performance.* Homewood, IL: Irwin.

Porter, L. W., Lawler, E. E., & Hackman, J. R. 1975. *Behavior in organizations.* New York: McGraw-Hill.

Porter, L. W., & Steers, R. M. 1973. Organizational, work, and personal factors in employee turnover and absenteeism. *Psychological Bulletin,* 80: 151–176.

Roethlisberger, F., & Dickson, W. J. 1939. *Management and the worker.* Cambridge, MA: Harvard University Press.

Ryan, R. M., & Deci, E. L. 2000. Self-determination theory and the facilitation of intrinsic motivation, social development, and well-being. *American Psychologist,* 55: 68–78.

Skinner, B. F. 1953. *Science and human behavior.* New York: Macmillan.

Stajkovic, A. D., & Luthans, F. 1998. Self-efficacy and work-related performance: A meta-analysis. Psychological Bulletin, 124: 240–261.

Stajkovic, A. D., & Luthans, F. 2003. Social cognitive theory and self-efficacy: Implications for motivation theory and practice. In L. W. Porter, G. A. Bigley, & R. M. Steers (Eds.), *Motivation and work behavior* (7th ed.): 126–140. Burr Ridge, IL: Irwin/McGraw-Hill.

Steers, R. M., & Porter, L. W. 1974. The role of task-goal attributes in employee performance. *Psychological Bulletin,* 81: 434–452.

Steers, R. M., & Rhodes, S. R. 1978. Major influences on employee attendance: A process model. *Journal of Applied Psychology,* 63: 391–407.

Steers, R. M., & Sanchez-Runde, C. 2001. Culture, motivation, and work behavior. In M. Gannon & K. Newman (Eds.), *Handbook of cross-cultural management:* 190–215. London: Blackwell.

Sweeney, P. D., & McFarlin, D. B. 1993. Workers' evaluations of the "ends" and "means": An examination of four models of distributive and procedural justice. *Organizational Behavior and Human Decision Processes,* 53: 23–40.

Taylor, F. 1911. *Scientific management.* New York: Harper.

Thorndike, E. L. 1911. *Animal intelligence.* New York: Macmillan.

Thurow, L. 1992. *Head to head: The coming economic battle among Japan, Europe, and America.* New York: Morrow.

Tolman, E. C. 1959. Principle of purposive behavior. In S. Koch (Ed.), *Psychology: A study of science,* vol. 2: 239–261. New York: McGraw-Hill.

Triandis, H. C. 1995. Motivation and achievement in collectivist and individualistic cultures. In M. Maehr & P. Pintrich (Eds.), *Advances in motivation and achievement,* vol. 9: 1–30. Greenwich, CT: JAI Press.

Vroom, V. H. 1964. *Work and motivation.* New York: Wiley.

Weick, K. E., Bougon, M. G., & Maruyama, G. 1976. The equity context. *Organizational Behavior and Human Performance,* 15: 32–65.

Notes

We are indebted to the staff of *AMR* and to the editorial panel for their time and effort on behalf of this special forum.

1. For recent reviews of the research literature on work motivation, see Kanfer (1990), Mitchell (1997), Ambrose and Kulik (1999), and Mitchell and Daniels (2002).

2. For a more detailed examination of the evolution of work motivation theories, see Pinder (1998) and Porter, Bigley, and Steers (2003).

3. See a special issue of *Harvard Business Review* (January 2003) focusing on the importance of employee motivation as a key strategic asset in competition and corporate performance.

RICHARD M. STEERS is the Kazumitsu Shiomi Professor of Management in the Lundquist College of Business, University of Oregon. He received his PhD from the University of California at Irvine. His current research focuses on employee motivation and cross-cultural management. **RICHARD T. MOWDAY** is the Gerald B. Bashaw Professor of Management in the Lundquist College of Business, University of Oregon. He received his PhD from the University of California at Irvine and focuses his teaching and research on leadership in organizations. **DEBRA L. SHAPIRO,** formerly the Willard Graham Distinguished Professor of Management at UNC–Chapel Hill, is now professor of management and organization in the R. H. Smith School of Business, University of Maryland at College Park, and a member of the Academy of Management's Board of Governors. She received her PhD from Northwestern University. Her research focuses on issues regarding how to manage conflict in organizations that tend to motivate unproductive employee behaviors and the cross-cultural challenges of managing conflict effectively.

Managing in the New Millennium: Interpersonal Skills

Patricia M. Buhler

Management is defined as "getting things done through others." Without strong interpersonal skills, then, it is not possible to be a successful manager. Interacting with others is an essential building block of management effectiveness. Unfortunately, few management development courses specifically address how to interact with others. Instead, the majority of these programs focus on the technical skills of management—addressing such skills as how to engage in strategic planning, how to structure organizations, or how to manage a budget. The development of interpersonal skills is often left to the individual.

What were traditionally labeled "soft skills" in the past, have now been identified as the "hard" skills in today's business environment. One of these skills is interpersonal skills. Nearly every aspect of business—and management in particular—requires an ability to interact effectively with others. Organizations themselves are collections of people. Teams are utilized more extensively today than ever before. Without finely developed people skills, then, a manager's performance and ability to be successful is substantially hindered.

A variety of research studies have emphasized the importance of these interpersonal skills. Katz's research on managerial competencies identified three key skills important to success. These are technical, human, and conceptual skills. The technical skills involve performing the actual work of the organization. The human skills are the interpersonal skills and the conceptual skills involve the ability to see the "big picture." While these three skills are important at all management levels, the technical skills become less important as one moves up the organizational hierarchy (and further away from the operations employees). The conceptual skills, in contrast, become more important. And according to Katz, the human skills are identified as equally important throughout the management ranks.

Managers can enhance their interpersonal skills by addressing several key components. They can develop their emotional intelligence, learn to recognize the uniqueness of each employee, acknowledge the impact of the details (and the "small stuff"), learn to listen, empower others, and build trust.

Emotional Intelligence

The business literature in the last decade has focused on the need for emotional intelligence in the workplace—moving beyond the importance of one's general intelligence. Daniel Goleman, founder of Emotional Intelligence Services, has suggested "the people who will become the leaders, the people who will become the star performers, are the ones who have the strength in the key emotional intelligence abilities." Effective relationships can be better built with emotionally intelligent employees. The probability of developing effective relationships increases as individuals are more aware of their own emotions and can read the emotions of others since emotions are not checked at the door as employees go to work.

Emotional intelligence (identified by the acronym EI) requires first mastering capabilities in self-awareness. Recognizing one's own emotions is the foundation for later understanding others. The second component is self-regulation. Once people are aware of their emotions, they must then learn to manage those emotions and the conditions that elicit their emotional responses. Those two components are then used to self-motivate and understand the role of emotions in performing at high levels. The fourth component is empathy. This involves "walking in another's shoes" so to speak and understanding their perspective and their feelings. Finally, these prior components enable individuals to develop effective relationships.

Recognizing the Uniqueness of Each Employee

While it is often easier to take the approach of "one size fits all," when it comes to people it simply does not work in today's diverse workplace. To build more effective relationships, each individual must be treated as the unique individual they are. This requires investing time in getting to know each employee and coworker.

Identifying what drives the behavior of others enables the astute manager to better interact with them. Getting out of the office helps to gain an understanding of others and ultimately how to better interact with them.

Getting to know others involves people at all levels in the organization. While sometimes ignored or overlooked, building effective interpersonal relationships includes managing upward in the organization. It is each manager's responsibility to manage relationships in all three directions—downward, laterally, and upward. Too often, managers assume that the only relationship they need to manage involves their employees.

The Small Stuff Is the Big Stuff

Remembering the details is critical in developing interpersonal skills. A failure to "sweat the small stuff" can actually be a mistake. It is, indeed, the small stuff that can make a big difference to employees. For example, when delivering rewards, the small ideas can often generate the biggest payoff. A simple hand-written thank you note to an employee or a peer can reap big benefits and mean a lot to the recipient.

Too often, managers take the easy way out by using budget constraints to explain why they can not reward employees. It takes more thought and more creativity to design a reward program based on individuals and their uniqueness. This does, however, depend upon the recognition or the uniqueness of each employee.

Learn to Listen

Listening continues to be a lost art. People tend to be better talkers than listeners. This may occur, in part, due to the fact that many consider listening to be a passive activity instead of approaching it as an active process with sincere involvement and participation. The keys to active listening involve hearing not just the words that are spoken, but listening to the feelings and then responding to those feelings.

When listening, it is critical to watch and observe the nonverbal cues. Volumes are communicated nonverbally. The words actually spoken are the smallest part of the communication. To actively listen and receive the full message intended by the sender, the nonverbal components must be read. Body language or tone of voice can drastically change the real meaning of the words actually spoken.

In most cases, people who are not actively engaged in talking are spending their time thinking about what they are going to say next rather than listening. When really listening, people learn more and "plug into" others. Covey's advice in his best selling book, *The 7 Habits of Highly Effective People,* is worth noting. "Seek first to understand and then to be understood." When managers engage in active listening and attempt to understand the perceptions of others, they are generally more effective in building effective relationships.

Empowering Others

Organizations give a great deal of lip service to empowering their workforce. Some may think if they delegate the distasteful tasks to employees that they are empowering them. It is much more, however. Those managers who truly empower others build effective relationships. But this is hard work requiring courageous personalities who trust others. To empower a workforce requires courage to give up power. It also involves rethinking the traditional perspective of power. Today's mindset that supports empowerment suggests that power be more evenly distributed throughout the organization. This also supports participative management.

While empowering others can be highly effective, it only works if others have the knowledge, skills, and abilities to be able to perform. This means that managers must invest in others—and their development. In a business environment that favors downsizing, this is a particularly important lesson. If others are to be empowered and perhaps take on additional responsibility, they can only be successful if they have the skill set to perform. If the appropriate training and development is not provided, this will not empower others, but rather will frustrate them.

A key component of empowering others also involves sharing information. Sharing information goes hand-in-hand with empowerment. It is necessary for people to have the appropriate information to make informed decisions and to perform effectively when they are empowered. Managers, then, must be brave enough to distribute information to others (rather than hoarding it in a power play).

Delegating is another critical element of empowering others. Delegation is an art in itself that is critical to building effective relationships. An inability to delegate is even said to be one of the top reasons for the failure of many managers.

Empowering others can be liberating and rewarding for both the manager who empowers others and for those who are being empowered. This communicates a level of trust in others that is usually well received—and motivating.

Building Trust

John C. Maxwell suggests in his book, *The 17 Essential Qualities of a Team Player,* that people must take the lead in serving others and trusting others. While many excuse themselves by waiting to return trust or service once it has been bestowed on them, they must instead trust others first and serve others first. Then others will trust them and serve them.

The first step in building trust is to demonstrate trustworthiness. Effective relationships depend upon trust. This requires that individuals demonstrate dependability and commitment.

Finally—Taking a Cue from *Fish!*

The Fish Philosophy provides an essential element of building effective interpersonal skills. The foundation of the Fish philosophy as proposed by Stephen Lundin and his co-authors in the best selling book, *Fish!,* is choosing an attitude. This is a daily choice each person makes. A positive attitude and enthusiasm go a long way to developing effective relationships in today's business environment. And only by developing those relationships will managers be able to get things done.

From *Supervision,* July 2005, pp. 20–22. Copyright © 2005 by National Research Bureau, 320 Valley Street, Burlington, Iowa 52601. Reprinted by permission.

Managing Employee Relations

Develop interpersonal communications and conflict-management skills to better manage employee relations.

GREG ROPER

When was the last time you took a good look at your workforce. What did you see? You probably saw a rapidly changing group of employees that is getting more diverse by the day. The accelerated growth of diversity in the workforce over the past 20 years has spawned new developments in managing employee relations, making it one of the biggest challenges facing managers.

To meet this challenge, managers must improve skills such as active listening, adaptability and decision-making. These core skills can assist supervisors and managers in tackling difficult issues that may arise within their workforce.

However, while the skills mentioned above are key, this article focuses on the two most important skills for managing employee relations: interpersonal communications and conflict management.

Interpersonal Communications

The first skill for managers to understand and practice is interpersonal communications, because it is the foundation for all actions in the workplace and it allows the supervisor or manager an opportunity to build relationships with the overall workgroup without alienating anyone in the work environment. Working with diverse groups of people requires a tremendous amount of interaction. If these interactions are positive, they can help create the right workplace climate, attitudes, beliefs and behaviors.

In addition, because interactions occur daily, it is important for managers to have the respect of their employees. If this respect is absent, the supervisor or manager will have a difficult time getting things accomplished.

In a June 2004 *Harvard Business Review* article titled "Understanding 'People' People," Timothy Butler and James Waldroop identify four dimensions to optimize interpersonal communications:

- **Influence.** This dimension is for those who thrive on constant interaction with people. The interaction allows individuals the opportunity to develop and extend their personal sphere of interpersonal influence. This provides professional satisfaction with the ability to influence,

negotiate and leverage valuable information as a method to enhance ideas. Think of these individuals as having highly developed salesmanship skills because they have the ability to constantly keep people highly motivated, no matter what the situation.

- **Interpersonal facilitation.** This dimension describes those who are perceived and known as "people persons." They are very aware of the interpersonal aspects of the work environment and are intuitive, because they are constantly monitoring the situation behind the scenes. Those who focus on this dimension pose critical questions to themselves, such as: What is going to be our strategy to ensure positive employee relations? Moreover, what employee relations issues are going to impact the business and what is the proper way to address them? "People persons" use these questions and subsequent answers to look for ways to improve organizational effectiveness through proactive solutions.

> **Listening skills are the foundation to managing conflict. Focus on what the person says, not your response to what is said.**

- **Relational creativity.** This dimension focuses on nurturing and developing relationships with diverse groups through visual and verbal imagery. An example of this would be the leader of a marketing team who develops and implements a marketing strategy designated for a particular consumer segment, or the plant manager who prepares a speech that the CEO of the organization will deliver to employees, as a method to excite employees about the organization's new direction.
- **Team leadership.** This dimension is for those who are committed to maintaining and fostering good employee relations with the workforce. They enjoy the day-to-day

interaction as a method of feeling good about themselves. Those who embrace this dimension don't care for individual tasks such as writing reports, working on a computer, or any other activity that doesn't allow them to engage others as a means to feel satisfied and fulfilled.

With respect to the four relational dimensions, it is important to note that a manager can have a profound interest in one, two, three or all four dimensions. It is also important to understand that managers need to keep these dimensions in mind when engaging diverse groups, developing people and creating employee relations strategies.

Conflict Management

The second skill for managers to leverage is conflict management. Learning to leverage this skill can help in resolving employee relations issues quickly and effectively, and can create greater satisfaction with the workgroup. There are seven components to effective conflict management:

- **Speak your mind and heart.** As a manager, you need to speak up and say what you think. As obvious as this point seems, people have a difficult time articulating their needs, wants and desires. This exacerbates the conflict because the communication gets distorted and people become frustrated. An example of this would be an employee who is very upset with their manager's management style. He goes to the manager to discuss how he feels, but, instead of focusing on the issue, the manager brings up other issues, which distorts the communication and frustrates the employee. Remember, instead of avoiding the problem, address it and speak up.

- **Listen well.** Listening skills are the foundation to managing conflict. Your focus should be on what the person says, not your response to what is said. Focus on what is positive in the conversation instead of negative, and inform the other party of what you are doing.

- **Express strong feelings appropriately.** Conflict of any type creates a surge in emotions such as happiness, anger, despair and sorrow. Your job as the manager is to manage those emotions through respect and careful examination of what the person is experiencing. Never attack the individual talking. Say, "Dave, I understand your conviction on this matter, and I am willing to work through it so that we can bring closure to the issue," instead of, "Dave, I am tired of your complaining and the poor attitude exhibited by you and your co-workers. To me, this is a done issue." Remember, you are trying to establish a relationship with your workforce.

- **Remain rational for as long as you can.** This means keeping yourself focused on resolving the conflict and remaining connected to the individual throughout the conversation. Then, summarize the situation and ask questions. For example, say, "John, I heard you say that you and Susan are having issues communicating. Allow

me to meet with Susan so that I can assist in addressing your concerns."

- **Review what has been said.** Ensure that all issues regarding the conflict are clarified, and if they are not, ask questions to get answers to the things you don't know. For example, say, "To get at the crux of the issue, I need answers to my questions. Why did Ken hurl a racial insult at Mohammed?"

- **Learn to give and take.** The conversation must be two-sided, not with you doing all of the talking. This will help provide a short- or long-term solution to the conflict. An example of this would be saying, "Linda, you made a good point, now please hear me out," instead of, "Linda, you need to listen to me. I don't need your input. I will solve this problem." Get employees involved so they buy into the process.

- **Avoid all harmful statements.** When you verbally attack, you create enemies and put individuals on the defensive. This means that you are reducing the chances of quickly resolving any conflict. Just remember the Hippocratic Oath: "Do no harm."

As stated in the seven points above, conflict management requires a great deal of listening, clearly articulating the issues, asking questions and providing solutions. Using these techniques to improve your conflict management skills will go a long way in fostering positive employee relations with a workforce.

"Employee relations in the workplace will continuously test the mental fortitude and physical endurance of managers in all industries," says Billy D. Ihrig, group director of labor and employee relations at Ryder Inc. in Miami. "Understanding the importance to getting at the root causes of employee relation issues will be the impetus for improved employee relations, increased credibility with the workforce and the establishment of a positive workplace for years to come."

The Payoff

This article has described two anchor skills—interpersonal communications and conflict management—that managers can use to improve employee relations in the workplace. Incorporating interpersonal communications and conflict management into your employee relations strategy could result in interactions that are more positive and less combative.

Remember, no organization wants to be known as one that doesn't foster strong employee relations. To survive in a highly competitive business environment, organizations want to attract and retain the best talent from all walks of life and be known as the employer of choice.

GREG ROPER, PhD, is a registered organizational development professional and region director of human resources at Frito Lay Inc. with over 12 years of experience in managing employee relations and change. He has research and writing interest in diversity, employee relations and employee involvement.

Banishing Bullying

Communication training, well-publicized policies and even theater productions help reduce interpersonal aggression in workplaces.

SADIE F. DINGFELDER

The logo for the Ramsey County, Minn., government is a big red R, which stands for the county's name on building signs and letterhead. However, the R takes on a double meaning on employee identification pins: It hovers over the word "respect," and is just one way the county fosters a work environment that is inhospitable to bullying, says Don Gault, a member of the county's public health department.

"We have a policy of respect, and we back it up with trainings that teach people to listen to each other," says Gault, who also serves as a member of the county's Workplace Action Team, the group responsible for such initiatives.

In fact, Ramsey County takes a variety of approaches to preventing workplace aggression. It even occasionally brings in a theater group to illustrate the ways that miscommunication can escalate in a workplace. Such a broad strategy is probably the most effective way to address workplace bullying, observes Kevin Kelloway, PhD, a psychologist at St. Mary's University in Canada who researches the topic.

"The way you limit [bullying] behavior is not by developing an exhaustive list of things you can't do, but by taking a more positive approach, saying 'This is the way we treat other people here,'" says Kelloway.

Businesses are increasingly tapping psychologists' expertise to foster healthy, respectful workplaces, Kelloway notes. For instance, he has found that companies increasingly call him for help changing their climates. They may be motivated by a number of factors, such as avoiding lawsuits, decreasing employee sick-day use and reducing turnover, he notes.

"We are seeing a trend where there is a shortage of qualified professionals," says Kelloway. "Companies are competing for talent, and . . . people recognize they can go elsewhere instead of tolerating behavior they may have tolerated in the past."

Further support for the idea that improving work climate can decrease aggression and bullying comes from a recent Department of Veterans Affairs pilot program. In it, psychologists and other professionals taught employees communication skills using a technique known as Collaborative Action Inquiry, which encourages groups to collect data on a problem and then cycle through stages of action and reflection. After the training,

employees at the pilot sites, including hospitals and claims-processing centers, reported less aggression and increased employee satisfaction.

In one case, the intervention reduced the average time for a claim to be processed, notes project consultant Joel Neuman, PhD, a psychologist in the School of Business at the State University of New York, New Paltz. Workers accomplished this feat by listening more carefully to one another: For example, they used a "talking stick" that gave one person the floor and reduced interruptions in meetings.

"The only way to address day-to-day forms of aggression—verbal aggression, psychological aggression, emotional abuse—is to change the nature of the conversations people are having with each other," he says.

Rooting Out Root Causes

Beginning in 1999, Neuman and his colleagues aimed to help 11 workplaces in the VA system increase communication and civility. But a team of outside experts can't just go into an office and tell a company how to reduce bullying, says Loraleigh Keashly, PhD, a psychologist at Detroit's Wayne State University who also consulted on the project. Unique issues contributed to disrespectful behavior at each of the VA workplaces, she notes.

"At one claims-processing center, the root causes were problems with communication and unfair promotion," says Keashly. "Favoritism was poisoning the climate there; union employees felt they weren't being heard by upper management."

So Keashly, Neuman and their colleagues asked both the union and management to nominate a group of employees to serve on an "action team" that would address the problem. The researchers then gave everyone in the center a survey that measured, among other things, how often the employees felt they were the target of disrespectful behavior, such as hostile glaring, malicious gossip and eye-rolling. The consultants then presented the results, which showed that some aggressive acts occurred more frequently there than at similar VA facilities.

With guidance from the researchers, the action teams analyzed the data and determined that rank-and-file employees were frustrated because they felt unheard by management. So they instituted an intervention program called "Flake-off Fridays," in which the center's assistant director invited a randomly selected group of employees to meet and chat with him. During these hour-long meetings, employees asked questions, brought up concerns or just enjoyed some time away from their desks.

"The only way to address day-to-day forms of aggression—verbal aggression, psychological aggression, emotional abuse—is to change the nature of the conversations people are having with each other."

Joel Newman, State University of New York, New Paltz

After the institution of Flake-off Fridays, the researchers administered a follow-up survey and found that bullying and other aggressive behavior had decreased at the claims center. The average amount of time it took to process a claim also decreased, reports Keashly about the as-yet-unpublished data.

The researchers repeated this process of surveys, meetings, intervention and follow-up at 10 other VA workplaces with similar results, says James Scaringi, the VA's special project program manager.

Though the teams' projects were no doubt part of the improvements, the process of developing the interventions—through respectful though sometimes heated discussions—also contributed to reduced bullying, notes Keashly. During the planning meetings, the psychologists taught the action teams to, for instance, speak up when someone said something that was unfair about another employee, she notes.

"Not only was the intervention they designed having an impact, but the way they were operating was catching on with other people," she says.

Backing It Up

The public health department of Ramsey County also aims to change how people communicate with each other by running training sessions that emphasize listening and communication.

In one exercise, small groups of co-workers go through a list of behaviors, such as "You get angry, go into a private room and kick the wall," and rate how violent they are on a scale of one to 10. After considering the examples, the group members discuss their answers.

"We have done this with thousands of people, and what we have found is each time we do it people have very different responses," says Gault. "What you learn from it is that people you work with have different takes on these things. One person might think kicking a wall is a healthy way to relieve anger, while others may think it is violent."

The exercise usually leads to discussion of what behavior is appropriate at work. The goal, however, is not to come to a final definition of respectful behavior, but to expose employees to each others' perspectives, Gault says.

While such discussions are useful, having a policy that explicitly defines and imposes sanctions for bullying can help fortify attempts to improve communication, says Kathryne Dupré, PhD, a Memorial University of Newfoundland business professor who researches the causes of workplace aggression ("Bullying stems from fear, apathy"). Ramsey County has such a policy, which is stated on posters and in the employee manual, and so do many businesses that APA has lauded through its Psychologically Healthy Workplace Award, notes David Ballard, PsyD, MBA, the directorate's assistant executive director for corporate relations and business strategy. Each year, the program nationally recognizes companies that safeguard employees' health and well-being. One such example is IBM's T.J. Watson Research Center, which won in 2006 in part because of its efforts to foster cooperation and respect in the workplace, he notes. (See the May *Monitor* or www.phwa.org for a full list of the winners.)

"IBM does a variety of things to address the issue and create a culture of trust in the organization, including creating a work environment where intimidation is not tolerated and formalizing this through their core values and employment guidelines," he notes.

The company's Business Conduct Guidelines state that IBM will not brook any intimidating behavior, and the company backs that up with disciplinary action, Ballard says. In fact, IBM won media coverage in 2003 when it fired a group of factory workers who were bullying their new boss.

"It's not just the existence of a policy but the belief that the organization will enact it," Dupré says.

UNIT 4
Developing Effective Human Resources

Unit Selections

Key Points to Consider

- Organizations spend a great deal of money on training and development. Why do many organizations feel it is necessary to provide courses in-house? Why do other organizations spend money on outside programs? Why might the training programs of some firms be inadequate, even though a great deal of money is spent on them? What are some of the new techniques being used in corporate education? What are some of the questions organizations should be asking of their training and development operations?

- What are your career plans, and how do you plan to implement them? How has career development changed over the years? Do you think you are likely to have a number of careers in the future? What do you think will be the impact of the Internet? Are you planning on going into one of the growth areas in the economy?

- Do you think the concept of diversity is a good idea? Why or why not? How should diversity be attained? What are some of the problems with diversity?

Student Web Site
www.mhcls.com/online

Internet References
Further information regarding these Web sites may be found in this book's preface or online.

Center for Organization and Human Resource Effectiveness
http://www.iir.berkeley.edu./cohre/cohre.html

Discrimination and Diversity
http://www.domz.org/society/work/worplace.discriminatiorydiversity

Employment Interviews
http://www.snc.edu/socsci/chair/336/group3.htm

Feminist Majority Foundation
http://www.feminist.org

Every organization needs to develop its employees. This is accomplished through a number of activities, including formal corporate training, career development, and performance appraisals. Just as the society and the economy will continue to change, so will the human resource needs of organizations. Employees and their employers must work together to achieve the firm's goals. They must plan together to make the maximum use of their abilities so as to meet the challenges of the changing social and workplace environments.

American industry spends approximately the same amount of money each year on training and developing employees as is spent by all colleges and universities in the United States combined. It also trains roughly the same number of people as there are students in traditional post-secondary education. Corporate programs are often very elaborate and can involve months or even years of training. In fact, corporate training and development programs have been recognized by academia for their quality and excellence. The American Council for Education has a program designed to evaluate and make recommendations concerning corporate and government training programs for college credit. Corporations themselves have entered into the business of granting degrees that are recognized by regional accrediting agencies. For example, McDonald's grants an associate's degree from "Hamburger U." General Motors Institute (now Kettering University) offers the oldest formalized corporate-sponsored/related degree-granting program in the United States, awarding a bachelor's in industrial management; Ingersoll Rand has an Executive MBA Program in cooperation with Indiana University and a PhD program in policy analysis is available from the Rand Corporation.

American industry is in the business of educating and training employees, not only as a simple introduction and orientation to the corporation, but as a continual and constant enterprise of lifelong learning so that both firms and employees can meet the challenges of an increasingly competitive world. Meeting these challenges depends on knowledge, not on sweat, and relies on the ability to adapt to and adopt technological, social, and economic changes faster than competitors do. But, for training to be truly effective and beneficial for the organization, management must be able to set priorities that will be effective and appropriate for the firm. Corporations must also take advantage of the latest in instructional technology, recognizing the value of performance simulations, and address the problem of employees who do not respond well to the new methods of instruction.

There is an important difference between jobs and careers. Everyone who works, whether self-employed or employed by someone else, does a job. Although a career is made up of a series of jobs and positions over an individual's working life, it is more than that. It is a sense of direction, a purpose, and a knowledge of where one is going in one's professional life. Careers are shaped by individuals through the decisions they make con-

Banana Stock / PictureQuest

cerning their own lives, not by organizations. It is the individual who must ultimately take the responsibility for what happens in his or her career. Organizations offer opportunities for advancement and they fund training and development based on their own self-interest, not solely on workers' interests. Accordingly, the employee must understand that the responsibility for career development ultimately rests with him- or herself.

One of the ways that organizations can assist in the career development of their employees is to engage in appropriate and effective performance appraisals. This process benefits both the employee and the employer. From the employers' perspective, it allows the organization to fine tune the performance of the individual and to take appropriate action when the performance does not meet an acceptable standard. From the employee's perspective, appraisals allow the individual to evaluate his or her situation in the organization. Appraisals will indicate, in formal ways, how the individual is viewed by the organization. It is, for the employee, an opportunity to gauge the future.

One of the pressing issues today is diversity. The American, and for that matter, the global workforce is made up of many different people with many different backgrounds. All of them have a wide degree of potential, none of which is based on race, creed, gender, or ethnic origin. It is very dangerous for any organization to ignore any potential labor pool whose talent can be used in a competitive environment, especially if that talent can be used competitively against the organization. Organizations that ignore diversity do so at their peril. The next Henry Ford, Bill Gates, or Warren Buffett could come from anywhere, and given today's world, it is far less likely to be a white male, than twenty or thirty years ago. It is, in fact, far more likely to be a minority group member, or female, as might be deduced from "The Face of Diversity Is More Than Skin Deep," or "Four Generations in the Workplace."

To ignore the development of employee potential of any organization is to court disaster—not only for the organization, but for the employee. People who have stopped developing themselves are cheating themselves and their employers. Both will be vulnerable to changes brought on by increased competition, but the workers will be the ones who join the statistics of the unemployed, or should be left behind.

Who's Next?

Creating a formal program for developing new leaders can pay huge dividends, but many firms aren't reaping those rewards.

SUSAN J. WELLS

What would you do if all of the senior managers in your company departed unexpectedly tomorrow? Would the firm be thrown into a leadership crisis? Or would there be a group of successors ready to take the helm?

Bill Moore, vice president of organizational development at K. Hovnanian Enterprises Inc. in Red Bank, N.J., one of the nation's largest homebuilders, asked those questions of his company's CEO and senior management team last year. He got very few reassuring answers.

But, by asking the question, Moore did get the attention and the action he wanted. Within several months, the CEO endorsed a wide-ranging succession plan that all six top executives committed to push throughout the $2.6-billion company.

Under the year-old plan, successor candidates have been identified for group, region, division and area presidents companywide. At least 50 leader candidates have been tapped, and the company is confident that nearly half of them will be ready to move into senior management within one to two years, Moore says. (For more on K. Hovnanian's succession planning program, see "Case Study: A Growing Business Needs More Managers.")

While the successful efforts to groom leaders at K. Hovnanian are inspiring, they represent the exception, rather than the rule. Studies show that many organizations are not acting on the critical need to develop management talent.

Consider these recent findings:

- Only 29 percent of 428 HR professionals polled this year have implemented succession planning or replacement charts. Nearly a third say their organizations aren't doing anything to prepare for the impending wave of retiring older workers and the impact those departures will have on the workforce, according to the "Older Workers Survey," conducted by the Society for Human Resource Management of Alexandria, Va., with the National Older Worker Career Center of Arlington, Va., and the Committee for Economic Development of Washington, D.C.

- Of 200 HR professionals polled between February and June of this year by DBM, an HR consulting firm based in New York, 94 percent say their organizations have not adequately prepared younger workers to step into senior leadership positions.

Most companies are realizing only now that their sole competitive edge is the bench strength of current and future leaders, says Bobbie Little, senior vice president of global leadership and learning for DBM. As a result, many have no formal succession planning program in place.

Companies that consistently use a formal process to help workers advance also are consistently high-performing firms.

That is troubling because there is evidence that succession planning can pay dividends in many ways, and not just for high-potential employees. By identifying the abilities and qualities needed to move up, and by communicating these to the workforce at large, employers may help to boost retention and corporate performance across the board.

In fact, according to a study of more than 100 companies by Hewitt Associates, an HR consulting firm in Lincolnshire, Ill., the companies that consistently use a formal process to help workers advance also are consistently high-performing firms, as measured by total shareholder return.

Formal Plans Are Best

Experts agree that formal succession management planning—except in the smallest of organizations—is vital.

The absence of a formal plan denies employers two critical levers for building great talent, says Mare Effron, global leader of the leadership consulting group at Hewitt Associates. Without formal plans in place, "you can't proactively have leaders develop the skills they need to assume the next level of responsibility, because you don't know what roles you might move them into," he says. And, "you can't communicate to leaders what their potential future is in the organization, giving the appearance that you either don't care or aren't strategic enough to know."

The Hewitt study found that only 55 percent of firms consistently used a formal approach to identify high-potential leaders, Effron says. However, all of the firms in the top quartile of total shareholder return consistently used such an approach.

"We are often asked by smaller firms: 'Do I really need all these processes in place? I only have 500 people or 1,500 people.' Our answer is that the fundamental rules apply no matter the size of your organization; it's simply much easier in a smaller organization," Effron says.

For example, when a *Fortune* 100 company gathers its succession planning data each year, it might take months and involve thousands of hours of HR investment, he says. "In a smaller company, you can do this around the conference table in an afternoon, but the basic steps still need to be in place for it to be successful."

However, management succession plans at most companies aren't as well-established as they should be, concludes a study based on responses from 908 directors from 209 boards of *Fortune* 1,000 companies conducted last fall by executive search firm Korn/Ferry International in New York. Directors say having a "formal management succession process in place" is one of the most important factors in good corporate governance, but only 64 percent have a management succession committee or process—and only 50 percent believe they're effective, the study found.

Common Traps

Why don't more companies have successful succession management programs? Experts say such programs often fall prey to several common traps.

For example, among companies that actually commit to a succession plan, few follow through with the rigorous implementation required. In fact, 70 percent of succession plans fail due to execution errors, according to a 2002 report, "Succession Planning for Results," from business research firm Cutting Edge Information in Durham, N.C.

> **'This is a startling change from those heady days when corporate America deluded itself into thinking it could predict an individual's career path.'**

Lack of executive-level support is another challenge to a successful program, says Bill Byham, co-author of *Grow Your Own Leaders* (Financial Times Prentice-Hall, 2002) and CEO of Development Dimensions International Inc. (DDI), an HR consulting firm in Bridgeville, Pa. "Succession management has to be a senior management program" driven by all senior leaders, he says.

Moore, whose program at K. Hovnanian Enterprises Inc. has been so successful, agrees that top-level commitment is vital. "To assure the success of the succession planning process, you must have 100 percent support and buy-in of the CEO," he says. "He or she must be the driver of your entire process."

However, buy-in from the top alone is not enough. Effron says an over-designed process can be the death knell for succession management programs.

"This is normally a 'textbook' design that incorporates every possible bell and whistle into the process," he says. "Many times this means lots of forms, too many criteria for evaluating potential, extensive training on the process and a high time demand on the manager."

Managers perceive this as simply more bureaucracy, he says, and participate only grudgingly—even if the CEO supports the process.

"When we see succession planning work, it's integrated into the yearly performance review process, so that managers are evaluating current year performance and future years' potential—succession likelihood—at the same time," he says.

HR's Role

As demands for leadership development grow—due to changing market conditions, corporate growth or the impending retirements of large numbers of baby boomers—HR's role becomes increasingly important. While consultants and practitioners disagree about the best level of HR involvement, most succession management efforts evolve and grow from HR's urging.

And while HR needs to guide the process, it also needs to involve others. Hewitt's Effron says HR should:

- **Co-design the process with the line.** Ideally, succession planning shouldn't emerge from HR alone. A design team of HR and line leaders should co-design the process, with HR bringing examples and content knowledge to the table, and the line serving as the "voice of the customer." The team should test, measure and analyze feedback before rolling out the plan across the organization, he says.
- **Manage the infrastructure.** HR must keep, track and report data to support the process. HR can also track the success of placements, provide updates on depth levels in the organization and analyze diversity.
- **Be an active voice in the process.** Leadership development staff or HR must speak up in succession planning meetings as an equally knowledgeable, equally authoritative participant.

"Succession management must be spearheaded by HR—it is the only logical choice," says George Cauble Jr., SPHR, director of human resources for Henrico County, Va., which has a workforce of nearly 4,000.

Faced with rising numbers of employees eligible for retirement and dwindling numbers of younger employees to replace them, Cauble two years ago led the implementation of a succession plan that created an organizational culture of

Filling Soon-to-Be-Empty Jobs

Henrico County, Va., recently took a close look at its workforce and saw two demographic trends on a collision course: Its upper managers were becoming eligible to retire in record numbers and a decreasing number of younger employees were available to grow into higher-level positions.

Younger employees (40 and under) made up just 44 percent of the workforce in 2000, compared to 66 percent in 1983. What's more, an HR analysis forecast that 29 percent of upper-level managers would be eligible for full retirement and 78 percent for reduced-benefit retirement by 2005, says George Cauble Jr., SPHR, director of HR.

Those statistics spurred Cauble to develop a two-phase succession-management program: Phase 1 teaches supervisors how to guide employees through an individualized professional development process. Phase 2 helps upper-level managers create strategies for developing subordinate managers.

'We decided to attempt to involve and develop as many people as possible in our organization'

"After much research, we decided to attempt to involve and develop as many people as possible in our organization—while the typical model is to only select and develop the few," Cauble says. "Our approach created an environment where leadership development was truly a high priority and has become a part of our workplace culture."

The county's HR department won an award from the Society for Human Resource Management's Richmond chapter for its succession management work last year. Also, over the last 17 consecutive years, the department has grabbed an unprecedented 34 National Association of Counties Achievement Awards.

To roll out its program, the county held eight information sessions over four months and offered managers a half-day training session on how to lead developmental conversations with employees, analyze employee assessment tools and supervise employee development.

Some managers below the department head level didn't want to participate because they didn't plan to move up. "To counter this, we made it clear that development was important for the current job just as much as it was for prospective higher-level jobs," Cauble says.

The county now boasts near 100 percent participation, he says.

—Susan J. Wells

ment heads. The group identified key leadership positions, and HR followed up with additional training on implementation.

The results have been "spectacular," Cauble says. For the fiscal year that ended in June 2003, the county filled 57 percent of all openings internally through promotions and career advancements, including seven upper management posts. (For more information about the county's program, see "Case Study: Filling Soon-to-Be-Empty Jobs," left.)

Finding the Unsung Heroes

Where do companies start to identify employees who should be targeted for advancement? DDI's Byham advocates forming what he has dubbed "acceleration pools."

Much like a championship athletic team that first finds the best available players and then decides where to put them in the lineup, this strategy pulls candidates from a wide range of leadership levels.

"Given sufficient resources and attention, an acceleration pool provides the leverage to both respond to the immediate talent gap and grow outstanding talent for the future," he says. "This is a startling change from those heady days when corporate America deluded itself into thinking it could predict an individual's career path."

Candidates chosen for their basic skills are developed through training and job experiences to maximize their potential contributions to the organization at large, rather than to a specific position, Byham says.

"Companies like this better than 'high-potential pools' because that term implies that people not in the pool don't have high potential," he says. Rather, an acceleration pool indicates that a worker's growth is being accelerated, not that others lack potential.

With its Leadership Potential Index, DDI rates an individual's potential by measuring four core factors and gauging strengths in each:

- **Leadership promise.** Has a motivation to lead, brings out the best in people and exemplifies authenticity.
- **Personal development orientation.** Is receptive to feedback and has learning agility.
- **Balance of values and results.** Fits the culture and has a passion for results.
- **Master of complexity.** Practices adaptability and conceptual thinking and navigates ambiguity.

'If employers truly seek to develop their leaders, criteria for advancement must be made clear.'

To Tell or Not to Tell

The question of whether or not to tell high-performing workers they've been tapped for executive grooming is a subject of continuing debate.

learning and development at all levels. The plan also created a structured developmental process for upper managers and provided practical tools for advancement.

Cauble and his staff conducted information sessions for all department heads, deputy county managers and assistant depart-

A Growing Business Needs More Managers

For K. Hovnanian Enterprises Inc., developing a surefire succession plan is key to filling its fast-growing home-building empire with a crop of next-generation leaders.

"We initiated our program to make sure we have leaders in place to grow our company," says Bill Moore, vice president of organizational development. Its growth needs are great: *Fortune* magazine recently named the Red Bank, N.J.-based company as the nation's 15th fastest-growing company. It has acquired seven other home-building companies in the last three years.

The company formed a succession planning committee that includes the chief executive officer, chief operating officer, chief financial officer, vice president of HR, senior vice president of corporate operations and Moore. This panel selects and approves candidates and tracks their progress throughout a one- or two-year employee development program.

Candidates who completed the program and were promoted have been 100% successful.

Before the committee reviews candidates, members gather data on each—including feedback from 12 to 14 direct reports, colleagues and senior managers. This confidential e-mail survey is designed to assess leadership ability.

Next, the panel examines the candidate's employment history and experience for technical and managerial skills. The goal: To discover and fill any gaps in work history.

The committee lays out this information in a two-page spreadsheet and assigns grades ranging from 1.0 to 5.0. Any grade of 3.9 or below requires an individualized training plan.

After the committee accepts a candidate's nomination, Moore and the candidate hone in on any necessary training or coaching and map out an action plan. Candidates must spend 10 percent to 20 percent of their work time on this personal development plan.

Next, Moore says, the committee places each candidate into one of three categories indicating readiness to move up: ready in two years, ready in one year or ready now.

The succession plan has netted measurable results, Moore says. Internal candidates who completed the program and were promoted have been 100 percent successful, compared to executives hired from the outside, whose success rate is closer to 50 percent, he says.

—Susan J. Wells

There are advantages and disadvantages to each choice, says William J. Rothwell, professor in charge of workforce education and development at Pennsylvania State University's University Park campus and author of *Effective Succession Planning* (Amacom, 2000).

An advantage to not telling is that employers keep their options open. "As business conditions change, managers may feel that a different kind of person is needed to fill a key vacancy or do the work," Rothwell says. The key disadvantage: "Superstars may leave the organization because they don't see a future for themselves."

By contrast, when top performers are told they are being considered for advancement, they are more likely to stay because they see a possible future for themselves, says Rothwell. The key disadvantages to sharing such information are that star workers may stop performing because they believe a promotion is "in the bag" or that managers may inadvertently commit themselves to an oral contract to promote the worker.

Rothwell predicts that more companies will be forced to tell promising leadership candidates about their selection as a retention strategy. However, companies must consider how to do that.

"The telling must be done in a legally defensible way," says Rothwell. "Managers need coaching from HR and from the legal department." For example, managers "must, above all, avoid promising anything in a blanket way to mollify an otherwise outstanding performer so as to retain him or her," Rothwell says.

There are two potential legal risks here: First, employment-at-will laws in most states give employers the freedom to dismiss an employee at any time for virtually any reason. Employers should not surrender that right with direct promises, he says.

Second, employers need to avoid making any implied promises that could unintentionally create a job contract.

Bottom line: A succession program should never pledge job security or guarantee promotions; it merely indicates that a worker's potential has been noted.

Keeping Secrets

The potential drawbacks of communicating succession planning status have prompted many companies to keep the process secretive, says Tom McKinnon, executive consultant at Novations/J. Howard & Associates, a diversity consulting and training company in Boston.

A recent Novations/J. Howard survey showed that 37.5 percent of companies tell executives they have been targeted for potential advancement, while 45.8 percent do not. Only 16.7 percent of employers polled make the criteria for inclusion known throughout the organization.

Such corporate secrecy has its down side, McKinnon says.

"If employers truly seek to develop their leaders, criteria for advancement must be made clear," he says. "If employers don't define the criteria or help people develop the skills, the only ones who will get promoted will be those who remind leaders of themselves."

The Hewitt study of 100 companies showed that 64 percent of high-performing employers tell employees of their status as up-and-coming leaders—and that 75 percent of these companies also tell employees when they're no longer considered for advancement.

Effron says deciding whether to tell has generated more discussion than any other finding in the study.

"While higher-performing companies tell their best talent that they are high potential and the benefits of that status, there's more to this than just the conversation," he says. "At the companies that tell, most of them are very committed to having a great working environment for all employees. They don't want a two-class system to emerge because certain people will get some extra attention, so they start with the fundamental premise that everyone is treated well and everyone will know where they stand regarding performance."

Knowing where you stand on the performance curve and what you need to do to be considered leadership material helps prohibit retention problems, Effron says. Clear communication about status and future in the organization is important.

"Also, the companies that are best at this also tell high potentials what this status doesn't mean. It doesn't mean that you're going to be CEO next year. It doesn't mean you permanently have this designation," he says. "It likely means you'll have increased burden placed on you to prove the potential you have."

Because smart companies are also confident they've accurately assessed potential, there's little danger of having to revisit the conversation.

In the end, succession work is never done, notes DBM's Little. The good news: You can see results from a succession plan in the first year.

"You know your program is working when line managers take ownership over from human resources and senior managers are driving the process regularly and consistently," she says.

SUSAN J. WELLS is a business journalist based in the Washington, D.C., area with 18 years of experience covering business news and workforce issues.

Avoiding Stereotypes

Four Generations in the Workplace

C. Stone Brown

Age diversity and intergenerational conflicts are getting lots of press these days as four generations converge on the workplace simultaneously. A handful of corporations have been addressing this issue for years but most are just beginning to understand the ramifications.

Several of the Top 50 Companies for Diversity have been ahead of the curve and have been putting age-diversity practices into play for the past five to 10 years.

Take a look at Pitney Bowes, the No. 1 company on the 2004 Top 50 Companies for Diversity list.

"We began to think about this issue of the aging work force and generational differences several years ago," says Johnna Torsone, Pitney Bowes' senior vice president and chief human resources officer. The company started to address this issue with its senior management through speakers, forums and workshops.

By being proactive, Pitney Bowes hasn't faced any major intergenerational conflicts, but Torsone has been experimenting with different tools to bring awareness to the issue.

In addition to forums and presentations, as part of its leadership-development courses, Pitney Bowes conducted a series of interactive role plays on intergenerational issues. It's not something the company plans to revisit any time soon. "I think it was stereotypical . . . I think people felt that way. We didn't continue it," she says.

The most effective tool thus far, Torsone says, was a series of focus groups on intergenerational issues.

"There was more commonality in the things that really matter to people than sort of the hype that's out there. The thing I did learn is that the junior people got annoyed at some of the people that would say, 'Well, you are too junior to do that,' using that kind of terminology. They wanted to be given an opportunity to prove themselves . . . they really resented that terminology." She says although all generations wanted an opportunity to show what they can produce, this was particularly important to younger workers.

Ultimately, these focus groups impact how Pitney Bowes trains its managers.

"When we talk about diversity, we try to sensitize them to the notion that everyone wants to feel like they are being stretched to do the most that they can do, and attracted to an environment that makes people feel they can do things, [as] opposed to saying, 'Well, here is why you can't do them,'" she says.

The challenge for many companies, though, is how to effectively confront and resolve age issues without stereotyping workers.

> **"You can't stereotype an entire group but, certainly, there is evidence that there are trends that are very different in terms of the attitudes toward work and outside of work."**
>
> Lois Rubin, Unilever Foods

Torsone doesn't believe this should be a major challenge for organizations. "The best way to counter stereotypes is focus the diversity message on the uniqueness of each individual and to give examples which belie the stereotype."

A lot of stereotypes can be traced back to generational profiles or stereotypes that are picked up through the media or even training. The profiles generally follow that the older workers (veterans and boomers) tend to be more loyal and hardworking but resistant to change. Whereas, the younger people (GenXers, millennials) embrace technology and tend to be creative and performance-driven.

A breakdown of the generations used in the book *Generations at Work: Managing the Clash of Veterans, Boomers, Xers and Nexters in Your Workplace* has veterans born between 1922 and 1943, boomers born between 1943 and 1960, GenXers born between 1960 and 1980 and millennials born after 1980. Other generational writers put the boomers between 1946 and 1964.

Just as we think of workers of different races, ethnicities and genders bringing diverse life experiences and perspectives into the work environment, it follows that each generation has identifiable behavior patterns. What are some of the cues that a company has generational issues? How can companies resolve age conflicts without stereotyping employees?

"You can't stereotype an entire group but, certainly, there is evidence that there are trends that are very different in terms of the attitudes toward work and outside of work," says Lois

Rubin, manager of diversity, Unilever Foods. "And I think that is one of the biggest differences when we talk about the generational differences."

"Generational diversity is just another dimension of diversity that companies came to a little bit later than race and gender. So it was just a natural evolution of the diversity conversation."

Jennifer Allyn, PricewaterhouseCoopers

Her company first addressed age issues last year at its diversity council meeting. "We are looking at the generational [cultural] issues and talking about them and I think that is where you start . . . you raise awareness," she says.

Intergenerational conflicts, similar to issues revolving around race, gender and ethnicity, are an indication that management is not effectively addressing these issues or is ignoring them.

There should have been awareness training that communicates to employees that maybe the veteran or baby boomer wants to improve his or her computer skills but needs a patient instructor, or that the GenXer, who is hard working, measured by his or her performance, relates to work differently because he or she watched the older generation burn themselves out on a job.

What researchers have found is that it's counterproductive to judge generational differences as a right way or wrong way of doing tasks or learning, because there are differences in how generations feel about work, learn new tasks and process information.

But too often, there is the human tendency to think "different" is wrong, similar to how we view race and gender differences, and that is typically where companies are just beginning to grapple with age-related issues.

PricewaterhouseCooper (PWC), which ranked No. 33 on DiversityInc's 2004 Top 50 Companies, has a work force comprised of 75 percent GenXers and millennials and has focused its attention on the interaction of these two generations.

"Generational diversity is just another dimension of diversity that companies came to a little bit later than race and gender," says Jennifer Allyn, PwC's director, Center for an Inclusive Workplace. "So it was just a natural evolution of the diversity conversation."

The challenge thus far for PwC hasn't been GenXers necessarily clashing with boomers, but simply trying to probe what the generations expect from their job.

"We address it different ways . . . we did a study to understand the expectations of new associates, in terms of what the work environment is like at the firm. We interviewed associates and managers to get a sense of how these two different generations experienced [work] and what they expected out of the firm," says Allyn.

Allyn says what jumped out in PwC's findings is how important work-life balance is to the millennial generation.

"While work-life is not a matter of children or marriage . . . it's that 'It's my first job out of college and I'm living in a new city and I'm trying to have a life outside work.'" This has presented some challenges for PwC.

"That is a big catalyst for change for us, especially in a client-service environment; obviously it's [a] very demanding, more hours-driven place. So how can we say to people, 'We value flexibility, we want this to be a place where you can succeed both professionally and personally?'"

The key is to raise the level of awareness about age diversity, in whatever way it takes, says Raines, co-author of *Generations at Work*. She has consulted for other DiversityInc Top 50 Companies, such as Sprint (No. 11 on the 2004 list) and Merck (No. 13 on the 2004 list).

"It can be a little more complicated than that and certainly there are all kinds of things you can do. But if we just become aware that it's generational . . . that [awareness] can be done by reading a book, or board gem, videos, and all sorts of resources to become a little bit more aware."

Sharing trans-generational knowledge between veterans, baby boomers, GenXers and millennials is similar to people of different cultures, races or ethnicities sharing ideas, values and beliefs. If companies begin the conversation with their employees with that model in mind, they resolve age conflicts before they start.

The Face of Diversity Is More than Skin Deep

Catherine M. Dalton

Diversity. The word itself can invoke a wide range of reactions, some supportive and others less so. An intriguing aspect of diversity is that while we might achieve agreement at the macro level as to what constitutes diversity, such agreement is significantly less likely at the micro level. That is, diversity wears many faces, and the nature and character of the face looks very different depending on the individual.

For some, the face of diversity is defined by skin color. For others, it is based on gender, ethnicity, sexual orientation, or religious preference. In some ways, however, these issues touch only the surface of diversity, its meaning, and its importance. Based on my experience, diversity is complex and rich, while at the same time being quite simple and straightforward.

For me, the face of diversity is a white, male, 70-year-old Midwesterner. It is a face that few might associate with diversity; after all, by the reckoning of most, it is the face of the majority, not the face of a minority. At the surface, such a conclusion seems fair. However, on closer examination it becomes crystal clear that this face is the very embodiment of diversity. It is a face I know well; it is the face of my father.

I have learned more about the importance of diversity from my father than from anyone else, perhaps precisely because he appears to be such an unlikely advocate of diversity. We all fall victim to stereotypes, and diversity is an area that does not enjoy immunity from them. A member of the "majority" is not necessarily less likely to understand, appreciate, or advocate diversity than a member of the "minority."

My lessons in diversity started at an early age. As a young child of the 1960s, I was witness to the growth of the Civil Rights movement in the U.S. It was a time in history when taking Robert Frost's "road less traveled" could prove a challenging path. Ms. Rosa Parks, who passed away in 2005 at the age of 92, provides a moving example of an individual who bore the costs of taking the road less traveled when, after a long, tiring day at work in December 1955, she refused to yield her seat on a Montgomery, AL city bus to a white man. She was summarily arrested, and subsequently faced constant threats and lost her department store job. Her simple act, however, sparked the Civil Rights movement and demonstrated that while path breakers seldom travel an easy road, their courage paves the way for countless others who might then more easily follow.

Diversity Starts at Home

One of my earliest experiences in diversity appreciation occurred in the 1970s. Having grown up in the Midwest, in the heart of suburbia, I had little exposure to racial diversity on a day-to-day basis. It is fair to say, however, that racial integration was not embraced by most suburbanites at the time. As such, when my father, a liberal arts professor at a small liberal arts university, brought home an African priest from work one day, suitcase in hand, it provided the whole family a valuable experience in diversity, including lessons in both the costs and benefits of embracing diversity.

It would be grossly unfair of me to say that my father was metaphorically color blind. He was, and is, not; in fact, few individuals are as skilled at seeing the broad spectrum of color that life provides. That said, I suspect that my father never considered the potential costs of inviting Father Bill, a priest from Kenya, Africa, to live with us while he earned a master's degree at the university where my father worked. My father only saw an individual, in a foreign country, who desperately needed a temporary home. He did not see, first and foremost, a black man. That simple, perhaps impetuous (at least according to my mother, who received no advance warning of our guest's arrival) decision to invite Father Bill into our home bore significant costs, as most of our neighbors did not share my father's enthusiasm for our houseguest. Father Bill was shunned, my parents were shunned, and my siblings and I were shunned by many of our neighbors.

Was it worth it? Absolutely. Who else in the neighborhood received a direct education in life in an African village? Who else in the neighborhood heard personal accounts of wrestling an alligator? More importantly, who else in the neighborhood had firsthand experience with the hope that Martin Luther King, Jr. expressed for his four children: that they would be judged for the content of their character, not the color of their skin? When my family looked at Father Bill, I assure you that we saw a person, not a "color."

I had similar experiences throughout my childhood, largely compliments of my father. My family shared our home at various times with a parade of fascinating individuals that included Gina, an exchange student from Bogotá, Colombia who was studying at the university where my father works, and seven of the nine members of the Nguyen family, who were able to escape just prior to the fall of Saigon, South Vietnam. Each addition to the family created interesting challenges (e.g., while not always easy, 15 people actually can peacefully co-exist in a five bedroom house for a two-year period, even though half speak only English and half speak only Vietnamese). More importantly, each addition to our family provided lifelong lessons in the value of tolerance, respect, and flexibility.

Those lessons during my "developmental years" have served me extraordinarily well in my professional life. While I may not have embraced diversity, writ large, in the same enthusiastic fashion as my father, I certainly have an appreciation for it; in particular, the value that diversity brings to organizations.

Diversity = Survival

Biologists have long understood the importance of diversity; in fact, nature provides potent lessons in its power. Biological diversity addresses the variety of living organisms, and their relationships with each other and the broad environment. Biologists talk about diversity within specific types of organisms, diversity across organisms, and diversity of ecosystems. The organizational corollary might be diversity across individuals, departments, strategic business units, organizations, and industries.

In both contexts, a central issue is that diversity is essential for survival. In the biological world, Darwin's "survival of the fittest" attests to the need for diversity in species. With no discernible distinction in living organisms, whether plant or animal, a potent invader can lead to the death of the species. Consider the constantly growing list of extinct and endangered animals or the devastation of plant species due to pests, disease, pollution, or destruction of habitat. Each loss is a loss of resources, real or potential.

Consider also a lack of diversity in organizations. A cynic may argue that organizations can survive quite well with no diversity. Imagine, for example, an early 20th century manufacturing firm employing only young, white males. Perhaps such an organization can survive in the short-term. However, ponder that same organization in the early 1940s when countless healthy, young, white males found themselves mired, voluntarily or otherwise, in World War II. "Rosie the Riveter" filled their places, enabling those firms to survive an otherwise devastating intervention.

Competitive strategy, too, is built on the concept of diversity. Take an industry in which all firms compete on the same basis, have access to the same resources, and sell to the same customer base. This homogeneity virtually forces such firms to eventually compete on a tenuous basis such as price. As many firms in many industries have experienced, that is almost always a losing proposition in the long run. It is heterogeneity, the ability to distinguish the firm's products and/or services from those of other firms, that enables organizations to garner and maintain a loyal customer base.

The Face of the Customer

Another compelling reason for embracing diversity in organizations is to better serve customers. Consider the case of a consumer products company whose products are largely purchased by women, but whose key decision-makers are all men. Taken to the extreme, contemplate that these same male executives are all in their middle 50s, college educated largely at Ivy League schools, and from middle- to upper-class backgrounds.

What I have described is the typical large firm top management team, even in 2005. According to Catalyst, a research and advisory organization dedicated to the advancement of women in the workplace, well under 10% of top jobs in large U.S. corporations are held by women. The numbers for minorities are equally as dismal.

At issue is not necessarily that any key decision making group should include a woman or a member of a racial minority. What is at issue, however, is that there is a significant body of research on top management teams that demonstrates heterogeneous (diverse) teams tend to produce superior outcomes as compared to homogeneous teams. Diversity infuses discussions with a wider variety of perspectives and ideas, leading to greater innovation. Granted, decision processes are lengthier and more difficult to manage with a diverse group of decision-makers. However, the alternative is likely to be a quick decision process that seldom leads to change or innovation. Were customers' needs static, such a top management team composition might be viable.

Importantly, diversity must extend beyond the traditional foci of race and gender. While it is true that these factors are strong forces and visible means for achieving diversity, it is also true that they scratch only the surface of diversity. This is akin to the biologist's conception of within-species diversity. It would seem, at best, naïve to assume that all women, for example, think alike. As a woman, I can confidently assert that we do not. A central challenge for organizations, then, is to determine the types of diversity that are relevant to the firm and its customers and to ensure that the appropriate perspectives are included in the organization.

A Sprint versus a Marathon

Recent events have reminded me that achieving diversity is much more of a marathon than a sprint. In her rookie season, Indy Racing League driver Danica Patrick was publicly derided by Formula One President Bernie Ecclestone, who suggested that women had no business racing with men, despite Ms. Patrick's fourth place finish in the 2005 Indianapolis 500. He then likened women

to domestic appliances, noting that they should all be "dressed in white" (I prefer clothing with a bit more variety, thank you very much, Mr. Ecclestone). Those familiar with Mr. Ecclestone's 2000 commentary on women driving in Formula One ("What I would really like to see happen is to find the right girl, perhaps a black girl with super looks, preferably Jewish or Muslim, who speaks Spanish") would likely be unsurprised by his lack of sensitivity.

Consider also Neil French, former Creative Director of WPP Group, who, following making comments about female ad executives, resigned that position in 2005. When asked at an industry dinner why he believed there were not more women represented among the ranks of creative advertising directors, Mr. French opined that "they're crap" and "don't deserve to make it to the top." Another candidate for sensitivity training.

My own experiences have provided potent reminders of how much work remains to be accomplished in the area of diversity. This is certainly true as regards gender diversity, an issue that hits the mark for me. While I own far more examples than I will burden the reader with, one that is particularly notable for its recency involved a communication I had with the Director of Corporate Relations for a major corporation. He asked me if the use of gender-neutral language in *Business Horizons,* a standard practice in many journals, is "a university PC thing." Like many others, that exchange reminded me that I had better tighten up the laces on my running shoes and strap on the water bottle, because it's going to be a long race.

R-E-S-P-E-C-T

The use of gender-neutral language in *Business Horizons* is not a "PC thing"; rather, it is, in the words of Aretha Franklin, a "RESPECT" thing. It is about creating an environment in which everyone feels welcome. That, to me, is the very essence of diversity. Too often, people get mired in a belief that diversity means they need to compromise their own value set. I believe that diversity simply means I need to understand and respect others and their choices, although I don't necessarily have to agree with them.

This belief, too, is a direct reflection of the lessons I learned from my father. He is the very model of someone who actively chooses, on a day-to-day basis, to embrace diversity in its many forms. Even at his current age, he continues to teach classes on the subject and engage in activities that will help him better understand diversity. My father appreciates that diversity can often best be understood when experienced. His own experiences have included everything from living with a group of university students in the inner city for a semester, to participating in service learning experiences in Nicaragua, Honduras, Ghana, and Appalachia, to volunteering as an assistant basketball coach for an inner-city basketball team, to serving meals in an inner-city soup kitchen.

Not only can learning, growth, and appreciation occur though such experiences, but one's comfort zone can expand exponentially. Inasmuch as we often fear what we don't understand, the more I experience, the more I understand, and the easier it is for me to respect others who are "different" from me. Imagine the power of leveraging such respect in the organizations in which we work. To do so is to imagine the power of diversity.

What do you see when you consider the face of diversity?

UNIT 5

Implementing Compensation, Benefits, and Workplace Safety

Unit Selections

Key Points to Consider

- Companies are involved in worldwide competition, often with foreign organizations with much lower wage rates. What should management do to meet this competition? What do workers need to do to meet this competition?

- When companies merge, what do you see as some of the problems that could happen from an HR perspective?

- How would you implement a merit/incentive program in a staff department such as research and development or data processing? In a line department such as sales or production?

- Explain why you believe some senior executives might be overpaid. Do you feel some are underpaid? Cite examples and reasons for your conclusions.

- What strategies should employers implement to control the rising costs of benefits while still getting the maximum value for their employees? How would you address the health care crisis for an organization?

- Healthy and safety is one of the primary concerns facing any organization. What are some of the innovative ways that corporations have found to provide better health care while at the same time reducing costs?

Student Web Site
www.mhcls.com/online

Internet References
Further information regarding these Web sites may be found in this book's preface or online.

BenefitsLink: The National Employee Benefits Web Site
http://www.benefitslink.com/index.php

Equal Compensation, and Employee Ownership
http://www.fed.org

Equal Pay Act and Pay Inequity
http://www.infoplease.com/spot/equalpayact1.html

Executive Pay Watch
http://www.aflcio.org/corporateamerica/paywatch/

Job Stress
http://www.workhealth.org/news/nwprahn98.html

Social Security Administration
http://www.ssa.gov

WorkPlace Injury and Illness Statistics
http://www.osha.gov/oshstats/work.html

Money makes the world go around . . . the world go around!

—From "Money" in the musical *Cabaret*

Individuals are usually paid what others perceive their work to be worth. This situation is not necessarily morally correct. In fact, it does not even have to be logical, but it is reality. Police officers and college instructors are often underpaid. They have difficult jobs, requiring highly specialized training, but these jobs do not pay well. Other professions pay better, and many illegal activities pay better than law enforcement or college teaching.

When a company is trying to determine the salary of individuals, two markets must be considered. The first is the internal structure of the firm, including the wages that the company pays for comparable jobs. If the organization brings a new employee on board, it must be careful not to set a pay rate for that individual that is inconsistent with those of other employees who are doing the same or similar jobs. The second market is the external market for employees. Salary information is available from many sources, including professional associations and the federal government. Of course, both current and prospective employees, as well as organizations, can easily gain access to this information. To ignore this information and justify pay rates only in terms of internal structure is to tempt fate. The company's top producers are the ones in whom the competition is the most interested, and no organization can afford a mass exodus of its top talent. Organizations must develop a "Philosophy of compensation."

One recent development in the area of compensation is a return to the concept of pay for performance. Many firms are looking for ways to directly reward their top performers. As a result, the idea of merit pay has gained wide acceptance in both industry and government. Pay for performance has been used in industry for a long time, most commonly in the sales and marketing area, where employees have historically worked on commission plans based on their sales productivity. Organizations are constantly looking at these types of programs, as may be seen in "Ten Steps to Designing an Effective Incentive Program." Theoretically, merit pay and other types of pay for performance are effective, but they can easily be abused, and they are often difficult to administer because measuring performance accurately is difficult. Sales and production have numbers that are easily obtained, but research and development is a different situation. How does a firm measure the effectiveness of research and development for a particular year when such projects can often take several years for results to be achieved?

One issue that has evolved over the past several years is the question of pay for top executives as seen in "Pay Setters." During times of economic recession, most workers are asked to make sacrifices in the form of reduced raises, pay cuts, cuts in benefits, other compensation reductions, or layoffs. Many of these sacrifices have not been applied to top management. Indeed, the compensation for top management has increased

Courtesy of Tara McDermott

substantially during the past several years. Are chief executives overpaid, and if so, how did they get that way, and who should set their pay?

The fastest-growing aspect of employee compensation is benefits. Benefits are expensive to any firm, representing an ever-increasing burden to employers. As a result, many firms are reducing benefits and attempting to find more effective ways to spend their benefit dollars, as discussed in "Benefits and the Bottom Line." Also, the needs of the employees are changing. As our society ages, there is greater interest in health benefits and pensions, and less interest in maternity benefits. Another facet of the issue is that employees are seeking greater benefits in lieu of salary increases, because the benefits, with some exceptions, are not usually taxed as discussed in "Employee Benefits of the Future."

Health and safety are also major concerns of employers and employees. The workplace has become more violent as workers act out against their employers for unfairness—whether real or imagined. Some firms have had to address the anger of employees and other problems. The problems facing companies may even extend beyond the workplace and employers may face liability when domestic violence comes to the workplace. Today, issues concerning safety and health in the workplace include AIDS, burnout, and substance abuse. These issues reflect not only changing social conditions but also a greater awareness of the threats presented by unsafe working conditions. An attempt to address some of these issues has been to practice what is essentially preventive medicine with wellness initiatives and other programs, as seen in "Doc in a Box" and "Building a Mentally Healthy Workforce." While there was initially some doubt about their effectiveness, the results are now in, and wellness programs do work.

All told, salaries, wages, and benefits represent a major expense, a time-consuming management task for most firms, and health and safety requirements are a potential area of significant loss, in terms of both dollars and lost production.

Philosophizing Compensation

Develop an overarching statement to ensure that your pay practices are applied consistently and effectively.

CHARLOTTE GARVEY

Most compensation philosophies have the same basic objectives: to attract, retain and motivate the best employees. But where you go from there determines whether the philosophy is a paper abstraction that sits on a shelf or a vital tool that allows you to equitably and consistently implement your compensation programs.

A well-crafted compensation philosophy "helps tell the story of who you are as an organization and what you value as an organization," says Lynne Sport, director of human resources and administration for the Carnegie Endowment for International Peace, a Washington, D.C.-based, not-for-profit think tank. Sport, who has worked in HR for nearly 20 years in a variety of sectors, including financial services and technology, says the philosophy can help guide HR compensation managers in assessing where the company fits in the marketplace when it comes to trying to attract talent.

A compensation philosophy should provide consistency in three areas: among departments, over time and as the company grows.

"Our comp philosophy is the overarching umbrella that all the compensation programs should fall under," says Karen Macke, senior vice president of compensation and benefits at The Hartford Financial Services Group Inc., a Connecticut-based insurance and financial services corporation with about 28,000 employees in the United States. "If a program falls outside the umbrella, you've got to question if the program is right for the organization."

Having a compensation philosophy can help shield HR professionals from pressures exerted by individual managers who want to customize compensation within their department or division. Without a clear philosophy in place, "you'll always be inundated by the business manager of a profitable business [line] who says, 'I want my own plan,' and you have no way of addressing that," says Paul Shafer, business leader and compensation expert with consulting firm Hewitt Associates in Norwalk, Conn.

The Hartford's philosophy identifies what the company's pay programs are trying to achieve, along with what elements must be consistent throughout the organization. The company does allow for some customization for "unique business situations," Macke notes, such as incentive plans for salespeople. But any unique programs must still align with The Hartford's business strategy and the desired culture of the organization, Macke says.

David Balkin, chairman of the management division at the University of Colorado's Leeds School of Business in Boulder and a compensation expert, suggests that a philosophy should provide a strategy "that links the different compensation programs and pieces together." Basing compensation decisions on historic company practices—in other words, the "We've always done it that way" approach—"doesn't work in a very dynamic economy with global and technological pressures," he says.

Another factor driving the decision to develop a philosophy is the size of the company, says Hewitt's Shafer.

In small companies, such as startups in the technology field, "you have a founder or a small group of senior people who tend to know everybody in the company" and who make "personal" decisions about individual pay, Shafer says. But once a company's workforce grows significantly, "those who are responsible for making the pay decisions oftentimes start losing touch with who all the people are," he notes. "They need a philosophy to be able to govern the program so it can be administered in a fair and equitable manner."

Close Collaboration

While HR generally is in the driver's seat when developing a compensation philosophy, that development often is done in close collaboration with high-level management to ensure executive buy-in and to develop a philosophy that meshes with the company's business objectives.

'You should put a compensation philosophy within the framework of your target philosophy.'

Kristen Vosburgh, PHR, manager of benefits and compensation at the Cary, N.C.-based business intelligence software company SAS, says that HR and compensation specialists should drive the process, "with feedback and validation from managers."

Sport adds, "HR is clearly in the best position to drive the process. We are the ones who understand the marketplace, have the compensation survey tools, have the knowledge about the jobs, understand the labor market issues and understand the legal issues." But "you can't have a process without senior management buy-in," she notes.

Once HR and top leadership are committed to developing a philosophy, Shafer says he likes to get senior leaders of the organization together to push them to identify and quantify the attributes of a compensation program that they think are important, such as the mix of pay elements. Most senior managers will tell you their philosophy should be to "attract, motivate and retain the best people," Shafer notes, but he adds, "That's too general. It really doesn't give you much guidance." Once the managers identify what they value in terms of compensation, Shafer says his firm works with the client's HR leaders to craft a philosophy statement that is acceptable to management and HR.

The process of considering changes in the philosophy also often is a collaborative process between HR and management. Vickie Davis, manager of compensation and benefits at the Babcock and Wilcox Co. (B & W), a Barberton, Ohio-based energy services company with about 1,100 employees at its U.S. headquarters, says the company's philosophy is reviewed every year prior to the salary-planning process.

While business leaders focus on possible changes relating to business objectives, it's HR's job to examine potential resource issues that might, for example, require a company to consider paying a premium for talent. If there was a scarcity in the available labor pool that would prompt a change in compensation philosophy, HR leaders "certainly would be the catalyst for that because we would be aware of it first," Davis notes.

Shafer urges HR managers to step back when considering their philosophy to look at the broader framework of attracting and retaining employees. "You should put a compensation philosophy within the framework of your talent philosophy," he says, by assessing fundamental issues such as whether the company is trying to develop homegrown talent or invest in attracting outside talent.

"It's cheaper to grow your own tomatoes than to go buy them in the market," Shafer observes. "But if it's the middle of winter and you need a tomato, you really don't have much choice."

HR needs to review how the company currently is evaluating jobs and paying employees, including consideration of market positioning of the jobs, and assess potential variances in pay compared to the market. HR managers also need to consider if current pay practices are working or whether adjustments are needed to attract and retain employees based on current wage rates, Vosburgh notes. Some of the more obvious signals that pay practices aren't working are employee turnover and an inability to successfully hire top job candidates.

Online Resources

For help creating a compensation philosophy, see the online version of this article at www.shrm.org/hrmagazine/05January. There you will find Prudential Financial's compensation philosophy statement and a new study showing that a growing number of workers indicate better health care coverage is more important than higher pay.

Company culture and business needs also must plug into the analysis, says Vosburgh. For example, she notes that at SAS, which employs about 5,300 people in North America, "We do aspire to pay our people competitively, but there is a cultural need to be egalitarian," so that need has shaped the compensation philosophy.

"Except for certain [research and development] and critical jobs where we may target base salary above the market median, we look at the local market median for the base salary," explains Vosburgh.

'Intangible Compensation'

Innovative companies are developing philosophies that communicate all that their workplaces have to offer. Vosburgh says SAS's philosophy focuses only partially on pay. "We have not given up on the paycheck. Base salary is important," she says. "However, our benefits, annual company contribution to profit sharing, a 401(k) safe-harbor contribution and on-site amenities are also a significant portion of the package."

The University of Colorado's Balkin notes that SAS has been included on many "best places to work" lists in part because of this broader compensation philosophy that emphasizes total rewards.

Similarly, as a not-for-profit organization, the Carnegie Endowment for International Peace does not offer high pay, Sport notes. What it does offer is the "intrinsic value" of working for an organization that emphasizes quality of life and robust benefits, including generous retirement and vacation programs. "We place a really high value on quality of life," she says, suggesting that a pleasant work environment perhaps should be considered "intangible compensation."

'Transparency and Clarity'

Once a philosophy is in place, many companies work hard to communicate it to their employees across the board. "For us, transparency and clarity in communication are critical to employees," says The Hartford's Macke. "The philosophy that helps define the comp program can't be motivating to employees if it isn't understood."

At B & W, enhanced communication turned out to be crucial in getting managers and employees to understand the company's new emphasis on pay for performance, which resulted in better performers receiving a larger proportion of salary and bonus dollars.

"Managers had difficulty embracing the philosophy at first," says B & W's Davis. Although the pay-for-performance system had rolled out several years earlier, Davis says it became clear by 2002 that more aggressive communication measures were needed to bring about increased acceptance of the approach.

Davis worked with B & W's communications staff to write a basic philosophy statement and to post it on the company's intranet. HR managers also began coaching line supervisors and providing them with talking points to help them in salary-related discussions with employees.

"The driving force behind putting [the philosophy] out there is the feeling that the employees needed to see it in writing, needed to understand it, so that they would understand it wasn't arbitrary," Davis says. Managers have achieved "a better comfort level" in discussing compensation with employees but, she acknowledges, it has been an evolution.

The reality of many workplaces is that some jobs are valued more, and therefore are compensated better, than others.

"We've gone from a culture that didn't talk about compensation to one that does," she notes. Employees "may not agree with how it has impacted them, but they do at least understand that it's not arbitrary, there is a process, there is a philosophy that everyone is trying to adhere to."

Possible Problems

But communicating openly with employees could leave companies vulnerable. The University of Colorado's Balkin, who has appeared as an expert witness on behalf of plaintiffs in pay discrimination cases, urges caution when considering just how open to be. The philosophy could come back to haunt the employer if the employer has failed to abide by it, he suggests.

In a litigation setting, "If I know what the compensation philosophy is and I see [an employee] who was treated as an exception to that policy, I would use that as additional evidence that discrimination took place," he says. "If you don't act consistently [within an open system], there's a liability there."

In addition, if those you expect to communicate the philosophy to the rank and file are not up to the task, think twice about how far you spread the word, says SAS's Vosburgh. "If the managers are not equipped to effectively communicate the philosophy, then the philosophy should be limited to management only," she says, adding, "Managers should possess basic compensation knowledge before a stated philosophy is publicized companywide."

Compensation often is a hot-button issue among employees, and the compensation philosophy should be constructed to address potential problems. The reality of many workplaces is that some jobs are valued more, and therefore are compensated better, than others.

When employees ask why jobs are ranked differently, "those are hard, hard questions to answer," says Sport. "But if you put together a good philosophy, they're very defensible." When she worked at a boutique financial services firm, she says, "we placed a very high value on talent, and that talent was unique." As a result, the key people in financial positions were very well compensated in terms of salaries and bonuses, while other employees were paid about market rate.

"But it was justifiable," Sport notes, because the compensation philosophy emphasized the value of those employees. "Without those key financial people, we wouldn't be in business."

CHARLOTTE GARVEY is a freelance writer, based in the Washington, D.C., area, who reports on business and environmental issues.

Do Your Employees Qualify for Overtime?

The Answer May Surprise You

DEE GILL

S he's well compensated. He's a manager. They're all on salary. These are some of the common reasons employers give to explain why they do not pay their employees overtime. But in many cases these reasons are not legally valid.

That's something business owners have been learning the hard way. Indeed, the number of overtime lawsuits has exploded over the past couple of years. In 2005, class-action suits involving wages surpassed discrimination cases as the most widespread work force class action, according to a recent study by Chicago law firm Seyfarth Shaw. During the same year, the Department of Labor collected $166 million in back wages, mostly overtimepay—a 26 percent increase from 2001. Large companies, such as Cingular Wireless, have doled out millions in back overtime wages recently. Smaller companies are being forced to pay up as well.

The litigation has been fueled, in large part, by changes to the Fair Labor Standards Act in 2004. The Department of Labor updated the antiquated act, which first came into effect in 1938, in order to eliminate references to outdated jobs (think straw bosses and keypunch operators) and establish guidelines for contemporary workers. Among other changes, the agency determined that employees must make at least $455 a week to be ineligible for overtime pay, a sharp increase over the previous benchmark of $250 a week. As a result, 1.3 million workers suddenly qualified for extra pay, according to the DOL.

But the effects of those changes are really being felt now. Not only are more workers "aware of the changes, but employment lawyers are increasingly on the lookout for potential overtime suits. "What we're seeing now are claims that are driven by an increase in awareness," says Paul DeCamp, administrator of the Wage and Hour Division at the Department of Labor. "All of a sudden, people are realizing that they have rights to overtime that they didn't know about." Paul Lukas, partner at Minneapolis law firm Nichols Kaster & Anderson, says that most clients come to his office complaining about wrongful termination or discrimination. But he ends each initial interview with questions about overtime pay, with an eye toward building a class-action case. And he's not alone. The revised overtime laws, Lukas says, have created a cottage industry. "Nothing wakes up lawyers faster than someone else making money on a certain kind of case," he says. "The word is that FLSA cases are lucrative cases."

Employers have been caught off guard by the rise in overtime disputes. "Employers frequently don't appreciate the value of spending time on these issues until it's too late," DeCamp says. Case in point: Eloy Torrez, president of SEI Group, an engineering firm in Huntsville, Alabama. Torrez thought he was being a good boss when he devised a pay plan that allowed him to avoid layoffs by adjusting his employees' salaries along with the ups and downs of government contracting. When business was flush, he paid staffers a salary, plus the equivalent of one hour of pay for each hour worked in excess of 40 hours a week. In a good year, he doled out as much as $30,000 extra per employee. But when contracts from clients like the U.S. Army and the Department of Homeland Security slowed down, Torrez scaled back some salaries, treating his staff of engineers, architects, accountants, and program managers as part-timers—paying them only for the hours they worked—but with full health benefits.

Torrez figured the system was great because it eliminated temporary layoffs and gaps in health coverage. But unbeknownst to him, it was also illegal. Because SEI's professional staffers were not receiving consistent salaries, they qualified for overtime pay—at least one and a half times their regular hourly wages—for every week they worked more than 40 hours. Last October, after an audit that lasted months, the Department of Labor ordered SEI to pay two years of back overtime wages totaling $464,342 to 103 of its 126 employees. "That's about half of this year's earnings," Torrez says. "This has been a huge burden for us."

Like many business owners, Torrez assumed that his staffers were ineligible for time and a half because they received salaries. But the updated overtime rules make it clear that salaried workers such as computer programmers and account executives

Excuses, Excuses

If you're using one of the following justifications to explain why you're not paying overtime, you could be breaking the law.

1. "He's on salary." Even salaried workers may have to be paid overtime if their jobs meet certain exemption criteria. The rule of thumb: If they don't make many independent decisions, they may qualify for time and a half.

2. "Longer hours are in her contract." Some employers try to avoid paying overtime by building extra hours into employment contracts. But employees can't opt out of overtime pay.

3. "He makes a lot of money." White-collar workers who earn more than $100,000 a year and meet the "independent judgment" criteria are ineligible for overtime only if they make at least $455 a week in guaranteed salary. In many cases, bonuses don't count.

4. "He's an outside sales rep." Outside salespeople are generally exempt from overtime pay. But if they spend more than half their time in the office, they may actually qualify.

may be eligible for overtime if their jobs meet certain exemption criteria. Those criteria are numerous and detailed, but the philosophy behind them is simple: Workers who do not spend most of their days performing tasks that require them to exercise "discretion and independent judgment" probably qualify for overtime pay. That could include anyone from a secretary who answers phones all day to a loan officer who relies on computer algorithms to determine an applicant's eligibility. Even managers and job site foremen who do not have strong input into hiring and firing decisions may be eligible to collect overtime.

Many employers realize they're in violation of the revised overtime laws only after they've been contacted by the Department of Labor. Most audits are the result of a complaint from a single worker that blows up into a companywide investigation. "If the DOL visits you, it will rarely be to look at the one employee complain," says Steve Trent, chairman of the labor and employment practice at Baker, Donelson, Bearman, Caldwell & Berkowitz in Johnson City, Tennessee. Audit results are rarely good news for companies. Those found to be in violation must pony up two years of back overtime wages, in addition to fines for repeat offenders. Lawsuits tend to be even more damaging: Lukas, for example, typically sues employers for two years of back overtime pay. If he can demonstrate that a business knowingly broke overtime laws—which he frequently does—his clients may be entitled to a third year of back wages.

To stay out of trouble, consider paying a labor attorney a few thousand dollars to vet your pay policies. And take a hard look at what your employees do all day, regardless of their job descriptions. If they don't make many independent decisions, there's a good chance they qualify for overtime pay. Also, think twice about offering flextime to hourly workers. If an employee with a flexible schedule works more than 40 hours in a given week, regardless of how much he or she worked the previous or following weeks, that person may qualify for overtime.

To learn more about the rules governing overtime pay, visit the Web site of the Department of Labor's Wage and Hour Division (wagehour.dol.gov) or call the DOL hotline (1-866-4-USWAGE).

Of course, you might not like what you discover. And correcting overtime mistakes isn't easy. Workers will probably ask about back wages when they find out they are eligible for overtime. To avoid a pricey lawsuit and bad press, some companies bite the bullet and hand over two years of back wages and pay overtime going forward.

Torrez, for his part, isn't sure how the Department of Labor found out about SEI's pay system. He recently switched his work force to guaranteed salaries with no overtime pay. When business slows down, Torrez says, he'll be forced to lay off workers. He's gotten plenty of complaints from staffers about the new system. "No one is happy about it," he says.

Ten Steps to Designing an Effective Incentive Program

BRUCE BOLGER

I t seems obvious that having motivated employees, channel partners (retailers or other distributors), and vendors can provide a competitive edge, yet surprisingly few organizations put a strategic emphasis on motivation. Those business leaders who do focus on motivation tend to do so out of faith, because the vast business, media, and academic community has paid comparatively little attention to the issues specifically related to motivating customers to buy, channel partners to produce, and all sales, service, and operations employees to work with maximum commitment toward achieving organizational goals.

The lack of business focus on motivation is demonstrated by the fact that few organizations have any one person responsible for motivating customers, employees, channel partners, and vendors. Is it the CEO, or head of human resources, sales, or marketing? Is that function written into anyone's job description? Is anyone measured by how well he or she motivates? The fact is that numerous people in an organization face the issue of motivation, often using their own approaches with little linkage to other organizational efforts. The HR department may have one approach for management and rank-and-file workers, while the sales department handles sales and channel-partner motivation, and marketing tackles customer motivation. "The Interaction Between Marketing & Human Resources and Employee Measurement & Incentives," a study conducted at the end of 2003 by the Forum for People Performance Management at Northwestern University, found that a large gulf existed between the motivational efforts of HR on the one side and sales and marketing on the other.

Based on the department from which the plan emanates, the need, or the audience, organizations use many different types of strategies to motivate people. These can include benefits, workplace environment, training, meetings, newsletters, compensation, recognition, and, in many cases, incentive programs. Maximizing overall motivation clearly involves a careful integration of these many factors.

Motivation clearly has an impact on performance, but it alone cannot guarantee success. A group of employees in a hamburger chain may love their work and provide great service, but motivation cannot replace the business lost if a nearby factory shuts down. What sets incentive programs apart from other motivation strategies is the ability to link the campaign to measurable, desirable actions or outcomes, such as increased effort by salespeople or increased customer loyalty due to better customer service. The specific objective of an incentive program is to drive measurable performance improvement.

Another element unique to the issue of motivation is the potential benefit of better integrating external motivation of consumers and internal motivation of employees, as well as specific tactics, such as meetings, print communications, and promotions. This integration, which focuses activities on the targeted audiences and desired behaviors and not the interests of tactical managers defending their budgets, requires a level of alignment that may not be present at many large companies today. Very few organizations have in place a management structure that clearly bridges internal and external audiences and the internal departments that serve them.

Business planners traditionally have often placed too much emphasis on incentives and not enough on the other elements that can affect performance.

The process of motivating people to improve performance can involve a variety of tactics, but all have in common the goal to produce a measurable action or outcome in the target audience. So the focus starts on the audience, by asking who do we want to motivate, and then proceeds to what are we asking them to do, how will we help them succeed, and how will we measure success and reward people in order to reenergize them for the new challenges beyond?

What Is an Incentive Program?

The lack of focus on motivation has created a fuzzy world of nomenclature related to incentive programs and other recognition and consumer promotion programs. Definitions and terms vary depending on the industry, audience, and individual businesspeople; these terms include *sales contents, recognition, rewards, tangible rewards, premiums,* and *dealer loaders.* Incentive programs comprise internal or external marketing campaigns designed to promote specific actions on the part of a specific audience to produce measurable outcomes through the integrated use of motivational strategies, including awards, communication, involvement, feedback, and recognition.

Actions promoted by incentive programs can include:

- Make more sales calls.
- Put up displays.
- Buy more of a product.
- Attend an event.

Outcomes can include:

- Increased sales,
- Expanded productivity,
- Improved quality, or
- Improved cycle times (how long it takes to get something done).

When referring to incentive programs, businesspeople and media often use the term *incentives,* as if the strategy focuses primarily on giving something to someone for doing something. This may be the case, but unless the campaign addresses the other issues related to increasing motivation, the program likely will fail. Business planners traditionally have often placed too much emphasis on incentives and not enough on the other elements that can affect performance.

What Motivates?

Because the issue of motivation stretches across an organization's entire audience, the answer depends on the audience: sales force, operations employees, administration or research, channel partners, or consumers. To simplify the answer, we'll break this into internal and external audiences.

Internal Audiences

Despite the lack of research and attention paid to the relationship between motivation and business performance, over the years numerous researchers have looked at different aspects of the issue. A study conducted in 2003 by the International Society of Performance Improvement, entitled "Incentives, Motivation, and Workplace Performance," provides an excellent summary of what is known on the subject. Commissioned by the SITE Foundation, a not-for-profit research foundation focused on incentive research, the study was undertaken to provide a comprehensive review of past academic research as well as provide a snapshot of current business practices via both a broad-based and in-depth survey of U.S. organizations. The study of current organizations found several elements critical to achieving performance improvement through motivation.

Incentive programs should instill a feeling of importance, because everyone's job counts when it comes to improving performance.

- *Emotion.* The study found that the workplace mood has a fundamental impact on performance. How employees feel about their jobs, work environment, and company directly affects their level of service and productivity. Further support for this hypothesis comes from a 2002 survey of U.S. workers, entitled "2002 Motivation for Excellence," which found that 85 percent of employees see a link between their level of motivation and the quality and quantity of their work. When properly designed, incentive programs have a positive, measurable impact on the emotional state of participants.

- *Communication.* The data support the existence of a direct link between performance and the degree to which participants understand the desired goals and steps they can take to help get there. Incentive programs should foster a greater understanding of organizational goals and how each participant's actions can contribute to overall success.

- *Buy-in.* The study found that performance thrives when employees feel engaged in the goal. Incentive-program proponents specifically use the campaign development process to foster engagement by involving employees in the design process.

- *Feasibility.* The study found that programs rewarding individuals based on their own achievement, rather than rewarding a predetermined number in so-called tournament or closed-ended programs, provide much better results.

- *Work utility.* The research confirms the intuitive link between work satisfaction and sense of purpose. Incentive programs should instill a feeling of importance, because everyone's job counts when it comes to improving performance.

- *Employee capability.* People quickly become discouraged if they want something but lack the skills to get it; motivation goes hand-in-hand with a participant's sense of ability. So every incentive program should include training that complements the actions requested by the program.

Analysis and feedback provide the method for utilizing the invaluable information that comes from directing people toward specific goals. What happens, or does not happen, provides a road map for better results in the future, no matter what the outcome.

External Motivation

Recently, much more research has been conducted regarding the understanding of customer behavior. Although much debate continues on many granular issues, a solid basis of evidence suggests the following key factors can come into play, depending on the audience and individuals. Curiously, many of these external marketing elements relate to internal audiences.

- *Availability.* Do consumers even know the product or service exists, and is it easy to find it? Availability could be a function of willingness of channel partners to carry a product, which in turn could be determined by how they are treated by sales or other employees.

What customers say to employees may be one of the most overlooked areas of business intelligence in helping organizations better understand what they can do to please.

- *Function.* Does the product or service fill a big enough need and do what it says it will do? Function can be a product of innovation that comes from a committed employee base looking for new ways to please the customer.
- *Value.* Is the price paid comparable to similar products in the market? Value can also be viewed in terms of productivity and the efficiency of internal employees.
- *Emotion.* Many people respond to what they perceive to be fun, exciting, and hip, and want to feel valued and recognized. Marketing strategies that address emotion often require the involvement of employees or channel partners.
- *Convenience.* Is the product relatively easy to buy and use with a minimum of problems? Convenience can suffer greatly when internal employees have little interest in customer satisfaction or understanding of what they can do to foster it.
- *Identification.* Can customers or prospects emotionally identify with the "brand," and do they feel comfortable interacting with the company's people or image? Many organizations spend millions to build a brand through advertising, only to have it thwarted by employees who interact with customers but whose attitudes can't always be covered up by a uniform, dress code standards, and one-week intensive training programs.
- *Communication.* Do customers and external channel partners understand your latest products, services, and value propositions? Communication is a two-way street, with marketers advertising and marketing to external customers, who in turn communicate to the internal employees they encounter on a day-to-day basis. What customers say to employees may be one of the most

overlooked areas of business intelligence in helping organizations better understand what they can do to please.

- *Integrity.* If there is a problem, how does the company handle it? Many marketing departments overlook the extent to which the internal audience—employees, salespeople, and channel partners—can influence these outcomes.

When properly constructed, consumer incentive programs get a better response if they address both external and internal audiences.

The Linkage to Performance

Companies do many things to motivate employees, but incentive programs are designed to drive specific actions that lead to increased performance.

In addition, incentive programs are among the very few business strategies whose cost varies according to the outcome. Whether your organization uses benefits, meetings, newsletters, advertising, promotions, recognition, training, or many other related strategies, your cost will likely be the same no matter what the outcome. With properly designed incentive programs, your cost will have a direct correlation to results, meaning that, under ideal circumstances, you pay more if your program succeeds, and much less if it doesn't.

The design steps will show how to direct motivational energy toward the achievement of specific, measurable goals. Also, performance measures are described that your organization can use to determine the specific value derived from an incentive program.

Steps to Designing a Program

The following overview covers the basic elements of incentive program design, no matter what the audience.

1. Design a Strategic Plan

The overall strategy of an incentive program is to perform a specific action to obtain a specific result. Your incentive program should address specific objectives with a specific strategy and tactics so that you have measurable results. The strategic plan should read like a business plan, outlining all of the elements covered below, along with the items that produce a return on investment.

2. Identify the Audience

Before you can do anything to set up an incentive program, you need to pinpoint the audience(s) that can drive the desired performance. Often, including more target groups can have a greater impact than you might think. For instance, customer service people might have a direct bearing on the efforts of your salespeople to increase sales. Retail personnel at a retail outlet might have a direct impact on whether or not customers see the point-of-sale displays that outlet agreed to put up. Employees in the shipping department might play just as much a role in helping you meet customer production deadlines as those in the assembly operation. No matter what department you're in, you can benefit by looking at all of the people who can affect your goals.

Your incentive program should address specific objectives with a specific strategy and tactics so that you have measurable results.

When identifying your audience, don't forget to take into account the anecdotal but useful 20-60-20 rule: 20 percent of your best performers will probably continue to perform no matter what you do, because they already perform under the current circumstances. Another 60 percent can go either way. The final 20 percent probably won't budge no matter what you do.

3. Conduct Appropriate Fact Finding

This process lies at the root of identifying what actions will yield the desired results. You need to find out how motivation can drive the behaviors your objectives require and what obstacles potentially stand in the way. This step often includes employee involvement programs or focus groups with consumers to determine what your targeted audience can do (or not do) to help you achieve your goal. This step helps you make sure your program addresses whatever hidden factors might stop people from doing the things you need them to do. The output of this process provides the basis for developing your program structure by confirming the specific actions required by the specific audience that can lead to the specific results.

Many programs overlook the value of integrating communications with incentive program design.

---

4. Create the Program Structure

Think of this step as the blueprint for your strategy. It spells out precisely what people have to do to reach their goal—how the organization will assist them, how people will be rewarded and recognized, and how you will measure the return on investment. There are essentially two types of incentive program structures underlying almost any type of program:

- Open-ended programs enable anyone to win based on his or her own actions and, therefore, give participants the greatest potential control over their success. The research confirms that these programs generally have greater motivational value because they offer accessibility to the broadest possible audience.
- Closed-ended programs have a predetermined number of winners. They have the benefit of letting you offer a larger, more impressive award with a fixed, predictable

budget, but research clearly shows that they often discourage a large portion of participants who quickly count themselves out of the running.

Many companies use closed-ended programs in conjunction with open-ended programs as a means of fostering loyalty among top performers by making them feel valued and appreciated.

5. Integrate Communications

Many programs overlook the value of integrating communications with incentive program design. The incentives used in conjunction with the program help draw attention to company communications, and company communications help direct people toward the behaviors and training tools that can help them succeed. Communication can take the form of imprinted promotional products delivered with training; announcements; standings reports showing how well partners or teams are performing; meetings, including local, regional, national, or international; newsletters (print or e-mail); personal letters; brochures; and more.

6. Select Rewards

Award selection depends largely on your objectives. If the goal is to compensate employees for work they accomplish year after year, cash is clearly the currency of choice. But if the goal is to recognize people for special behavior that may not be rewarded in subsequent years and to foster communications, alignment, etc., then it may pay to use noncash awards that won't become confused as compensation and, therefore, expected year after year.

So, the question becomes, How do noncash awards compare with cash rewards when the goals include rewarding exceptional behavior, enhancing communications, and better aligning employee actions with external marketing promises? In a survey of incentive-award users released in September 2003, the majority of users surveyed believe that merchandise and travel awards get remembered longer and are more promotable than cash and that cash awards have the least residual value. These findings support the use of noncash awards when the goal involves getting attention and deriving derivative value in terms of focus and commitment levels. If memorability has no place in your recognition strategy, cash may be a better solution.

Both common sense and research support the theory that presentation is as important as the award itself, because people respond best to genuine appreciation for their efforts.

7. Develop a Budget

Several rules of thumb help guide incentive planners to more measurable, cost-effective programs. First, set up your program so that your fixed costs consist primarily of strategic planning, communications, training, and tracking and administration and that your rewards and recognition are based on incremental performance generated by participants, customers, channel partners, or employees. Return-on-investment measures below can help you determine how much to payout in awards, but companies generally budget top awards to equal about 3 percent to 5 percent of a recipient's annual earnings to get attention. Under this scenario, only about 20 percent of the program's budget has a fixed cost; the rest varies based on performance improvement.

Open-ended programs can be more difficult to budget, because how much you spend depends on how much individuals or groups perform, which no one can accurately predict. On the other hand, your budget only goes up if your results go up; and if your program is structured correctly, you won't pay nearly as much for your program if results fall short. Most other marketing options have a fixed cost no matter what the outcome. Closed-ended programs are easy to budget, because you set the predetermined number of winners, but that also may mean you'll pay full freight for your program even if you don't achieve your objectives.

Both common sense and research support the theory that presentation is as important as the award itself, because people respond best to genuine appreciation for their efforts.

8. Develop Measures

In the early 1990s, the American Productivity and Quality Center created the Master Measurement Model for the SITE Foundation in order to guide planners toward the development of measurable programs. The model has the following elements.

1. Determine the processes to be measured in a numeric way. Measures could include unit sales, dollar sales, repeat customers, defect percentage, customer satisfaction scores, cycle times, etc.
2. Decide on two to three related processes or outcomes to be measured, and make sure that you measure related issues, such as sales, sales presentations conducted, repeat business or number of repairs per day, timeliness of repair report submission, or number of suggestions made to repair the update manual.

3. Create a basis for comparison. What is the rate of unit sales, dollar sales, repeat customers, defects, customer satisfaction, or cycle times to which your program's performance will be compared?
4. Translate the numerical goal into a unit of measure that can easily be tallied against a previous, comparable period.
5. Weight that measure based on how important it is to the overall program objective. A sales incentive campaign might weight the goals as follows: 50 percent for sales; 25 percent for sales presentations; and 25 percent for repeat customers. (See Figure 1.)

9. Track Results

Tracking and administration of incentive-program design ironically can create some of the biggest challenges and opportunities. The challenges relate to the practical issues of collecting and sharing data. Fortunately, the Internet, intranets, and enterprise software or customer relationship applications have made this task much easier, and administration is now further supported via the proliferation of online incentive technology. Some of the available online incentive technology has easily customizable functions enabling you to set up the type of measurement and award allocation features outlined under step 8.

The most important elements of tracking and administration include:

- Implementing the program business plan according to the time line;
- Having an up-to-date database of each participant;
- Setting up a simple system for collecting and reporting data;
- Sending out all standing and other reports on schedule;
- Making sure all awards get distributed on schedule;
- Running tracking reports to determine award redemptions and costs;
- Calculating results and return on investment as indicated above;
- Feeding back market or other knowledge obtained from the program.

Performance Feedback Report					
	Base Data	New Data	New Base	Weight	Result
Measure A	12.11	12.52	103.44	.50	51.7
(This indicates an improvement in performance of 3.4 percent, translating into a unit measure of 51.7.)					
Benefit Report for Field Service Reps					
	Base Data	New Data	Improvement	$ per Unit	Benefit
Measure A	14.32	15.17	.85	$50K/1	$42.5K
(By multiplying the unit improvement by the estimated benefit per unit, you arrive at an estimate of the benefits derived from your program.)					

Figure 1   Performance feedback report and benefit report for field service reps

Source: The Master Measurement Model of Employee Performance, created for the SITE Foundation by the American Productivity and Quality Center.

One of the key benefits of an incentive program is the ability to collect valuable data not only about results, but also about the processes necessary for success. Often, an incentive program helps collect useful data you might not ordinarily get unless people (especially channel partners) have an incentive to do so.

10. Analyze Results and Solicit Feedback

Your program might have both quantitative and qualitative measures of success. Quantitative measures are reflected in the actual results; qualitative measures might come from some other indices, such as results from employee or customer surveys, customer or employee turnover rates, revenue or other productivity measures per employee, etc. These qualitative results can represent byproducts with an additional value to the organization over that achieved through the actual results.

During the analysis and feedback phase, you want to look at your program results against your business plan and attempt to isolate any outside factors that could have affected performance, either accounted for or unaccounted for in your plan. Review actual results and whatever qualitative information you gleaned so that you can prepare a recommendations report for any future programs.

This process can include a per-participant review to see whether any patterns have emerged about group or individual performance that could provide ideas for improvement in the future.

If you have used both results and process measures, you have powerful tools to determine the precise impact of your incentive program. If the results went up, but the processes being measured went down in quantity or quality, then you can assume that the results had little to do with the program. If, on the other hand, the processes showed improvement but results went down, you can conclude that some outside circumstance other than motivation or work effectiveness contributed to the outcome. Also, if you can continue to track data following the end of the formal program, you can continue to monitor what happens to results and process measures to see what happens without the incentive program.

Many companies that use incentive programs do so in the belief that there's almost always a value to promoting important behaviors and that the use of rewards helps sustain commitment to positive behaviors over time.

Bruce Bolger is a founder of the Forum for People Performance Management and Measurement in the Department of Integrated Marketing Communications at the Medill School at Northwestern University. He is also managing director of the Incentive Performance Center, a not-for-profit organization dedicated to improving the effectiveness of incentive programs, and president of Selling Communications Inc. (Irvington, New York), a target marketing, media, and technology company. He is also author of *Principles of Incentive Program Design* (Association of Incentive Marketing, 2004), from which this article has been adapted.

Pay Setters

Chairmen of compensation committees give the lowdown on why executive pay keeps going up.

Frank Maley

Tom Smith ran a big grocery chain for 13 years and was paid handsomely for it. In 1998, his last full year as CEO of Salisbury-based Food Lion Inc., he earned $3 million, according to the formula Business North Carolina uses to calculate executive pay. Adjusted for inflation, that would have been equal to about $3.6 million in 2005. That would put Smith at 20th on this year's ranking of CEO pay at the 75 largest public companies in the state.

He also starred in some of Food Lion's television commercials, so couch potatoes around the state quickly grew familiar with—some, perhaps tired of—his boyish mug interrupting their favorite shows. Since retiring in 1999, he has dropped out of the public eye but not completely out of corporate boardrooms. These days, Smith helps set pay for executives at Concord-based CT Communications Inc. as chairman of its compensation committee.

He's not unusual. Eight of the 10 highest-paid CEOs on the list—compiled by the Charlotte office of human-resources consultant Findley Davies Inc.—run companies where the compensation-committee chairmen are current or former CEOs. Four are, or were, CEOs of public companies. The theory is that few know as much about CEO compensation as CEOs. Few have reason to care as much. But is it wise to let CEOs, past and present, set their peers' pay?

"There are two points of view there," says Paul Hodgson, a compensation specialist at The Corporate Library, a Portland, Maine-based company that researches corporate governance. "One is that it is the fox guarding the henhouse and that they're unlikely to be harsh with their fellow CEOs and say, 'We need to be more modest about our pay levels here.' Alternatively, they may actually have more authority in that situation and therefore be able to stand up to another CEO."

Whether it's the best practice, CEOs often are judged by their peers, and in any given year their pay could go either way. Twenty-three CEOs on our list took pay cuts in 2005, sometimes even when their company produced a positive total return, but 46 got a pay boost—seven even though their companies produced negative returns. The median pay change for CEOs at the state's 75 largest public companies was 13.1% in 2005. That's a smaller increase than the previous year but larger than the median total return in 2005—measured from the first trading day of the fiscal year to the last—of 6.4%. And with a median pay package of $1.4 million, those CEOs won't get much sympathy from their shareholders.

To get fat pay packages, though, CEOs don't need shareholder sympathy, just their acquiescence and a strong demand for their

Working for Their Keep

Even though he was the top-paid CEO, Ken Lewis was a bargain for his shareholders, Paul Anderson worked just for dividends.

CEO/Company	Total compensation (000s)	Net income per dollar of compensation
1 Paul M. Anderson, Duke Energy	$ 0.0	nm
2 Kenneth D. Lewis, Bank of America	$26,524.4	$620.7
3 G. Kennedy Thompson, Wachovia	20,396.4	325.7
4 Robert A. Niblock, Lowe's	9,428.8	293.9
5 Susan M. Ivery, Reynolds American	3,677.8	283.3
6 Robert P. Ingle, Ingles Markets	101.0	263.2
7 John A. Allison IV, BB&T	7,748.7	213.4
8 Christopher J. Kearney, SPX	5,514.0	197.7
9 Daniel R. DiMicco, Nucor	7,297.4	179.6
10 Robert B. McGehee, Progress Energy	4,115.3	169.4

talents. "Our system operates on the basis of the free market and of competitiveness," says Bill Holland, former CEO of United Dominion Industries, a Charlotte-based maker of industrial equipment, and compensation-committee chairman at Lance Inc., a Charlotte-based snack maker. "Top-level executives command a lot of money. That's just a fact."

Setting CEO pay is a complicated process that usually takes several months and is part of a larger task of deciding what to pay all of a company's top executives. "I do not like to see these incentives for the CEO much different than ones for the other top executives," Smith says. "The amounts might be different, but the same things that guide him or her need to guide the other executives."

At CT Communications—a local phone company that has branched into Internet access, wireless communications and long-distance service—discussion of CEO Michael Coltrane's 2005 pay started in mid-2004. The compensation committee instructed Findley Davies to launch a survey of compensation at companies in the same industry—preferably eight or more. "The way I like it is if you can knock out the upper and lower extremes and still have a good listing of companies to balance out, because you never find a company that you can match up with exactly," Smith says.

In most years, CT's consultant presents the completed survey to the committee in September and fields questions about it. The committee may request additional information. In November, the full board of directors discusses the company's goals. Around the first of December, the committee meets again and tries to translate those goals into a pay package that will motivate top executives and place them in the right spot on the industry spectrum. "If you've got a CEO and your company is doing average, I think you should pay him near the median," Smith says. "But if you've got one that's producing results better than those other eight, or better than seven out of the eight, then you should move the CEO higher."

As at many public companies, CT's Coltrane receives a fixed salary plus a bonus and other pay based on performance. In 2005, his annual bonus was contingent on the company hitting goals in, among other things, operating revenue; operating earnings before interest, taxes, depreciation and amortization; operating free cash flow; and customer growth. His long-term incentives were based on three-year growth in operating revenue, operating EBITDA, earnings per share and total shareholder return compared with a peer stock index.

The process varies from company to company. But many rely on consultants and try to peg CEO pay to company performance within its industry. The process is more detailed and defensible at many than it once was but still can produce results that are puzzling when pay is compared with company performance in the same year. Coltrane, for example, got a 57% raise in 2005, when CT's total return was a paltry 1.4% and its net income dropped slightly. Most of the increase came from an option grant and long-term incentive payouts aimed at boosting future performance and weren't influenced only by 2005 results.

Company performance can be affected by industry trends, long-term goals and extraordinary circumstances. CT's bottom line was stagnant, but it's in an increasingly competitive industry—with long-distance carriers, cell-phone companies and cable-television operators wanting bigger shares of local phone markets—and net income took a hit from the cost of laying more fiber-optic cable, which Smith says will help it compete long-term.

Likewise, it's hard for outsiders to easily understand the deal Lance gave David Singer. He received about $6 million in 2005, ninth on our list. That's more than six times what his predecessor, Paul Stroup, made in 2004 and more than seven times what Singer made in 2004 as chief financial officer of Charlotte-based Coca-Cola Bottling Company Consolidated. It was 35% more than Holland made in his penultimate year as CEO of United Dominion, though Lance is less than a third the size United Dominion was in Holland's day, before it was purchased in 2001 by SPX, now based in Charlotte.

Lance didn't exactly sparkle in 2005. Its total return was a minuscule 1.1%, and net income dropped 26%, though part of that decrease stems from the purchase of Tom's Foods, a Columbus, Ga.-based competitor, for $38 million in October, Holland says.

Singer's pay had to be big, in part, to lure him from Coke Consolidated, where he was CFO 19 years, Holland says. Besides, Lance historically hadn't paid well. Most of Singer's 2005 pay was in restricted stock that won't vest for five years. "A great deal of his compensation was equity-based and will either pay out or not pay out. It's valued at a point in time. But based on how the company performs, he may or may not earn that money."

Although he once did the same kind of executive work as Singer, Holland is certain he can be impartial. After all, he answers not to Singer but to the company's shareholders. "If a particular board or a particular committee is not in step with what their shareholders think they should be able to kick them out. And that happens." It's more difficult at Lance than at some companies because its directors aren't voted on annually, but staggered terms for directors also can help prevent precipitous purges by shareholders, Holland says.

Since it passed in 2002, the Sarbanes-Oxley Act has made boards and CEOs more accountable for corporate finances and more conscientious about explaining CEO pay. In July, the U.S. Securities and Exchange Commission issued rules that will force companies to clarify executive compensation even more. Among other things, they must report a dollar value for all equity-based compensation and a total compensation figure comparable with those at other companies. The new rules will close most loopholes companies have used to avoid disclosing full CEO compensation, Hodgson says, but he doesn't expect them to give complete details about the performance measures used to set pay.

He would like shareholders to have a stronger voice in setting CEO pay, such as nonbinding votes on compensation-committee reports. A negative vote wouldn't overturn the decision but would send a message to board members. Holland says such a vote could set bad precedent and blur the lines between shareholders, directors and management. "You could get down to saying, 'Is the company setting the right capital-expenditure budget? Are they aggressive enough in their growth plans?'"

No matter how fully it's disclosed, CEO pay isn't likely to go down soon. People capable of running big public companies are in short supply, and heightened interest in CEO pay could, paradoxically, lead to more pay, says Hank Federal, principal and Southeast compensation-practice leader for Toledo, Ohio-based Findley Davies. "With the ever-increasing scrutiny around the businesses and what they do and how they pay these executives, they have less and less room for any kind of error. Therefore, it is contracting the pool of very qualified CEOs. When you've got people demanding and needing high-qualified CEOs and a shrinking pool, what does that typically do? It raises prices."

Doc in a Box

Wellness specialists credit health-monitoring kiosks with saving time, money and lives.

Dawn S. Onley

Automated health screening stations at Frank Fuentes' workplace are helping keep him off blood pressure medication and out of the doctor's office.

Fuentes, an office equipment coordinator at American Honda Motor Co. in Torrance, Calif., credits the noninvasive, computerized monitoring stations with giving him and other Honda em-ployees the key to managing their own health: timely information.

Fuentes says he has used the screening stations consistently over the past decade to monitor his blood pressure and to get alerts when he has picked up weight. "I was on medication once before. They told me I couldn't get off it until I lost weight," Fuentes says, adding that he checks his blood pressure every few days now at one of the stations. "By doing the reading, I can tell whether I need to exercise."

Computerized Screening Inc. (CSI) of Sparks, Nev., sells the Health Station used by American Honda and other employers to help employees like Fuentes get fast health assessments at their worksites.

American Honda has used the stations for more than 10 years. Workers in the security department requested that the machines be installed in the workplace after seeing how they were used in supermarkets.

American Honda safety specialist John Duehring says that at first the company leased the kiosks, but they proved to be such a major hit, with thousands of uses each month, that officials decided to purchase them to complement a corporate wellness structure that includes an on-site fitness center, wellness seminars and free exercise classes. Honda now owns 11 Health Stations spread across more than half a dozen major facilities and plans to buy nine more stations, Duehring says. Employees use the stations in cafeterias and break rooms.

Touch-Screen Testing

The Health Station comes in basic and advanced models and measures users' blood pressure, heart rate and weight noninvasively. To use the machines, employees sit down at what resem-bles a combination workbench and mini-entertainment center with touch-screen computers that will walk users through a variety of tests.

To measure blood pressure, users put their arms into a standard blood pressure cuff and rest their elbows on a table in front of them. In some models, a scale built into the seat measures weight. Health Stations, depending on the options purchased, also can monitor other signs such as spirometry, the measurement of lung strength and capacity used by physicians treating breathing issues such as asthma.

Other tests, driven by question-and-answer sessions with the computers, look at users' lifestyles and health choices, such as their level of exercise or smoking habits. The answers help the station generate a personalized health risk appraisal, which places users in government-defined health risk categories.

Bob Sullivan, CSI's executive vice president, says an upgraded version offers enhanced features including Internet links, through a secure server, to let users reach their health care providers or pharmacists on the web. This model also features a drug encyclopedia and a database that ensures medications are compatible. Some models include connectivity that allows videoconferencing right at the station. Stored in the stations are hundreds of health tips and educational videos on everything from alternative medications to nutritional supplements and herbal remedies.

The stations contain customized information on local health care providers including physicians, hospitals and crisis centers.

Use of the Health Station is "completely patient driven," Sullivan says. "The patient is involved in his own health care. This is giving people the ability to understand what their health status is."

In keeping with medical information privacy law, neither employers nor the vendor can access employee-specific information in the kiosks.

Prices for Health Station models range from the Model 3K at $3,495 to the Model 6K at $6,995. Options, such as more tests and information databases, vary depending on the employer's needs, Sullivan says. CSI has 3,500 stations in workplaces, supermarkets and other locations across the United States and Canada. According to the 26-year-old company, its health-monitoring stations are in about 60 percent of *Fortune* 500 companies.

There is at least one other manufacturer of such health monitoring machines. Medical Screening Services Inc. of Niles, Ill., markets its Vita-Stat health stations, which measure blood pressure, heart rate and weight, calculate body mass, and provide educational information on hypertension, exercise, weight and diet.

Fuentes says he likes being able to monitor his blood pressure. But he says he wishes his company machine gave users a weekly or monthly tip on what they should eat as well as on new medical discoveries.

Some employees are skeptical of the station's readings, Fuentes adds. "Some of the people are not aware that the machine gives you a true reading. People are a little apprehensive about trying to use it. They can have high blood pressure without knowing it."

Keeping Data Private

CSI's Health Stations also allow users to establish their personal medical records in the station's system. The user can bring in records of doctor's visits, hospitalizations or prescription drug use and load that data into some models.

Employees need not worry that their bosses could peruse their personal medical information, Sullivan notes. The Health Insurance Portability and Accountability Act (HIPAA) requires increased security for employee health information and imposes criminal and civil penalties for employers that don't comply. In keeping with HIPAA, Sullivan says, neither employers nor CSI can access employee-specific information. The Health Station encrypts such information, and users can access it only with a personal identification number known solely to the employee.

Employers can choose how their Health Station model stores data, Sullivan adds. Some stations are truly stand-alone, with all data stored at the station at the employer's site, while others store data on servers based at CSI. "But we do nothing with the patient-identified data internally, nor do we have access to it," he says.

Although employers cannot access an employee's individual data from the stations, employers can get aggregate data to see what employee populations are using the monitoring stations and what their health concerns are. Then employers can use that data to develop health programs to address issues identified in the data, according to Sullivan.

For employers who wonder if they might be liable should an employee use a monitoring station and then fall ill, Sullivan notes that each time a CSI Health Station gives a user a measurement such as blood pressure, it also displays a disclaimer that points the user to a physician or health care professional for any follow-up.

Cost-Effective Wellness

About four years ago, a blackjack dealer at the Cal-Neva Resort & Spa in Lake Tahoe, Nev., suffered a heart attack and passed out at work. The dealer survived, but the incident prompted senior wellness officials at the upscale casino and resort to take additional steps to promote employee wellness.

The resort, which had long mandated CPR classes for managers and had external defibrillators on-site, was already proactive about employee health, but after the dealer's heart attack, officials felt they could do even more, says Rick Talbot, Cal-Neva's chief of security and director of employee wellness and safety. Cal-Neva purchased a Health Station to give employees and resort visitors a way to monitor their health.

That move may have prevented another calamity last October when the resort's director of engineering, who felt under the weather, decided to test his heart rate. The director, who suffers from ongoing heart problems, sat down at the Health Station and quickly learned that his heart rate was racing at more than 200 beats per minute.

Cal-Neva is considering purchasing another monitoring station. Talbot, who acknowledges he's in a high-stress job, says he uses the station daily to monitor his own blood pressure and heart rate. About 3,000 users each month access the resort's station. Talbot adds that the station helps not only employees but also resort guests, many of whom are unaccustomed to the high altitude of Lake Tahoe.

"We're at 6,200-feet elevation, and the air's a little thin," Talbot explains. "We get older folks here. I've taken guests, complaining of shortness of breath, to the machine myself."

Sullivan recalls the story of a man at another workplace who was noticeably red in the face and was told by another employee to check his blood pressure at their company's health-monitoring station. When he did, he learned it was off the chart, and he had to have immediate bypass surgery, Sullivan says.

Talbot believes the stations save his employer money and increase productivity, although Cal-Neva doesn't keep statistics on how much it believes it saves due to the stations.

"This is saving health care dollars. Just think of what you save if you save [on] hospitalization for cardiac arrest [if the machine catches heart irregularities before an attack]. It's a real lifesaving possibility," Sullivan says.

While American Honda also doesn't have any metrics in place to measure whether the monitoring stations have helped reduce absenteeism or increase productivity among the workforce of 3,040, Duehring says user feedback shows that employees use the kiosks widely. For example, just at the company's headquarters, there are 1,000 uses of the machine a month. And Duehring says he hears from employees all the time—asking for more machines.

'We provided a complete wellness program to the entire staff of our corporate headquarters at minimal cost and great efficiency.'

"All we go by is how many people are using the machines," he says. "We know that when we have the machine set up in one area and we move it, we get a lot of phone calls."

AstraZeneca, a pharmaceutical manufacturer headquartered in Wilmington, Del., is another employer using the monitoring stations. Amy Milhorn, senior manager of corporate health services, says the three CSI Health Stations her company owns definitely have saved her and her staff time. Milhorn has three full-time and two part-time nurses on her staff who don't have to do as many blood pressure readings and other tests as they used to.

"Instead of employees coming to the nurses to get readings, they use the machines," Milhorn explains.

"CSI provided the basis for a program that enabled us to cost-effectively reach all employees," says Milhorn, whose company has 5,500 employees. "We provided a complete wellness program to the entire staff of our corporate headquarters at minimal cost and great efficiency. We spent far less than if we hired additional health care practitioners, and [we] reached a much greater number of people in a lesser amount of time."

DAWN S. ONLEY is a Washington, D.C.-based freelance writer who specializes in technology issues in private-sector and federal workplaces.

Building a Mentally Healthy Workforce

Psychologists highlight effective interventions to help counter the rising cost of mental health problems in the workplace.

Melissa Dittman

Psychologists and occupational health leaders highlighted programs aimed at alleviating work-family conflicts and workplace stress at a recent conference organized by the National Institute for Occupational Safety and Health and more than 20 co-sponsors, including APA. The 2004 Steps to a Healthier U.S. Workforce Symposium brought together leaders from the occupational safety and the health promotion communities to explore ways to improve employees' health and safety.

One session at the event included promoting employee well-being through such means as flexible work schedules and team-based employee problem-solving.

The need is evident: The number of employees nationwide reporting psychiatric disabilities is steadily growing and costing companies in lost productivity and employee absenteeism, according to psychologists who spoke at the session.

For example, at Bank One—now J.P. Morgan Chase—employees' mental health issues from 2000–2002 accounted for the second leading cause of short-term disability and were second in total of days absent from work—behind only pregnancy.

Depression, in particular, is the most reported psychiatric disability, and contributes to the most absences, limiting employees' cognitive reasoning and interpersonal skills, said clinical psychologist Daniel J. Conti, PhD, an employee assistance program director at J.P. Morgan Chase. By 2020, depression is expected to rank second in leading causes of worldwide disability; in 1990, it ranked fourth, according to the "The Global Burden of Disease" (Harvard University Press, 1996).

As such, Conti said companies need to not only take into account the productivity lost through employee absenteeism due to such mental health problems, but also the productivity lost while an employee is present but limited at work due to health problems—which he referred to as "presenteeism." He stressed the need for companies to change management and organizational work methods to help decrease such losses.

Doing that requires workplaces to examine returns on mental health components of their medical plans, and it requires employees to shift their work attitudes and behaviors, Conti noted.

Employer flexibility is also key to minimizing mental health problems among employees, said Lynne Casper, PhD, of the National Institute of Child Health and Human Development.

"Workplace policies can have an effect on people's health, how they live their life and their ability to manage their work and family obligations," she said.

Team-Building Interventions

Indeed, tedious job tasks, job insecurity or inflexible work schedules can demoralize some employees or lower their motivation, speakers noted.

To address such issues, psychologist David M. DeJoy, PhD, director of the Workplace Health Group, conducted a study on healthy work organization in retail. DeJoy and his colleagues surveyed employees at 21 stores—all part of the same company—to identify employees' concerns about issues such as their work schedules. From there, the researchers formed a team of eight to 12 employees at each store to develop store-specific interventions to respond to those concerns. Such interventions included programs geared to build skills to enhance employer and employee communication, improve morale, manage conflict and solve problems related to, for example, customer-service issues.

> **"Workplace policies can have an effect on people's health, how they live their life and their ability to manage their work and family obligations."**
>
> Lynne Casper
> National Institutes of Health

According to self reports from employees and employers, the interventions led to better communication as well as improved employee satisfaction with work schedules, job content and feelings of increased involvement in workplace decisions, said DeJoy, a professor of health promotion and behavior at the University of Georgia. The team-based intervention also had some positive effects on store sales and employee turnover.

Working Parent Programs

Researchers have shown that programs—such as Triple P (Positive Parenting Program)—geared to help working parents balance work and family life also can contribute to improved employee mental health.

Triple P provides evidence-based support strategies for parents of children from birth to 12 years old, said psychologist Ron Prinz, PhD, Carolina Distinguished Professor at the University of South Carolina. The program features individual or small group sessions focused on helping parents better plan and prioritize their family and work responsibilities and gain confidence in their parenting skills. Australian psychology professor Matthew Sanders, PhD, and his colleagues at the University of Queensland developed Triple P.

Triple P, in particular, derives from research showing that parents with high work stress tend to have low job self-efficacy, less positive parent-child interactions, less parental satisfaction and more coercive parenting styles, Prinz said.

Triple P can counter some of that, according to preliminary data. Parents who participated in Triple P group sessions at work were able to reduce work stress and child behavior problems and also improve their overall self-efficacy, Prinz said.

However, child care isn't the only source of family life stress. At IBM, for example, the company found a 200 percent increase from 1986 to 2001 in employees needing elder care for aging loved ones. To help, the company created a national referral and resource service to help employees find elder care.

Flexible Work Schedules

IBM also introduced flexible work schedules—such as giving many employees the option to work part-time or at home—based on another of its survey findings that such scheduling contributes to improved worker satisfaction. Now one-third of IBM employees do not work primarily at a traditional IBM office. Working from home, in particular, has gained acceptability among employees and employers, said Michael D. Shum, IBM's director of Global Workforce Diversity Operations.

Indeed, IBM researchers have found that employees who work at home have the least difficulty with motivation and retention and are more willing to put in extra effort in their job. Plus, 55 percent of the employees surveyed agreed that working from home at least one day per week is acceptable, and 64 percent said they are likely to work from home in the next five years.

"This whole face-time culture of a manager having to watch a person work is changing," Shum said. "We still have a long way to go, but we're making progress."

Employee Benefits of the Future

Melissa Proffitt Reese, Linda Rowings, and Tiffany Sharpley

Employee benefits provide a significant portion of an employee's total compensation and are an important element in any employee's job satisfaction. To maximize the positive impact of benefits on employees, employers must reconsider benefit packages and how such benefits are communicated to employees. This will help ensure they meet the needs and wants of the four generations of individuals who will be working side by side. This article:

- describes the generations that will be working together and what businesses will need from each generation;
- examines ways employers can attract and retain different generations;
- discusses ways in which employers can and should consider the costs associated with providing benefits; and
- provides design ideas for an employee benefit package that will motivate multiple generations.

Which Generations Will be Working Together in the Workforce?

Historically, businesses have relied on the ability of multiple generations to work together to make the business a success. Typically, there have been at least two, if not three, generations working simultaneously in the workforce. In the near term, business communities will have four generations working together in the workforce. The generations are commonly known as: the "Traditionalists," "Baby Boomers," "Generation X," and "Generation Y." Although experts express differences as to who falls within these different categories, generally the Traditionalists were born prior to 1946, the Baby Boomers were born between 1946 and 1964, Generation X-ers were born between 1965 and 1977, and Generation Y-ers were born between 1978 and 1989.

Traditionalists

The Traditionalists are expected to retire within the next five years. They lived through World War II and appreciate security. Traditionalists typically have historical knowledge of their business industry and company and tend to be loyal to their company. Traditionalists are known for positive traits such as: stability,

attention to detail, thoroughness, loyalty, and hard work.[1] Other less flattering characteristics include dislike of ambiguity and change, reluctance to buck the system, being uncomfortable with conflict, and reticent when they disagree.[2]

Baby Boomers

The Baby Boomers are known for being hard workers and making the necessary sacrifices. Baby Boomers are very busy growing their organizations and their own individual careers. Baby Boomers are often viewed (especially by Generation Y-ers) as primarily focusing on money with "lip service" paid to family/work/life balance. Many Baby Boomers are "empty nesters" and have significant discretionary income, while others are struggling to simultaneously work, raise children, and assist aging parents. Baby Boomers are positively described as service-oriented, driven, willing to "go the extra mile," good at relationships, eager to please and good team members.[3] However, Baby Boomers are also known to be uncomfortable with conflict, reluctant to go against peers, overly sensitive to feedback, judgmental of those who see things differently, and self-centered.[4]

Generation X

Generation X is smaller in number than the Baby Boomer generation and has generally struggled more with the work/life balance issues. This generation is seen as feeling more of a need to actually achieve a work/life balance, which did not seem achievable by the Baby Boomer generation. Generation X-ers tend to be self-sufficient and are technologically literate. Generation X-ers are positively described as adaptable, independent, unintimidated by authority, and creative.[5] This generation's less attractive qualities include impatience, a lack of people skills, inexperience, and cynicism.[6]

Generation Y

Generation Y, also known as the Millennials, is the up-and-coming generation. Generation Y is expected to very shortly outnumber Generation X and perhaps the Baby Boomer generation in the workforce. This generation prides itself on spending more time with family and less time at work. Generation Y individuals not only understand technology, but are truly experts with respect to using technology. Also, Generation Y-ers are expected to change jobs repeatedly over the course of their careers. Generation Y is positively known for collective action, optimism, tenacity, and multitasking capabilities.[7] Generation Y is also thought to need supervision and structure and lacks experience, especially with respect to handling difficult people.[8]

What Does Business Need from Each of the Generations?

Each generation described in the previous section brings a unique set of skills to the workforce. The Traditionalists provide historical knowledge of the industry as well as experience and wisdom from the past that needs to be shared with the next generations. The Baby Boomers are currently leading and managing their companies and focusing on their own careers. Generation X individuals provide strong support to the Baby Boomer generation and perform duties very independently with a strong work ethic. Generation Y is expected to fill the gap that will be left when the Baby Boomer generation retires. As mentioned above, Generation Y is very large in population (unlike Generation X). Therefore, companies will rely on Generation Y for their futures. Unfortunately, Generation Y is not seen as independent as Generation X, and has a need for supervision and structure. Therefore, since the labor, and ultimately the leadership, of Generation Y will be necessary to maintain the workforce, organizations need to focus now on mentoring and training Generation Y to prepare them with the skills that the business will need in the upcoming decades.

What Can an Employer Do to Attract and Retain the Different Generations?

Employee benefits are such a large cost for employers that it is imperative to spend these dollars effectively. Thus, benefits should be designed and communicated to address the different generations' needs and desires. The "one size fits all" approach of the past will not be effective for such diverse generations.

Furthermore, according to the Bureau of Labor Statistics, the American workforce is expected to grow only one percent annually over the next decade, meaning that finding qualified workers will be an ongoing issue for employers. Offering a more flexible workplace and benefits will make it easier to attract and retain the right workers.

Flexible Scheduling

Despite their differences, a common characteristic of all generations of workers is a desire for more flexibility. For example, many Traditionalists wish to ease into retirement, while Boomers are frequently responsible for caring for aging parents, Generation X-ers often desire time for participating in school activities with their children, and numerous Generation Y-ers want time for community service. Many employers have found that they can increase work schedule flexibility while maintaining productivity.

One of the more common approaches to increasing work schedule flexibility is flextime. Most flextime programs require the employee to be present for certain "core" hours, such as from 9:00 A.M. to 3:00 P.M., while providing the opportunity for an employee to elect a start time as early as 7:00 A.M. and a departure time of 3:30 P.M. or as late as 9:00 A.M. with a departure time of 5:30 P.M. While flextime makes scheduling meetings more problematic, it can provide better service to customers in other time zones. Somewhat similar to flextime, compressed work week programs allow employees to work four 10-hour days each week, or nine nine-hour days per two-week period, with the tenth day of the period off. Typically, employees are expected to schedule medical appointments and home maintenance on their days off, which increases productivity; skeptics, however, have expressed concerns that productivity decreases during the longer days.

Another approach is job sharing. Job sharing frequently involves two employees, each working 2½ or three days per week to perform a single job. This allows the employees to perform a full-time job on a part-time basis. If the job-sharing workers have different strengths and the job is structured to utilize each person's particular skills, the employer will also benefit from the job sharing. A key element to the success of this approach is the ability of the sharing employees to communicate effectively with each other. Typically, benefits for those who job share are pro-rated. Each worker would need to meet the applicable eligibility requirements to receive retirement, life, health, and disability benefits.

Telework has grown in popularity in recent years, due to employee interest, as well as concerns about pollution and gas prices. In addition, improvements in technology have made it possible to perform many jobs without physically being in the office one or more days per week. Many federal government agencies use telework. The federal Web site *www.telework.gov* has a number of helpful elements, including a telework guide, frequently asked questions, and telework training sessions for employees and managers. If an employer is considering implementing a telework program, it should consider what equipment it will provide, policies regarding use of that equipment by family members (which may raise privacy and security concerns), approval of overtime, supervision, training, and worker safety. Employers who have implemented telework programs have found that many at-home workers miss the social interaction of the workplace, and thus implement monthly on-site meetings and schedule on-line meetings to alleviate the loss of interaction. Telework also reduces opportunities for mentoring and may further erode the social skills of the on-line generation (*i.e.*, Generation Y).

To avoid the high cost of replacing valued workers, a number of corporations (notably IBM and PricewaterhouseCoopers) have implemented extended leave and sabbatical programs (for as long as five years).[9] While mothers of small children are the most frequent users, younger employees often appreciate the ability to complete higher education degrees on a full-time basis.

Unique Benefits

While some employers have found success with adding flexibility to work schedules, others have added unique "perks." Employers seeking to attract and retain younger workers may want to consider free food or beverages on a daily or weekly basis, casual dress every day, movie tickets and small gift certificates, and tuition reimbursement. Employers seeking to attract and retain older workers may want to offer free financial planning, elder care assistance, and wellness programs. Employers targeting families might offer monthly on-site celebrations for the whole family, lactation rooms, adoption assistance, child care referrals or on-site day care, paid maternity or paternity leave, child care reimbursement for overtime or business travel, and infertility assistance. Other creative employers have offered group legal, auto, and homeowners insurance (and allowed their employees to payroll deduct the premiums), subsidized fitness center memberships, paid parking and mass transit passes, domestic partner benefits, pet insurance, rest areas (complete with pillows and blankets), and concierge services, such as on-site dry cleaning, oil changes, and massages.

Traditional Benefits

With respect to more traditional employee benefits, Traditionalists want and expect benefits that reward longevity, such as defined benefit pension plans. Conversely, Generation Y-ers, who anticipate multiple job changes over the course of their careers, prefer portability in the form, for example, of 401(k) or profit-sharing plans with short vesting schedules and health savings accounts, which will allow them to preserve and take with them their retirement and medical savings as they move from job to job.

What Do the Differences in Generations Mean to Benefit Communications?

Traditionalists and Baby Boomers expect significant direction from their employers on benefits matters, and are less than comfortable with technology. For these groups, the traditional handouts, booklets, and meetings are most effective. If on-line enrollment and Internet-based education is used, employers need to be certain these groups are comfortable with the processes needed to access the information.

Generations X and Y, in contrast, have great faith in technology and their own decision-making abilities. The individuals in these generations have grown up with computers. These groups demand Internet-based education and a variety of options. Employers need to be mindful of the large amount of misinformation readily accessible through the Internet, and need to make sure that their message is disseminated and received. Benefits departments must (if they have not already) implement electronic methods of communicating with participants, provided employees have computer access at work. For companies with employees without computer access (*e.g.,* employees who are on the road or who work in a manufacturing plant), print materials mailed to homes may still be most effective.

Another impediment to electronic (and effective) communications is the current Internal Revenue Service and the Department of Labor requirements for providing plan information to participants. Current requirements limit the instances in which communications can be given electronically and require that very technical information be included. Thus, summary plan descriptions and certain notices that go to employees are too technical and complicated to grab the attention of the younger generations, and frequently overwhelm the older generations. The best type of communication is a cross between the "Highlights" type of information employees often receive at times of open enrollment, and a summary plan description which includes specific details as regulated by the Department of Labor. In the future it will be most effective to communicate using a combination of print and electronic methods (*e.g.,* postcards, booklets, newsletters, text messages, e-mails, podcasts, Webcasts, etc.) and in a way that minimizes the complexity of the material.

What Do the Costs of Offering Employee Benefits Mean to Your Business's Bottom Line?

The first step in evaluating an organization's employee benefit package is to take inventory of the benefits (and costs of these benefits) currently offered. When calculating the cost, an employer should be sure to include the administrative cost of the benefit. For example, under a retirement plan, costs include not only the funding of the plan, but also the cost of plan administration (regardless of whether a third-party administrator or an internal administrator manages the plan). In addition, there may be actuarial costs and legal costs, such as costs incurred to provide proper plan documentation, submissions to the Internal Revenue Service, notices to participants, and other areas of compliance. A review of costs should be conducted for each employee benefit that is provided to employees (including vacation days, approved leaves, retirement plans, group life, health, and disability, and perks). Once the benefit costs are determined, an employer can begin to evaluate what is truly important to each particular generation, and determine which benefits should be maintained or enhanced and how they should be changed or modified. To a large extent, the benefits offered by U.S. employers are shaped by tax favorable treatment. As employers go through this evaluation process, they may find a need to lobby Congress or state legislatures to modify the tax or legal requirements associated with the benefits being offered.

What Do Employee Benefit Packages Designed to Motivate Four Generations of Employees Look Like?

The overall objective when designing employee benefit packages for the future should be to empower employees to make their own decisions for benefit packages that fit their needs and lifestyles. Traditionally, employee benefit packages have been designed with a paternalistic approach. Instead of providing choices for employees, employers have historically dictated what the benefits package will be—the "employer knows best" approach. This has meant the employer presents the benefit and the employee's choice is simply whether or not to sign up for a particular benefit in the benefits package. Unfortunately, this approach has become obsolete with the advent of two-income families, single-parent households, and a multi-generational workforce. To maximize the impact of the employer's benefit contributions, employees should be given an opportunity to choose the benefits that are most meaningful to them. For those who worry that employees cannot or will not handle choices appropriately, this empowerment concept is not untested with respect to employee benefits. The key to success, however, is strong and consistent communication from the employer regarding options and issues to consider when selecting benefits.

Let's discuss some possible options for employers to consider:

Option 1: Elimination of "Traditional" Employee Benefit Plans. An employer could simply terminate all of its benefit plans and replace those benefits with a specific dollar amount to each employee to use as the employee sees fit. For example, an employer could provide employees with $15,000 a year extra in compensation to cover any health care, retirement, PTO leave, or other employee needs. This approach provides the ultimate flexibility to employees and completely eliminates employer involvement for employee benefit plans. While superficially attractive, under the current U.S. tax structure, the employee and employer would lose significant tax advantages, thus leading to an increased tax liability and potentially decreasing compensation for the employee overall. Additionally, if employees were required to find their own individual coverage, under the current benefits system, individuals with medical problems could have significant difficulty obtaining coverage. Given this country's poor savings rate, the pure compensation approach also raises issues about how to handle those who fail to purchase individual health, life, and disability coverage or save for retirement.

To the extent this lump-sum approach is attractive to employers and employees, Congress should be approached to create a tax-advantaged method to providing additional flexibility for employees to pick and choose the benefits that are most valuable to them, while freeing the employer from the time of administration of benefits and the pressure to spend funds to provide under-appreciated benefits. In addition, third-party administrators and other vendors that currently provide employers coverage for employees would need to create products that could provide such *ad hoc* individual coverage on a tax-free basis (assuming Congress passed the necessary legislation).

Option 2: Maintain Current Employee Benefit Plan Structure with Modifications. The least radical strategy to motivate the multiple generations in the workforce would be for an employer to make modifications to its current employee benefit plan structure. For example, if an employer has a traditional health plan, the employer could consider offering health reimbursement arrangements (HRAs) or health savings accounts (HSAs), either as an option or as the sole health plan. To help bridge the increased deductible gap from a traditional health plan to an HRA or HSA, the employer should use at least a portion of the premium savings from purchasing a high deductible health plan to initially fund the HRA or HSA. HRAs and HSAs shift significant costs and responsibility onto the consumer (*e.g.,* the employee), but currently it is very difficult for employees to know the cost of medical expenses and how best to shop around for the best price and treatment option. An employer could assist by lobbying for increased disclosure of health care costs and outcomes.

Option 3: Non-Traditional "Unique" Employee Benefits. In addition to modifying their "traditional" employee benefit plans (Option 2 above), employers could offer unique benefits to attract the new generations and retain their older workers. As discussed earlier in this article, an increasing number of employees are demanding a flexible work schedule and work environment, and employers are finding that allowing these employees to work remotely from home (which may or may not be located in the same city as the "office") is feasible. Video chat rooms can be used for business meetings or just socializing with colleagues. Ensuring that all documents needed by employees are available electronically (*e.g.,* 401(k) enrollment forms, health plan enrollment forms, flexible benefit claim forms, summaries of material modifications, etc.) is essential for employers who have telecommuting employees.

Working Women recently published a list of benefits/perks offered by companies voted the "100 Best Companies." The perks offered by the best employers to work for include a number of the non-traditional benefits mentioned above, such as elder care and child care resource and referral, massage therapy, dry-cleaning service, take-home meals, parental leave *beyond* the Family Medical Leave Act requirements, paid adoption leave, infertility treatment assistance (*in vitro*), child care reimbursement for business travel, and emergency sick-child care.[10]

Conclusion

The options discussed above are only the beginning of the benefit designs that can be (and should be) considered as organizations move into the new era of a four-generation workforce. The emphasis should not be as much on the options, but on embarking on a new way of thinking about employee benefits. Organizations should no longer rely on the traditional benefit plan structures and features. To be competitive and attract the best and brightest workforce, employers must create innovative benefit packages that appeal to a broad range of workers.

Notes

1. Ron Zemke, Claire Raines, and Bob Filipczak, *Generations at Work* 46 (2000).

2. *Id.*

3. *Id.*

4. *Id.*

5. *Id.* at 110.

6. *Id.*

7. *Id.* at 144.

8. *Id.*

9. *The Best vs. the Rest,* Working Mother, October 2006, 82.

10. *Id.* at 74.

MELISSA PROFFITT REESE is co-managing partner of the law firm of Ice Miller LLP. LINDA ROWINGS is senior counsel, and TIFFANY SHARPLEY is an associate, at the firm. Residing in Ice Miller's office in Indianapolis, the authors can be reached at melissa.reese @icemiller.com, linda.rowings@icemiller.com, and tiffany. sharpley@ icemiller.com, respectively.

Benefits and the Bottom Line

Take a good, hard look at your benefits package to make sure you're doing what's best for employees and your company.

Phillip M. Perry

Controlling the rising cost of employee benefits is a challenge that never seems to get easier. Though escalating health insurance premiums get the lion's share of attention, business owners must consider the full range of worker benefits, which together comprise 37.2 percent of the average payroll, according to the U.S. Chamber of Commerce.

Of course, doing away with benefits is not an option. Hourly workers and salaried staff demand them as part of the employment agreement. The challenge is to offer attractive plans that encourage quality employees to remain on board while maintaining a healthy bottom line.

To do this, make sure you aren't paying for benefits your staff doesn't need, advise various consultants. Being all things to all people is more expensive than narrowing in on what your employees really want. To find out the latter, survey your employees. This will help you put your energy where there's 'value added,' as opposed to offering a little bit of everything.

Web to the Rescue

Your goal is to select the most affordable quality plans and administer them as cost effectively as possible. Technology can help.

"A number of new Web-based services offer plans and quote prices so certain choices can be made over the Internet," says Tim Harrington, a principal with Mercer Human Resource Consulting, a Chicago-based consulting firm that has tracked benefits costs for more than 25 years.

The automation inherent in the Internet allows Web-based services to offer comparison-shopping of products from a broad range of carriers. They can also reduce the overhead involved in processing employee claims, educate new employees on your benefits plans, and answer common questions.

Various Web services handle benefits such as health insurance and retirement plans, and offer clients the opportunity to create custom Web pages for use by their employees. In many cases these services allow employees to access information on the plans without having to call their human resources departments, saving your business time and money.

Health Insurance

Health insurance, by far the most popular benefit, is offered by 96 percent of employers, according to Business and Legal Reports, a human resources research organization based in Old Saybrook, Conn. Premiums for such coverage rose an average 7.7 percent in 2006, a rate more than twice as great as workers' wages (3.8 percent) and overall inflation (3.5 percent). The figures were announced in the 2006 Employer Health Benefits Survey from the Kaiser Family Foundation.

When containing costs, your first line of defense is to join purchasing groups.

"When you join forces with other employers you bring more leverage to the negotiating table," says Larry Boress, president of the Midwest Business Group on Health, a Chicago-based consortium of 80 employers.

The second step on the cost savings journey is to shift costs to employees. Cost sharing occurs when employees make greater co-payments and/or pay higher annual deductibles for services received.

Employees become more prudent consumers of health care when they pay a greater portion of the costs. At the same time, insurance companies fund less of the total annual health care expense. Both phenomena translate into lower risk for the carrier and lower premiums for the employer.

Life Insurance

Life insurance is both inexpensive and popular, with 89 percent of employers offering it. Because it's a commodity item, employers should shop around for the best rate. You may find you can save money by purchasing group life from one carrier and accidental death and dismemberment from another. Be aware that some life carriers have divisions that compete with each other. One division may offer both life and AD&D while another may offer just life. The prices of the life insurance may differ in the two divisions, so shop around.

A common but costly error is to save time by purchasing different forms of insurance from the same broker. If you don't have time to comparison shop and need to use a broker, ask other employers which ones have proven to be highly knowledgeable about carriers.

Workers Compensation

Workers compensation is a mandated benefit that can erode your bottom line if you don't watch it carefully. Premiums are increasing nationwide at about 10 percent to 15 percent annually, according to a spokesperson for Sullivan Curtis Monroe, an insurance brokerage in Irvine, Calif.

"It's starting to hit businesses in the pocketbook," he reports. "They are asking 'What can we do now?'"

Premium increases represent only one part of your cost. Other, indirect costs can be two to three times as great. They include the overhead to administer a claim, supervisory time in investigating an accident and lost time from the injured individual. Here are suggestions for cost containment measures:

- **Run physical tests for applicants.** Include "range of motion" tests for jobs that require much lifting, stopping and standing.
- **Improve your workplace.** Adjust work stations to reduce claims that result from repetitive stress injuries.
- **Choose an experienced carrier.** Don't just buy insurance from the carrier with the lowest price. Choosing the cheapest carrier can end up costing you more when it fails to handle claims properly. Instead, look for a company with a good claims-handling history. Meet with the individuals who will handle your claims, and determine their operating philosophy. And get feedback from other businesses that have experience with that carrier.

You can also reduce premiums, or keep them from increasing unnecessarily downstream, by taking some proactive steps.

"Overcharges by insurance companies are very common," says Edward Priz, principal of Advanced Insurance Management, Riverside, Ill.

To keep them from occurring, Priz says you need to audit your own classification codes to assure accuracy with the workplace conditions to which your personnel are exposed.

You also need to assure the accuracy of your "experience modification factor." That term refers to the number used to modify your charges, based upon the accident history of your workplace. Consider having an outside auditor review your records.

Disability Income

Workers compensation protects your workers from financial disaster if they're injured on the job. But what if the injury takes place outside of work? That's where long- and short-term disability comes to the rescue. It can be a valuable benefit, offered by 68 percent of employers nationwide.

How can you control the rising costs for this insurance? The Washington Business Group on Health, an organization that assists businesses in this area, has three suggestions:

- **Form early "return to work" policies.** You want to encourage people to return to work as soon as possible. That's because the costs of an illness go far beyond disability payments and insurance premiums. They also include lost productivity, overtime for employees required to accomplish the missing person's work, and re-training time.
- To encourage early return, develop workplace programs that will accommodate workers who suffer from temporary disabilities. Many employers have these in place for staff members covered by workers comp, but have not extended the programs to cover people absent under short-term or long-term disability. Now is the time to do so.

- **Pick the right plan.** Be aware of policies that encourage workers to stay home longer. For example, some plans allow no payments unless a person stays out for two weeks, at which time the payments become retroactive to the first day. Under these plans, individuals often stay out longer because it is in their self-interest.
- **Select your carrier wisely.** Not all insurance companies are equal. Select a company that will help you increase your productivity by helping injured people return to work more quickly.

Ask the right questions of any prospective company: Do they spend money on rehabilitation? Do they have good medical resources? Do they have doctors and nurses on staff? What training do they provide their people? Check with other businesses in your area to discover what insurers they use and their level of satisfaction.

Finally, put disability insurance in context. It's all about productivity. You can push down cost by choosing a plan that is less expensive, but the result may be longer periods of time during which people are away from the workplace. The savings you pick up on the health side can be cancelled out by losses on the productivity side.

Cohesive Approach

Left uncontrolled, the rising costs of employee benefits can erode your bottom line and lead to staff discontent when draconian measures are needed to cap spiraling expenses.

Take action now to review your entire benefits package. Survey your staff to find out what benefits they really want, in important. And finally, share information on costs with your employees. When employees know the effect benefits have on the health of your company, they'll be more willing to help by cost sharing and responsible utilization of benefits.

Internet Services

Here are some Internet services that can help employers reduce employee benefits costs by streamlining the recordkeeping process.

- www.employease.com [Variety of benefits.] Services include maintaining a centralized database of employees, managing enrollments, issuing benefit statements, and allowing employees 24-hour access to data. Claims it can be used with any carrier.
- www.benefitmall.com [Health insurance, payroll, other benefits.] Maintains a network of brokers who sell products from more than 100 health insurance carriers. Allows employers to visit sites and compare prices and features of various health insurance plans.
- www.healthmarket.com [Health insurance.] This service offers self-directed health plans that by-pass the usual managed care organizations. Employers and employees each contribute a set number of dollars annually to the plans, which have signed on doctors and hospitals.

From *Industrial Distribution,* Vol. 96, No. 1, January 1, 2007, pp. 32+ . Copyright © 2007 by Industrial Distribution. Reprinted by permission of Reprint Management Services.

UNIT 6

Fostering Employee/ Management Relationships

Unit Selections

Key Points to Consider

- Taking disciplinary action is often one of the most difficult and unpleasant activities that a manager must do. If you were a manager, how would you take disciplinary action? If you were the employee being disciplined, what would you do? What would you do about an employee who suddenly lashes out at another for no particular reason?

- What are some of the advantages of hiring temporary employees? Have you ever considered an internship? Why is it good for the employer? For the intern?

- Should managers be concerned about ethics? Why or why not? Do you think that unethical behavior can be economically justified? Why would managers knowingly engage in unethical and/or illegal behavior thinking they can get away with it?

- There is a labor market that is essentially unregulated and out of the reach of the law. Do you think this should be controlled? Who do you think is responsible here?

Student Web Site

www.mhcls.com/online

Internet References

Further information regarding this Web site may be found in this book's preface or online.

Management, Leadership and Supervision
http://humanresources.about.com/od/managementandleadership/

The American labor movement has a long history dating back to the start of the Industrial Revolution. That history has been marked by turmoil and violence, as workers sought to press their demands on business owners, whether represented by managers or entrepreneurs. The American labor movement exists because working conditions, pay, and benefits were very poor during the early years of the Industrial Revolution in both the United States and the rest of the world. It should be remembered that the American labor movement is only a small part of a broader, worldwide labor movement that includes most Western, European societies. The working conditions under which the first American industrial workers labored would be unacceptable today. Child labor was common. There are documented instances of 6- and 7-year-old children, chained to machines for 12 hours a day, 6 days a week, who threw themselves into the machines—choosing death over life in the dehumanized and mechanized existence of the early factory. Conditions in some factories in the North prior to the Civil War were so infamous that Southern congressmen used them as a justification for the institution of slavery. Slaves sometimes lived in better conditions than the factory workers of New England and many other Northern states.

Unions exist because workers sought a better working environment and a better standard of living. Companies often took advantage of employees, and the government sided with management and the owners, frequently quelling strikes and other forms of labor protest initiated by the workers. Such incidents as the Pullman Strike, the Hay-Market Square Riot, and the Homestead Strike exemplify the struggle of the American labor movement to achieve recognition and success in the attempt to improve the lives of all workers, whether unionized or not. The victories of labor have been hard fought and hard won. But, labor has not been without blemish in the struggle for worker's rights. The Marion County Turkey-Shoot, in Southern Illinois, probably the most violent day in American labor history, involved coal miners deliberately chasing strikebreakers from the mines and killing them.

During the past hundred years, the fortunes of the American labor movement have varied, and now workers' fortunes may be taking an even deeper downward turn, with attempts at unionization becoming even more difficult. Unions have been able to achieve their gains through the mechanism of collective bargaining. The individual has very little bargaining power when compared to a company, especially huge companies such as General Motors or General Electric. Collective bargaining allows workers to pool their collective resources and power to bargain with the corporation on a more equal footing. Unfortunately for the unions, many of the industries in which they are strongest are in decline. New leadership is necessary if the American labor movement is to survive and rebound in the next century and if it is to serve as a useful organ of society.

A union's ultimate weapon in contract negotiations, the strike, represents a complete breakdown of discipline from management's perspective. Disciplinary situations are almost always unpleasant, and today they can often lead to court cases, with all of the attendant legal questions and problems. A key to effective disciplinary action is documentation of employees' actions and the steps that were taken to correct them. How to go about "Setting up a Disciplinary Procedure" is outlined in the first article of this unit. Management needs to implement procedures and policies to assure employees are treated fairly and equitably in the workplace to deal with "Hard-Core Offenders."

The American labor movement has come a long way since the first strike by printers in Philadelphia in 1786. The journey, while difficult, has led to greater justice in the workplace and an increased standard of living for the nation as a whole. Unions have experienced both declines and increases in membership, but they have endured as a powerful social, political, and economic force. Whether or not they will again successfully "reinvent" themselves and adapt to a changing environment is a major question.

During the past fifteen years, primarily as a result of the dislocations in the job market, temporary workers became available to organizations. There are certain advantages to this situation for the employer, especially when looking to hire a new permanent employee out of school, as seen in "Interns on the Payroll."

There is also the issue of ethics. How companies treat their employees and their customers is going to be of increasing concern in the future. Ethical behavior will be at a premium, and managers know that it will be part of the job. Unfortunately, some managers of organizations will always make the economic/legal calculation that doing something that is illegal or unethical at best will benefit them, if not their shareholders, customers, and/or employees. "Business Ethics: The Key Role of Corporate Governance" will always be a problem no matter what the laws may be or how they're enforced. Someone will always try to get away with some sort of illegal, unethical, or dishonest activity. Flawed human nature will always play a role.

The underground and lower-end labor market also plays a role in the ethical treatment of employees. An estimated twelve million undocumented aliens in the United States have to work somewhere and often do for less than minimum wage. They do it because they work for unethical employers who know that they are in the United States illegally and therefore are not protected by employment laws, so they are therefore exploited. This is creating an underclass of workers who perform "Unregulated Work" at below the legal wage. This is not only subsidizing these unethical employers, but it is giving them an unfair advantage in the marketplace by lowering their costs when competing against employers paying legal wages, and driving down the wages of legitimate workers.

Setting up a Disciplinary Procedure

CHARTERED MANAGEMENT INSTITUTE CHECKLIST

Introduction

This checklist is aimed at those wishing to implement a disciplinary procedure within their company or organisation.

It is essential that an employer acts reasonably in dealing with misconduct and ill-discipline. A fair and thorough disciplinary procedure can help protect an employer against an unfair dismissal claim and the ensuing costs of a successful claim. Legislation aside, it is good personnel practice to deal with employee ill-discipline quickly and fairly, and to offer guidance on improving behaviour, so that problems do not fester and grow.

Although this checklist focuses on the mechanics of a disciplinary procedure, it is important to remember that good management, for example spotting problems before they become serious and identifying development needs to improve performance, can prevent many cases reaching this stage.

National Occupational Standards for Management and Leadership

This checklist has relevance for the following standards:
B: Providing direction, Unit 8; D: Working with people, Units 1 and 2

Definition

A disciplinary procedure provides employers with a structured approach for dealing with ill-discipline at work. The procedure defines the types of ill-discipline it covers, the presentation and documentation of warnings, representation at disciplinary interviews, time limits for investigation, and rights of appeal.

Action checklist

1. Designate a Disciplinary Procedure Management Committee (DPMC)

The Committee should include, depending on the size of the organisation, at least one person from the personnel department, and from each level of management within the organisation, and a representative from each trade union to which employees belong. The Committee will manage the design, implementation and running of the disciplinary procedure. Appoint a coordinator (preferably a member from personnel, but certainly someone with project management experience who commands respect, has excellent communication and negotiation skills and can get things done) to oversee the project.

2. Define the terms of reference

Identify the employees covered by the procedure (for example, all non-directors) and the managers who will be responsible for the disciplinary interviews. Define ill-discipline (both minor and serious misconduct), clarify legal obligations, and agree on the process which can lead to dismissal.

3. Draw up the procedure

Use the experiences, soundings and research of the Committee to devise a procedure. Try to obtain samples of procedures used in other organisations and remember to write as simply as possible so that it is easy to understand. If necessary, consider using external expertise.

The procedure should contain the following:

- **Purpose.** An initial paragraph giving the reasons for having a procedure, highlighting the benefits to employees of a consistent set of rules and the importance of discipline in the workplace.

- **Types of misconduct.** This should give staff an indication of the type of misconduct that would invoke the disciplinary procedure. Distinguish between minor offences and those which are serious or may constitute gross misconduct:

Minor	Serious
Smoking (where appropriate)	Vandalism
Time-keeping	Fraud
Misuse of company facilities	Alcohol/Drugs
Dress	Violence, bullying

- **Warnings.** Depending on the seriousness of the offence an employee will be faced with a series of warnings:

   Oral (confirmed in writing)
   Written
   Final written

The ultimate penalty after this will be dismissal, although sanctions short of dismissal such as transfer, demotion or loss of pay may be considered.

The warnings will be given to the employee after an interview, usually with the employee's line manager. Many procedures stipulate a length of time after which, if the employee does not re-offend, the warning lapses, but this can leave the door open to abuse of the system. For this reason it is best not to set a time limit, and to keep the warning on file. Remember that the disciplinary procedure should not be invoked unless informal warnings from the line manager have had no effect, or unless the offence is considered to be so important that instant disciplinary action must be taken. In cases of gross misconduct an employee may be suspended from work, on full pay, pending an investigation, then dismissed.

- **Representation at meetings.** A colleague or trade union representative can, by right, accompany or represent the employee at each warning interview. Consider stipulating that the union should be involved unless the employee specifically objects. On occasions when the offence also constitutes a criminal offence, a solicitor should be allowed to be present.

- **Investigations.** All abuses of discipline must be investigated before a warning of any kind is issued. At the very least this involves hearing the employee's side of the story. It is possible to suspend the employee on full pay while the investigation is taking place.

Set a time limit to carry out investigations into gross misconduct, such as deliberate malpractice. This should be not more than 10 days after the offence was committed.

- **Documentation.** Detailed minutes should be taken at all interviews and kept along with copies of any investigation into the misconduct and any warnings issued. This documentation is not only useful for checking whether an employee's behaviour improves; it can also be used as evidence, in the event of an industrial tribunal, that correct procedures have been followed.

- **Plans of action.** In the case of minor offences every effort must be made to help the employee overcome problems, obviating the need to pursue the process further. The procedure should make it clear that plans of action will be agreed between the employee and the line manager at each interview to enable improvements in discipline. A date will be given for an evaluation interview, at which, if progress has not been made, a more severe warning can be issued.

- **Appeals.** Employees should be given the right to appeal against any warning they receive, as long as it is made in writing to their line manager within five working days of the issue of the warning.

4. Draw up an implementation timetable
In a large organisation it is often better to pilot the disciplinary procedure on one site or in a large department before full implementation.

5. Provide training for managers and supervisors
Training should be given to all managers and supervisors who may have to deal with disciplinary issues. Ensure that they understand the mechanics of the procedure and try to make sure that there is a consistency of approach. Give training not only in conducting a disciplinary interview effectively but also on general discipline and control; this will help solve as many problems as possible without the need for the full procedure.

6. Communicate the procedure to all employees
If you have disciplinary rules, by law they must be notified to employees. Ensure that staff are aware of the procedure (a letter should be sent to all employees along with a copy of the procedure), and know when the procedure will come into effect. Explain that the procedure has been introduced to benefit employees by providing them with a consistent way of dealing with ill-discipline. The same information should be given to new recruits and included in the staff manual.

7. Implement the procedure
Ensure a member of the DPMC is available to answer any questions that may arise, especially during the critical period following the communication of the procedure.

8. Evaluate the procedure
Regular evaluation of the procedure will contribute towards improving it. The number of times the procedure is used should be recorded, and any managers who seem to have difficulty in handling discipline should be identified. Employees who have been disciplined under the procedure should be asked for their views on it.

9. Make changes and give feedback on the results
Changes should be made in the light of the evaluation. These may include extra training for some managers, or re-writing some of the steps or phases. Communicate the changes made to employees.

Managers should avoid:

- Taking disciplinary action until the case has been investigated.
- Setting the procedure in stone by ignoring the need for regular reviews.
- Allowing the procedure to replace the need for good management.

From *Chartered Management Institute Checklist*, (Checklist 102) March 2006. Copyright © 2006 by Chartered Management Institute. Reprinted by permission.

The ABC's of Employee Discipline

WILLIAM COTTRINGER, PHD

I n any business or industry, it is important to establish high standards of performance and conduct. From time to time supervisors are required to discipline employees in order to enforce the expected work standard.

Carrying out employee discipline can have a major impact on the company and on individual employee's lives. It is critical to take the appropriate action in being fair and considering all the relevant facts.

By following this simple ABC system for disciplining employees, you will be successful in assuring a good work performance standard and helping your company meet its business goals by providing quality products or services in whatever industry you are part of.

Act

A common mistake supervisors make is to not take appropriate preventative action to catch a work problem in the making, when the employee can still be "rescued." Problems such as chronic lateness, poor performance, lack of teamwork and negative attitudes can not be corrected without immediate action from the beginning. Two months later is too late. All disciplinary actions should be proceeded by a clear communication of expectations and prompt feedback when those expectations are not being met.

Of course, some work rule violations are non-negotiable and once all the facts are collected. immediate action must be taken—which is usually termination. This is true in cases such as theft, serious insubordination, substance abuse, serious safety violations, verbal abuse of clients, taking company secrets and other behaviors that are unlawful, jeopardize the safety and welfare of employees or put the business in serious risk.

In other situations, an employee may need to be suspended or removed from the site until a proper investigation can be conducted.

Cases such as these may involve suspected theft reported by a client, a sexual harassment complaint, a work accident or other conduct that might put the company business or other employees in jeopardy.

Other violations should follow a system of progressive discipline, in which the least harsh corrective action is implemented first and then harsher ones to follow. The object is to get the employee's attention before the performance problem becomes a chronic habit. Be fair, consider all relevant facts and then act. Act first by providing prompt and clear feedback about the specifics of the problem, explain why the problem can't continue, communicate the desired expectation and set the consequences for continued failure. Then make sure you follow up.

Employee discipline is an essential part of effective management. There are good reasons to act including:

- To change problem behavior
- To maintain performance standards
- To meet business goals
- To protect rights and due process
- To identify any unclear procedures
- To correct wrong workplace conditions

Be Fair

Employee discipline has to be carried out in a consistent and fair manner or otherwise it may do more harm than good. Before you decide to discipline an employee over a work rule violation, ask a few key questions:

- Does the employee understand exactly what is expected and is he or she able to do the job?
- Are there any performance barriers or other legitimate problems that need to be removed?
- Is the violation strictly willful misconduct or intentional poor performance?
- Have personality issues been separated from performance ones?
- Is the rule or policy reasonable and necessary for the safe, legal and productive operation of the company?
- Has the rule or policy been properly communicated and distributed to all employees? Are all employees aware of the rule and do they really understand it? Has there been adequate training?
- Has the rule been consistently enforced in the past?
- Have other employees been disciplined for the same offense throughout the company?
- Has there been a thorough, prompt and unbiased investigation conducted?
- Have all witnesses been contacted who can help prove or disprove the violation?

- How condemning is the evidence? Who is most credible and why?
- What needs to be done that will balance the needs of the individual employee and the good of the over all organization?

You may want to create your own checklist of questions to ask in order to help you remain objective and fair. As a supervisor you are required to avoid doing anything that might be perceived as being inconsistent and unfair. One mistake in the area can be costly.

Consider the Facts

Another common mistake supervisors make is to arrive at a judgment of guilt and plan the punishment before taking the time to do a thorough investigation. It is imperative to get at all the relevant facts. Sometimes the last bit of evidence that is most likely to be missed can change the entire direction of a case. Below are several questions you should ask in order to determine the most appropriate disciplinary action to take, once you have completed a good investigation to verify the offense.

- How condemning is all the evidence? How serious was this offense? What were the actual consequences? What was the intention? How deliberate was it?

- What kind of prior record does the employee have?
- Are there any mitigating or aggravating circumstances of the violation?
- What is the attitude of the employee toward the violation?
- What is the likelihood of the employee changing for the better?
- What has been the practice in the past with similar violations?
- Will the disciplinary action or lack of it adversely effect the company operation?
- Are the intended disciplinary measures appropriate for the offense, all things being considered?

Be proactive in preventing minor performance and conduct issues before they become serious problems.

Take the time to be fair, consider all relevant facts and then act appropriately to carry out a system of employee discipline that will encourage all employees to help the company achieve its goals.

WILLIAM COTTRINGER, PhD, is a business consultant, sport psychologist and college teacher in St. Louis, Missouri. He is the author of *You Can Have Your Cheese & Eat It Too,* published by Executive Excellence. He can be reached at 1(618) 288-4956 or ckurtdoc@charter.net.

From *Supervision,* by William Cottringer, (64:4) April 2003, pp. 5, 7. Copyright © 2003 by National ResearchBureau, 320 Valley Street, Burlington, Iowa 52601. Reprinted by permission.

Hard-Core Offenders

Egregious employee behavior can lead to expensive lawsuits and crippled employee morale. Here's how to stop it before it starts.

LINDA WASMER ANDREWS

Most workplace harassers, bullies and abusers gradually inch over the line that separates acceptable and unacceptable conduct. Occasionally, though, someone bolts across that line with such audacity that you're left shaking your head in stunned disbelief.

That's the way "Carol" still feels three years after interrupting a meeting between two co-workers in her office. She says one of the men stood up, yelled at her and literally *kicked* her out of the cubicle.

"I flew across the room and fell over another co-worker's desk," she says. "I was mortified. I fled to my own cubicle, sobbing hysterically out of shock and in great pain." Carol says she sustained a "sacral contusion"—a bruise near her tailbone—but the more serious injury was to her sense of trust and safety.

"When my supervisor asked this man why he kicked me, he explained that he was under a great deal of stress from his divorce and took it out on me," she says. "They basically just slapped his hand and told him not to do that again. They refused to fire him, and I didn't feel safe coming back to work as long as he was still in the office."

Ultimately, Carol—who, like others in this article, prefers not to be identified—lost her job. She says this physical confrontation, combined with another incident involving a client, contributed to the loss of her job. She also says she currently has a workers' compensation suit pending.

Outrageously egregious conduct frequently carries a steep price tag for employers. At times, companies even may be hit with punitive damages, which are intended both to punish the company and to deter others from similar conduct. In such cases, the legal damages alone can soar into the millions.

But even when no legal action is taken, extreme misbehavior can poison morale—decreasing productivity, increasing absenteeism and turnover, driving up health care costs for stressed-out employees, and generally dragging down the company's bottom line.

It doesn't have to be this way, however. The sooner you spot the warning signs of egregious behavior, the better your chances of being able to stop it before it starts.

Over-the-Top Costs

Unfortunately, it's easy to become complacent, to fall into the trap of assuming that "it couldn't happen here"—at least until it actually *does* happen at your workplace. Before you know it, your company could be paying hefty financial penalties for employees' outrageous conduct. Consider these examples of unacceptable workplace behavior—and the prices employers paid because of them—as reported recently by the U.S. Equal Employment Opportunity Commission (EEOC):

- Seven Afghan Muslim employees at two car dealerships in Solano County, Calif., said they had been harassed and were called offensive names such as "the bin Laden gang," "sand niggers," "terrorists" and "camel jockeys." Their suit resulted in a $500,000 settlement with the dealerships.
- A major soap manufacturer wound up paying $10 million after it was alleged in a lawsuit that about 100 female employees had been sexually harassed—including being propositioned and groped, for example—at one Illinois facility.
- An 18-year-old male salesclerk for a baby products retailer in New Jersey alleged that he was subjected to a sexually hostile environment—he was called "fag," "faggot" and "happy pants," and he was forcibly stripped of his trousers by co-workers. The retailer settled for $205,000.

Of course, even when litigation isn't an issue, extremely offensive or abusive behavior has a price. "I believe that legal liability is actually the least of the concerns," says Craig Pratt, SPHR, a management consultant in Oakland, Calif., and co-author of *Investigating Workplace Harassment: How to Be Fair, Thorough and Legal* (SHRM, 2002).

'I didn't feel safe coming back to work as long as he was still in the office.'

Good Employees Gone Bad

Egregious acts are usually committed by chronic offenders. Occasionally, though, a model employee will suddenly snap. James Stone, a labor and employment attorney at the McDonald Hopkins law firm in Cleveland, recalls one such incident:

"An employee deliberately drove through a large flock of birds in the parking lot, killing many. Other people, including non-employees, observed the event. It was a rather gruesome situation, and the employee was fired on the spot, with no investigation at all."

It turned out the employee was a military veteran who apparently had suffered a wartime flashback. As a result of the hasty discharge, "the employer was left dealing with a lawsuit and a costly settlement," says Stone. "In general, with this kind of egregious conduct, it's best to put the employee on suspension with or without pay. It's easy to overlook mitigating factors when extreme conduct occurs. Nevertheless, sometimes they're present, and a little time allows the company to consider those factors and make a reasoned, rather than an emotional, decision."

(For more information on responding to potentially violent actions at work, including the potential repercussions of immediate terminations, see the *HR Magazine* November 2002 cover story, "Bulletproof Practices.")

"I think far and away the biggest impact is what happens to people's motivation," says Pratt. "If you've ever been in a situation where you feel offended by the behavior of a co-worker—especially if you feel intentionally targeted—you know that you can't bring your best effort to work. Emotionally, intellectually and behaviorally, you're just not going to be all there."

Persistent harassment or abuse can cause long-term stress in its victims, in turn exacting a mental and physical toll. In vulnerable individuals, the results are occasionally devastating. "Cindy," for instance, is a former English teacher who says she was subjected to systematic intimidation by a school official. "He stalked me on the job," she says. "He got in my face and screamed at me," she says. "I went from poised and self-possessed to acting like a battered wife at work."

Cindy says the scare tactics were combined with "an arduous workload, disparate treatment, stabs in the back and innuendos to others that I was losing it—and, by God, I did!" Eventually, she suffered what she calls a "nervous breakdown." Her therapist diagnosed it as post-traumatic stress with a conversion disorder—a psychiatric condition in which emotional distress gives rise to very real neurological symptoms. In Cindy's case, the symptoms took the form of brief, involuntary muscle twitches that a decade later still affect her ability to speak and eat.

Targets of abuse such as Cindy and Carol are not the only ones who suffer, however. Co-workers who are bystanders may become stressed-out, too. In addition, "employees who observe or hear about harassment that goes unchallenged may feel anxious, fearing that they will be next, or depressed, feeling

like the organization doesn't care about its employees," says Kathleen Rospenda, a psychology professor at the University of Illinois at Chicago. Work soon becomes the last place they want to be.

Says Rospenda: "Unchecked harassment creates a climate of disrespect"—and that's not a climate conducive to high motivation or a person's best effort.

Trends to Avoid

Mistreatment at the hands of co-workers or supervisors is nothing new, of course. Certainly, the lecherous male boss who can't keep his eyes and hands off the female staff has been around for centuries and is still going strong. However, other prime targets for harassers and abusers may shift with the political winds. Be alert for these emerging trends in workplace victimization:

"Homosexual" victims. In many workplaces, the harshest abuse is reserved for individuals who are perceived as homosexual—regardless of whether they are or are not.

'I went from poised and self-possessed to acting like a battered wife at work.'

The majority of such cases seem to involve male-on-male harassment, says Dale Carpenter, an associate professor at the University of Minnesota Law School who specializes in sexual orientation issues.

Carpenter also believes that such male-on-male harassment is often more severe than other types. "I think it's probably accurate to say that such harassment tends to be especially virulent and frightening to the targets," he says. "There's typically more physical intimidation and more relentless teasing involved."

Carpenter recommends watching for teasing that is based on "an individual's failure to conform to gender expectations, such as calling a man a 'sissy.' That's a warning signal that an illegal environment of harassment may be in the process of being created."

(For a look at recent cases in which employees successfully sued on the basis that they were discriminated against for failing to meet gender stereotypes, see "Religion vs. Sexual Orientation" and the Court Report section in the August 2004 issue of *HR Magazine*.)

Teenage victims. A spate of recent lawsuits has involved teenage plaintiffs, some of them young girls who were groped, asked for lap dances or even raped. "We had one district office where all but one of the cases litigated in a year involved young workers," says Naomi Earp, vice chair at the EEOC. That set off alarm bells at the agency, which launched a new Youth@Work educational campaign in September.

In some cases, young workers are the victims of egregious abuse by other young employees. In such cases, lack of work experience could be a factor, says Earp. "If you have a 16- or

Boys Will Be Boys

Some of the worst cases of sexual harassment come from workplaces that are male-dominated, where women may be reduced to sex objects and "weaker" men may be mercilessly tormented amidst all the jockeying for the alpha male position.

Lisa Kearney, a psychology resident at the South Texas Veterans Health Care System in San Antonio, has studied this phenomenon. Like many social scientists, she believes it can often be traced to "male gender role conflict"—in other words, the pressure men feel to conform to society's traditional definition of what it means to be a man. She says this definition tends to emphasize power, competition and material success at the expense of emotional expression and a healthy work/life balance.

Harassment, in this theory, is a way of letting everyone know who is powerful—and who isn't.

For HR managers in mostly-male workplaces, extra care may be needed to keep the power plays from getting out of hand. In her research, however, Kearney found that one-time anti-harassment programs may not do the trick. While such programs tend to increase men's ability to recognize harassment, they don't necessarily decrease men's tolerance for it.

Instead, she suggests longer-term training in which employees are repeatedly exposed to messages about the negative impact that harassment can have on both individuals and the workplace as a whole. To make such training more appealing and relevant to male employees, she suggests, package it as part of a broader educational initiative that promises to teach "better ways of managing the stress in your life."

17-year-old worker with an 18- or 19-year-old supervisor, it could be argued that both the employee and the manager are relatively new to the workplace and may not fully understand the rules of behavior there," she explains. For HR professionals in companies that employ teenage workers, Earp recommends reviewing policies and training to make sure "they speak in a language teens will understand and that resonates with that audience."

It may be particularly important to get that message to teenage workers before summer, when the number of U.S. workers ages 15 to 17 swells to 4 million from 3 million.

Muslim victims. "There is something very personal and exceptionally demeaning about being targeted based on your religious beliefs. It just hits home more deeply for folks," says Linda Ordonio-Dixon, a senior trial attorney at the EEOC's San Francisco District Office. Since Sept. 11, 2001, much of the religion-based harassment has been directed at Muslims, and it's a trend that shows no sign of abating soon.

For example, Ordonio-Dixon worked on a case in which four Pakistani Muslim workers at a California steel plant alleged

they were ridiculed during their daily prayers, mocked for their traditional dress and called names such as "rag head."

"The harassment went on for a number of years, it was conducted in concert with the supervisors, and there was a significant amount of emotional distress experienced by the claimants," says Ordonio-Dixon. The result: a $1.1 million settlement. The lesson: Don't ignore fundamental anti-harassment policies and procedures.

What Was She Thinking?

When confronted with their bad behavior, the worst harassers and abusers often claim they either didn't realize it was unwelcome or had intended it as a joke. "Lisa" says that was the case with her former boss, the editorial director at a professional association who claimed she was joking when she made repeated comments comparing Lisa to a prostitute and a "slut."

But that explanation didn't fly, says Lisa, when the editorial director continued making the comments *after* Lisa complained.

What drives some people to keep saying and doing such wildly offensive things?

Nili Sachs, a psychotherapist in Rockford, Minn., who consults on sexual harassment issues, believes egregious behavior often has its roots in a lack of empathy. "That's the common denominator of all the harassers I've ever interviewed, read about or seen in therapy," Sachs says. Such people can say and do outrageous things that cause intense fear, shame or humiliation because they're psychologically incapable of feeling the other person's pain. They also tend to lack insight into their own motivations.

"These people may have absolutely no idea how insensitive they are," says Sachs.

The implication is that many chronic offenders may not be entirely feigning ignorance about the havoc they wreak. When confronting such individuals, you may need to spell out the problem in very clear, concrete terms.

Online Resources

Visit the online version of this article at www.shrm.org/hrmagazine/04December to see:

- Court cases showing how punitive damages are assessed and how employees who don't conform to gender stereotypes can bring suit if they are mistreated.
- Links to the Equal Employment Opportunity Commission's Youth@Work Initiative, which may help employers prevent egregious behavior from younger employees.
- Links to organizations that offer information regarding harassment and workplace bullying.

Then there are the co-workers and colleagues who used to be the kids who took others' lunch money and today are still bullies at heart. For these office bad boys and girls, "it's all about controlling another person," says Gary Namie, principal consultant at The Work Doctor, a Bellingham, Wash.-based company specializing in workplace bullying issues. Bullies, says Namie, "don't have control of their own lives."

According to Namie, such people often have deep-seated feelings of powerlessness and low self-esteem. To keep those disturbing feelings at bay, they may go for a cheap power fix by provoking fear, hurt or shame in those around them. The only way to control these controllers is to create a workplace where such behavior simply isn't tolerated.

Pro-Harassment Policies

While the personality of the perpetrator certainly plays a role, egregious behavior doesn't occur in a vacuum. If dealt with promptly and decisively, such behavior often can be nipped in the bud.

On the other hand, if a company fails to respond effectively, anyone who might be prone to cruel or vile behavior may feel that a green light has been given, and the behavior can quickly escalate to the next level.

That's apparently what happened at an auto body shop in Massachusetts, where a female technician working in a shop full of men was repeatedly harassed by a male coworker. "He was constantly saying vulgar things, making sexual advances, touching her inappropriately," says Eric Parker, a partner in the Boston law firm of Parker Scheer who represented the woman in a lawsuit against the body shop.

Parker says the woman reported the incidents, and her tormentor was fired—only to be rehired. Finally, one day, as the woman was working underneath a dashboard with her legs protruding from the open driver's door, the man knelt down and bit her right between the legs.

Parker says: "The woman was fully clothed, and there was no breaking of the skin, but she suffered considerable emotional anguish as a result of the attack. She was good and scared." The man was later arrested and pled guilty to charges of sexual assault; the lawsuit against the company was settled for $141,000.

A message that misconduct will be tolerated or even condoned is probably the No. 1 factor contributing to egregious workplace behavior. In this case, the man's rehiring certainly sent a loud and clear signal that there would be no real consequences for sexually harassing a co-worker. By letting one person's offensive behavior slide, a company tacitly encourages not only that individual but also other potential harassers and abusers in the workforce.

"Intentionally or unintentionally, you're setting up benchmarks," says Karen Karr, an employment attorney at the Steptoe & Johnson law firm in Phoenix. "Your employees look to you for guidance on what's acceptable and what's not." The absence of a clear "stop" sign often is interpreted as "go."

At times, a company's inaction may be due to denial that a problem exists or minimization of the problem's severity. At other times, however, it may be symptomatic of a broader lack of respect and concern for employees. In such workplaces, Namie says, "fear is the dominant emotion. Success is defined as a zero-sum competition, in which one person's gain is always at another's expense."

Namie says there may also be an overemphasis on meeting quotas: "The message is, as long as you make your numbers, you're free to do with people what you want."

It Couldn't Happen Here

For the HR person at a company where numbers rule and disregard for employees is rampant, it may be tempting to take a head-in-the-sand approach. In the long run, however, this means not only betraying the human values that draw most people to the field in the first place, but also undermining the company's best interests.

"The first thing to do is get buy-in from the person at the very top of the organization," says Aimee Kaye, president of Sageview Consulting, an HR outsourcing firm in New York. "You want an organization that is free of abusive and hostile environments. But executive management people don't just do what HR people want because it's the right thing. You can't approach it that way. You have to show them how it's ultimately going to affect the bottom line."

That should be easy to do, considering all the potential costs associated with egregious behavior. Once you've secured the support of those at the top, it's easier to send a strong message to all those below.

Just having an anti-harassment policy, complaint mechanism and investigation procedure in place isn't enough, however. You need to make sure that they're actually used, which means having safeguards to protect complainants from retaliation.

"For a policy to work effectively, the organization needs to not just say that retaliation is prohibited, but actually model it," says Patricia Eyres, a speaker and consultant with Litigation Management and Training Services in Long Beach, Calif. Once complaints have been investigated and substantiated, appropriate corrective action also needs to be taken. Otherwise, employees get the demoralizing impression that nobody really cares what happens to them at work.

Since the best cure is always prevention, effective anti-harassment training is vital as well. For your policy, procedures and training to be most effective, however, they must be relevant to your workforce. This means they may need to be updated periodically to adapt to the changing times. Two emerging danger zones you may want to address are:

- E-mail, which is all too often used for distributing offensive "jokes" and explicit pornography.
- Home offices or remote satellite offices where employees and their assistants may be operating with very little supervision.

Truly egregious behavior may seem like the exception to the rule, but actually it's often the rule taken to its logical extreme. The sooner you get involved, the better the odds you can prevent a relatively minor incident from spiraling into something much more sinister and destructive.

For many HR professionals, this may go somewhat against the grain. "Most of us don't want to impose our own moral judgment on our co-workers. We tend to see ourselves as live-and-let-live types," says Pratt. "But by not getting involved right away, my experience has been that these types of problems can go rapidly out of control. Early confrontation, in my view, is the critical HR practice here."

LINDA WASMER ANDREWS is a freelance writer in Albuquerque, N.M., who has specialized in health and psychology issues for two decades. She holds a master's degree in health psychology from Capella University and is pursuing a PhD in health psychology through Northcentral University.

Interns on the Payroll

Giving career-minded students purposeful work helps you spot the cream of the crop for hiring later.

ROSEANNE WHITE GEISEL

Call them professionals-in-the-making. They're the students or recent graduates hired for a summer or a semester to serve as interns in companies and organizations throughout the country. HR managers who help bring them on board and monitor their work say they're smart, motivated and hardworking, and that they contribute significantly while they're learning on the job.

Interns can help advance company projects that have been back-burnered for lack of regular employees' time, experts say. They also can energize a workplace with their enthusiasm for the business and, despite their inexperience, can even supply an expertise of their own—such as familiarity with the latest technologies. And in many companies, the best of them come to be regarded as promising potential candidates for full-time positions.

Amy Van Kirk, director of national campus recruiting for the U.S. operations of PricewaterhouseCoopers (PwC), the New York-based accounting and consulting company, says that "interns are probably the key" to developing a high-quality workforce.

Having an internship program can be one of the biggest pluses for a company, some experts say, because it can help HR in its mission of making sure the company hires the best and the brightest. Such a program can raise a company's profile among students on the campuses from which it draws interns, it can keep the company's name in front of colleges' career officers, and thus it can keep channels open between employers with jobs to fill and talented graduates looking for full-time employment.

In fact, colleges can be integral in building and maintaining an internship program. Forging a relationship with colleges and universities that can, become rich source of strong candidates is "just like any other business partnership," says Tom Leonti, a manager for North American Manufacturing Co. Ltd., a Cleveland-based engineering company.

Leonti says he wanted Case Western Reserve University students "to know who we were." So the company invited the head of Case's engineering department for a tour to provide a look at company operations and a sense of the types of can-

didates best-suited for working there. Leonti has hired interns for his combustion-products department and figures other students "would hear good things about North American from their classmates" who had interned there.

Recruiters for Arthur J. Gallagher & Co. Inc., a commercial insurance and reinsurance brokerage headquartered in Itasca, Ill., not only establish relationships with college career centers but also give presentations to insurance, finance and sales classes, says Terry Hennen, director of training and communications.

Allstate Insurance Co. in Northbrook, Ill., develops internship relationships with schools that offer actuarial science programs. It helps keep the insurer visible to hard-to-find actuarial grads looking for full-time jobs, says Wanda Wiebke, Allstate's director of recruitment and selection.

Internship candidates come not only through college ties, however, but also from employee referrals and word-of-mouth, Wiebke notes. Recruiting tasks, she adds, are shared by the departments that hire interns and by human resources.

Just as in hiring regular employees, so too in bringing interns into the workplace: It requires HR to tailor job descriptions to the company's needs—but with the aim of assigning interns work that's beneficial for them and that taps their individual talents as much as possible. HR also can help interview candidates, provide orientation for those who are selected and help evaluate their performance.

Shaping the Program

The cornerstone of a solid internship program is its alignment with the company's objectives or with those of a particular department. At PwC, for example, each service line submits goals for its interns, and those goals are helpful in the hiring process, says Van Kirk.

PwC has developed an "internship toolkit" for recruiters and mentors. The written materials in the toolkit provide advice on mentoring, conveying best practices, communicating effectively with interns and determining which interns should receive offers for full-time employment.

Paychecks and Payoffs

Interns are doing real work, and mostly they're earning real money.

Arthur J. Gallagher & Co. Inc., a commercial insurance brokerage in Itasca, Ill., hired about 100 interns last summer and paid each about $3,600 for their nine-week stay. Gallagher has always paid interns since starting its program nearly 40 years ago. "Some of these kids are working their way through college," says Terry Hennen, director of training and communications, adding that the company would not want finances to make the internship a hardship.

The 107 interns at Allstate Insurance Co. this past summer received a percentage of the company's entry-level salary of $32,000. The percentage was determined by the years of college or graduate school the intern had completed, says Wanda Wiebke, director, recruitment and selection. In addition, because all interns work at the company's headquarters in Northbrook, Ill., they are offered free housing in a local hotel.

The New York-based accounting and consulting company PricewaterhouseCoopers (PwC), which takes on about 1,800 interns a year, not only pays interns but also allows those who then take full-time jobs with the firm to use the start date of their first internship as the start date for their retirement plan benefits, says Amy Van Kirk, director of national campus recruiting.

But employers' investments in interns far exceed salary and other purely financial benefits. Companies enable interns to learn from the masters of their industries and to ask questions of top executives—an access that often is not available to full-time employees.

Allstate's interns have lunch sessions with the chairman and other key officers. Gallagher's interns hear top corporate officers speak during training sessions, and they bring their time at the company to a close with a barbecue at the home of the company's president, Pat Gallagher.

And Van Kirk notes that PwC interns who receive a full-time job offer also get a "transition week" at the Disney Institute of Management in Orlando, Fla., where they receive management training that emphasizes teamwork, excellence and leadership.

Another important step in shaping an internship program is to set orientation and training requirements. At many large companies, interns receive both general group orientation and training as well as job-specific training in the departments to which they are assigned.

After interviewing internship candidates on campus, Gallagher brings the best prospects in for another round of interviews at the offices where they would work—whether at headquarters or at other locations. Those interviewed at headquarters meet with about six people, Hennen says. "We're looking for people who are go-getters."

Then all interns from all locations are brought in during their second week for training. They hear 20 to 25 presentations by Gallagher staff members, including Chairman Bob Gallagher and President Pat Gallagher.

Orientation and training for new nursing school graduates at Henry Ford Health System, a complex of hospitals and health provider organizations in the Detroit area, is completed in stages. Prior to passing their licensing exams, they are assigned to a dedicated preceptor. "We train and mentor them, and, under close supervision, they begin to deliver patient care," says Maureen Henson, SPHR, director of employment and recruitment strategies.

Accompanying the mentorship at Henry Ford is a classroom program of four to 10 weeks, depending on each graduate's experience in health care. The program is produced by the nursing development faculty, which has more than a dozen members and serves three of the health system's hospitals.

Getting down to Business

In keeping with their aim of attracting and developing future professionals, companies are giving interns real work to accomplish. In effect, interns these days are not making any more trips to the photocopier than are other employees involved in the core business activities.

The current nursing students or interns at Henry Ford support the nursing unit as patient sitters, Henson says. They stay with patients to assist them with meals or just to make sure they are safe—a particularly important responsibility, especially in the care of homeless or indigent patients who may not have family members or friends visiting. "It gives the students an exposure to the fast pace of a [complex-care] setting in the inner city," Henson says.

Henry Ford also has interns on the business side of the organization. Henson's two human resource interns this past fall helped revise the employment application, took part in rewriting and automating job descriptions, and provided logistical support to recruiters. A formal internship program involving Henry Ford's business functions will be inaugurated in the coming year.

The Gallagher firm also gives interns important work to do. "We really get our interns involved," says Hennen. Interns spend eight of their nine weeks in the program rotating through various areas of the company. They are assigned every half-day to a different professional "whose job it is to give them a beneficial experience" and teach them best practices, he says. They may accompany staff members on prospecting or service calls, or they may help with proposals, Hennen says.

In fact, Leonti of North American Manufacturing says the work that his firm gives interns during their eight months with the company is part of what attracts them in the first place. "These young people are very, very smart and very aggressive. You have to keep them challenged. When they leave in August, they can talk about the project they've worked on," he says.

Meaningful projects lead to meaningful internships, says Allstate's Wiebke. Interns are used in all departments during their 10 weeks with the company, she says, and each is assigned to a project or a team. "Some departments really value [the interns] because of the skill sets the interns bring," she adds.

Noteworthy among those skill sets, experts say, are interns' abilities in information technology and other technical specialties. They arrive for internship duties with the benefit of up-to-the-minute classroom teaching in such areas. Says Henson: "Interns bring the latest computer skills."

Those who have interned at the company are much more comfortable in the corporate environment when they start full time.

Henson adds that interns also bring another helpful quality—the perspective of their generation. Managers on the business side of the Henry Ford organization, she says, can gain a lot by dealing with, and thereby learning about, members of Generation X (born from 1968 to 1979, after the baby boomers) and Generation Y (approximately 1980 to 1995). Members of those generations, she says, need more-immediate gratification, a greater sense of accomplishment for their work. "Their expectations are different, and yet they bring such incredible talent and imagination to the job," Henson says. And although young interns in those brackets may have to be coached sometimes on corporate etiquette, she says, they bring good critical thinking skills into the workplace.

Wrapping It Up and Moving On

As internships draw to a close, performance evaluations must be completed. Many companies rely on a formal procedure. For example, everyone who works with a Gallagher intern in a given week completes a 24-question evaluation form in addition to a schedule on which the intern's activities are logged.

At Allstate, each intern is evaluated by someone in the department where he or she worked, and the type of evaluation depends on the intern's assignment. Evaluations of interns are briefer than those for full-time employees, Wiebke notes.

Because North American Manufacturing has at most only a few interns at any time, Leonti likes to go over the engineering school's evaluation form with each student in person. "I like to give them some pointers," he says.

Generally, colleges that require students to serve internships are then involved in evaluations of the students' performance in the workplace. When colleges do not get involved in evaluations, however, supervisors' evaluations of interns remain within the company and are not sent to the interns' colleges.

The next step at some companies with internship programs is to decide who gets offers for full-time employment. About 85 percent of the members of each intern class at PwC receive offers, and 90 percent of those who get offers accept them, Van Kirk says. At the Gallagher firm, about 50 percent receive job offers.

The HR Connection

From finding, hiring, training and evaluating interns to identifying those who eventually could join the company full time, HR plays a major role in internship programs. Yet HR managers typically say they do not consider handling internship tasks a burdensome increase in their workload. Rather, they view it as one of HR's integral functions. "It's part of what we do in recruiting," says Van Kirk.

And having interns in the workplace can boost employees' spirits, says Hennen. "People like to see a college person get turned on to the business."

There's also the bonus of training a potential full-time employee in everything from corporate culture to client service. HR managers say those who have interned at the company are much more comfortable in the corporate environment when they start full time.

Says Henson at Henry Ford: "It serves industry well to bring in talent, develop them, mentor them and expose them to various pieces of the workplace. We end up learning from them as well."

ROSEANNE WHITE GEISEL is a freelance business writer and editor in Arlington, VA.

Business Ethics: The Key Role of Corporate Governance

With growing global pressure for enforceable business ethics and social responsibility, what role should a board of directors play in setting the corporation's tone and policies? Worldwide, the authors find that boards have been on the leading edge in making business ethics an effective priority for companies.

JOHN D. SULLIVAN, PHD AND ALEKSANDR SHKOLNIKOV

Although concern with ethics has always been a part of doing business, business leaders today are beginning to think about ethics as a set of principles and guides of behavior rather than a set of rigid rules. In this sense, business ethics is not only an attempt to set a standard by which all of the employees of a company can know what is expected, but it is also an attempt to encourage employees, managers, and board members to think about and make decisions through the prism of a shared set of values.

Business ethics and corporate governance have become key factors influencing investment decisions and determining the flows of capital worldwide. In part, this is the result of scandals in both developed and developing countries. However, in a more positive sense, the growing demand for good governance also flows from the lessons learned about how to generate rapid economic growth through market institutions. From this perspective, the emphasis on anti-corruption and good governance is based both in moral standards as well as utilitarian considerations of improved market performance.

While ethics and an ethical business culture are at the heart of the corporate governance framework, the two are approached somewhat differently. Corporate governance is concerned mainly with creating the structure of decision-making at the level of the board of directors and implementing those decisions. In this sense governance can be thought of as steering the corporation. In fact, the very word governance itself comes from the Greek word for steering.

Moreover, corporate governance is about accomplishing the core values of transparency, responsibility, fairness, and accountability. Because these values are also key concerns for business ethics, the two can be seen as being directly related. However, the corporate governance aspect deals with setting up the structures through which these values are attained, while ethics is both a guide for behavior and a set of principles (or a moral code).

In its most basic form, corporate governance is about creating a set of principles and a decision-making system to govern the modern corporation. A key challenge of governance is to ensure that the owners, or the stockholders, could control and demand accountability from the hired management. Following the Asian financial crisis and

other international crises, the Organisation for Economic Cooperation and Development (OECD) came to develop the "OECD Principles of Corporate Governance" that today are accepted as the international standard.

The relationship between ethics codes and corporate governance has surged to the fore. Just having a code is not enough— it must be enforced on a day-to-day basis.

The implementation of the OECD Corporate Governance Principles requires a whole set of supporting and enforcing market institutions. On the one side, corporate governance demands the participation of private actors, including auditors, accountants, and credit rating agencies. On the other side, it involves the functions of government, securities regulators, capital market authorities, and the like.

The relationship between ethics codes and corporate governance has surged to the fore. In the governance principles of the World Bank, for example, ethics, although not directly listed, is an unstated assumption that runs through many pieces of it. The New York Stock Exchange (NYSE) has released new corporate governance rules that specifically declare that "listed companies must adopt and disclose a code of business conduct and ethics for directors, officers, and employees, and promptly disclose any waivers of the code for directors or executive officers."

This was done in response to Enron and other major corporations, where the board of directors waived a substantial code of ethics. What happened at Enron shows a determining factor in all ethics codes—simply having a code is not enough. It is just as important to enforce that code in day-to-day operations. The NYSE provision, in that regard, focuses on both aspects of an ethics code—definition and implementation.

Business ethics sets out a standard by which all employees can know what is expected. It also encourages them to make decisions through a shared set of values.

Given the new mandates on business, companies find themselves pressed to develop strong codes of ethics to guide the behavior of board members, managers, and employees. Multinational corporations are also being required to set standards for those in their supply chains, in some cases higher standards than the laws of the countries in which they do business.

As noted earlier, business ethics is an attempt to set out a standard by which all of the employees can know what is expected. Yet it is also an attempt to encourage employees, managers, and board members to think about and make decisions through the prism of some shared set of values. What then are the sources from which these values can be derived?

Laws and regulations of the countries in which companies operate constitute one of these sources. Another is the notion of social responsibility or *corporate citizenship,* which is the preferred term in the business community. Corporate citizenship involves building a decision-making system that takes into the account not only internal operating procedures, but also the impact of corporate behavior on its stakeholders—employees, investors, and communities.

One starting point to consider in developing initiatives to strengthen business ethics is the difference between bright lines and values. This is a relatively new distinction. Bright lines are those standards that attempt to set out specific and very finite rules which companies and individuals cannot break. Examples include the OECD Anti-Bribery Convention, which can be translated into national laws and rules on anti-bribery standards. Companies could take a considerable amount of time to develop these bright line standards or to try to identify them themselves.

Transparency International (TI), working with major corporations, has developed its own set of bright line standards called the TI Business Principles, applicable to companies of various sizes, industries, and geographical locations. Similarly, the International Chamber of Commerce (ICC) has also developed a set of rules of conduct to combat extortion and bribery. Although bright line rules are often very specific, each company still needs to develop accountability practices to ensure that employees are indeed following these rules.

In terms of general guidelines for behavior, there are a number of different sources for business ethics programs. Historically, one of the more prominent is that developed by Reverend Leon Sullivan, which began with the anti-Apartheid movement in South Africa and has since evolved into a global set of principles (*www.GlobalSullivanPrinciples. org*). Reverend Sullivan's principles have been adapted and expanded by the United Nations' Global Compact into 10 principles. The U.N. Global Compact goes considerably beyond the bright line rules and deals with the larger issue of values.

Another similar set of principles was developed by the Caux Round Table, an organization where business leaders from different countries came up with a set of general principles for business behavior. Another set of guidelines, the OECD Multinational Corporation Guidelines, go even further, attempting to encourage or mandate corporate behavior in a variety of areas, ranging from the environment to contributions to society and providing leadership in developing a nation. (The OECD Guidelines can be found at *www.oecd.org*.)

Codes of corporate ethics, codes of corporate conduct, and codes of corporate governance overlap in many ways, with many different organizations offering guidance and advice. The most encompassing list comes from the Ethics Resource Center located in Washington,

D.C. *(www.ethics.org),* which provides guidance on the issues companies should address.

The various codes and sources of corporate ethics try to capture three core areas:

- Existing laws and regulations.
- Building good business relations.
- Key concerns of society and improved corporate citizenship.

Corporate citizenship starts with a corporate code of ethics. A code of corporate ethics outlines the values and beliefs of an organization and ties them to its mission and objectives. A good code not only describes an operational process and regulates the behavior of managers and employees, but it also sets long-term goals, communicates the company's values to the outside stakeholders, and motivates employees.

A code of ethics is more than simply a statement of a company's moral beliefs. A well-written code is a true commitment to responsible business practices in that it outlines specific procedures to handle ethical failures. Codes of ethics today address a variety of issues including work environment, gender relations, discrimination, communications and reporting, gift giving, product safety, employee/management relationships, involvement in the political sphere, financial practices, corruption, and responsible advertising.

To be effective, codes of ethics should be more than just a document on a shelf. They need to be created in a way that ethical behavior is encouraged and that employees take pride in making ethical decisions. Codes of ethics should provide guidance into relationships between stakeholders and corporate decision-making. More importantly, employees at every level must strive to uphold the standards put forth by the code of ethics and the top management should exemplify those standards.

Over the past several decades we have witnessed profound changes in the way business operates in countries around the world. One of the more notable areas is the business community's treatment of corruption-related issues. The private sector has become one of the leaders in global efforts to curb corruption, developing landmark and far-reaching transparency and accountability standards as well as mechanisms to enforce them. While ethical codes play an important role in driving transparency and accountability, other initiatives that extend beyond internal rules have also made their mark in combating corruption.

One source for ethical values is the laws and regulations of countries in which companies operate. At the same time, quality of laws and regulations (as well as their enforcement) has a direct bearing on the levels of corruption in a particular country. The World Bank's *Doing Business* survey of more than 100 countries, for example, clearly showed that heavy business regulation and procedural complexities in the judiciary are associated with higher levels of corruption. The Heritage Foundation/Wall Street Journal annual Index of Economic Freedom also illustrates that higher degrees of economic freedom are correlated with lower corruption.

The Conference Board has conducted a study of business ethics around the world and the role of boards of directors in carrying out board oversight of ethics programs. The Conference Board identified the following elements in the role of the board:

- Codes of conduct.
- Communication of standards through training.
- Methods to encourage employees to report possible violations to management.
- Enforcement mechanisms (investigation and discipline).
- Oversight and review to achieve ongoing improvement.

In fact, the Conference Board found that not only were these elements quite common, but in many countries the program was actually established by board resolution. In the United States, 66 percent of American companies established the ethics program as the result of

Who Sets Your Ethical Course?

The Board—And Many Other Players

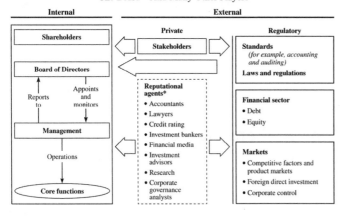

*Reputational agents refer to private sector agents, self-regulating bodies, the media, and civic society that reduce information assymmetry, improve the monitoring of firms, and shed light on opportunistic behavior.

Source: The World Bank

the action of the board of directors, while in Japan 96 percent took a similar stance.

Boards of directors should develop ways of monitoring compliance and ensuring that these ethics codes are not simply a standard put on the company's Web site, but not communicated and implemented throughout the company. One of the ways to do that is by carrying out program audits.

In U.S. companies, some 45 percent have carried out program audits (this can be expected to increase). In contrast, in Japan 64 percent of such companies have carried out program audits. The number is even higher at 67 percent in India, and in Western Europe, where it is over 75 percent.

Directors' ethics training is becoming quite common throughout the world, with many multinationals routinely offering ethics programs for their boards.

Complementing these program audits is the concept of directors' ethics training. The Conference Board survey found that directors' ethics training is becoming quite common throughout the world, from a low of 42 percent in Western Europe to a high of 94 percent in Japan. Many multinational companies are now routinely offering ethics training programs for their boards. The subjects covered include:

- Fiduciary duties.
- Corporate opportunities.
- Principal regulations governing company business.
- Personal liability.
- Corporate law.
- Stock exchange regulations.
- Insider trading.
- Business secrets.
- Employee training programs.

The role of the board, therefore, is seen as central to establishing and maintaining a corporate ethics program, and by corollary is a central feature in overall corporate governance guidelines and codes. This trend can be expected to continue, driven both by national legislation, international conventions, and the expectations of investors.

Debates in coming years will center on the relative roles of business, government, and non-governmental organizations in establishing codes of conduct and in reporting requirements as well as individual industry standards.

From the point of view of the business community, however, the major issue to consider is the central importance of corporate governance and business ethics in maintaining a market economy. Adam Smith, David Hume, and other philosophers and early economists were very much concerned with the role of ethics and the role of business behavior.

We can look at ethics as the solution to one of the central problems of development. In the move from a "cash and carry" or barter economy to an economy where transactions can be conducted over time and distance, business ethics are central to ensuring that contracts are adhered to. Ethics hold down the costs of doing business and improve the flow of capital to emerging markets.

Still, business should be mindful, as should nongovernmental organizations, that too much pressure is not put onto the multinational corporations to enforce laws and regulations which are actually the concerns of national government. For example, the emerging trend to hold business accountable for human rights violations in developing countries is worrisome. In some cases, it may deter multinationals and other sources of investment from investing in an emerging market. We have to find a way to meet high ethical standards and, at the same time, ensure that the risks assumed by corporations do not inhibit the further development of the emerging markets.

JOHN D. SULLIVAN, PhD is executive director of the Center for International Private Enterprise (CIPE). **ALEKSANDR SHKOLNIKOV** is a CIPE program officer. [www.cipe.org]

Unregulated Work

Is enforcement the next battle in the fight for workers' rights?

SIOBHÁN MCGRATH AND NINA MARTIN

Guillermo regularly puts in 70-hour weeks as a prep cook in a New York City restaurant. He came to the United States from Ecuador six years ago because he heard that "you can earn something for your family." But these aspirations soured after he wasn't paid for three weeks. Small sums of money and continued promises from the boss keep Guillermo returning to work each day for his 12-hour shifts.

Non-payment of wages plagues Guillermo and his co-workers, but their employer uses other tactics to reduce labor costs as well. Guillermo explains, "Workers have to punch out as if they had worked eight hours. So after eight hours, they punch out and then work four more hours. It is almost like a threat that if you don't punch the card, you're fired." With an average wage of about $300 per week, these long hours translate into just over $4 per hour. Some of Guillermo's co-workers have left the restaurant for other jobs, usually at food establishments, but often the working conditions they face are frustratingly similar.

Brenda, an African-American grandmother, is a child care worker in Brooklyn. Formerly a home health care worker, Brenda's own health no longer permits her to make the long commute to her patients' homes. Caring for children in her home seemed like a good way to replace this lost income. The parents of the children she cares for receive subsidized child care as they move from welfare to work. Brenda has no sick days or vacation days, and she only has health insurance through her husband's job.

Worse, her pay often dips below minimum wage. But the city's Human Resources Administration, which cuts her check, maintains that this does not break the law. Even though the city effectively sets her pay, it classifies her as an "independent contractor," rather than an employee. So Brenda doesn't have the same rights as a regular employee, such as the minimum wage, overtime, or paid leave.

Unfortunately, the experiences of Guillermo and Brenda are far from unique. Violations of employment and labor laws are a growing problem in U.S. workplaces. Employers in many sectors of the economy are breaking the law in order to cut costs, gain a competitive edge, and boost profits, and workers are suffering the consequences. In some industries, the abuses have become so common that they are now routine practice. And enforcement by the government has steadily declined, so that more and more workers are facing abusive and unsafe conditions at work. Anyone who pays attention knows that U.S. workers in certain industries and occupations have long been vulnerable to employer abuses. But today, illegal and abusive practices are becoming common in a far larger swath of the economy, and the will and resources to enforce worker-protection laws are shrinking.

We are part of a large research team working out of three universities that is studying this phenomenon—what we call "unregulated work"—in New York City and Chicago. Over the past two years we have conducted in-depth interviews with over 400 workers, employers, government officials, community groups, union staff, and policy advocates. The next phase of our project will be a survey of workers in unregulated jobs, in order to estimate the size of this hidden zone of the economy. To date, we have found unregulated work in 14 industries. While many people are familiar with the conditions faced by garment workers and construction day laborers, the tentacles of unregulated work stretch into many other sectors of the economy, including workplaces as diverse as restaurants, grocery stores, security companies, nail salons, laundries, warehouses, manufacturers, building services firms, and home health care agencies.

We have documented considerable variety in how employers violate laws. They pay their workers less than minimum wage, fail to pay them overtime, refuse to pay them for all hours worked, or simply don't pay them at all. They disregard health and safety regulations by imposing unsafe conditions, forcing employees to work without providing necessary safety equipment, and failing to give training and information. The list of ways employers break the law goes on: they refuse to pay Unemployment Insurance or Workers' Compensation; they discriminate against workers on the basis of race, gender and immigration status; they retaliate against attempts to organize; they refuse medical leaves.

Such stories of substandard working conditions may sound familiar—they carry strong echoes of the experiences of workers at the beginning of the *last* century. At that time, the solution was to pass laws to create wage minimum standards, protect workers who speak up for their rights, and eventually, guarantee workplace safety and outlaw discrimination. That these very laws are now being so widely violated poses new challenges. While efforts to pass new laws raising workplace standards are still critical, a new battle has emerged to ensure that existing laws are enforced.

What Explains Unregulated Work?

The rise of unregulated work is closely tied to many of the same factors that are thought to be responsible for declining wages and job security in key sectors of the economy. Over the last 30 years, for example, global economic competition has been extinguishing the prospects of workers in manufacturing. Local manufacturers struggle to drive down their costs in order to compete against firms located in Asian or Latin American countries where wages and safety standards are lower.

Yet unregulated work cannot be explained simply as a by-product of globalization. It's true that the competitive pressure felt in manufacturing may ripple through other parts of the economy, as wage floors are lowered and the power of labor against capital is diminished. But we found businesses that serve distinctly local markets—such as home cleaning companies, grocery stores, and nail salons—engaging in a range of illegal work practices, even though they are insulated from global competition.

Declining unionization rates since the 1970's also contribute to the spread of unregulated labor. One effect has been a general rise in inequality accompanied by lower wages and workplace standards: a weaker labor movement has less influence on the labor market as a whole, and offers less protection for both unionized and non-union workers. More directly, union members are more likely to report workplace violations to the relevant government authority than non-union workers, as a number of studies have shown. So it makes sense that employers are increasingly committing such violations in the wake of a long-term decline in the percentage of workers in unions.

> **While efforts to pass new laws raising workplace standards are still critical, a new battle has emerged to ensure that existing laws are enforced.**

But even the powerful one-two punch of globalization and de-unionization provides only a partial explanation. Government policy is also instrumental in shaping unregulated work—not only employment policies per se, but also immigration, criminal justice, and welfare "reform" policies that create pools of vulnerable workers. In this environment employers can use a variety of illegal and abusive cost-cutting strategies. Perhaps most significantly, they are deciding whether or not to break the law in an era of declining enforcement, when they are likely to face mild penalties or no penalties at all.

Immigration Policy

The deeply flawed immigration policy in the United States creates a labor supply that is vulnerable at work. For example, employers often convince undocumented workers that they have no rights at the workplace. If undocumented workers demand to be paid the minimum wage, their employers threaten not just to fire them, but also to "call immigration." Armed with such threats, employers break the law with little fear of being held accountable. Yet this strategy is only possible because US immigration policy currently denies an estimated 10 million undocumented immigrants legal recognition, thereby ensuring a steady stream of vulnerable workers. In spite of the protections they have on paper, undocumented workers consistently report feeling that government assistance is off-limits because of their immigration status.

The victims of unregulated work are not, however, limited to undocumented immigrants. Immigrants who are authorized to work are also a significant part of this workforce. Employers sometimes simply assume that people from certain countries are undocumented. Some workers are hampered by a lack of proficiency in English. Many new arrivals also lack knowledge of U.S. labor and employment laws and employers can, and do, exploit this ignorance.

For example, the newly arrived Polish women we interviewed who work at A-1 Cleaning in Chicago are usually very pleased to have quickly found work that does not require a full command of English. A Polish immigrant founded the home cleaning company, using his ties in the community to find new workers. But this is not a story of ethnic solidarity. This employer often fails in his duty to inform these workers that their rights under U.S. law include such novel concepts as a minimum wage and overtime pay, and routinely violates these rights. If employees don't fully understand workplace regulations and their rights under the law, an unscrupulous employer can get them to work for less than minimum wage.

Prison, Welfare, and Discrimination

Immigrants are not the only workers made more vulnerable to workplace exploitation by government policies. Many workers, like Brenda, were born and raised in the United States but face barriers to employment in the more regulated part of the labor market. Predictably, race, ethnicity, and gender play a role in determining who ends up in the unregulated workforce. In addition, people leaving the welfare rolls or coming out of prison are especially vulnerable: they are pushed to find work as soon as possible, yet the stigma attached to having been on welfare or in prison limits the options available to them. For "ex-offenders," this is compounded by the fact that they are legally barred from certain jobs. Similarly, some features of welfare reform policies, such as abrupt or arbitrary benefit cut-offs, or "work first" policies that force people to take the first job offered, only make it more difficult to find a satisfactory job. Ironically, the only stable employment history some workers are able to build is in unregulated work, but because they are "off the books" this does not translate into better prospects in formal jobs, so they stay mired in exploitative jobs.

Employers also keep workers trapped in unregulated jobs through illegal discrimination. In New York City's restaurant industry, for example, a white college student applying for a job will be given a front-of-the-house job such as waiting tables, seating people, or operating the cash register. A Mexican worker, regardless of language skills or immigration status, will instead be funneled into a back-of-the-house job such as dishwashing, cooking, or janitorial work. These behind-the-scenes workers are then more vulnerable to violations and extremely unlikely to be promoted to better positions.

Externalization and Exclusion from Legal Protection

New business strategies in recent decades have produced a clear shift towards the "externalization" of work. Various forms of subcontracting and outsourcing are now widespread, and allow employers to evade responsibility for mistreating workers. When workers complain about abusive or illegal practices, the firm and its subcontractor can always point fingers at each other. Overall, the growth of outsourcing has driven many jobs into spaces where the reach of regulation is weak or nonexistent.

Employers also insulate themselves from workers' demands for improved working conditions by hiring temporary workers or using subcontractors. Some use placement agencies to do their dirty work, routinely asking them to screen workers on the basis of gender, race, age and other characteristics. In one of the most egregious examples we discovered, some employment agencies in New York demand sensitive health information from job seekers. A group of workers explained to us that these agencies also post signs refusing job applications from western Africans or South Africans. In this way, they seem to believe that they are screening out potentially HIV-positive candidates for their clients. One of the main services these agencies provide, then, is to discriminate simultaneously on the basis of national origin and disability.

Tapping into a contingent workforce of day laborers allows many employers to keep their costs to an absolute minimum. The emergence of day labor corners in many cities is one of the most visible examples of unregulated work. Day laborers are hired for a variety of jobs, including construction, cleaning, and moving. Besides the often dangerous and difficult working conditions they face, day laborers may work for employers who scrimp on promised wages or fail to pay them at all. (See "Just in Time: Emerging Alliances between Unions and Day Laborers," *Dollars & Sense,* March/April 2004, for an in-depth look at day laborers' efforts to organize.)

Chicago's largest day labor corner is on the city's northwest side, in the parking lot of a gas station. Known colloquially as the "slave station", the corner is the morning destination for large numbers of men who hope to find a day's work. Many of the men are Polish; others are Mexican, Ecuadorian, Guatemalan, and Ukrainian. They have often just arrived in the city and have large debts incurred while traveling to the United States.

Contractors actively try to bid down wages of workers by playing them off against one another. While the going wage in the area for these jobs is between $8 and $10 per hour, day laborers are sometimes forced to accept as little as $4 per hour rather than go without work.

Some workers are especially vulnerable to employers' abuses because they are located outside the reach of some, or even all, legal protections. For example, although domestic workers are covered by minimum wage laws and other protections, they are not covered by the National Labor Relations Act, and so they don't have the right to organize. This means that their employers are effectively given free reign to fire them for complaining about their jobs or demanding better treatment. Farm workers are similarly vulnerable, since they are exempt from protection of many labor laws.

Employers are increasingly misclassifying their workers as "independent contractors" in order to evade workplace regulations. The problem, as Cathy Ruckelshaus of the National Employment Law Project points out, is that this classification is only supposed to be applied to independent businesspersons. "You have to ask yourself, especially in the case of some of the low-wage workers," she says, "whether these people are actually running their own businesses or not." Child care workers, construction day laborers, janitors, street vendors, delivery people and bathroom attendants have been placed into this category, when in fact they were dependent upon their employer for scheduling, job assignments, equipment and training—signaling their status as traditional employees.

The Enforcement Problem

Our fieldwork indicates that unregulated work is a growing feature of business strategies at the bottom of the labor market. Very few attempts have been made to estimate the prevalence of workplace violations, but our preliminary findings are in line with evidence gathered by other researchers. For example, in the late 1990s the U.S. Department of Labor (DOL) carried out several surveys to assess compliance with the Fair Labor Standards Act (FLSA)—the law that regulates the minimum wage, overtime, and the use of child labor. Among their results: in 1999, only 42% of restaurants in Chicago and only 35% of garment shops in New York City were in compliance with FLSA.

Unfortunately, just as employer violations appear to be increasing, the resources allocated to enforcement are waning. Data we recently received from the Department of Labor shows that while the number of workplaces in the United States more than doubled between 1975 and 2004, the number of compliance actions by the DOL's Wage and Hour Division (WHD) declined by more than a third. As Howard Wial, a senior researcher at the Brookings Institution, writes, "The general picture that emerges . . . is that there has been a long-term decline in the adequacy of enforcement resources, which has probably resulted in a long-term decline in the amount of attention that the WHD pays to low-wage workers."

So employers are unlikely to be the target of WHD inspections, and if they are, penalties are unlikely to be high enough to provide a deterrent. An unprincipled employer may find that it is cheaper to break the law—and run the slight risk of getting caught—than it is to comply. David Weil, an economist at Boston University, conducted a cost-benefit analysis of compliance in the garment industry, including data on the annual likelihood of inspection, the average underpayment per worker, and the median civil penalty. He found that for an apparel contractor with 35 workers, "the potential cost of not complying [with minimum wage requirements] is $121 versus a benefit of $12,205, implying that an apparel employer should clearly choose not to comply."

The problem of unregulated work is not just a "race to the bottom." It is a race that is taking place *below* the bottom. The legal floors on wages and working conditions are increasingly irrelevant to American employers. For the workers who populate this segment of the labor market, there is no guarantee that workplace laws will protect them.

Workers Push Back

The good news is that on the ground, community groups and other advocates are taking action. Workers are protesting for the wages owed them even as they are filing complaints with the Department of Labor or filing suits in court. In New York, workers have also collaborated with the state Attorney General's office, which has undertaken a number of initiatives to bring law-breaking employers into compliance. Immigrant workers in particular are organizing, either with unions or through Worker Centers, on the basis of industry and occupation. Day-labor groups across the country are creating "job centers," where wage rates and rules for hiring are collectively set and enforced by workers.

Some employment agencies also post signs refusing job applications from western Africans or South Africans. They seem to believe that they are screening out potentially HIV-positive candidates for their clients.

Advocates are also using legislation to pressure the relevant government agencies to enforce the law to protect workers. Cam-

paigns are also underway to pass state legislation that would tie businesses' operating licenses to their compliance with labor and employment laws. In 2003, a new law in California increased employers' responsibility for violations carried out by their subcontractors. And a local law passed the same year in New York City increased the responsibility of employment agencies for the actions of their clients who hire domestic workers.

Clearly, a greater commitment to workplace enforcement, backed up by sufficient resources, will be necessary to combat the increasing number of violations of workers' rights. Yet more enforcement alone will not be enough. A deeply flawed immigration policy also needs to be fundamentally changed, so that all workers enjoy the minimum standards under the law, regardless of their citizenship status. In practice, our current immigration system accepts people into the country but then effectively denies them rights in the workplace. This creates a steady stream of vulnerable workers. Comprehensive immigration reform, with a sound path to legalization, is an essential component of efforts to guarantee workers' rights. Similarly, comprehensive changes to welfare and penal policies would make people returning to the workforce less vulnerable to exploitation in the unregulated workforce.

The growth of unregulated jobs has created a new terrain in the battle for workers' rights. While continuing efforts to raise the minimum wage and improve workplace standards are critical, in practice employers are routinely violating the standards that already exist. A greater commitment to enforcement, comprehensive reform in a range of areas of government policy (including immigration, penal, and welfare policy), and efforts to close the loopholes employers are currently taking advantage of, will all be necessary to fulfill the promise of protective labor legislation.

Siobhán McGrath is a Policy Research Associate with the Economic Justice Project at the Brennan Center for Justice. She holds a Master's degree in Economics from the New School for Social Research. **Nina Martin** is a Researcher at the Center for Urban Economic Development (CUED). She is a PhD candidate in the College of Urban Planning & Public Affairs at the University of Illinois at Chicago and holds a Master's degree in Urban Planning from the London School of Economics.

The Brennan Center and CUED, together with the Department of Black and Hispanic Studies at Baruch College (CUNY), have been working together to document the growth of unregulated work in New York City and Chicago. The names of workers have been changed.

From *Dollars & Sense*, September/October 2005, pp. 16–19, 34–35. Reprinted by permission of Dollars & Sense, a progressive economics magazine. www.dollarsandsense.org.

Accounting for Corporate Behavior

JOHN A. WEINBERG

The year 2002 was one of great tumult for the American corporation. As the year began, news of accounting irregularities at energy giant Enron was unfolding at a rapid pace. These revelations would ultimately lead to the demise of that firm and its auditor Arthur Andersen. But Enron was not an isolated case, as other accounting scandals soon followed at WorldCom and Global Crossing in the telecommunications industry and at other prominent companies in different sectors. In July of 2002, Forbes.com published a "corporate scandal sheet" listing some twenty companies that were under investigation by the Securities and Exchange Commission (SEC) or other government authority.[1] Of these cases, the vast majority involved misreporting of corporate earnings.

These allegations certainly created the appearance of a general phenomenon in corporate finance, and the resulting loss of confidence in financial reporting practices arguably contributed to the weakness of markets for corporate securities. The fact that many of the problems were surfacing in industries that had been at the center of the new economy euphoria of the late 1990s contributed to the sense of malaise by shaking investor confidence in the economy's fundamental prospects. In most of the recent cases, the discovery of accounting improprieties was accompanied by a spectacular decline of high-flying stocks and, in a number of cases, criminal charges against corporate executives. Consequently, the state of corporate governance and accounting became the dominant business news story of the year.

To some observers, the recent events confirm a sense that the stock market boom of the 1990s was artificial—a "bubble" backed solely by unrealistic expectations with no grounding in economic fundamentals. According to this view, investors' bloated expectations were nourished by the fictitious performance results reported by some firms. In the aftermath of these events, Congress enacted a new law known as the Sarbanes-Oxley Act to reform corporate accounting practices and the corporate governance tools that are intended to ensure sound financial reporting.

The attention received by the various scandals and the legislative response might easily create the impression that a fundamental flaw developed in the American system of corporate governance and finance during the late 1990s. It *does* appear that the sheer number of cases in which companies have been forced to make significant restatements of their accounts, largely as the result of SEC action, has risen in recent years. Beginning in 1998 with large earnings restatements by such companies as Sunbeam and Waste Management and with a heightened commitment by the SEC, under then chairman Arthur Levitt, to police misleading statements of earnings, the number of cases rose significantly above the dozen or so per year that was common in the 1980s.[2] While the frequency and magnitude of recent cases seem to be greater than in the past, accounting scandals are not new. Episodes of fraudulent accounting have occurred repeatedly in the history of U.S. financial markets.

In the aftermath of the stock market crash of 1929, public attention and congressional investigation led to allegations of unsavory practices by some financial market participants during the preceding boom. This activity led directly to the creation of the Securities and Exchange Commission in 1934. One of the founding principles of this agency was that "companies publicly offering securities . . . must tell the public the truth about their businesses."[3] The creation of the SEC, however, did not eliminate the problem, and scandals associated with dubious accounting remained a feature of the financial landscape. In 1987 a number of associations for accounting and finance professionals organized a National Commission on Fraudulent Financial Reporting. The commission studied cases from the 1980s and characterized the typical case as involving a relatively small company with weak internal controls. Although incidents of fraud were often triggered by a financial strain or sudden downturn in a company's real performance, the companies involved were usually from industries that had been experiencing relatively rapid growth. So while the size of companies involved in recent cases may be atypical, the occurrence of scandals in high-growth firms fits the established pattern.

Does fraudulent financial reporting represent the Achilles' heel of U.S. corporate finance? This essay addresses such questions by examining the problem of financial reporting in the context of the fundamental problem of corporate governance. Broadly stated, that fundamental problem is the need for a large group of corporate outsiders (shareholders) to be able to control the incentives of a small group of corporate insiders (management). At the heart of this problem lies a basic and inescapable asymmetry: insiders are much better informed about the opportunities and performance of a business than are any outsiders. This asymmetry presents a challenge that the modern corporation seeks to address in the mechanisms it uses to measure performance and reward managers.

While the tools of corporate governance can limit the effects of the incentive problem inherent in the corporate form, they cannot eliminate it. Ultimately, there are times when shareholders just have to trust that management is acting in their best interest and realize that their trust will sometimes be violated. Still, management has a powerful interest in earning and preserving the trust of investors. With trust comes an enhanced willingness of investors to provide funds, resulting in reduced funding costs for the business. That is, the behavior of corporate insiders is disciplined by their desire or need to raise funds in financial markets. This discipline favors efficient corporate governance arrangements.

As discussed in the next section, there are a variety of tools that a corporation might use to control managerial discretion, ranging from the makeup and role of the board of directors to the firm's relationship with its external auditor. To say that such tools are applied efficiently is to say that managers will adopt a tool as long as its benefit outweighs its cost. In the absence of government intervention, the forces of competition among self-interested market participants (both insiders and outsiders) will tend to lead to an efficient set of governance tools. It bears repeating, though, that these tools do not eliminate the fundamental problem of corporate governance. The observation of apparent failures, such as the accounting scandals of 2002, is not inconsistent, however, with a generally well-functioning market for corporate finance. Still, such episodes often provoke a political response, as occurred during the Great Depression and again in 2002 with the Sarbanes-Oxley Act. Through these interventions, the government has assumed a role in managing the relationship between shareholders and management.

The final sections of the essay consider the role of a government authority in setting and enforcing rules. After reviewing the functions of the SEC, discussion turns to the Sarbanes-Oxley Act, the provisions of which can be classified into two broad categories. Parts of the act attempt to improve corporate behavior by mandating certain aspects of the design of the audit committee or the relationship between the firm and its external auditor. The discussion in this essay suggests that there is reason to doubt that such provisions, by themselves, can do much to reduce fraud. Other parts of the act deal more with enforcement and the penalties for infractions. These provisions are more likely to have a direct effect on incentives. An open question is whether this effect is desirable. Since reducing fraud is costly, it is unlikely that reducing it to zero would be cost effective from society's point of view. Further, it is unrealistic to expect the new law to bring about a substantial reduction in instances of fraud without an increase in the resources allocated to enforcement. Given that it is in the interest of corporate stakeholders to devise mechanisms that respond efficiently to the fundamental problem of corporate governance, one might doubt that the gains from government intervention will be worth the costs necessary to bring about significant changes in behavior.

1. The Nature of the Modern Corporation

In the modern American corporation, ownership is typically spread widely over many individuals and institutions. As a result, owners as a group cannot effectively manage a business, a task that would require significant coordination and consensus-building. Instead, owners delegate management responsibilities to a hired professional. To be sure, professional managers usually hold some equity in the firms they run. Still, it is common for a manager's ownership stake to be small relative both to the company's total outstanding equity and to the manager's own total wealth.[4]

This description of the modern corporation featuring a separation between widely dispersed ownership and professional management is typically associated with the work of Adolf Berle and Gardiner Means. In their landmark study, *The Modern Corporation and Private Property,* Berle and Means identified the emerging corporate form as a cause for concern. For them, the separation of ownership and control heralded the rise of a managerial class, wielding great economic power but answerable only to itself. Large numbers of widely dispersed shareholders could not possibly exert effective control over management. Berle and Means' main concern was the growing concentration of economic power in a few hands and the coincident decline in the competitiveness of markets. At the heart of this problem was what they saw as the impossibility of absentee owners disciplining management.

Without adequate control by shareholders in the Berle and Means view, managers would be free to pursue endeavors that serve their own interests at shareholders' expense. Such actions might include making investments and acquisitions whose main effect would be to expand management's "empire." Managers might also use company resources to provide themselves with desirable perks, such as large and luxurious corporate facilities. These actions could result in the destruction of shareholder wealth and an overall decline in efficiency in the allocation of productive resources.

The experience of the last seventy years and the work of a number of writers on the law and economics of corporate governance have suggested that the modern corporation is perhaps not as ominous a development as imagined by Berle and Means. A field of financial economics has developed that studies the mechanisms available to shareholders for exerting some influence over management's decisions.[5] These tools represent the response of governance arrangements to the forces of supply and demand. That is, managers implement a governance mechanism when they perceive that its benefits exceed its costs. The use of these tools, however, cannot eliminate the fundamental asymmetry between managers and owners. Even under the best possible arrangement, corporate insiders will be better informed than outsiders.

The most obvious mechanism for affecting an executive's behavior is the compensation arrangement between the firm and the executive. This tool, however, is also the most subject to problems arising from the separation of ownership and control. Just as it would be difficult for owners to coordinate in directly running the firm, so it is difficult for them to coordinate employment contract negotiations with managers. In practice, this task falls to the board of directors, who, while intended to represent owners, are often essentially controlled by management. In terms of this relationship, management can benefit by creating a strong and independent board. This move signals to owners that management is seeking to constrain its own discretion. Ultimately, however, shareholders face the same challenge in assessing the board's independence as they do in evaluating management's behavior. The close contact the board has with management makes its independence hard to guarantee.

Another source of control available to owners comes from the legal protections provided by corporate law. Shareholders can bring lawsuits against management for certain types of misbehavior, including fraud and self-dealing, by which a manager unjustly enriches himself through transactions with the firm. Loans from the corporation to an executive at preferential interest rates can be an example of self-dealing. Of course use of the courts to discipline management also requires coordination among the widespread group of shareholders. In such cases, coordination can be facilitated by class-action lawsuits, where a number of shareholders come together as the plaintiff. Beyond suing management for specific actions of fraud or theft, however, shareholders' legal rights are limited by a general presumption in the law that management is best positioned to take actions in the firm's best business interest.[6] For instance, if management chooses between two possible investment projects, dissatisfied shareholders would find it very difficult to make a case that management's choice was driven by self-interest as opposed to shareholder value. So, while legal recourse can be an important tool for policing certain types of managerial malfeasance, such recourse cannot serve to constrain the broad discretion that management enjoys in running the business.

Notice that this discussion of tools for controlling managers' behavior has referred repeatedly to the coordination problem facing widely dispersed shareholders. Clearly, the severity of this problem depends on the degree of dispersion. The more concentrated the ownership, the more likely it is that large shareholders will take an active role in negotiating contracts and monitoring the behavior of management. Concentrated ownership comes at a cost, though. For an investor to hold a large share of a large firm requires a substantial commitment of wealth without the benefits of risk diversification. Alternatively, many investors can pool their funds into institutions that own large blocks of stock in corporations. This arrangement does not solve the corporate governance problem of controlling incentives; however, it simply shifts the problem to that of governing the shareholding institutions.

In spite of the burden it places on shareholders, concentrated ownership has won favor as an approach to corporate governance in some settings. In some developed economies, banks hold large shares of equity in firms and also participate more actively in their governance than do financial institutions in the United States. In this country, leveraged buyouts emerged in the 1980s as a technique for taking over companies. In a leveraged buyout, ownership becomes concentrated as an individual or group acquires the firm's equity, financed through the issuance of debt. Some see the leveraged buyout wave as a means of forcing businesses to dispose of excess capacity or reverse unsuccessful acquisitions.[7] In most cases, these transactions resulted in a temporary concentration of ownership, since subsequent sales of equity eventually led back to more dispersed ownership. It seems that, at least in the legal and financial environment of the United States, the benefits of diversification associated with less concentrated ownership are great enough to make firms and their shareholders willing to face the related governance challenges.[8] Still, there is considerable variation in the concentration of ownership among large U.S. corporations, leading some observers to conclude that this feature of modern corporations responds to the relative costs and benefits.[9]

A leveraged buyout is a special type of takeover, an additional tool for controlling managers' incentives. If a firm is badly managed, another firm can acquire it, installing new management and improving its use of resources so as to increase profits. The market for corporate control, the market in which mergers and acquisitions take place, serves two purposes in corporate governance.[10] First, as just noted, it is sometimes the easiest means by which ineffective managers can be replaced. Second, the threat of replacement can help give managers an incentive to behave well. Takeovers, however, can be costly transactions and may not be worth the effort unless the potential improvement in a firm's performance is substantial.

The threat of a takeover introduces the idea that a manager's current behavior could bring about personal costs in the future. Similarly, a manager may have an interest in building and maintaining a reputation for effectively serving shareholders' interest. Such a reputation could enhance the manager's set of future professional opportunities. While reputation can be a powerful incentive device, like other tools, it is not perfect. There will always be *some* circumstances in which a manager will find it in his best interest to take advantage of his good reputation for a short-run gain, even though he realizes that his reputation will suffer in the long run. For example, a manager might "milk" his reputation by issuing misleading reports on the company's performance in order to meet targets needed for additional compensation.

The imperfections of reputation as a disciplining tool are due to the nature of the corporate governance problem and the relationship between ownership and management. Any tools shareholders have to control management's incentives are limited by a basic informational advantage that management enjoys. Because management has superior information about the firm's opportunities, prospects, and performance, shareholders can never be perfectly certain in their evaluation of management's actions and behavior.

2. Corporate Governance as an Agency Problem

At the heart of issues related to corporate governance lies what economists call an agency (or principal-agent) problem. Such a problem often arises when two parties enter into a contractual relationship, like that of employer-employee or borrower-lender. The defining characteristic of an agency problem is that one party, the principal, cannot directly control or prescribe the actions of the other party, the agent. Usually, this lack of control results from the agent having superior information about the endeavor that is of mutual interest to both parties. In the employer-employee relationship, this information gap is often related to the completion of daily tasks. Unable to monitor all of their employees' habits, bosses base workers' salaries on performance to induce those workers to put appropriate effort into their work.[11] Another common example of an agency problem includes insurance relationships. In auto insurance, for instance, the insurer cannot directly monitor the car owner's driving habits, which directly affect the probability of a claim being filed. Typical features of insurance contracts such as deductibles serve to enhance the owner's incentive to exercise care.

In interpreting corporate governance as an agency problem, it is common to identify top corporate management as the agent and owners as the principal. While both management and ownership are typically composed of a number of individuals, the basic tensions that arise in an agency relationship can be seen quite clearly if one thinks of each of the opposing parties as a single individual. In this hypothetical relationship, an owner (the principal) hires a manager (the agent) to run a business. The owner is not actively involved in the affairs of the firm and, therefore, is not as well-informed as the manager about the opportunities available to the firm. Also, it may not be practical for the owner to monitor the manager's every action. Accordingly, the control that the owner exerts over the manager is primarily indirect. Since the owner can expect the manager to take actions that maximize his own return, the owner can try to structure the compensation policy so that the manager does well when the business does well. This policy could be supplemented by a mutual understanding of conditions under which the manager's employment might be terminated.

The agency perspective is certainly consistent with a significant part of compensation for corporate executives being contingent on firm performance. Equity grants to executives and equity options are common examples of performance-based compensation. Besides direct compensation, principals have a number of other tools available to affect agents' incentives. As discussed earlier, the tools available to shareholders include termination of top executives' employment, the possibility of a hostile takeover, and the right to sue executive management for certain types of misbehavior. Like direct compensation

policy, all of these tools involve consequences for management that depend on corporate performance. Hence, the effective use of such tools requires that principals be able to assess agents' performance.

In the usual formulation of an agency problem, the agent takes an action that affects the business's profits, and the principal pays the agent an amount that depends on the level of those profits. This procedure presumes that the principal is able to assess the firm's profits. But the very same features of a modern corporation that make it difficult for principals (shareholders) to monitor actions taken by agents (corporate management) also create an asymmetry in the ability of shareholders and managers to track the firm's performance. Since owners cannot directly observe all of the firm's expenses and sales revenues, they must rely to some extent on the manager's reports about such measures of performance. As discussed in the next section, the problem of corporate governance is a compound agency problem: shareholders suffer from both an inability to directly control management's actions and an inability to easily obtain information necessary to assess management's performance.

The characterization of corporate governance as an agency problem might lead one to doubt the ability of market forces to achieve efficient outcomes in this setting. But an agency problem is not a source of market failure. Rather, agents' and principals' unequal access to relevant information is simply a condition of the economic environment. In this environment, participants will evaluate contractual arrangements taking into account the effects on the incentives for all parties involved. An individual or a firm that can devise a contract with improved incentive effects will have an advantage in attracting other participants. In this way, market forces will tend to lead to efficient contracts. Accordingly, the economic view of corporate governance is that firms will seek executive compensation policies and other governance mechanisms that provide the best possible incentive for management to work in shareholders' best interest. The ultimate governance structure chosen does not eliminate the agency problem but is a rational, best response to that problem, balancing the costs and benefits of managerial discretion.

3. Accounting for Corporate Performance

All of the tools intended to influence the incentives and behavior of managers require that outsiders be able to assess when the firm is performing well and when it is performing poorly. If the manager's compensation is tied to the corporation's stock price, then investors, whose behavior determines the stock price, must be able to make inferences about the firm's true performance and prospects from the information available. If management's discipline comes from the threat of a takeover, then potential acquirers must also be able to make such assessments.

The challenge for effective market discipline (whether in the capital market or in the market for corporate control) is in getting information held by corporate insiders out into the open. As a general matter, insiders have an interest in providing the market with reliable information. If by doing so they can reduce the uncertainty associated with investing in their firm, then they can reduce the firm's cost of capital. But it's not enough for a manager to simply say, "I'm going to release reliable financial information about my business on an annual (or quarterly or other interval) basis." The believability of such a statement is limited because there will always be some circumstances in which a manager can benefit in the short term by not being fully transparent.

The difficulty in securing reliable information may be most apparent when a manager's compensation is directly tied to accounting-based performance measures. Since these measures are generated inside the firm, essentially by the same group of people whose decisions are driving the business's performance, the opportunity for manipulation is present. Certainly, accounting standards set by professional organizations can limit the discretion available to corporate insiders. A great deal of discretion remains, however. The academic accounting literature refers to such manipulation of current performance measures as "earnings management."

An alternative to executive compensation that depends on current performance as reported by the firm is compensation that depends on the market's perception of current performance. That is, compensation can be tied to the behavior of the firm's stock price. In this way, rather than depending on self-reported numbers, executives' rewards depend on investors' collective evaluation of the firm's performance. Compensation schemes based on this type of investor evaluation include plans that award bonuses based on stock price performance as well as those that offer direct grants of equity or equity options to managers.

Unfortunately, tying compensation to stock price performance hardly eliminates a manager's incentive to manipulate accounting numbers. If accounting numbers are generally believed by investors to provide reliable information about a company's performance, then those investors' trading behavior will cause stock prices to respond to accounting reports. This responsiveness could create an incentive for managers to manipulate accounting numbers in order to boost stock prices. Note, however, that if investors viewed earnings management and other forms of accounting manipulation as pervasive, they would tend to ignore reported numbers. In this case, stock prices would be unresponsive to accounting numbers, and managers would have little reason to manipulate reports (although they would also have little incentive to exert any effort or resources to creating accurate reports). The fact that we do observe cases of manipulation suggests that investors do not ignore accounting numbers, as they would if they expected all reports to be misleading. That is, the prevailing environment appears to be one in which serious instances of fraud are occasional rather than pervasive.

In summary, the design of a system of rewards for a corporation's top executives has two conflicting goals. To give executives an incentive to take actions that maximize shareholder value, compensation needs to be sensitive to the firm's performance. But the measurement of performance is subject to manipulation by the firm's management, and the incentive for such manipulation grows with the sensitivity of rewards to measured performance. This tension limits the ability of compensation plans to effectively manage executives' incentives.[12]

Are there tools that a corporation can use to lessen the possibility of manipulated reporting and thereby improve the incentive structure for corporate executives? One possible tool is an external check on a firm's reported performance. A primary source for this check in public corporations is an external auditor. By becoming familiar with a client and its performance, an auditor can get a sense for the appropriateness of the choices made by the firm in preparing its reports. Of course, every case of fraudulent financial reporting by corporations, including those in the last year, involves the failure of an external auditor to detect or disclose problems. Clearly, an external audit is not a fail-safe protection against misreporting. A significant part of the Sarbanes-Oxley legislation was therefore devoted to improving the incentives of accounting firms in their role as external auditors.

An external audit is limited in its ability to prevent fraudulent reporting. First, many observers argue that an auditor's role is limited to certifying that a client's financial statements were prepared in accordance with professional accounting standards. Making this determination does not automatically enable an auditor to identify fraud. Others counter that an auditor's knowledge of a client's operations makes the auditor better positioned than other outsiders to assess the veracity of the client's reports. In this view, audit effectiveness in deterring fraud is as much a matter of willingness as ability.

One aspect of auditors incentives that has received a great deal of attention is the degree to which the auditor's interests are independent of the interests of the client's management.[13] Some observers argue that the objectivity of large accounting firms when serving as external auditors is compromised by a desire to gain and retain lucrative consulting relationships with those clients. Even before the events of 2002, momentum was growing for the idea of separating the audit and consulting businesses into separate firms. Although the Sarbanes-Oxley Act did not require such a separation, some audit firms have taken the step of spinning off their consulting businesses. This step, however, does not guarantee auditor independence. Ultimately, an auditor works for its client, and there are always strong market forces driving a service provider to give the client what the client wants. If the client is willing to pay more for an audit that overlooks some questionable numbers than the (expected) costs to the auditor for providing such an audit, then that demand will likely be met. In general, a client's desire to maintain credibility with investors gives it a strong interest in the reliability of the auditor's work. Even so, there will always be some cases in which a client and an auditor find themselves willing to breach the public's trust for a short-term gain.

Some observers suggest that making the hiring of the auditor the responsibility of a company's board of directors, in particular the board's audit committee, can prevent complicity between management and external auditors. This arrangement is indeed a standard procedure in large corporations. Still, the ability of such an arrangement to enhance auditor independence hinges on the independence of the board and its audit committee. Unfortunately, there appears to be no simple mechanism for ensuring the independence of directors charged with overseeing a firm's audit relationships. In 1987 the National Commission on Fraudulent Financial Reporting found that among the most common characteristics of cases that resulted in enforcement actions by the Securities and Exchange Commission was weak or inactive audit committees or committees that had members with business ties to the firm or its executives. While such characteristics can often be seen clearly after the fact, it can be more difficult and costly for investors or other outsiders to discriminate among firms based on the general quality of their governance arrangements before problems have surfaced. While an outside investor can learn about the members of the audit committee and how often it meets, investors are less able to assess how much care the committee puts into its work.

The difficulty in guaranteeing the release of reliable information arises directly from the fundamental problem of corporate governance. In a business enterprise characterized by a separation of ownership and control, those in control have exclusive access to information that would be useful to the outside owners of the firm. Any outsider that the firm hires to verify that the information it releases is correct becomes, in effect, an insider. Once an auditor, for instance, acquires sufficient knowledge about a client to assess its management's reports, that auditor faces incentive problems analogous to those faced by management. So, while an external audit might be part of the appropriate response to the agency problem between management and investors, an audit also creates a new and analogous agency problem between investors and an auditor.

An alternative approach to monitoring the information released by a firm is for this monitoring to be done by parties that have no contractual relationship with the firm's management. Investors, as a group, would benefit from the increased credibility of accounting numbers this situation would provide. Suppose that a small number of individual investors spent the resources necessary to assess the truthfulness of a firm's report. Those investors could then make trades based on the results of their investigation. In an efficient capital market, the results would then be revealed in the firm's stock price. In this way, the firm's management would suffer the consequences (in the form of a lower stock price) of making misleading reports. The problem with this scenario is that while only a few investors incur the cost of the investigation and producing the information, all investors receive the benefit. Individual investors will have a limited incentive to incur such costs when other investors can free ride on their efforts. Because it is difficult for dispersed shareholders to coordinate information-gathering efforts, such free riding might occur and is just a further reflection of the fundamental problem of corporate governance.

The free-riding problem that comes when investors produce information about a firm can be reduced if an individual investor owns a large fraction of a firm's shares. As discussed in the second section, however, concentrated ownership has costs and does not necessarily resolve the information and incentive problems inherent in corporate governance. An alternative approach to the free-riding problem, and one that extends beyond the governance arrangements of an individual firm, is the creation of a membership organization that evaluates firms and their reporting behavior. Firms would be willing to pay a fee to join such an organization if membership served as a seal of approval for reporting practices. Members would then enjoy the benefits of reduced funding costs that come with credibility.

One type of membership organization that could contribute to improved financial reporting is a stock exchange. As the next section discusses, the New York Stock Exchange (NYSE) was a leader in establishing disclosure rules prior to the stock market crash of 1929. The political response to the crash was the creation of the Securities and Exchange Commission, which took over some of the responsibilities that might otherwise fall to a private membership organization. Hence, a government body like the SEC might substitute for private arrangements in monitoring corporate accounting behavior. The main source of incentives for a government body is its sensitivity to political sentiments. While political pressure can be an effective source of incentives, its effectiveness can also vary depending on political and economic conditions. If government monitoring replaces some information production by private market participants, it is still possible for such a hybrid system of corporate monitoring to be efficient as long as market participants base their actions on accurate beliefs about the effectiveness of government monitoring.

Given the existence of a governmental entity charged with policing the accounting behavior of public corporations, how much policing should that entity do? Should it carefully investigate every firm's reported numbers? This would be an expensive undertaking. The purpose of this policing activity is to enhance the incentives for corporate managements and their auditors to file accurate reports. At the same time, this goal should be pursued in a cost-effective manner. To do this, there is a second tool, beyond investigation, that the agency can use to affect incentives. The agency can also vary the punishment imposed on firms that are found to have violated the standards of honest reporting. At a minimum, this punishment simply involves the reduction in stock price that occurs when a firm is forced to make a restatement of earnings or other important accounting numbers. This minimum punishment, imposed entirely by market forces, can be substantial.[14] To toughen punishment, the government authority can impose fines or even criminal penalties.

To increase corporate managers' incentive for truthful accounting, a government authority can either increase resources spent on monitoring firms' reports or increase penalties imposed for discovered infractions. Relying on large penalties allows the authority to economize on monitoring costs but, as long as monitoring is imperfect, raises the likelihood of wrongly penalizing firms. The Sarbanes-Oxley Act has provisions that affect both of these margins of enforcement. The following sections describe enforcement in the United States before and after Sarbanes-Oxley.

4. Government Enforcement of Corporate Honesty

Before the creation of the Securities and Exchange Commission in 1934, regulation of disclosures by firms issuing public securities was a state matter. Various states had "blue sky laws," so named because they were intended to "check stock swindlers so barefaced they would sell building lots in the blue sky."[15] These laws, which specified disclosures required of firms seeking to register and issue securities, had limited impact because they did not apply to the issuance of securities across state lines. An issuer could register securities in one state but offer them for sale in other states through the mail. The issuer would then be subject only to the laws of the state in which the securities were registered. The New York Stock Exchange offered an alternative, private form of regulation with listing requirements that were generally more stringent than those in the state laws. The NYSE also encouraged listing firms to make regular, audited reports on their income and financial position. This practice was nearly universal on the New York Stock Exchange by the late 1920s. The many competing exchanges at the time had weaker rules.

One of the key provisions of the Securities Exchange Act of 1934 was a requirement that all firms issuing stock file annual and quarterly reports with the SEC. In general, however, the act did not give finely detailed instructions to the commission. Rather, the SEC was granted the authority to issue rules "where appropriate in the public interest or for the protection of investors."[16] As with many of its powers, the SEC's authority with regard to the treatment of information disclosed by firms was left to an evolutionary process.

In the form into which it has evolved, the SEC reviews financial reports, taking one of a number of possible actions when problems are found. There are two broad classes of filings that the Corporate Finance Division of the SEC reviews—transactional and periodic filings. Transactional filings contain information relevant to particular transactions, such as the issuance of new securities or mergers and acquisitions. Periodic filings are the annual and quarterly filings, as well as the annual report to shareholders. Among the options available to the Corporate Finance Division if problems are found in a firm's disclosures is to refer the case to the Division of Enforcement.

Given its limited resources, it is impossible for the SEC to review all of the filings that come under its authority. In general, more attention is paid to transactional filings. In particular, all transactional filings go through an initial review, or screening process, to identify those warranting a closer examination. Many periodic filings do not even receive the initial screening. While the agency's goal has been to review every firm's annual 10-K report at least once every three years, it has not had the resources to realize that goal. In 2002 around half of all public companies had not had such a review in the last three years.[17] It is possible that the extraordinary nature of recent scandals has been due in part to the failure of the SEC's enforcement capabilities to keep up with the growth of securities market activity.

5. The Sarbanes-Oxley Act of 2002

In the aftermath of the accounting scandals of 2002, Congress enacted the Sarbanes-Oxley Act, aimed at enhancing corporate responsibility and reforming the practice of corporate accounting. The law contains provisions pertaining to both companies issuing securities and those in the auditing profession. Some parts of the act articulate rules for companies and their auditors, while other parts focus more on enforcement of these rules.[18]

The most prominent provisions dealing with companies that issue securities include obligations for the top executives and rules regarding the audit committee. The act requires the chief executive and financial officers to sign a firm's annual and quarterly filings with the SEC. The signatures will be taken to certify that, to the best of the executives' knowledge, the filings give a fair and honest representation of the firm's financial condition and operating performance. By not fulfilling this signature requirement, executives could face the possibility of significant criminal penalties.

The sections of the act that deal with the audit committee seek to promote the independence of directors serving on that committee. To this end, the act requires that members of the audit committee have no other business relationship with the company. That is, those directors should receive no compensation from the firm other than their director's fee. The act also instructs audit committees to establish formal procedures for handling complaints about accounting matters, whether the complaints come from inside or outside of the firm. Finally, the committee must include a member who is a "financial expert," as defined by the SEC, or explain publicly why it has no such expert.

Like its attempt to promote audit committee independence, the act contains provisions regarding a similar relationship between a firm and its auditor. A number of these provisions are intended to keep the auditor from getting "too close" to the firm. Hence, the act specifies a number of nonaudit services that an accounting firm may not provide to its audit clients. The act also requires audit firms to rotate the lead partner responsible for a client at least once every five years. Further, the act calls on the SEC to study the feasibility of requiring companies to periodically change their audit firm.

With regard to enforcement, the act includes both some new requirements for the SEC in its review of company filings and the creation of a new body, the Public Company Accounting Oversight Board. The PCAOB is intended to be an independent supervisory body for the auditing industry with which all firms performing audits of public companies must register. This board is charged with the task of establishing standards and rules governing the operation of public accounting firms. As put forth in Sarbanes-Oxley, these standards must include a minimum period of time over which audit work papers must be maintained for possible examination by the PCAOB. Other rules would involve internal controls that audit firms must put in place to protect the quality and integrity of their work.

Sarbanes-Oxley gives the PCAOB the task of inspecting audit firms on a regular basis, with annual inspection required for the largest firms.[19] In addition to examining a firm's compliance with rules regarding organization and internal controls, inspections may include reviews of specific audit engagements. The PCAOB may impose penalties that include fines as well as the termination of an audit firm's registration. Such termination would imply a firm's exit from the audit business.

In addition to creating the new board to supervise the audit industry, the act gives the SEC greater responsibilities in reviewing disclosures by public companies. The act spells out factors that the SEC should use in prioritizing its reviews. For instance, firms that have issued material restatements of financial results or those whose stock prices have experienced significant volatility should receive priority treatment. Further, Sarbanes-Oxley requires that no company be reviewed less than once every three years. Other sections of the act that deal with enforcement prescribe penalties for specific abuses and extend the statute of limitations for private securities fraud litigation.

The goal of the Sarbanes-Oxley Act is to alter the incentives of corporate managements and their auditors so as to reduce the frequency of fraudulent financial reporting. In evaluating the act, one can take this goal as given and try to assess the act's likely impact on actual behavior of market participants. Alternatively, one could focus on the goal itself. The act is presumably based on the belief that we currently have too much fraud in corporate disclosures. But what is the right amount of fraud? Total elimination of fraud, if even feasible, is unlikely to be economically desirable. As argued earlier, reducing fraud is costly. It requires the expenditure of resources by some party to evaluate the public statements of companies and a further resource cost to impose consequences on those firms determined to have made false reports. Reduction in fraud is only economically efficient or desirable as long as the incremental costs of enforcement are less than the social gain from improved financial reporting.

What are the social benefits from improved credibility of corporate information? A reduction in the perceived likelihood of fraud brings with it similar benefits to other risk reductions perceived by investors. For example, investors become more willing to provide funds to corporations that issue public securities, resulting in a reduction in the cost of capital for those firms. Other things being equal, improved credibility should also lead to more investment by public companies and an overall expansion of the corporate sector. Again, however, any such gain must be weighed against the corresponding costs.

Is there any reason to believe that a private market for corporate finance, without any government intervention, would not result in an efficient level of corporate honesty? Economic theory suggests that the answer is no. It is true that the production of information necessary to discover fraud has some characteristics of a public good. For example, many people stand to benefit from an individual's efforts in investigating a company. While public goods can impede the efficiency of private market outcomes, the benefits of information production accrue to a well-defined group of market participants in this case. Companies subject to heightened investigative scrutiny enjoy lower costs of capital.

In principle, one can imagine this type of investigative activity being undertaken by a private membership organization. Companies that join would voluntarily subject their accounting reports to close review. Failure to comply with the organization's standards could be punished with expulsion. This organization could fund its activities through membership fees paid by the participating companies. It would only attract members if the benefits of membership, in the form of reduced costs of capital, exceeded the cost of membership. That is, such an organization would be successful if it could improve at low cost the credibility of its members' reported information. Still, even if successful, the organization would most likely not eliminate the potential for fraud among its members. There would always be some circumstances in which the short-run gain from reporting false numbers would outweigh the risk of discovery and expulsion.

Before the stock market crash of 1929, the New York Stock Exchange was operating in some ways much like the hypothetical organization just described. Investigations after the crash, which uncovered instances of misleading or fraudulent reporting by issuers of securities, found relatively fewer abuses among companies issuing stock on the NYSE.[20] One might reasonably conjecture that through such institutions the U.S. financial markets would have evolved into an efficient set of arrangements for promoting corporate honesty. While consideration of this possibility would make an interesting intellectual exercise, it is not what happened. Instead, as often occurs in American politics, Congress responded to a crisis with the creation of a government entity. In this case, a government entity charged with policing the behavior of companies that issue public securities. The presence of such an agency might well dilute private market participants' incentives to engage in such policing activities. If so, then reliance on the government substitutes for reliance on private arrangements.

Have the SEC's enforcement activities resulted in an efficient level of corporate honesty? This is a difficult determination to make. It is true that known cases of misreporting rose steadily in the 1980s and 1990s and that the events of 2002 represented unprecedented levels of both the number and the size of companies involved. It is also true that over the last two decades, as activity in securities markets grew at a very rapid pace, growth in the SEC's budget lagged, limiting the resources available for the review of corporate reports. In this sense, one might argue that the level of enforcement fell during this period. Whether the current level of enforcement is efficient or not, the Sarbanes-Oxley Act expresses Congress's interest in seeing heightened enforcement so as to reduce the frequency of fraudulent reports.

How effective is Sarbanes-Oxley likely to be in changing the incentives of corporations and their auditors? Many of the act's provisions set rules and standards for ways in which firms should behave or how they should organize themselves and their relationships with auditors. There is reason to be skeptical about the likely effectiveness of these provisions by themselves. These portions of the act mandate that certain things be done inside an issuing firm, for instance, in the organization of the audit committee. But because these actions and organizational changes take place inside the firm, they are subject to the same information problems as all corporate behavior. It is inherently difficult for outsiders, whether market participants or government agencies, to know what goes on inside the firm. The monitoring required to gain this information is costly, and it is unlikely that mandates for changed behavior will have much effect without an increase in the allocation of resources for such monitoring of corporate actions, relationships, and reports.

Other parts of the act appear to call for this increase in the allocation of resources for monitoring activities, both by the SEC and by the newly created PCAOB. Together with the act's provisions concerning penalties, these portions should have a real effect on incentives and behavior. Further, to the extent that these agencies monitor firms' adherence to the general rules and standards specified in the act, monitoring will give force to those provisions. If the goal of the act is to reduce the likelihood of events like Enron and WorldCom, however, monitoring might best be applied to the actual review of corporate reports and accounting firms' audit engagements. Ultimately, such direct review of firms' reports and audit work papers is the activity that identifies misbehavior. Uncovering and punishing misbehavior is, in turn, the most certain means of altering incentives.

Incentives for deceptive accounting will never be eliminated, and even a firm that follows all of the formal rules in the Sarbanes-Oxley Act will find a way to be deceptive if the expected payoff is big enough. Among the things done by the SEC and PCAOB, the payoff to deception is most effectively limited by the allocation of resources to direct review of reported performance and by bringing penalties to bear where appropriate. Any hope that a real change in corporate behavior can be attained without incurring the costs of paying closer attention to the actual reporting behavior of firms will likely lead to disappointment. Corporate discipline, whether from market forces or government intervention, arises when people outside of the firm incur the costs necessary to learn some of what insiders know.

Notes

1. Patsuris (2002).
2. Alternative means of tallying the number of cases are found in Richardson et al. (2002) and Financial Executives Research Foundation Inc. (2001). By both measures, there was a marked increase in the number of cases in the late 1990s.
3. From the SEC Web page.
4. Holderness et al. (1999) present evidence of rising managerial ownership over time. They find that executives and directors, *as a group,* owned an average of 21 percent of the outstanding stock in corporations they ran in 1995, compared to 13 percent in 1935.
5. Shleifer and Vishny (1997) provide a survey of this literature.
6. This point is emphasized by Roe (2002).
7. Holmstrom and Kaplan (2001) discuss the role of the leveraged buyouts of the 1980s in aligning managerial and shareholder interests.
8. Roe (1994) argues that ownership concentration in the United States has been constrained by a variety of legal restrictions. While this argument might temper one's conclusion that the benefits of dispersed ownership outweigh the costs, the leveraged buyout episode provides an example of concentration that was consistent with the legal environment and yet did not last.
9. Demsetz and Lehn (1985) make this argument.
10. Henry Manne (1965) was an early advocate of the beneficial incentive effect on the market for corporate control.
11. Classic treatments of agency problems are given by Holmstrom (1979) for the general analysis of moral hazard and Jensen and Meckling (1976) for the characterization of corporate governance as an agency problem.
12. Lacker and Weinberg (1989) analyze an agency problem in which the agent can manipulate the performance measure.
13. Levitt (2000) discusses this point.
14. Richardson et al. (2002).
15. Seligman (1982, 44).
16. Seligman (1982, 100).
17. United States Senate, Committee on Governmental Affairs (2002).
18. A summary of the act is found in Davis and Murray (2002).
19. Firms preparing audit reports for more than one hundred companies per year will be inspected annually.
20. Seligman (1982, 46).

References

Berle, Adolf, and Gardiner Means. 1932. *The Modern Corporation and Private Property.* New York: Commerce Clearing House.

Davis, Harry S., and Megan E. Murray. 2002. "Corporate Responsibility and Accounting Reform." *Banking and Financial Services Policy Report* 21 (November): 1–8.

Demsetz, Harold, and Kenneth Lehn. 1985. "The Structure of Corporate Ownership: Causes and Consequences." *Journal of Political Economy* 93 (December): 1155–77.

Financial Executives Research Foundation Inc. 2001. "Quantitative Measures of the Quality of Financial Reporting" (7 June).

Holderness, Clifford G., Randall S. Krozner, and Dennis P. Sheehan. 1999. "Were the Good Old Days That Good? Changes in Managerial Stock 20 Federal Reserve Bank of Richmond Economic Quarterly Ownership Since the Great Depression." *Journal of Finance* 54 (April): 435–69.

Holmstrom, Bengt. 1979. "Moral Hazard and Observability." *Bell Journal of Economics* 10 (Spring): 74–91.

———, and Steven N. Kaplan. 2001. "Corporate Governance and Merger Activity in the United States: Making Sense of the 1980s and 1990s." *Journal of Economic Perspectives* 15 (Spring): 121–44.

Jensen, Michael C., and William H. Meckling. 1976. "Theory of the Firm: Managerial Behavior, Agency Costs and Ownership Structure." *Journal of Financial Economics* 3 (October): 305–60.

Lacker, Jeffrey M., and John A. Weinberg. 1989. "Optimal Contracts Under Costly State Falsification." *Journal of Political Economy* 97 (December): 1345–63.

Levitt, Arthur. 2000. "A Profession at the Crossroads." Speech delivered at the National Association of State Boards of Accountancy, Boston, Mass., 18 September.

Manne, Henry G. 1965. "Mergers and the Market for Corporate Control." *Journal of Political Economy* 73 (April): 110–20.

Patsuris, Penelope. 2002. "The Corporate Scandal Sheet." Forbes. com (25 July).

Richardson, Scott, Irem Tuna, and MinWu. 2002. "Predicting Earnings Management: The Case of Earnings Restatements." University of Pennsylvania Working Paper (October).

Roe, Mark J. 1994. *Strong Managers, Weak Owners: The Political Roots of American Corporate Finance.* Princeton, N.J.: Princeton University Press.

———. 2002. "Corporate Law's Limits." *Journal of Legal Studies* 31 (June): 233–71.

Seligman, Joel. 1982. *The Transformation of Wall Street: A History of the Securities and Exchange Commission and Modern Corporate Finance.* Boston: Houghton Mifflin.

Shleifer, Andrei, and Robert W. Vishny. 1997. "A Survey of Corporate Governance." *Journal of Finance* 52 (June): 737–83.

United States Senate, Committee on Governmental Affairs. 2002. "Financial Oversight of Enron: The SEC and Private-Sector Watchdogs." Staff report (8 October).

This article first appeared in the Bank's 2002 Annual Report. It benefited from conversations with a number of the author's colleagues in the Research Department and from careful and critical readings by **Tom Humphrey, Jeff Lacker, Ned Prescott, John Walter,** and **Alice Felmlee.** The views expressed herein are the author's and not necessarily those of the Federal Reserve System.

UNIT 7

International Human Resource Management

Unit Selections

Key Points to Consider

- How does the smaller world affect the practice of human resource management?

- How do you think developed societies should respond to the outsourcing of jobs to lesser-developed societies, and what can or should they do to help individuals whose jobs have been outsourced?

- What do you think the impact is of illegal immigrants on the U.S. or other developed countrys' labor markets?

- What are some considerations of transnational firms in the human resource area?

- How would you expect organizations in the future to view the market for potential employees?

- How would you expect organizations to view compensation of international employees?

Student Web Site

www.mhcls.com/online

Internet References

Further information regarding these Web sites may be found in this book's preface or online.

Cultural Globalization
http://www.inst.at/studies/collab/breidenb.htm
Globalization and Human Resource Management
http://www.cic.sfu.ca/forum/adler.html
India Finance and Investment
http://www.finance.indiamart.com
International Business Resources on the Web
http://www.globaledge.msu.edu/ibrd/ibrd.asp
International Labour Organization
http://www.ilo.org
Labor Relations and the National Labor Relations Board
http://www.snc.edu/socsci/chair/336/group2.htm

The world is changing and getting smaller all the time. At the beginning of the twentieth century, the Wright brothers flew at Kitty Hawk, and some 25 years later, Charles Lindbergh flew from New York to Paris, alone, nonstop. In 1969 the spacecraft *Eagle One* landed on the moon, and Neil Armstrong said, "One small step for man, one giant leap for mankind."

Indeed, the giant leaps have become smaller. The world has shrunk due to transportation and communication. Communication is virtually instantaneous—not as it was during the early part of the 1800s, when the Battle of New Orleans was fought several weeks after the peace treaty for the War of 1812 had been signed. For centuries, travel was limited to the speed of a horse or a ship. During the nineteenth century, however, speeds of 60 or even 100 miles an hour were achieved by railroad trains. Before the twentieth century was half over, the speed of sound had been exceeded, and in the 15 years that followed, humans circled the globe in 90 minutes. Less than 10 years later, human beings broke free from Earth's gravity and walked on the moon. The exotic became commonplace. Societies and cultures that had been remote from each other are now close, and people must now live with a diversity unknown in the past.

A shrinking world also means an expanding, global economy, because producers and their raw materials and markets are now much closer to each other than they once were. People, and the organizations they represent, often do business all over the world, and their representatives are often members of foreign societies and cultures. Human resource management in just the domestic arena is an extremely difficult task; when the rest of the world is added to the effort, it becomes a monumental undertaking.

U.S. workers are competing directly with workers in other parts of the world, as discussed in "Globalization and the American Labor Force." Companies often hold out for the lowest bidder in a competition for wage rates. This often forces the wage rates down for higher-paying countries, while only marginally bringing up the wages of the lower-paying societies—a development that is bound to have a direct impact on the standard of living in all of the developed countries of the world. In the United States, immigration has become a major issue as more illegal immigrants from lesser-developed countries pour into the United States to take the low-end jobs, creating an almost separate society within the country, as seen in "Immigration and the U.S. Economy: The Public's Perspective."

As more firms become involved in world trade, they must begin to hire foreign workers. Some of these people are going to stay with the firm and become members of the corporate cadre. In the global economy, it is not uncommon for Indian employees to find themselves working for American or European multinational corporations in, say, Saudi Arabia. This presents the human resource professional with a problem of blending the three cultures into a successful mix. In this example, the ingredients are a well-educated Asian, working in a highly traditional Middle-Eastern society, for a representative of Western technology and culture. The situation involves three different sets of values, three different points of view, and three different sets of expectations on how people should act and be treated. A people strategy that spans the globe is a necessary approach to any organization doing business on a worldwide scale. As seen in "Don't Settle for Less: Global Compensation Programs Need Global Compensation Tools," there is bound to be a blending of ideas on such issues as compensation, benefits and pensions. This will occur not only on a regional level, such as with the EU or NAFTA, but probably on a global level in the more distant future as organizations vie for top talent, no matter where they have originated.

American industry does not have a monopoly on new ideas in human resources. Other societies have successfully dealt with many of the same problems. While U.S. firms certainly will not adopt every idea (lifetime employment as practiced in Japan seems the most obvious noncandidate), they can learn much from organizations outside the United States. Human resource managers need to engage in "Learning from Our Overseas Counterparts" if they are going to meet the needs of their employees and contribute to the success of the corporation.

Faster and better communication and transportation are leading to a more closely knit social, cultural, and economic world, where employees' global employment skills can make the difference between the success or failure of an organization.

But this closer world is also a more dangerous world. Recent events in the War on Terror have demonstrated the dangers associated with doing business abroad, outside of the confines of one's home country. Family and personal security have become a far larger issue than they were in the past and security is now a consideration for all individuals whether they are working domestically or outside of their home country. But we cannot turn our back on the world. The world, because it is the one largely created by the success of Western culture, ideas, and technology, is going to come to the United States and Europe whether the West wants it or not. The only alternative is to be ready for it. As it says in the *Art of War,* "That which you cannot change, accept with open arms."

Globalization and the American Labor Force

The global economy has changed the way national economies recover from recessions and create jobs. This article focuses on the impact of technology and the presence of educated workers in developing countries. Our basic idea is that these two factors have created a market for highly skilled and educated workers that is international in nature and extremely competitive. This article describes this development, analyzes its impact on the United States, discusses public policy alternatives developed in the United States, continental Europe, and Great Britain, and offers some initial ideas that could lead to a solution.

FRED MAIDMENT
Ancell School of Business, Western Connecticut State University

Over the past three years or so, the U.S. economy has struggled to come out of a recession that started as the Bush administration took office in 2001,[1] following a period of historic economic growth and expansion. The U.S. economy peaked in the summer of 1999 and declined slowly until the country experienced three consecutive quarters of negative economic growth as President George W. Bush took office. The economy then began a slow recovery that was set back by a series of events including Sept. 11 and revelations of corporate wrongdoing (e.g., Enron, Global Crossing, and Arthur Anderson) that came to light as the economy was beginning to rebound from the relatively mild recession of 2001. In addition, the dot-com bubble—one of the greatest stock market speculation bubbles of all time—burst, taking with it many of the assets of individual and institutional investors, causing them to be far more cautious and less likely to invest on future promises of high returns.[2]

The post-2001 recovery has been slow and painful. Although the nation may be seeing the beginnings of a truly significant recovery, job-growth figures have been disappointing.[3] Although there are many reasons for this lack of job growth, this article argues that a systemic change has occurred: that there is now a global economy, not only for markets and raw materials, but for labor. The jobs that workers held in the United States prior to the last recession are returning, but they are not necessarily returning to American workers.

The Disappointing Job Picture

While economic growth figures for the United States in 2004 are impressive, the question remains, "Where are the jobs?" These are some recent figures:

Month	Net New Jobs Added to Payroll
November 2003	57,000
December 2003	1,000
January 2004	112,000
February 2004	21,000
March 2004	308,000
April 2004	288,000
May 2004	249,000
June 2004	112,000
July 2004	32,000
August 2004	144,000

Jobs have always been a lagging indicator, i.e., they follow rather than lead economic growth. Employers would rather have their employees work overtime than hire additional workers when an economic upturn begins because hiring new workers is expensive and, if the upturn is not real, or is cut short, terminating new hires is expensive and painful. Although the numbers reported above are all positive and can be subject to different interpretations (as we saw in the recent presidential campaign), they fall below the numbers of new jobs necessary to keep up with changes in the population.

The Link to Technology

For years, the manufacturing sector of the U.S. economy has been sending jobs to less-costly locations. For example, jobs in the textile and auto industries first left the Northeast and the upper Midwest for the South. Now, the textile industry is in the process of departing from the United States almost completely, and the auto industry is becoming so globalized that it is hard to tell whether a car was made in America, Japan, Korea, or Europe. But the jobs affected in these more-traditional downsizings have almost always been jobs that require limited skills. A job that can be learned in 30 minutes on an assembly line will always be in danger of going to the lowest bidder. It does not take long for a relatively unskilled worker in the Third World to reach the level of proficiency of a much more-expensive employee working in a developed country.

Technology has not only enabled manufacturing workers to become far more productive, but it has also enabled much of that work to be done outside the developed world in plants in the Third World. More recently, in the high technology service industries, the back-office work was moved to workers outside of the developed world. This is especially true in information technology, finance, and other service sectors.[4] Those jobs are never going to return to the United States or to any other developed country.

From Technology to Education

But this is material that is well-known. The focus of this article is the new forces that have come into play. For the first time in developing countries there are critical masses of highly skilled, well-educated workers who are capable, willing, and perfectly able to perform complicated and advanced tasks at a very high level.[5] Throughout most of history, this type of person has been found in substantial numbers only in advanced economies. But that has changed, partly as a result of more than 50 years of student exchanges between the United States, Europe, and the developing world, especially China and India.

The original exchange students went to the United States and Europe to study at the end of World War II and a stream followed. Some of them stayed, but many of them returned to their homes, where they became teachers and often leaders in their societies. As the generations have passed, universities have been established in countries such as China and India that produce engineers, teachers, accountants, doctors, scientists, and other professionals who are often as skilled as those produced in the West. Perhaps their equipment is not as current as that of MIT or Caltech, but the faculty went to school there or was taught by faculty that went to school there. They read the same journals, go to the same meetings, have many of the same ambitions (for comparison purposes, think of the United States, circa 1920, with middle-class families getting their first cars, houses, and even indoor plumbing), and work on many of the same projects, including putting people into space, as the Chinese recently did.[6]

Thus, the institutions of higher education in the developing world have created a significant number of highly qualified workers, and, as is well-known, the costs and standards of living in India and China and other developing countries are very much lower than that of the United States or other developed countries. An engineer or a computer programmer in one of these countries would, obviously, be paid far less than a U.S., Japanese, or European counterpart.

Multinational corporations are fully conversant about the differences in labor costs and the capabilities of their employees and have started to take advantage of them on a wide variety of fronts. Today, smaller organizations are also taking advantage of this, often through the euphemism of "third-party provider," especially in information technology.[7] India's and China's workforces are at least three-and-one-halftimes larger than the American workforce. Even if the technologically advanced workforces in China and India are only one-third of the relative size of that in the United States, then both China and India have as many technology workers as the United States has.

The Historical Lesson

There is historic precedent for the situation facing the developed countries. At the end of World War II, both Germany and Japan were completely devastated. Yet, they still had a large number of highly skilled, well-educated, and trained workers. While their traditional forms of capital had been obliterated by the war, their human capital, while damaged, had more-or-less survived. With the assistance of the United States, through the Marshall Plan and other programs, these two countries were back on their economic and political feet in less than a decade, producing goods and services that were often competitive on the world market, and in 25 years, giving American industry a real challenge.

Existing Public Policy Responses
The Continental European Approach

The European approach to the more competitive global environment is far more protective of labor than the U.S. approach. This orientation stems from the historic relationship among European unions, their employing corporations, and the governments.[8] The union movement in Europe is far more politically involved than its American counterpart. There are political parties in many of the countries in Europe that are called "Labor" parties, and they tend to be somewhat more closely aligned with more liberal social causes and issues, including extensive holidays, family leave, and significantly fewer working hours. In Germany, for example, it is not uncommon, for a member of the labor union to have a seat on the board of directors of the corporation, something that might bring on a heart attack for an American CEO.

For European corporations, this means that it is very difficult to terminate employees, because they have many protections against being fired. The result is that corporations in Europe hire new employees only when they absolutely must, and once an employee has a job s/he does not leave. This has resulted in at least two unintended consequences.

First, unemployment in Europe has remained relatively high for the past 15 years, especially among the young, as compared to the United States.[9] The major economies of Germany, France, and Italy have had unemployment rates of around 10% or more.[10] Second, this very restrictive labor market, along with very high rates of taxation, has resulted in very low economic growth in Europe over the past 15 years. During the 1990s, the European Union grew by only a little over 8%, while the U.S. economy grew by over 60%.[11] As Michael Burda of Humboldt University in Berlin said, "You have to work to grow,"[12] [p. A1].

The American Approach

American public policy toward corporate and workplace issues has had three major components. First, stated in its most simple form, the policy has been to keep government out of most of the affairs of business, as long as competitive conditions in the marketplace were maintained. Since the latter part of the 19th century, the country has at least paid lip service to an antitrust policy, focusing on the prohibition of marketing and industrial practices that would restrict trade. These antitrust laws addressed conditions that had developed in the 1800s. These laws were later augmented by New Deal legislation in the 1930s and still later by the social legislation of the Johnson years. These policies were based on the assumption that the relationship between corporations and the people is essentially adversarial in nature; that companies do not necessarily have the best interests of their employees and customers at heart. Many European countries and, in particular, Japan, have not followed this path, and have instead encouraged the development of large, often multi-industry cartels, such as Mitsubishi and Hitachi.

Second, with the exception of unionized organizations, American firms operate under the doctrine of employment at-will. Essentially, this means that employees can be hired or terminated for any reason. While this doctrine has been modified over the years to account for racial, gender, and other forms of specific discrimination such as those covered by the ADA, Title VII, and the ADEA, it is still alive, if not fully well. This allows American organizations to be far more flexible in their hiring practices than their continental European counterparts. There have been efforts to reform the employment at-will doctrine, notably the Model Employment Termination Act,[13] but these efforts have so far been largely unsuccessful. When reform arguments of substantial cost savings were presented, they were ignored by U.S. industry, which holds the doctrine of employment at-will near and dear to its heart.[14] Even in unionized environments, American companies are not as restricted as many continental European organizations. What this means is that American organizations can expand or contract their workforces far more easily than their continental European or Japanese counterparts. Unlike in continental Europe or Japan, it places the burden of responding to changes in the economy on the workers, not on the corporations, because in the United States, workers must respond by taking the initiative and making themselves more marketable in the workforce. In continental Europe and Japan, more of the burden is placed on the corporations because it is more difficult to shed workers when the economy slows.

Third, although the doctrine of employment at-will remains viable, public policy has permitted the development of two major classes of exceptions. First, since the 1930s, the government has provided at least some support to the organized labor movement, and it has permitted unions to bargain collectively over topics that would restrict the application of employment at-will. Thus, collective bargaining agreements consistently contain provisions calling for the arbitration of disputes over employee discharge or for seniority rules that influence who will be let go if there is a downturn. However, the U.S. labor movement has never been as politically involved as are the labor movements in many of the other developed countries, and it has never penetrated industry to the extent that unions have in countries such as Great Britain, France, Germany, Italy, and the Scandinavian nations. Today, only a relatively small percentage of American workers are members of a labor union, and those workers do not have the public policy protections their European counterparts possess.

In the United States today, it is well-known that union organizing attempts are often blunted by employer use of tactics of questionable legality,[15] and efforts on the part of organized labor to influence elections have rarely succeeded. Some of the more recent failures include organized labor's efforts to elect Vice President Al Gore as president in 2000; campaigning for losing Democratic congressional candidates in 2002, and supporting losing Congressman Dick Gephardt in the 2004 Iowa caucuses.[16] These failures have exposed organized labor's lack of political muscle in the United States.

The results of the American approach are: 1) the U.S. economy has grown faster than virtually any other large developed economy in the world over the past 15 years, especially during the decade of the 1990s; 2) U.S. unemployment has been about half that of Germany, Italy, or France during the 1990s.[11] Even during the past recession, the U.S. unemployment rate would have been the envy of these three nations;[17,18] and 3) American workers have become far more productive. Over the past 25 years American workers have actually increased the amount of time spent on the job, while their European and Japanese counterparts[19] have gone in the other direction. According to a United Nations study, American workers now spend more than 500 hours per year more on the job than the average German worker and about 125 hours more per year than the average Japanese worker. Only South Korean and Czech workers exceed the amount of time spent on the job by American workers. With the Czechs, the difference is about the same as it is between the Americans and the Japanese workers. South Korea is the only industrialized country where workers still work a six-day week, and the government is attempting to move the country to a five-day week, partially because the government feels that this will actually improve the economy because the people will have more time to spend their money.[20]

The British Approach

The approach in Great Britain has been somewhat different from the United States and the other major European economies. In the United Kingdom, it has been more difficult to terminate employees than in the United States, but easier than in the rest of the European Union. At the same time, the British have experienced generally lower tax rates than the rest of Europe, but higher than that of the United States. The combination has lead to an unemployment rate that compares very favorably with that of the United States[11] and an economic growth rate of almost 40% for the 1990s.[10,11] In fact, the European Union, as a whole, would actually have experienced slight negative growth for the decade of the 1990s had it not been for the British economy.[21] However, the United Kingdom may be more like its E.U. partners in the future as the officials in Brussels have started to bring the policies of all of the members of the European Union more in line with each other.[22] Also, the proposed B.U. constitution would appear to move that policy forward.[23]

Evaluation

Neither the American approach to coping with the rate of technological changes and challenges nor the European approach is completely satisfactory. As we have seen, the European approach, coupled with a high rate of taxation, trades high unemployment and low economic growth for job security for those who have jobs. The U.S. approach has produced higher levels of economic growth, a relatively low tax rate, and a lower unemployment rate. However, the cost has been paid in terms of job security, high employee stress, and low employee morale, loyalty, and commitment. The British approach of lower taxation than its E.U. partners, but higher taxation than the United States, coupled with a less-restrictive labor policy than continental Europe, but a more-restrictive policy than the Americans, has resulted in low unemployment and very respectable economic growth. The real question concerns how to achieve economic growth and low unemployment rates without some of the dysfunctional consequences. While there are some who may say that these goals are mutually exclusive, the recent British example demonstrates that they do not have to be.

Under the Thatcher government, the British instituted a series of reforms that were, at the time, very painful to many in the United Kingdom. These actions resulted in the privatization of many industries that had formerly been state monopolies, and the resulting discipline of the marketplace stemming from that privatization made those industries far more competitive than they had been in the past. As such, workers no longer had the same kind of job security frequently associated with state-run monopolies/government jobs. Companies had to compete. While British unions, unlike their American counterparts, possessed sufficient political power to temper this privatization by restricting the ability of the newly privatized and existing companies to hire and fire at will, the firms were able to gain more control over their labor force than their continental European counterparts have been able to achieve. This was then combined with the British approach of comparatively moderate taxation, especially by European standards, that has led to relatively high economic growth and low unemployment.

During the 1990s the British experienced 39% economic growth for the decade.[11] While this did not match the growth rate of the United States, it was farberter than that of the other major economies of Europe. British taxes are high when compared to those in the United States, but not as high as in much of the rest of Europe, and the unemployment rate during the 1990s compared very favorably with that of the United States. Flexibility in hiring and firing in Great Britain was somewhere between the United States and continental Europe. The British may soon have to conform to the rest of the European Union in their employment practices, even though they have opted-out of the European Union's 48-hour maximum workweek.[24] Should they choose to vote yes on the new E.U. constitution, it will be interesting to see how these new rules will affect economic growth and unemployment over the next 10 years in the United Kingdom and continental Europe.[22,23]

Where Will the High-Tech Jobs Be?

In the United States, with the economy on the rise, most organizations should be considering hiring new employees, but the question is, in a global marketplace for products, services, materials, and labor, Where are they going to be doing the hiring? It is not uncommon for "American" corporations to have well over 50% of their employees, markets, and sales outside of the United States. Such common U.S. names as Ford, IBM, and Coca Cola would fall into this category, and more firms are joining them.[7] Companies in India are also outsourcing jobs when it is their interest to do so.[25] The global marketplace is a bazaar where all things are for sale, including the classic economic factors of production: land, labor, capital, and entrepreneurship. Buyers of these factors, like shoppers on the Internet or at the mall, will look for the best possible value for their money—which could very well mean replacing highly skilled and highly expensive American workers with less-expensive but also quite skilled employees in countries such as India or China.

Just as the textile industry moved production and the jobs out of New England and just as the auto industry created the "rust-belt" in the Midwest by moving production to less-costly locations, corporations are now doing the same with high-value/ high-tech service sector jobs. This is history repeating itself, with the difference being that these are service jobs that require a relatively high degree of education and training. And these jobs are going to people who are prepared to do them for far less money than the people in the United States. The question for policy makers is how to respond to this shift in the economic environment.

Economists call this an economic dislocation, but to the individual who has been "economically dislocated" it means the loss of one's source of income, damage to one's self-respect, and often an array of social and psychological problems for the person and the community. To the elected policy maker, the individual is a citizen, a constituent and, most importantly, a vote.

The primary responsibility of a corporation in a capitalistic market economy is profitability.[26] These organizations also have secondary responsibilities to various stakeholders of the organization, including their employees, customers, suppliers, the communities in which they do business, as well as others,[27] but their primary function today is to achieve survival and profitability in a highly competitive global marketplace. These organizations must ruthlessly control costs, while at the same time continuously maintain, enhance, and improve the quality of their products. These considerations encourage the export of, not only routine manufacturing jobs as in the past, but the high-technology jobs of today, and traditional U.S. public policy encourages this development. This country's historical hands-off policy toward jobs and even toward the migration of entire industries has been in the name of free trade, and the American economy, on the whole, has benefited. Now, however, the industries at risk include the financial sector, information technology, and other areas of high technology, considered to be important to the future of the American economy.

Existing policy proposals are inadequate. President Bush has proposed adding some funds to community colleges to help retrain individuals whose jobs have moved overseas,[28] but this is only a response to help people who have lost their jobs in the manufacturing sector, not in the high-tech/service sector. It seems unlikely that these high tech/service sector people would be candidates for welding jobs. Indeed, many of them could teach in the programs. Presidential candidate Kerry repeatedly raised the issue of outsourcing during his campaign, but he did not deal with the issue addressed in this article.

The governments of both the United States and Europe need an industrial policy that addresses the need for employment and economic growth. The European approach has not been successful in either area. The U.S. policy of *laissez faire* may not be adequate to deal with the changing marketplace, as the demand for highly skilled and educated labor becomes both global in nature and far more competitive. Advances in technology cannot be stopped, nor should they, and corporations will not stop seeking to increase their competitiveness by cutting their costs and increasing their profits. But a balance must be struck between what is fair to citizens/workers/consumers of a society and the benefits/costs/changes that advances in technology are certain to bring. The genie of technological advancement and communication is out of the bottle, and nobody wants to or is able to put it back in, but dealing with that genie will not be easy. There are bound to be economic dislocations as willing, capable, and educated workers in developing countries compete with workers in developed societies.

We think that the British have presented at least a middle way. Something closer to a solution to the problem of dealing with outsourcing/technological unemployment, while at the same time providing an environment that encourages economic growth and development—not as Darwinian as the American, but not as protectionist as their continental neighbors. It is still more difficult to terminate employees in the United Kingdom than in the United States, but it is still much easier than in the rest of Europe. The British approach gives firms the flexibility they need to respond to changes in the marketplace, while giving the employees a certain amount of protection from the whims and potential incompetence of management. This spreads the systemic risk of the marketplace to both the employer and the employee, forcing the employer to take a more active role in determining the future human resources needs of the organization, as well as the technological needs the organization will have to address to make those human resources competitive.

The employees still have the responsibility to maintain and improve their skills. The difference is that in the British model, there is more sharing of the burden of rapidly changing technology and the resulting outsourcing of the human resources needs of the company.

An Overall View

As a result of the forces discussed in this article, policy makers should consider the following when addressing the needs of the 21st century in employee management relations:

- Corporations have a duty not only to their stockholders to make a profit, but to their other stakeholders and the communities in which they do business;
- Technological change is going to be rapid and both predictable and unpredictable;
- The global marketplace will be hyper-competitive for the foreseeable future and companies must continue to pursue technological change and advancement while at the same time ruthlessly attempting to control costs.
- The cost of addressing the global economy of the 21st century must be paid. The only real question is who will pay for it.
- In the American approach, it is paid directly by the workers, who are subsidized, at least in part, by the government;
- In the continental European model it is paid by the corporations, who are also subsidized, directly or indirectly, by the government;
- In the British model, the labor force and the employers share responsibility, and there is some direct or indirect government support.

Policy makers must select the approach that will be most beneficial and cost-effective for their societies. Each approach to the problem of outsourcing technological unemployment has costs associated with it, and each has certain benefits. This author favors an approach more in line with the British model, since it spreads the systemic cost of outsourcing and technological unemployment more evenly among the concerned parties. However, it should also be recognized that American industry has demonstrated that it will be very reluctant to give up the doctrine of employment at-will even if it can be definitively demonstrated that it is in its best interests to do so, and that firms will be generally unwilling to assume any additional costs in the hypercompetitive global marketplace unless either required and/or given incentives to do so.

The history of American industry has demonstrated a reluctance to reform itself, and major reforms have been imposed only from the outside in the form of industrial policy. Unfortunately, these reforms have come only when the abuses of industry have finally demanded they be instituted. Policy makers need to take action to prevent these kinds of abuses from occurring. The need is obvious, but is the political will to act sufficient to avoid the inevitable crisis that has been necessary for action in the past?

Summary and Conclusions

The world has become a global marketplace that is more competitive and far less forgiving than the national economies of just a few decades ago. To survive in this hypercompetitive world, corporations must produce the highest quality goods possible while at the same time ruthlessly cutting costs, a major component of which is almost certain to be labor.

Outsourcing jobs to less-expensive venues is nothing new; manufacturing jobs have been outsourced for years. What is new is that service sector jobs, often requiring a high degree of education and training, are now being outsourced to countries where the cost of similarly educated and competent employees is much less than that in developed countries.

Since World War II, many people from the developing world went to the United States and Europe, were educated in the major universities, returned to their home countries and taught others. These educated and skilled workers in places like India and China have reached a critical mass and are now capable of doing many of the jobs that were once the sole domain of workers in developed countries. Corporations have realized this and have transferred much of the work to these less-costly locations because the technology of to day's environment allows them to do so at minimal cost. The workers are highly competent, motivated, and much less costly.

This has presented governments in developed countries with the problem of increased unemployment, not because the company has done away with the job, but because the job has left the country. There have been a variety of responses to these events. In the United States, the burden has fallen primarily on the employees to seek retraining and new jobs. In continental Europe, the burden falls primarily on the firms to retrain the human resources and to provide them with the technology to make them competitive in the global economy. Great Britain has found a middle way, however, that provides the basis for our recommendations concerning the future of labor relations in the 21st century.

Government policy makers have a vested interest in how corporations treat their workers. If the government is going to accomplish its primary task of protecting the citizenry/workers/voters, it will have to take an active role in establishing an industrial policy that will do that, while at the same time allowing private industry to have the necessary flexibility to grow, prosper, and provide a standard of living that will benefit all of the citizens.

Notes

1. "Hayswire: NBER Mulls Revision of Recession Start Date Backwards," NCC, *American Intelligence Wire,* January 18, 2004.

2. V. J. Rancanelli, "Singing the Earnings Blues," *Barons,* November 5, 2001, V 81, I 45, MW p. 12.

3. R. Foroohar and T. Emerson, "A Heavier Burden: Even as Recovery Spreads Worldwide, Workers Are Finding Themselves Working Harder for Less Money," *Newsweek,* August 23, 2004, p. 36.

4. Russell Flannery, "Hiring Hall," *Forbes,* July 26, 2004, p. 80.

5. A. P. D'Costa, "Uneven and Combined Development: Understanding India's Software Experts," *World Development,* January 2003, pp. 211–227.

6. J. Plomfret, "China's First Space Traveler Returns Home a Hero," *The Washington Post,* October 16, 2003, p. A. 01.

7. L. Sullivan, "The 0 Word: Outsourcing Overseas: IBM Is Doing It. So Is Dell. Amazon, Cisco Systems, Motorola and Merrill Lynch Are Also in on It. Congress Is Filibustering on the Topic and Presidential Candidates Are Debating It. So What Exactly Is All the Excitement over Outsourcing Jobs Overseas?" *Risk Management,* July 2004, v 51, 7, p. 24–30.

8. C. P. Wallace, "Difficult Labor: German Unions Are Losing Support and Influence. Is Militancy or Moderation the Way to Regain their Clout?" *Time International,* August 4, 2003, v 162, 5, p. 51.

9. F. Maidment, "Germany and the United States: Two Countries, Two Directions," *European Business Review,* v 16, I. 3, 2004. pp. 267–271.

10. *European Marketing and Data Statistics, 2003,* Euromonitor, PLC, London, UK.

11. F. Maidment, "Labor's Role in Driving Economic Growth: A Comparison of the EU and NAFTA," *Proceedings of the Annual Meeting of the Northeast Business and Economics Association,* October 2–4, 2003, Parsippany, N.J., pp. 75–77.

12. C. Rhodes, "Short Hours Undercut Europe In Economic Drive," *The Wall Street Journal,* August 8, 2003, p. AI, col. 1.

13. Theodore J. St. Antoine, "The Model Employment Termination Act: A Fair Compromise," *The Annals of the American Academy of Political and Social Science,* November 1994, v. 536, pp. 93–102.

14. Lewis Maltby, "The Projected Economic Impact of the Model Employment Termination Act," *The Annals of the American Academy of Political and Social Science,* November 1994, v. 536, pp. 103–118.

15. B. Israel, "Post-Dispatch Tries to Bust Union," *St. Louis Journalism Review,* April 2003, v. 33, 255, p.31.

16. S. Greenhouse, "For Labor, a Day to Ask What Went Wrong?" *The New York Times,* January 21, 2004, p. A23.

17. Each country determines its unemployment rate somewhat differently, and if the United States calculated its rate the way any of these three European countries calculate their rates, the U.S. rate would be slightly higher. Also, for historic purposes, it is difficult to directly compare unemployment rates over time because all governments, from time to time, make changes in the way they calculate their unemployment rates [18].

18. F. Maidment, "Unemployment to Rival the Depression," *The New York Times,* January 30, 1983, Sec. III, p. 21.

19. "Koreans, Czechs, American Are Hardest Workers," *EAP Associates Exchange,* September-October 2001, v. 31, is, p. 32.

20. S. Prasso and M. Ihlwan, "Less Work, More Shopping," *Business Week,* September 9, 2002, p. 10.

21. F. Maidment, "Should Great Britain Join NAFTA?" *Proceedings of the New England Business Administration Association Annual Meeting,* May 2003, New Haven, Conn., pp. 42–44.

22. "News Analysis: EU Internal Comms Directive Looms," PRWeek, July 16, 2004, p. 17.

23. "The Ultra-Liberal Socialist Constitution," *The Economist,* September 18, 2004, v. 372, n. 8393, p. 59.

24. Steve Crabb, "The Art of Overdoing It," *The Grocer,* July 17, 2004, p. 68.

25. "Great News! India Is Outsourcing Jobs," *Asia Africa Intelligence Wire,* April 23, 2004.

26. M. Freedman, *Capitalism and Freedom,* University of Chicago Press, Chicago, 1962.

27. G. A. Steiner and J. F. Steiner, *Business, Government and Society,* McGraw-Hill Higher Education, Burr Ridge, Ill., 2001.

28. "Bush Brings Job Growth Message to Fairfax," *The Washington Post,* June 26, 2003, p.T.05.

Immigration and the U.S. Economy: The Public's Perspective

Immigration has long been one of the burning economic and social issues of American history. We think of ourselves as a nation of immigrants. But in times of economic pressure, we have turned off the immigrant valve. The many coauthors of the following piece, all opinion survey experts, analyze current surveys and historical ones. Mythology aside, how do Americans view immigration? Read on.

ROBERT J. BLENDON, ET AL.

President George W. Bush's recent immigration proposal has rekindled a heated debate about whether the United States should be more open or less open to new immigrants and under what circumstances. It also raises the issue of what should be done about illegal immigrants who have been living in this country for many years. Historically, the United States may be a nation of immigrants, but the type and number of immigrants and the circumstances under which they are admitted have been contentious public issues for well over a century.

This paper seeks to examine broadly where Americans stand today on the immigration issue. Using a myriad of recent and historical public opinion data, we seek to answer four critical questions: (1) Is America still a country welcoming to immigrants? (2) Do we see recent immigrants as being helpful or harmful to the nation's economy and culture? (3) Are illegal immigrants, the subject of much of today's debate, seen as being different from legal immigrants in the contribution they make to the country now and in the future? (4) What does the public want its government to do about future legal and illegal immigration?

The data presented here are derived from two main sources. The discussion of current attitudes is based mainly on a survey by National Public Radio, the Kaiser Family Foundation, and Harvard's Kennedy School of Government. The survey was conducted by telephone May 27–August 2, 2004, among a nationally representative sample of 1,888 adults, including 1,104 nonimmigrants and 784 immigrants. The fieldwork was conducted by International Communications Research (ICR). We also present current and historical data from thirty-seven other nationwide public opinion surveys from 1938 to 2004.

Historical Background: Earlier Immigration Debates in the United States

The passage of the Chinese Exclusion Act of 1892 and the Immigration Quota Act of 1920 marked the beginning of restrictions on immigration as the country grappled with how to control the influx. The advent of public opinion polling in the 1930s created a new era of immigration policy analysis by providing insight into the pulse of the public on this issue. A review of the polling literature finds that there have been four major debates on immigration policy since polling data have been available. These debates have been influenced by factors such as immigrants' ethnic origin, the circumstances under which immigrants are fleeing their homes, and the state of the U.S. economy.

The first wave of polls on immigration appeared in the late 1930s, a time of increasing conflict in Europe and during the Great Depression in the United States and abroad. During this time, polling questions focused on whether the United States should expand immigration quotas to admit refugees fleeing Nazi-controlled Europe (Simon and Alexander 1993). Surveys found that a large majority of the public opposed admitting these refugees. In 1938, two-thirds (67 percent) believed that German and Austrian refugees should be kept out of the country (Roper/*Fortune* 1938), and 72 percent disapproved of allowing a large number of Jewish exiles to come to the United States (Gallup 1938). The cultural background of the refugees appeared to make a difference in public sentiment. While 63 percent of the public approved of sending ships to bring English refugee women and children to the United States until after the war (Gallup 1940), only 26 percent approved of bringing refugee children from Germany (who would most likely be Jewish) to the United States (Gallup 1939).

In the immediate post-World War II years, the public was not very receptive to allowing refugees into the United States. Only 18 percent said that if they were a member of Congress, they would vote to allow 100,000 European refugees to enter the country in each of the next four years in addition to the 150,000 immigrants already permitted (Roper/*Fortune* 1947).

With the onset of the cold war, people in the United States became somewhat more receptive to refugees fleeing communism, but the public was still split. In 1953 about half (47 percent) approved of President Eisenhower's proposal to admit 240,000 asylum-seekers over a two-year period (NORC 1953). In 1955 a slight majority (52 percent) favored letting a limited number of refugees from communism enter the United States (NORC 1955). Even after the Soviet army crushed an attempted Hungarian revolution in November 1956, a majority (57 percent) of the public opposed changing the law to make it easier for refugees to come to the United States from communist-held countries (Gallup 1956). In 1958, 55 percent disapproved of permitting 65,000 of the 160,000 Hungarian refugees still left in Europe to come to the United States (Gallup 1958).

By the 1960s, with the nation's economy expanding, the public appeared more willing to make room for immigrants. In 1960, a large number of anti-Castro refugees were granted asylum in the United States (Simon and Alexander 1993). By this time, two-thirds of legal immigrants admitted to the United States were outside the quotas (Gorman 2004), and the annual volume of immigrants jumped from 38,000 in 1945 to about 300,000 in 1965 (Fetzer 2000). Despite these growing numbers, 64 percent of the public said that U.S. immigration policy should have provisions for admitting people who escape from communism (Gallup 1965). The passage of the landmark 1965 Hart-Cellar Immigration Act opened the door for more non-European immigrants by repealing the Quota Act, which had limited the annual number of immigrants who could be admitted from any country to 3 percent of the number of people from that country living in the United States in 1910.

Beginning in the 1970s, the immigration debate took another turn, as the country faced the most severe recession since World War II and the number of non-European immigrants continued to rise (Gorman 2004) (Figure 1). Between 1960 and 1980, the foreign-born Asian population quintupled and the foreign-born Mexican population quadrupled (Gorman 2004). Polls from this period found that the public in the United States was resistant to this cohort of immigrants, even those originating from communist countries. Asked whether 150,000 to 200,000 South Vietnamese who worked with the Americans in Vietnam and might be evacuated before a communist takeover should be permitted to live in the United States, 52 percent of the public said no (Gallup 1975). They were also unreceptive to a second wave of Cuban refugees, the Mariel boatlift of 1980, portrayed by the press as criminals, homosexuals, and mentally ill "undesirables" expelled by Castro (Cultural Orientation Resource Center 2004). Nearly three in five (57 percent) believed that these Cubans should not be allowed to enter the United States (Gallup 1980). Reflecting growing unrest about the country's immigration policies in light of economic conditions, three-fourths of the public believed that it is wrong for us to let in so many Cuban and other refugees when there were real troubles at home and unemployment was on the rise (ABC News/Harris 1980).

In the 1980s and 1990s, the increasing number of immigrants entering the United States without documentation sparked a new debate, this time about *illegal* immigration. Although illegal immigration had existed from the time of the Chinese Exclusion Act, the number of illegal immigrants skyrocketed in the late twentieth century. Growing unemployment in Mexico, as well as the end to the United States's *bracero* program for temporary workers, spurred millions of Mexicans to cross the border illegally to look for work (Gorman 2004). In addition, the rise of affordable air travel made it possible for immigrants to fly to the United States for a "vacation" or to study and never leave. In fact, as many as 30–40 percent of the 8–10 million illegal immigrants in the United States may have entered the country with legal visas but stayed beyond their expiration dates (Gorman 2004).

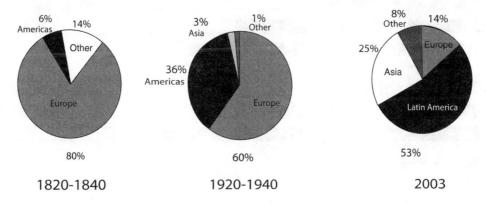

Figure 1   Immigration to the United States, by region of origin.

Source: LeMay 2004 (1820–40, 1920–1940); U.S. Census Bureau 2004 (2003).

Surveys show that the majority of the public in the United States favored a strong government policy against illegal immigration. In 1984, 55 percent of the public said that illegal immigrants should be arrested and deported, while 34 percent said that they should be given amnesty (Gallup 1984). In surveys conducted between 1977 and 1990, 71–79 percent of the public favored banning employment of undocumented immigrants (Gorman 2004). Negative sentiment toward illegal immigrants continued to grow. In 1994, California passed Proposition 187, forbidding state and local officials to provide health benefits and public education to illegal immigrants. At the time of the law's passage, 58 percent of the public nationwide favored a similar law in their own state (*Time*/CNN 1994).

We are now in the midst of the fifth debate on immigration. Conflicts over how to address illegal immigration still exist but now have been coupled with additional concerns over border control in the post-September 11 world.

Immigration Debates in Other Countries

The United States is not the only country grappling today with immigration controversies. Concern about this issue has been seen in Europe as well. A recent survey shows that half or more of the residents of Britain, France, and Germany think that immigrants are a bad influence on their country. At least four out of ten citizens in Spain and Japan feel the same way (AP/Ipsos 2004).

About seven in ten residents of the United States, Britain, Italy, France, Germany, and Spain say that large numbers of immigrants and refugees coming into their areas in the next ten years are an important threat. In 2002, in the aftermath of 9/11, a majority of adults in the United States (60 percent), Britain (54 percent), and Italy (52 percent) said this was an *extremely* important threat, numbers that have declined to about one in four in 2004 (26 percent in the United States, 29 percent in Britain, 25 percent in Italy) (GMF 2004) (Figure 2). But as in the United

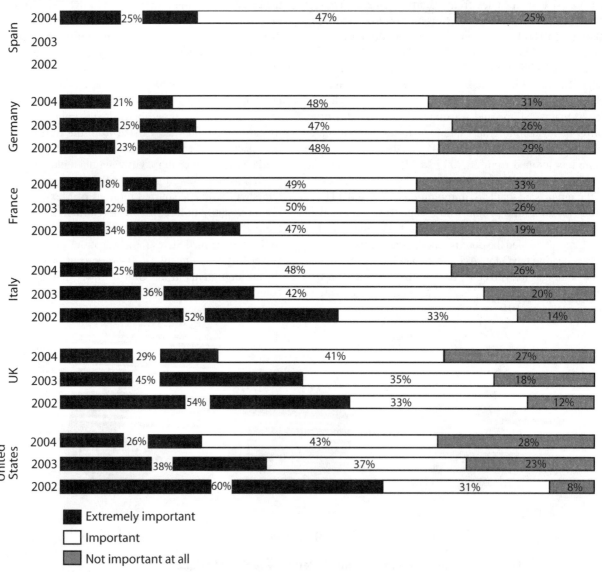

Figure 2   U.S. and European assessments of immigration as a possible threat.

Note: "don't know" responses not shown.

Source: GMF 2004.

States, concerns about the immigration issue are not likely to subside.

The Public's Views about the Flow of Immigrants into the United States

What do the data show about the public's views during this, the fifth immigration debate in the United States?

America is still a country that welcomes immigrants, but the public is divided about how many immigrants they want to come into the United States in the future. Two in five (41 percent) think legal immigration should be decreased, and nearly as many (37 percent) feel it should be kept at its present level. Fewer than one in five (18 percent) think more legal immigrants should be allowed into the country (NPR/Kaiser/Kennedy School 2004) (Table 1).

The public's preferences are not very different when they are asked simply about "immigrants" rather than "legal immigrants." In June 2004 about half (49 percent) said they thought immigration should be decreased, while 33 percent thought it should be kept the same. Only 14 percent thought immigration should be increased (Gallup 2004).

The events of 9/11 had an important but short-term effect on the public's views about the volume of immigrants into the United States. Between June and October 2001, the proportion saying that immigration should be decreased rose from 41 percent to 58 percent (Gallup 2004). Similarly, in the aftermath of 9/11, six in ten (59 percent) believed that legal immigration should be decreased (CBS/*NYT* 2001).

The proportion favoring a decrease in immigration was highest in 1993 (63 percent), just before the passage in California of Proposition 187. This is nearly double the proportion that wanted to decrease immigration in 1965 (33 percent) (Gallup 2004).

Immigrants' Impact on the Economy

The public as a whole is divided on the impact that immigrants have on the country. About half of adults nationwide (47 percent) say that immigrants today are a burden on the country because they take our jobs, housing, and health care, while about half (47 percent) believe that immigrants today strengthen the country because of their hard work and talents (Table 2). Native-born Americans are slightly more negative, with 52 percent saying

Table 1 The Public's Views about the Level of Immigration (%)

| | Legal immigration should be | | | Immigration should be[7] | | |
	Incr.	Kept at present level	Decr.	Incr.	Kept at present level	Decr.
1965	—	—	—	7	39	33
1977	—	—	—	7	37	42
1993	—	—	—	6	27	65
1995	—	—	—	8	28	62
1996	8[1]	35	50	—	—	—
1999	—	—	—	10	41	44
2000	—	—	—	13	41	38
2001 pre-9/11	—	—	—	14	42	41
2001 post-9/11	9[2]	29	59	8	30	58
2002	15[3]	27	55	12	36	49
2003	9[4]	37	48	13	37	47
2004 January	16[5]	34	45	—	—	—
2004 June	—	—	—	14	33	49
2004 May-August	18[6]	37	41	—	—	—

Sources:
[1]CBS 1996
[2]CBS/*NYT* 2001
[3]CCFR 2002
[4]CBS/*NYT* 2003
[5]CBS/*NYT* 2004
[6]NPR/Kaiser/Kennedy School 2004
[7]Gallup 2004
Note: "Don't know" responses not shown.

Table 2 The Public's Views about Whether Immigrants Today Strengthen or Are a Burden on the United States

	Immigrants today	
	Strengthen our country because of their hard work and talents (%)	Are a burden because they take jobs, housing, health care (%)
1994[1]	31	63
1996[1]	37	54
1997[1]	41	48
1999[1]	46	44
2000[1]	50	38
2002[2]	50	40
2003[3]	45	44
2004[4]	47	47

Sources:
[1]Pew 2000
[2]CIRCLE 2002
[3]Pew 2003
[4]NPR/Kaiser/Kennedy School 2004
Note: "Don't know" responses not shown.

Table 3 Americans' Views about Whether Recent Immigrants Take Away Jobs

	Recent immigrants		
	Take away jobs from Americans who want them (%)	Do not (%)	Don't know (%)
Total	46	52	1
By immigration status			
Nonimmigrant	51	48	1
Immigrant	17	81	3
By race/ethnicity			
White	50	48	2
Black	55	44	*
Latino	22	77	1
By education			
Not college graduate	50	49	1
College graduate	35	63	2
By income			
<$30K	55	44	1
$30–49.9K	44	55	1
>$50K	42	58	1
By economic condition in United States			
Excellent/good	36	62	2
Fair/poor	52	48	1
By personal finances			
Excellent/good	39	59	1
Fair/poor	52	46	1
By party; identification			
Republican	46	52	2
Democrat	46	53	1
Independent	55	44	*

Source: NPR/Kaiser/Kennedy School 2004.

immigrants today are a burden and 42 percent saying they strengthen the country (NPR/Kaiser/Kennedy School 2004).

When it comes to the impact of immigration on the U.S. economy, the public makes a clear distinction between legal and illegal immigrants. They are divided on the impact of legal immigrants on the nation's economy. About four in ten (42 percent) say that legal immigrants have helped the economy, and 23 percent say they have hurt it, while 30 percent believe they have had little impact. However, a majority (54 percent) believe that *illegal* immigrants have hurt the economy, while only 18 percent think they have helped it (NPR/Kaiser/Kennedy School 2004).

The public is divided on the question of whether recent immigrants to the United States take away jobs from Americans who want them: 46 percent say they do, 52 percent say they do not. People with lower household incomes (less than $30,000 per year) and who rate the condition of their own finances and nation's economy as only fair or poor are more likely to say that recent immigrants take away jobs than those with higher incomes and those who see their own finances and the nation's economy as excellent or good. African-Americans and whites are far more likely than Latinos, and nonimmigrants are far more likely than immigrants, to think that recent immigrants take away jobs (NPR/Kaiser/Kennedy School 2004) (Table 3).

Twelve percent of native-born Americans report that they or a family member has ever lost a job because a company hired

immigrant workers. Some 15 percent said they or a family member had not gotten a job because an employer hired a recent immigrant instead (NPR/ Kaiser/Kennedy School 2004).

Another economic question is whether most of the money made by recent immigrant stays in this country to help create jobs or goes back to the immigrants' home countries and aids the economy there instead. A majority of the public (58 percent) believe that recent immigrants send most of the money they earn in the United States back to the country they came from. About one-third (35 percent) think recent immigrants spend most of the money here in the United States (NPR/Kaiser/Kennedy School 2004).

The public is also concerned about recent immigration and taxes. Nearly six in ten (58 percent) believe that recent immigrants do not pay their fair share of taxes, while only one-third (33 percent) think they do (NPR/Kaiser/Kennedy School 2004).

Immigrants' Impact on the Culture

Many nonimmigrants believe immigrants are changing American culture and values when they ought to be adopting them, an issue raised by Samuel P. Huntington in *Who Are We?* (2004). Our survey asked whether people believed the United States is a country with a basic American culture and values that immigrants take on when they come here, or whether it is a country made up of many cultures and values that change as new people come here. Sixty-four percent of nonimmigrants said it is the latter, with 34 percent saying the former. Asked, however, what kind of country the United States *should* be, the numbers essentially reversed, with 62 percent saying it should be a country with a basic American culture and values, and 33 percent saying it should be a country made up of many cultures and values. And those who think the country is not as it should be were more likely than others to say that recent immigrants keep too much of their culture and traditions (48 percent–25 percent) (NPR/Kaiser/Kennedy School 2004).

Immigrants agree with nonimmigrants on what kind of country the United States *is,* but disagree on what kind of country it *should* be. A majority of immigrants like things the way they are, with 57 percent saying the United States should be a country made up of many cultures and values (NPR/Kaiser/Kennedy School 2004).

Concerns about Illegal Immigration

The public wants the United States to be open to legal immigrants in the future, but they are very concerned about illegal immigration. A majority of the public (54 percent) believe that most recent immigrants are in the country illegally (NPR/Kaiser/Kennedy School 2004). According to the Census Bureau, 9.1 million immigrants were admitted to the United States legally during the 1990s (U.S. Census Bureau 2003). During that same period, according to an estimate by the Immigration and Naturalization Service, 7.1 million unauthorized immigrants entered the United States (U.S. INS 2003).

About two-thirds (69 percent) say they are concerned about illegal immigration, including 31 percent who are very concerned. But the impact on jobs was not their number one concern. When asked why they were concerned, the top answer was that providing services like schools and health care to illegal immigrants

costs taxpayers too much (expressed by 85 percent of those concerned about illegal immigration). Three-fourths (76 percent) of those concerned said they were concerned that illegal immigration increases the likelihood of terrorism in the United States. This number compares with 60 percent of those who were concerned about illegal immigration because they felt that illegal immigrants take jobs away from Americans (NPR/Kaiser/Kennedy School 2004).

Whether one thinks most recent immigrants are here legally or illegally makes a big difference in how one perceives their effect on American society. Those who think most recent immigrants are here illegally are significantly more likely than those who think they are here legally to believe that recent immigrants do not pay their fair share of taxes (71 percent to 43 percent), are a burden on the country (59 percent to 35 percent), and take away jobs from Americans who want them (54 percent to 40 percent) (NPR/Kaiser/Kennedy School 2004).

The public in the United States today does not believe the historical stereotype that immigrants commit more crimes than non-immigrants do. Most of the public, including most non-immigrants, believe that neither legal nor illegal immigrants are more likely than native-born Americans to commit crimes (NPK/Kaiser/Kennedy School 2004).

Attitudes about Immigration Policy

The public feels strongly that it wants government to stem the flow of illegal immigrants in the future. But compared with other issues, immigration is not a high priority nationally. Immigration is not among the top ten issues the public says it wants government to address (Harris Interactive 2004).

Overall, 61 percent of the public (66 percent of nonimmigrants) think the federal government is not tough enough on immigration, while only 10 percent think the government is too tough. Immigrants (26 percent) and Latinos (29 percent) are the two groups least likely to say that the federal government is not being tough enough. According to the Census Bureau, 39 percent of the Hispanic population of the United States in 2000 was foreign-born (U.S. Census Bureau 2001). Interestingly, economic status does not seem to make a great deal of difference in attitudes on this issue. A majority of nearly every demographic group want the government to be tougher on immigration (NPR/Kaiser/Kennedy School 2004) (Table 4).

Although a majority of the public want the government to be tougher, they are divided on whether or not we should spend more to prevent illegal immigrants from coming to this country. About half (52 percent) think the federal government should spend more, with 14 percent saying it should spend less and 30 percent saying it should spend about the same amount (NPR/Kaiser/Kennedy School 2004).

Our survey asked specifically about a plan proposed by President Bush that would allow some illegal immigrants currently

Table 4   The Public's Views about Federal Immigration Policy

| | Federal government is | | |
	Not tough enough on immigration	About right	Too tough
Total	61%	26%	10%
By immigration status			
Nonimmigrant	66	24	7
Immigrant	26	37	32
By race/ethnicity			
White	66	24	6
Black	67	26	6
Latino	29	33	34
By education			
Not college graduate	64	24	9
College graduate	50	33	13
By income			
<$30K	57	29	11
$30–49.9K	61	26	10
>$50K	67	23	8
By economic condition in United States			
Excellent/good	62	28	6
Fair/poor	60	24	12
By personal finances			
Excellent/good	62	27	8
Fair/poor	60	24	12
By party identification			
Republican	70	22	3
Democrat	66	24	8
Independent	60	27	10

Source: NPR/Kaiser/Kennedy School 2004.

Note: "Don't know" responses not shown.

in the United States to stay in this country legally for several years as long as they hold jobs that no U.S. citizen wants. The plan would require these immigrant workers to return to their countries after their time under this program had expired. President Bush's Democratic opponent, Senator John Kerry of Massachusetts, also supported some kind of guest-worker program. There is a partisan difference in support for the Bush administration's proposal (58 percent of Republicans support it, compared with 33 percent of Democrats), although we should note that the question specifically mentioned President Bush. Overall, 44 percent of the public support the proposal;

52 percent oppose it (NPR/Kaiser/Kennedy School 2004). When asked in October 2004 which presidential candidate they trusted more to handle immigration, the public was almost evenly split, with 45 percent naming Bush and 43 percent choosing Kerry (Gallup/CNN/*USA Today* 2004).

Most people do not think that guest workers will return to their home countries when the law would require them to leave. Overall, nearly three-quarters (72 percent) say the workers will not return. Even among supporters of the plan, 61 percent say the workers will not return (NPR/Kaiser/Kennedy School 2004).

Opposition to the Bush plan does not seem to be overwhelming until you look at the salience numbers. The political danger of going ahead with a guest-worker plan seems much higher than any danger from doing nothing. Nearly three-quarters (73 percent) of those who oppose the plan, or 38 percent of the public overall, say they would be upset if it does go into effect; fewer than half as many of those who say they support the plan would be upset if it doesn't go into effect (36 percent of those who support the plan, or 16 percent of the public overall) (NPR/Kaiser/Kennedy School 2004).

Conclusions

Although immigration was not a major issue in the 2004 presidential campaign, the legal and illegal immigration controversy is not likely to go away. In spite of the problems many immigrants face in the United States and the dangers some face in getting to this country, most immigrants find life in the United States to be better than it is in their home country, at least in terms of opportunity. More than three-quarters (84 percent) of immigrants report that opportunities to get ahead are better in the United States than in their country of origin. Six in ten (62 percent) consider treatment of the poor to be better in the United States, and a plurality (47 percent) of immigrants consider schools to be better in the United States than in their home country. Immigrants from Mexico and Central and South America are especially likely to see each of these measures as being better in the United States than in their home country (NPR/Kaiser/Kennedy School 2004) (Table 5). As a result, large numbers of people are likely to be highly motivated to keep coming to the United States legally or illegally, unless conditions at home change.

Although historically the public in the United States has been more receptive to immigrants when the nation's economy gets better, current concerns about immigration are not based only on the loss of jobs to immigrant labor. The public is also concerned that providing services to illegal immigrants costs taxpayers too much, that immigrants do not pay their fair share in taxes, and that illegal immigration increases the likelihood of terrorism. A substantial number also seem concerned that immigration threatens American culture.

Table 5 How Immigrants Compare the United States and Their Country of Origin (%)

	Opportunities to get ahead		
	Better in the United States	**About the same**	**Better in country of origin**
Total immigrants	84	10	5
Mexican	94	4	2
Central/South American	89	7	3
Other	80	13	6
Treatment of the poor			
Total immigrants	62	16	17
Mexican	76	19	5
Central/South American	69	10	18
Other	54	15	28
Schools			
Total immigrants	47	15	33
Mexican	63	12	23
Central/South American	54	23	21
Other	38	15	40

Source: NPR/Kaiser/Kennedy School 2004.

Note: "Don't know" responses not shown.

Even with all these pressures to limit illegal immigration, this issue will be politically difficult to resolve. George W. Bush won 43 percent of the Latino vote in 2004, a 12 percentage point gain over 2000, showing that this growing share of the electorate is willing to shift allegiances between the parties (Connelly 2004). While a majority of the public want the federal government to get tougher on stopping future illegal immigration and not make it easy for those who are here illegally to work, the two political parties are competing for votes from the emerging Latino community, which does not see a need to toughen federal immigration policy and enforcement.

ROBERT BLENDON is a professor at the Kennedy School of Government, Harvard University, and the Harvard School of Public Health. **STEPHEN PELLETIER** is assistant director, **JOHN BENSON** is managing director, and **ELIZABETH RALEIGH** is research associate at the Harvard Opinion Research Program at the Harvard School of Public Health. **MOLLYANN BRODIE** is vice president, director of public opinion and media research, **ELIZABETH HAMEL** is senior research associate, and **DREW ALTMAN** is president of the Kaiser Family Foundation. **MARCUS D. ROSENBAUM** is a senior editor at National Public Radio.

From *Challenge,* Vol. 48, no. 2, March/April 2005, pp. 113–131. Copyright © 2005 by M.E. Sharpe, Inc. Reprinted by permission.

Learning from Our Overseas Counterparts

Adopt some practices that help keep your foreign colleagues flexible in the face of stringent workplace laws.

PAUL FALCONE

As U.S. citizens and employers, we all gripe about high taxes and the numerous workplace protection laws that make it challenging to manage difficult employees. That's especially the case in "employee-friendly" states like California, where courts and juries appear to assume that employers are guilty until proven innocent. And the grumbling continues like this: How are companies supposed to deal with restrictive and expensive laws like the Family and Medical Leave Act (FMLA), pregnancy disability leave and everything that comes with Title VII compliance?

It's a lot to deal with and keep track of as employment legislation constantly changes on the federal, state and local levels. However, take a gander across the pond, and you'll see that U.S. managers have it pretty easy in comparison. What challenges face our overseas management counterparts, and, more important, what can we learn from them in terms of how they deal with their own challenges?

International Sensitivity

As unique as our problems appear, U.S. managers may be surprised to learn of some of the woes facing their overseas counterparts. Nothing helps you appreciate your situation more than viewing it through the comparative perspective of others. So let's briefly scan the globe and highlight some of the more salient issues that plague our management counterparts in foreign countries.

The European Union (EU) currently has 15 member states and is poised to accept another 10 in May. The EU gives new meaning to the term "work/life balance," tipping more heavily onto the "life" for many of its workers. For example, EU countries start with four weeks of vacation; however, in some countries that's just the beginning. In France, for example, employees are guaranteed five weeks of vacation

per year, unless they are between 18 and 21 years old. Then they are entitled to a 30-day annual leave regardless of how long they have served in the company. Maternity leave is a minimum of 16 weeks (10 of which must be taken after the child is born) but can increase to 26 weeks for a woman's third pregnancy. More significant, the initial duration of unpaid parental leave in France is one year, which can be extended until the child's third birthday.

Maybe those sound like wonderful perks if you're an employee in the EU, but managing around four weeks of annual vacation and three years of child care leave (as opposed to our 12-week FMLA baby-bonding period) can certainly strain your business operations.

Try this one on for size: In Spain, workers who are laid off commonly receive nine weeks of severance for each full year of service. In the United States, it's a much more common practice to award one week of severance for each full year worked. That means a five-year Spanish employee who is about to be laid off (or "made redundant," as they say in most other parts of the world) would be entitled to 45 weeks of severance. Under such financial constraints, a layoff may not be as attractive an alternative for your company becoming more economically competitive after all.

To make matters worse, certain EU countries such as Germany mandate a "social plan" in light of a pending layoff. In addition to objective selection criteria like years of service, performance track records and education or specialized technical skills, German employers also must consider a worker's age and number of dependents. Generally speaking, the more difficult it would be for a worker to find employment elsewhere or the more children that a worker has to support, the greater the level of job protection. Employers are also obligated to create a retraining plan to help those redundant workers reenter the workplace with suitable skills to find employment elsewhere.

In Spain, workers who are laid off commonly receive nine weeks of severance for each full year of service.

Here's a twist to the high cost of employer-paid benefits: One in seven people in the EU works part-time. Because many part-timers are female, part-time employees hold the same employment status (including benefits) as full-time employees. Otherwise, the disparity in benefits could be seen as a form of sex discrimination. That's one of the reasons why employee benefits are evaluated at 70 percent of wages in France and 92 percent of wages in Italy (as opposed to 37 percent in the United States). Ouch!

And don't think these employment-related headaches are only limited to EU countries. Other parts of the world beyond Europe face employment-related challenges as well. In Japan, for example, female employees are entitled to a monthly (partially) paid absence called "menstruation leave." A great perk for employees, no doubt, but a challenge nonetheless for operational supervisors.

In Mexico, a Christmas bonus, consisting of at least 15 days' salary, is considered part of the salary. In fact, there are "13 months of annual salary" in many Latin American countries, just to make sure employees have enough money during the holidays to buy presents for their families.

Lessons Learned

Now that we're all a little more *au courant* with some of the challenges facing our non-U.S. counterparts, let's see how successful managers abroad face their key day-to-day issues. Clearly the result of so many employee rights is the concern that an entitlement mentality may plague European workers. Because of the prevalence in the European Union of strong unions and works councils that are empowered with information and consultation rights on behalf of covered workers, employees may be more apt to challenge management's directives. To make matters worse, many European employers are required by statute to provide detailed employment contracts to new hires outlining the terms and conditions of employment. Employees have been known on occasion to refuse additional work responsibilities if those duties were not clearly outlined in the original written agreement.

To delicately work around such restrictions, many European managers attempt to create a work environment where employees can find meaningful ways to contribute. "There are a number of universal traits that make a good manager, including flexibility, credibility and active listening skills" according to Rensia Melles, director of clinical products, global services at FGI, a provider of international employee assistance program (EAP) services in Toronto. "There is an increasing need for global managers to develop relationships with employees—and the context of how this is done will differ from culture to culture. However, managers everywhere need to consider putting less of a focus on discipline and more emphasis on coaching as a means of creating change and motivating staff. This acknowledgment of the individual often takes the form of guidance, mentoring and training."

In essence, by giving employees the flexibility to reinvent their jobs in light of the company's changing needs and to take ownership of their work, there is less chance that workers will take a strict adherence to their job duties or otherwise look for ways of avoiding work.

Finding qualified staff to replace workers who are on leave can be time-consuming and costly, and regulated temporary services no doubt play a role in the process. "Since companies must comply with statutory leave benefits, creative employers will take the opportunity to reorganize departments and realign resources with business needs. This is a good opportunity for change in the department and to motivate those employees on leave to return to new and challenging responsibilities in the workplace—possibly even earlier than originally planned," according to Deena Baker-Nel, senior manager of international assignment services at Deloitte in Los Angeles.

"Some companies meet with an employee before the leave even begins to discuss potential responsibilities upon return," says Baker-Nel. "Adding rotational assignments or new meaningful roles that employees view as critical to their career development can go a long way in motivating people to return early."

And because it's so costly to lay off workers and difficult to terminate for cause, many organizations forego the opportunity to shed individuals, even if it means going into an overbudget/overstaff situation. When facing the challenge of retaining substandard performers or genuinely "redundant" workers, employers may likely continue the employment relationship.

"In such cases, the company may have no choice but to rethink the individual's role," according to Heather Hand, senior vice president of global human resources at Sunrise Medical in Carlsbad, Calif. "For example, we were faced with a situation where a marketing director overseas had lost interest in her job. She rarely came out of her office and only dealt with her staff via e-mail. The cost of making her redundant was excessive, so we re-purposed her role in a way that she could focus more on her clients and spend less time managing people and dealing with creative services. We changed her title to director of affiliate relations, which allowed her to save face internally, and she tuned back in and became a solid team contributor. I don't know that we would have looked at that very same issue quite as creatively or strategically in the United States in order to come up with an employment solution that benefited both the employee and the company."

From time to time, it's important that U.S. managers increase their sensitivity of how others see the management world and thereby lessen their U.S.-centric view of things. U.S. challenges may seem unique, but there are other systems and ways of doing business that in some respects are superior to ours from a worker's standpoint and perhaps inferior from a managerial or competitive standpoint. In appreciating our differences, we can learn and share lessons that help keep our daily challenges in perspective.

PAUL FALCONE is director of international human resources at Paramount Pictures in Hollywood, Calif. He is the author of four books published by AMACOM, including *The Hiring and Firing Question and Answer Book* (2001) and *101 Sample Write-Ups for Documenting Employee Performance Problems: A Guide to Progressive Discipline and Termination* (1999). This article represents the views of the author solely as an individual and not in any other capacity.

From *HR Magazine,* February 2004 , pp. 113–114, 116. Reprinted with the permission of HR Magazine published by the Society for Human Resource Management, Alexandria, VA, via the Copyright Clearance Center.

Human Resource Management in a Global Environment: Keys for Personal and Organizational Success

An Interview with Eliza Hermann

CATHERINE M. DALTON

Eliza Hermann is Vice President Human Resources Strategy at BP plc, based in London, England. In 1986, her career in the energy business began when she joined Amoco Corporation, where she earned a series of promotions in the international oil business which exposed her to markets ranging from Argentina to Azerbaijan. She was a member of the team involved in the successful integration of Amoco when BP acquired the company in 1998. During the past several years at BP, she has served as Manager, Strategy and Business Transformation-Global Aromatics, leading a team responsible for strategic planning and business development in the company's Petrochemical segment, and more recently as Vice President, Human Resources for BP's global Gas, Power, and Renewables segment. Throughout her career, Ms. Hermann has traveled extensively, with particular focus on Asia, Western Europe, North America, South America, Russia, and the republics of the former Soviet Union.

Ms. Hermann holds a Master of Business Administration (MBA) degree from the Kelley School of Business, Indiana University and a Bachelor of Arts degree in social and behavioral sciences from Johns Hopkins University. She serves on the board of directors of Brightpoint, Inc., where she is Chairperson of the Compensation and Human Resources Committee, as well as a member of the Corporate Governance and Nominating Committee.

I recently had the opportunity to talk with Ms. Hermann about her experiences in human resources at BP and Amoco, as well as her experience as a corporate board member with Brightpoint. During our conversation, she shared her reflections on the centrality of human resources in major strategic initiatives, and her belief in the power of mentoring as a means for ensuring a flow of talent within a company.

Business Horizons: Firstly, thank you for taking the time to share your thoughts with our readership at Business Horizons. I would like to begin our conversation with your career at Amoco. I suspect it would be fair to say that the oil industry is, and was, a relatively non-traditional industry for a freshly-minted MBA, yet alone a woman, when you joined Amoco in 1986. As a result, what attracted you to Amoco and the oil industry, more generally?

Eliza Hermann: Actually, most major energy companies hire a number of new MBAs each year because business acumen and commercial skills are critical in this industry, along with science and technical skills. What may have been more unusual was the hiring of women. There were certainly not a lot of women in the industry in the early days and, frankly, even today it is fairly male-dominated.

How did you choose Amoco out of your many options when graduating with your MBA?

The simple truth is that Amoco chose me. Toward the end of my first year in the MBA program, a representative from Amoco called the Business Placement Office about hiring a summer intern; someone with knowledge about labor relations. I had such experience, so following a phone interview with an Amoco representative, I was hired and spent a summer interning in Chicago with the company. I really enjoyed the job and was impressed with my colleagues and the leadership that I met. I returned to Bloomington for the second year of the MBA program with a job offer in my pocket for when I finished the program. While I did interview a bit more broadly during my second year, I was fairly certain I would return to Amoco, and I did.

That certainly speaks very well of Amoco that you were so certain that you would return to the company full-time following your internship experience.

It was a very good experience interning with Amoco, and the single biggest factor why I wanted to go back was definitely the people. Also, I was attracted to Amoco because it was such a global business, and I'd been interested in international business as early as the seventh or eighth grade.

It sounds like you knew very early what career path you wished to pursue. You have had an extensive and highly successful career in human resources management. Did you always know that you were interested in human resources and, if so, what attracted you to this area of business?

When I was a sophomore in college at Johns Hopkins University in Baltimore, I had not yet decided what I would pursue as a career. To help defray college costs, I took a part-time job as a reader for a blind man who worked for the National Labor Relations Board, the government agency that handles union relations in the U.S. The job entailed making audio tapes that he could listen to, and I became fascinated by the material that I was reading to him, which included labor law cases and other labor research and journal articles. This job opened my eyes to labor relations, which I had not previously heard much about. I ended up working part-time for the NLRB for two years and, through that experience, realized that labor relations was but a small part of a larger arena called human resources, which I then became very interested in. Later on, my rationale for going back to business school was to earn an MBA and deepen my business knowledge, so that I could launch my career in corporate HR.

There is much discussion about the differences between line and staff jobs in organizations. Within this discussion, how would you characterize the importance of HR in organizations?

Without people, most businesses wouldn't be in business. HR focuses on driving much greater organizational and human capability and effectiveness for bottom-line business benefit.

With BP's acquisition of Amoco, you had the opportunity to experience in real time one of the more important corporate strategic changes organizations might experience. As you know, a merger/acquisition in some fashion affects everyone in both organizations. Can you share your thoughts on the role that you believe HR played in the successful integration of Amoco into the BP corporate structure?

One of the key success factors was very tight project management of all aspects of the deal, including the people aspects. For example, in HR we laid out a staffing process that started at the top of the company and cascaded down from there on a schedule, so that people would find out their new status as quickly as possible. In such situations, you don't want people living in an uncomfortable area of uncertainty for any longer than absolutely necessary. We worked very fast in the first two years or so to integrate or harmonize all the various people processes, or design new ones where we needed to. For example, the performance appraisal process, the job posting process, how people are treated; anything that was directly touching or affecting employees we worked very hard to get sorted out quickly. We also led a lot of change management work to help people cope with change. These were some of the areas of HR's contribution.

Was the acquisition particularly hard on Amoco employees, as they were acculturated into the BP system?

I think this varied by employee. There were some people who saw the acquisition as a really good thing, offering new opportunities. Others immediately saw it as a negative; being bought by a non-American company, people who might have been senior in the old headquarters in Chicago and knew they could never move. It was much more an individual set of reactions. There were also a lot of the classic stories about people leaving, either at the time of the acquisition or within the first two years after the acquisition. Lots of people left.

And these were not necessarily the people that you would want to leave, were they?

Most definitely not.

With your permission, I'd also like to talk about HRM in general, training in particular. There is considerable discussion and debate in the field of human resources management about the importance of training and how to make training "stick;" how to ensure that training is effective. Would you mind sharing your thoughts on the training function and how to ensure that organizational training is effective?

Firstly, I would probably reframe the question more broadly as overall learning and development. Training implies training classes. I don't know if you intend to focus on training classes or the broader arena.

Thank you for the opportunity to clarify. Let's focus on the broader arena.

OK. My belief is that the best way to actually make learning stick, whether it originates in the classroom or not, is to reinforce it. One of the best reinforcements is to be sure to apply it at work, quickly and frequently. And it is certainly helpful if there is a supervisor, peer, or colleague who is actively involved in helping the person apply the new learning effectively: giving feedback and follow-on coaching as needed, or just being a sounding board. So, I'd say those are two significant reinforcers that help make training effective. With regard to measuring effectiveness of training, this is very difficult, particularly for knowledge work, leadership, or behavioral skills.

Another belief about training is that it is not necessarily about the classroom experience or training experience itself, but also the opportunity to network with other individuals.

Absolutely. I am a huge believer in networking. And networking could be internal to a corporation or broadly external across many organizations. Either could be really important, depending on what the learning goal is.

Internal networks are good for learning within an organization, especially in a large company like BP. This is one thing BP does really well compared to others companies I've touched. Obviously, we are huge, we are global, we are very dispersed physically, but there are mechanisms that enable the creation of global communities of interest or communities of practice, to share learning, knowledge, and processes.

One aspect of your career that has almost certainly enabled a rich variety of learning opportunities is your extensive experience with international travel while with Amoco and, subsequently, BP. What do you think has been the greatest benefit you have realized from these experiences in non-domestic markets?

You learn pretty quickly that there is no one right way culturally, or what works well in one country or culture isn't going to work well in another. Cultural context is everything in the practice of HR. You develop a pretty quick appreciation for other peoples' beliefs and practices and how things get done.

One school of thought with regard to organizational structure and design is that the more decentralized the organization, for example, a decentralized organization such as BP, the more important it is at a corporate level to understand these cultural issues. Would you agree?

That's an interesting theory. I'm not sure that centralization/decentralization would make a difference in that.

Is it simply that it is a good guideline to be culturally sensitive, regardless of how the company is structured?

Yes, I think at any multi-country or multinational organization, sensitivity to local cultural context is going to be crucially important to the success of the business.

Extensive international travel such as yours undoubtedly brings with it some challenges. What are some of the more notable challenges, either personal or corporate, you have faced operating in such a wide variety of global markets?

With a Western, capitalistic decision making approach, it is very easy to think that other cultures or people in other countries should make decisions based on the same thinking around economics that we would, when in fact their negotiating positions might be driven by quite different needs or value sets. So what's uneconomic to us might be economic to them, or vice versa. One example might be Azerbaijan in the very early 1990s. Azeri leaders put an economic value on access to great training outside of their own country, whereas historically we might not have seen access to training as a big negotiating lever in constructing the terms of a deal. Another example more common in certain Asian cultures is the whole issue of saving face. This could become even more important than dollars and cents type thinking in certain situations. Another example involves the purpose of a meeting. Quite often, we may think the purpose of a meeting is to make a decision, but there are cultures where the purpose of the meeting is more a matter of form. The decision will already have been made beforehand, which then drives a lot of different meeting behaviors. If you are operating on the wrong assumption at the wrong moment, it's quite difficult to interpret the meeting behavior. Respect for hierarchy is another example. In some cultures, this is a big behavioral driver. A subordinate

might never openly, in a group setting, speak up unless agreeing with what the boss said.

You have been able to apply your HR expertise not only as a senior executive, but more recently as a corporate director for a company involved in multiple country markets. In fact, you are part of a trend of corporations actively seeking specialized expertise, particularly in the area of human resources, for the board of directors. How have you found your experience as a corporate board member at Brightpoint?

The ability to apply my HR technical/functional expertise on Brightpoint's board of directors is tremendously gratifying. I feel I am able to contribute not only my HR skills, but also in the area of coaching for better organizational effectiveness.

Do you find that HR has historically been an under-represented area on corporate boards?

My sense is that there are not large numbers of HR professionals on corporate boards, although I don't have any factual data on this. If HR people are under-represented, the one thing that does surprise me is that with all of the increased focus on CEO pay, there wouldn't be more of a call for HR or compensation experts. But, then again, boards can hire these individuals as consultants.

I would agree. Historically, boards have simply hired this type of expertise and have therefore concluded that such expertise or guidance is not needed on the board on an ongoing basis. In some respects, that is not misguided thinking from the perspective that it is good practice in the current governance environment that the board hire outside experts to provide context for critical board decisions.

It is interesting thinking. If you think about big construction engineering projects, who oversees and manages the whole contract with the outside engineering firm? Someone who knows engineering, of course. So it is interesting in the matter of compensation and compensation consultants that there might be some benefit in having someone manage that process who knows something about it, who can offer unique insight on the basis of solid experience in that area.

Speaking of the issue of compensation, congratulations on your appointment last year as Chairperson of the Compensation and Human Resources Committee at Brightpoint. Within that role, what do you see as the critical issues for an effective Compensation and Human Resources Committee?

Executive pay and succession planning.

A crucial aspect of human resource planning is effectively managing succession processes. Do you believe most organizations are effective at succession planning?

My assertion is that most are probably not as effective as they could be.

What would make them more effective?

The whole practice of succession planning has to be fully integrated into everything else to do with leadership performance assessment, leadership talent identification, assessment of upward potential, and leadership development. It all has to be one integrated approach that the top leadership takes very seriously as the backbone of their people process. This means it also has to be fully integrated with the business performance management process, of course. The important thing is that it is central; that it is integrated into the overall core business processes of the enterprise.

I would think that a key aspect of successful succession planning is effective mentoring of succession candidates.

In terms of leadership development, or employee development in any sense, I believe mentoring and coaching are very effective tactics.

Do you find that organizations effectively engage in mentoring and coaching?

I think that even the best organizations can probably do more. Fundamentally, I think that every supervisor, every team leader, everyone who is a manager of other human beings, as a part of their formal job should be coaching and mentoring the people who work for them. I think we have separated the concept of mentoring from that of coaching, and now think of mentoring as outside the reporting relationship, which is just a different form of coaching, or a different form of providing someone who is a sounding board or a source of advice or guidance. A lot of companies have effective mentoring programs. But I think that a formal mentoring program is never going to be 100% of the solution because the best mentoring relationships are often based on the chemistry and the relationship between the individuals, and you can't ever formally arrange that.

What advice would you give to someone looking for a coach or mentor?

The starting place is to look at one's professional network and think about who you already know or who you already talk with in a professional context, inside or outside the organization, and enhance the relationship. Ask the person for advice or feedback on the particular issue. I see it as a very organic process as opposed to "OK, now we're going to go into our mentoring conversation for the next 10 minutes." I see it much more as something that is just a part of everyday life.

There is a distinction between informal mentoring, which I think is actually much more powerful, and formal mentoring, which is formal programs where people are paired together and matched up. BP has a formal mentoring program; in fact, several of them. One of the more novel formal programs that I've participated in is reverse mentoring, where someone more senior is paired up with someone very junior, say a year or two out of university, and the senior individual is the mentee and gets to learn from the more junior person their issues and concerns from their perspective.

That sounds like a fascinating program. Our readers might enjoy hearing about how the reverse mentoring program works at BP.

It is voluntary on either person's part. Both the more senior people and the more junior people can volunteer if they would like to be paired up and participate. It is a formal program, so there is a structure built around it that lasts about a year. The pairings are made by someone in HR and the process is deliberately set out to have as diverse pairings

as possible. I participated two years ago. My mentor was a 20-something Azerbaijani accountant who was working in London for a couple of years to better develop his financial skills. He was very bright and had a deeply inquiring mind. We had a good year. There were a couple of "lunch and learn" sessions put on by the organizers; otherwise, we were left to our own devices to meet roughly every two months. I got some insight as to what he was thinking and what he was concerned about, and it was a very different mentoring experience.

What were your and your mentor's individual goals in entering this reverse mentoring experience?

For him, to learn more about how someone more senior looked at the organization and looked at career development, in particular. Insight into how BP decision-making works, how things actually get done. For me, as with all of the senior participants, to get the insight into how a more junior person would look at the organization.

You are clearly quite passionate about mentoring. Have you found other ways to serve as a mentor?

In BP, I am often asked if I will mentor others. I would say at any given time that I am mentoring around a dozen HR people. Some of these have been identified by us, the leadership of the HR function, as having significantly higher potential. But, in other cases, it may just be more junior people who I've come into contact with or who simply want a more senior mentor. I also mentor some Indiana University Kelley School of Business MBA students, two at the moment, although I keep in touch with two or three others who have already graduated. With the latter, it is not a program anymore, but a relationship that has carried on past the formal mentoring.

In either your formal or informal roles as a mentor, what do you find to be the most satisfying aspect of being a mentor?

When it is truly a two-way relationship where there is real conversation and collegial advice-giving in both directions. It's also very satisfying seeing these people get ahead in their careers, seeing them do what they want to do.

Through your mentoring experiences, you have undoubtedly facilitated others' career successes. What is it that you believe has enabled your own success as an HR professional?

There are certain elements of what I do that I am really passionate about, and because of this, I put a lot of energy, effort, and dedication into my job. In particular, I care very deeply about helping other people develop and get ahead in their careers, particularly professional women.

Have you relied on mentors throughout your career and, if so, how have they helped you professionally?

I've had lots of mentors, former bosses, and other senior colleagues with whom I've worked over the years. I'd say the people who I think of most actively as a coach or mentor to me now are a relatively small number of people: three, four, or five, and the frequency of our conversations varies widely. It's definitely not on a schedule and it's not a formal process.

When you do interact with them, is it because a specific issue has arisen and you would like their help?

It is more like a sounding board, in my case. It is because I want to run something past them and have them think about it from their perspective and think about different alternatives.

If you were tasked with mentoring your successor, what advice would you offer that individual?

Recognize up front the amount of time and attention to organizational politics, the informal systems and processes that influence so much about how things actually get done in an organization. Leaders need to cultivate the skill of navigating an organization so that they can be the best engineer, the best HR person, or the best finance person in the world. Without the knowledge, skill, and inherent curiosity about how to work with people and get things through an organization, they are not going to achieve their full potential.

Politics, by the way, is not a bad thing. Any enterprise has its own political system, if we can call it that. But, I think what makes the difference is the curiosity and the inquiry to learn how the political system works.

Thanks you so much for your time and willingness to share your thoughts with Business Horizons' readers.

From *Business Horizons,* Vol. 48, Issue 3, May/June 2005, pp. 193–198. Copyright © 2005 by Kelley School of Business at Indiana University. Reprinted by permission of Elsevier Ltd. www.elsevier.com.

Don't Settle for Less: Global Compensation Programs Need Global Compensation Tools

AL WRIGHT

To drive higher performing workforces, businesses are creating compensation programs that more directly align with their strategic business and financial goals. The result is increasingly complex compensation strategies, taking into account factors of geography, job function, skills, competencies, and goal achievement, all driving multiple pay types including base pay and variable bonus and stock components.

Certain Web-based technologies can minimize HR administration expenses, while maximizing the positive impact on employee behavior. Tools that automate compensation planning, off-cycle compensation administration, and importantly, persistent employee communication are rapidly gaining acceptance, particularly among companies that have a global presence and need a Web-based solution that can support intricate multinational requirements.

Compensation Planning Is an Increasingly Complex Business Process

As organizations grow in size and expand across the globe, they need to coordinate the allocation of salary increases and other forms of compensation to support long-term budgeting processes. The purpose of compensation planning is to ensure that salary increases are distributed equitably across the organization while staying within set budget guidelines. Yet, without the right tools in place, this can be an insurmountable task.

Each year companies set merit guidelines and budgets, balancing market factors, internal business factors, and the company's ability to pay. Then, managers are asked to rate their employees' performance and allocate merit increases along with other coinciding compensation programs such as bonus payments and stock option grants. Focal compensation planning periods have replaced, by and large, the practice of determining increases based on individual employment anniversaries.

Compensation planning is a business necessity for just about any company, but it can be a disproportionately difficult process for several reasons. First, the task of determining individual compensation often involves taking into account numerous company guidelines and compliance issues with regard not only to base pay, but to incentive pay (such as annual bonuses) and stock option plans. Each compensation program typically has its own set of guidelines for appropriate increases and awards in order to ensure that the organization is rewarding high performance. Salary increases alone can take the form of merit increases, adjustments to the salary range minimum, lump sum payments, equity adjustments, and promotions. In addition, each program has a separate budget or pool of available money or stock shares that managers need to administer. Internal equity among similar positions within groups and between groups must be taken into consideration as well. Finally, market pay rates and compliance for their U.S. and international locations need to be factored into compensation decisions.

Compensation Planning History

Beginning in the 1980s, companies frequently relied on spreadsheets to administer focal reviews. Human resources generalists and compensation analysts were called upon to create individual spreadsheets for each manager that listed the employees for which the manager had direct compensation planning responsibility. Managers then input salary increases, bonus payments, and stock option share recommendations into their spreadsheets. Compensation departments then had the arduous task of aggregating the spreadsheets from multiple locations and in multiple currencies and at different management levels of the organization for additional input, review, and approval. Reconciling budgets proved problematic for large organizations. Changes to employee data such as terminations or transfers complicated this process since the spreadsheets only contained static employee information.

The spreadsheet approach was so labor and time intensive for both line managers and human resources professionals that getting through the compensation planning process often took several months, hindering the organization's ability to focus on other important business issues. In addition, the lack of tools to assist the manager in making appropriate compensation decisions reduced their effectiveness in building a high performance organization.

The Business Case for Automating Compensation Planning

For many organizations, the labor costs of manually administering compensation planning processes have become prohibitive. The degree of difficulty for creating and combining spreadsheets for hundreds, or even thousands, of managers increases to a point where such a process becomes impractical to administer. The Cedar Group estimated that in North America alone, companies experienced a savings of $5.29 per average transaction with an automated compensation planning system.[1] Multiply that potential savings for companies with 10, 20, even 100,000 employees, and the return on investment is clear, with many companies realizing a payback period in under two years.

In addition to squandering resources, labor-intensive manual compensation planning leads to missed budget targets and payroll errors resulting from employee status changes. The costs of these problems are considerable. In contrast, some organizations have experienced "instant" returns on their investment in automated compensation planning solutions.

For example, prior to deploying a fully automated compensation planning solution, a large telecommunications company struggled with payroll errors resulting from employee terminations, transfers and status changes during the compensation planning period. By the time compensation planning was completed, the employee information was so out of date that the resulting merit increases were erroneous. The payroll department had to correct all the mistakes at an estimated cost of $400 per error. Implementing an automated compensation planning system eliminated the payroll errors since the employee data was continually refreshed in order to keep it current. The savings to the company in avoiding the payroll errors more than paid for the new compensation planning system in its first year.

Supporting Complex Compensation Plans

Automated compensation planning systems need to support base pay, variable pay and stock option plans across each geographic location. The main component of base pay is the annual merit salary increase that recognizes the individual's performance for the previous year. The amount of the merit increase is affected by the individual's performance rating and the corporate merit budget. Managers need the capability to enter merit increases as either a percent or an amount. Dynamically calculated "spending to the merit budget" information can be prominently displayed for the manager in an automated compensation planning system. Screen views that support the sorting of information can facilitate maintenance of internal equity for merit increases for employees with similar performance in the same position.

Associated with the merit increase is the lump sum payment. For high performing employees at the top of their salary range, lump sum payments can be awarded in lieu of a merit increase to their annual salary. In some organizations, employees can receive either a merit increase or a lump sum payment, but not both. Compensation planning systems can be flexible to support variations in merit increase and lump sum payment business rules.

Salary adjustments are often included in annual focal reviews, and these adjustments have several variations. An adjustment to the salary range minimum is often applied to an employee whose salary is below the minimum of the salary range. This "adjustment to minimum," typically does not debit the merit budget. In addition, equity adjustments are used to recognize an inequity in the employee's salary that cannot be corrected through a merit or promotional increase. Sometimes a separate adjustment budget is established. Compensation planning systems can support multiple adjustment types and the variations of their budget calculations.

Promotions sometimes occur during the focal review as well. Promotions typically include a change in the employee's salary grade to recognize the increased responsibilities and higher skill set required for a new job. Additional data is needed to support the promotion increase—including job code, job title, new grade and new salary range. Sometimes, in-grade promotions or reclassifications are also permitted in the focal review process. Compensation planning systems can facilitate accessing all the additional data required for both promotions and reclassifications.

Variable pay plans can differ greatly between organizations. Bonus plans vary from simple discretionary bonus payments determined by managers to formula driven bonus plans factoring bonus targets for positions, bonus guidelines based on performance ratings, and any number of corporate, business unit and individual objectives. In addition, many organizations have multiple bonus plans with differing eligibility rules. Due to the complexity of incentive programs, some compensation planning systems specialize in supporting just complex variable pay and incentive programs. Other compensation planning systems include variable pay support along with their support for base pay and stock programs so that the manager can plan the employee's total cash compensation.

Merit stock option plans are frequently included in focal compensation planning. An employee's stock option grant history is particularly helpful to managers for determining totals for vested and unvested stock option shares. Stock option guidelines typically recommend shares to be allocated to an employee based upon their position or grade along with their performance rating. Managers also need to allocate stock based on the available pool of shares. Stock pools are often calculated by multiplying a target number of shares per grade or position times an expected participate rate times the number of incumbents in the grade or position. Not all compensation planning systems include support for stock option allocation, guidelines or pool calculations.

Integrating Market Data into Compensation Planning

Many base pay programs incorporate the concept of merit guidelines. A matrix of performance ratings with associated merit increase guidelines is frequently provided to managers in order to assist them in making merit decisions that reward high performing employees within the annual merit budget. The employees' position in their salary range can also be integrated into the matrix so that for each portion of the salary range (e.g., quartile or tercile) for each performance rating, the manager has a guideline percent merit increase. Compensation planning systems can include merit guideline data in a decision support tool delivered at the time the manager is making the merit decision. In addition, these systems can display the specific guidelines for the individual employee based on their location within their salary range and the performance rating selected so that managers do not have to interpret a guideline matrix. Additionally, for compensation programs utilizing bands rather than grades, the compensation planning systems can display the market target salary for the position in order to provide a context for the manager's merit increase decision.

Supporting Global Compensation Requirements

For global organizations, such factors as rewards, salaries, incentives, and various forms of direct and indirect compensation must be aligned with the cultural and economic norms of each operating location. Effective global compensation planning depends on an understanding of environmental factors such as economic growth, inflation, unemployment, and prevailing pay practices in the countries where one operates. This leads many companies to ask the question: How do we create a compensation program that supports the way our company is structured, organized, and operated globally?

Because many companies have operations and offices outside the U.S., a global compensation planning system must support differing international compensation practices and requires that leaders think about compensation as a whole, regardless of the country location of the employees. The laws, customs, and philosophies regarding compensation vary tremendously from country to country, so exporting a U.S. style plan to other countries rarely makes sense. In fact, because of these variations, the Human Resource Certification Institute has developed the first Human Resource Certification for HR professionals with international and cross-border responsibilities at multinational organizations.

For example, outside the U.S., most countries plan salaries in monthly rather than annual amounts. Further complicating the cross calculation between annual and monthly salaries, the number of months included in the annual salary varies by country. Seasonal bonuses paid in these countries are counted as "extra months of salary." So the number of months included in the annual salary is different from Japan, to Germany, and so on.

Additional compensation components, such as statutory increases, are required for compensation decisions in some countries. Compensation planning systems can cross calculate monthly and annual salaries as well as display the necessary wage information specific to the individual and country. In addition, accurately converting between a benchmark currency—for example, the U.S. dollar—and the employee's local currency is critical so that planning can be executed in local currency while budget spending can be aggregated in the benchmark currency. Compensation planning systems can be architected so that database field sizes accommodate the conversion of currencies with large exchange rate variances (e.g., one U.S. dollar converts to approximately 1.6 million Turkish liras.) Finally, merit budgets

and merit guidelines vary per country due to economic conditions. Budget and guideline configuration for compensation planning systems can support these country specific variations.

Companies that adopt a compensation planning system for their global organization ensure equal standards and similar opportunities across geographic boundaries enabling leaders around the world to use an automated solution to determine their employees' compensation. This allows managers to evaluate employees in the same way, regardless of their location, as the process is applicable across business units, functions and international boundaries, while at the same time being appropriately calibrated to the local market in each country.

Furthermore, it allows employee compensation to be based upon a similar set of criteria, regardless of location. This simplifies the task for leaders who have to decide compensation for employees in several different countries with different currencies. This approach is quite different from organizations where each country has its own process, which makes it difficult to seamlessly move from one system to the next, and where valuable time is spent learning the special rules for each system.

Through reducing duplication and implementing best practices across the organization, costs are reduced and value is added in terms of consistency leveraging the capabilities of the organization on a global basis.

System Flexibility Is Critical

One thing is certain—compensation plans change over time. Compensation planning systems can adapt to changes in plan components, eligibility, business rules, budgets, guidelines, access dates, calculations, and even screen presentations. Adding or removing base pay components, bonus plans, or stock plans is necessary to provide flexibility for typical compensation program changes. Creating eligibility flags in the database for each compensation component enables changing participant eligibility at a granular level.

Business rules such as minimum and maximum increases or awards can also be changed. Some compensation planning systems offer an administrative application for compensation professionals to quickly and easily change merit budgets, bonus and stock targets and pools, guidelines and system access dates. Calculations for values such as an employee's total compensation can be adjusted as needed. Finally, the actual screen presentations can be easily altered to support the changes in the compensation programs. In fact, some compensation planning systems offer the flexibility to vary the screen presentation based on the employee population or an employee attribute such as Fair Labor Standards Act (FLSA) status.

Compliance Issues

Compliance issues are demonstrated in several ways. Some organizations separate compensation planning for exempt employees from the planning for non-exempt employees—terms not even recognized other than in the U.S.—in order to prevent managers from using merit budget from one group for a different group. Compensation planning systems can present different screen presentations for different groups to accommodate different employee populations as well as differences in the compensation plans themselves. Regulatory compliance for protected groups (e.g., gender, age, and minority status) can also be reinforced with compensation planning systems. Presenting merit increase spending by protected group, for example, builds awareness with managers of possible adverse impact situations. In some European countries, data privacy of sensitive employee compensation data is a legal responsibility. Password protected compensation planning systems can limit data access to those who have a legitimate business need for the information.

Completing the Compensation Solution

Compensation planning in common reviews is just one part of the compensation process conducted by managers. Off-cycle merit increases, adjustments, promotions, and bonuses are all common manager transactions that can be automated. Compensation applications can support focal planning and off-cycle transactions. Off-cycle compensation transactions can also require varying guidelines and approval processes. Manager self-service applications that automate off-cycle compensation changes come with sophisticated rules engines and workflow to accommodate the business rule differences between transactions. Compensation planning applications can work together with manager self-service applications to report valuable "year-to-date" information so that managers can assess their merit and bonus spending throughout the entire year.

Communicating pay decisions to employees on a regular basis reinforces the desired behavior promoted by compensation plans—i.e., increased job satisfaction and motivation. Total compensation statements provide employees with a clear statement of the full value of their compensation and benefits. Online total compensation statements can be updated to regularly reinforce the wealth-building opportunities offered by a company, thus fostering the retention of top talent. Companies find that online total compensation statements are one of the most appreciated and used applications an organization can provide its employees.

Implementation Tips

Organizations interested in deploying automated compensation management solutions in a manner that maximizes cost efficiencies should undertake certain strategies as they prepare for implementation. Among the most beneficial are the strategies listed below.

1. Plan sufficient time to implement an automated compensation planning system. Do not try to make a "last minute decision" which can compromise either the desired functionality of the application or the quality of the implementation.

2. Phase in functionality over time either by compensation component (base pay, variable pay, stock) or geographical region. Aggressively manage "scope creep" to ensure the success of each phase.

3. Consider what is the best practice in the industry when reinforcing manager behavior with a specific feature or a business rule in the system. Often the best opportunity to improve a business process is when implementing a new application.

4. Check the frequency of occurrence for exceptions to corporate practices in order to validate whether they warrant being addressed in the software application from a cost and time perspective. Trying to create an application that supports 100 percent of all exceptions can be cost prohibitive. Supporting "rare exceptions" can dramatically increase the cost of the system.

5. Examine the ramifications of rounding for all calculations—especially when converting from annual to monthly or hourly amounts as well as when converting currencies. Also consider how rounding calculations can affect the user of the system. Unexpected rounding of values can confuse managers.

6. Validate all required data (especially management hierarchy data) with the Human Resource Information System or supporting systems. The accuracy of the data used within the compensation planning application is extremely important. A single piece of invalid data can jeopardize the user's confidence in the entire system. Plan time in the implementation schedule to correct data feeds coming into and out of the compensation planning system.

7. Test, test, and then test some more. Create test plans that include all calculations, business rules, and data entry validation checks. Test plans must include all country or organization specific business rules and calculations. Test each scenario carefully. Also test the technical network and server infrastructure as well as each user Web-browser/operating system version combination.

8. Carefully plan change management communication. Make time to gather input from all major stakeholders in all regions or organizations in approving the supported functionality and the implementation plan, as well as any pending business process changes.

Note

1. The Cedar Group HR Self-Service Survey, 2002.

AL WRIGHT is a Senior Solutions Consultant for Workscape Inc.

Test Your Knowledge Form

We encourage you to photocopy and use this page as a tool to assess how the articles in *Annual Editions* expand on the information in your textbook. By reflecting on the articles you will gain enhanced text information. You can also access this useful form on a product's book support Web site at *http://www.mhcls.com/online/*.

NAME:

DATE:

TITLE AND NUMBER OF ARTICLE:

BRIEFLY STATE THE MAIN IDEA OF THIS ARTICLE:

LIST THREE IMPORTANT FACTS THAT THE AUTHOR USES TO SUPPORT THE MAIN IDEA:

WHAT INFORMATION OR IDEAS DISCUSSED IN THIS ARTICLE ARE ALSO DISCUSSED IN YOUR TEXTBOOK OR OTHER READINGS THAT YOU HAVE DONE? LIST THE TEXTBOOK CHAPTERS AND PAGE NUMBERS:

LIST ANY EXAMPLES OF BIAS OR FAULTY REASONING THAT YOU FOUND IN THE ARTICLE:

LIST ANY NEW TERMS/CONCEPTS THAT WERE DISCUSSED IN THE ARTICLE, AND WRITE A SHORT DEFINITION:

We Want Your Advice

ANNUAL EDITIONS revisions depend on two major opinion sources: one is our Advisory Board, listed in the front of this volume, which works with us in scanning the thousands of articles published in the public press each year; the other is you—the person actually using the book. Please help us and the users of the next edition by completing the prepaid article rating form on this page and returning it to us. Thank you for your help!

ANNUAL EDITIONS: Human Resources 08/09

ARTICLE RATING FORM

Here is an opportunity for you to have direct input into the next revision of this volume.
We would like you to rate each of the articles listed below, using the following scale:

1. **Excellent: should definitely be retained**
2. **Above average: should probably be retained**
3. **Below average: should probably be deleted**
4. **Poor: should definitely be deleted**

Your ratings will play a vital part in the next revision.
Please mail this prepaid form to us as soon as possible.
Thanks for your help!

RATING	ARTICLE	RATING	ARTICLE
	1. HR Is Dead, Long Live HR		24. Who's Next?
	2. Numbers Games		25. Four Generations in the Workplace
	3. Why We Hate HR		26. The Face of Diversity Is More than Skin Deep
	4. Alien Nation		27. Philosophizing Compensation
	5. Strange Bedfellows		28. Do Your Employees Qualify for Overtime?
	6. Understanding HRM-Firm Performance Linkages: The Role of the "Strength" of the HRM System		29. Ten Steps to Designing an Effective Incentive Program
	7. Strategic Human Resources Management in Government		30. Pay Setters
	8. The Best 4 Ways to Recruit Employees with Disabilities		31. Doc in a Box
	9. Making Reasonable Accommodations for Employees with Mental Illness under the ADA		32. Building a Mentally Healthy Workforce
			33. Employee Benefits of the Future
	10. The Devil Is in the Details		34. Benefits and the Bottom Line
	11. The Disability Advantage		35. Setting Up a Disciplinary Procedure
	12. Implementing Sexual Harassment Training in the Workplace		36. The ABC's of Employee Discipline
			37. Hard-Core Offenders
	13. Some of 'Our Boys Overseas' Have Gray Hair		38. Interns on the Payroll
	14. Fighting for Values		39. Business Ethics: The Key Role of Corporate Governance
	15. Too Old to Work?		
	16. Can You Interview for Integrity?		40. Unregulated Work
	17. Six Ways to Strengthen Staffing		41. Accounting for Corporate Behavior
	18. Balancing HR Systems with Employee Privacy		42. Globalization and the American Labor Force
	19. Tomorrow's World		43. Immigration and the U.S. Economy: The Public's Perspective
	20. The Future of Work Motivation Theory		
	21. Managing in the New Millennium: Interpersonal Skills		44. Learning from Our Overseas Counterparts
			45. Human Resource Management in a Global Environment: Keys for Personal and Organizational Success
	22. Managing Employee Relations		
	23. Banishing Bullying		46. Don't Settle for Less: Global Compensation Programs Need Global Compensation Tools

BUSINESS REPLY MAIL
FIRST CLASS MAIL PERMIT NO. 551 DUBUQUE IA

POSTAGE WILL BE PAID BY ADDRESSEE

McGraw-Hill Contemporary Learning Series
501 BELL STREET
DUBUQUE, IA 52001

ABOUT YOU

Name

Date

Are you a teacher? ❏ A student? ❏
Your school's name

Department

Address

City

State

Zip

School telephone #

YOUR COMMENTS ARE IMPORTANT TO US!

Please fill in the following information:
For which course did you use this book?

Did you use a text with this ANNUAL EDITION? ❏ yes ❏ no
What was the title of the text?

What are your general reactions to the Annual Editions concept?

Have you read any pertinent articles recently that you think should be included in the next edition? Explain.

Are there any articles that you feel should be replaced in the next edition? Why?

Are there any World Wide Web sites that you feel should be included in the next edition? Please annotate.

May we contact you for editorial input? ❏ yes ❏ no
May we quote your comments? ❏ yes ❏ no